FIFTEEN DECISIVE BATTLES
OF THE WESTERN WORLD

Napoleon I.
Photogravure From A Portrait By S. Tofanelli.

FIFTEEN DECISIVE BATTLES OF THE WESTERN WORLD

From Marathon to Waterloo

Edward Shepherd Creasy

Introduction by Eric Yesson, Ph.D.

BARNES
& NOBLE
BOOKS
NEW YORK

CONTENTS

ILLUSTRATIONS

INTRODUCTION

PAINTING rich portraits of imperial conquest, diplomatic intrigue, and battlefield genius, Sir Edward Creasy's *Fifteen Decisive Battles of the Western World: From Marathon to Waterloo* (1851) narrates epic military confrontations that forged human events from antiquity to the modern age. The book captured the imagination of readers in Victorian England and became one of the best-selling books of its generation, rivaling sales of Charles Darwin's *Origins of Species* (1859). Creasy's crisp and clear depictions of history's greatest battles effectively created a new genre in military history. *Fifteen Decisive Battles* traces how military conflicts gave rise to, sustained, and brought down history's greatest civilizations, empires, and nation-states. The numerous volumes that examine "turning points" and "what ifs" in military history owe a tacit debt to Creasy's book and its immense popularity.

Born in 1812, three years before Waterloo, Edward Shepherd Creasy was raised in Bexley, Kent, in southern England and was educated at Eton College and King's College, Cambridge. In 1837 (the year Queen Victoria ascended the throne) Creasy was called to the bar at London's prestigious Lincoln's Inn and later became an assistant judge at the Westminster sessions court. Creasy left his judicial post in 1840, accepting a professorship in modern and ancient history at the University of London. In addition to *Fifteen Decisive Battles*, Creasy published works on the Ottoman Empire and English military and political history during his tenure at

London. In 1860 he received a knighthood and was appointed chief justice for the British colony of Ceylon (Sri Lanka). In 1870, with his health failing, Creasy returned to England, and after a brief stint in Ceylon, he died in London in 1878.

Fifteen Decisive Battles was reissued no less than seven times between 1851 and 1856; dozens more editions appeared in subsequent decades. Creasy's work became something of a pop icon in its day, even making a cameo appearance in Gilbert and Sullivan's *The Pirates of Penzance* (1879):

> *I know the kings of England and I*
> *quote the fights historical*
>
> *From Marathon to Waterloo in order*
> *categorical*

More than a century and a half since its first publication, the book retains its widespread appeal. In 2003 *Fifteen Decisive Battles* gained a whole new audience after appearing on a list of national security books recommended by United States Congressman Ike Skelton.

The initial popularity of Creasy's study tells us a great deal about the reading habits and interests of Victorian England. Britain played a pivotal role in world affairs, and popular commentators routinely compared Britain to the great empires of history. Creasy's book appealed to those wanting to understand how Britain had achieved its tremendous influence and how long it would last. The public already appreciated that war had played a significant part in establishing the country's global position. The glorification of commanders who had fought in the Napoleonic Wars was well underway by mid-century. In 1845 a squalid corner of London called the "Mews" was transformed into Trafalgar Square. A statue of Admiral Horatio Nelson, who triumphed over the French and Spanish fleets at Trafalgar Bay in 1805, looms over the plaza, commemorating his role in defeating Napoleon's quest for European domination.

During his school days at Eton, the young Edward Creasy developed a fondness for another hero of the Napoleonic wars. Sir Arthur Wellesley, the first Duke of Wellington, led the allied force that finished off the French emperor at Waterloo in 1815. Wellington would famously remark that the "battle of Waterloo was won on the playing fields of Eton." Britain's officer corps was drawn largely from noble families that turned to elite institutions like Eton to educate their sons. The school prided itself on its rigorous intellectual and physical training regimen. During Creasy's days at Eton, Wellington was a cabinet minister and later prime minister, the school's most famous and honored graduate, and a living legend in British society. Creasy's schoolboy fascination with the military exploits of his fellow Etonian presaged his subsequent career as academic historian and author.

By choosing the plains of Waterloo as scene for his final chapter, Creasy tapped into the popular appeal for all things Wellington. But *Fifteen Decisive Battles* promises much more than another rendition of how Britain's greatest general defeated the French emperor. Creasy tells Victorian readers in the Preface preface that he is interested in understanding military contests that have had a "practical influence on our own social and political condition." He invites them to "speculate on what we probably should have been, if any one of those battles had come to a different termination." What would have happened if Napoleon had defeated Britain and its allies at Waterloo? Would mid-nineteenth nineteenth-century Britain have been as rich and powerful if her armies had not prevailed on that fateful day?

Creasy seeks to identify which military conflicts have had the greatest impact on world history. While never developing a full-fledged theory of history, he employs some basic rules of thumb that illuminate key turning points through the ages. Drawing upon a wealth of historical knowledge, Creasy pinpoints empires and states that significantly influenced the evolution of world politics and social organization. He then traces political and social change back to the key military confrontations that made such change possible.

The chart below spells out the key attributes of Creasy's fifteen battles (in chapter order).

Battle	Date	War	Historical Impact
Marathon	490 BC	Persian-Greek Wars	Greek victory over Persian empire leads to the "Golden Age" of Athenian democracy under Pericles
Syracuse	413 BC	Second Peloponnesian War	Defeat of Athenian forces propels Sparta over Athens as the pre-eminent power in ancient Greece
Arbela (Gaugamela)	331 BC	Macedonian Conquests	Alexander's victory over Darius' Persian army helps establish an empire stretching from the Indian Ocean to the Mediterranean
Metarus	207 BC	Second Punic War	Rome's defeat of Carthaginian forces guarantees its survival at home and the extension of its empire abroad
Teutoburg Forest	9 AD	Roman Empire Wars	Germanic tribes annihilate Varus' legions; central Germany never comes under Roman control
Châlons	451	Roman Empire Wars	Victory by Roman and German armies over Attila perpetuates Roman civilization and Christendom in western Europe

Battle	Date	War	Historical Impact
Tours	732	Moslem Conquests	Charles Martel defeats Muslim forces and preserves Christian rule in France; his grandson, Charlemagne, establishes the Holy Roman Empire
Hastings	1066	Norman Conquest of England	William's victory over Harold unites England with western France and transforms it into a European power
Orléans	1429	Hundred Years' War	Inspired by Jeanne d'Arc, French armies defeat England and expel her forces from French territory
Spanish Armada	1588	English-Spanish Wars	England's victory over the Spanish fleet scuttles Phillip II's invasion plans and preserves Protestant rule
Blenheim	1704	War of the Spanish Succession	Anglo-Dutch armies repulse French-Bavarian forces marching on Vienna; the defeat blocks Louis XIV's quest for European hegemony
Pultowa (Poltava)	1709	Great Northern War	Peter the Great's victory over Charles XII eclipses Swedish power in northern Europe, making Russia the dominant player there

Battle	Date	War	Historical Impact
Saratoga	1777	American Revolutionary War	America's victory turns the tide against the British and convinces France to recognize and assist an independent United States
Valmy	1792	French Revolutionary Wars	French troops repulse a Prussia-Austrian invasion force and propel the Revolution forward against Europe's monarchies
Waterloo	1815	Napoleonic Wars	Wellington's defeat of Napoleon in fields of Flanders ends the French emperor's quest to rule over Europe

If any of these outcomes had been reversed, then subsequent events might have played out quite differently. Creasy cites Edward Gibbon, the eighteenth-century English historian, in wondering if the Arabs had defeated Charles Martel at Tours whether "the interpretation of the Koran would now be taught in the schools of Oxford."

Creasy's methodological approach excludes some of history's most famous encounters on the battlefield. Many battles of seeming consequence, he notes, "appear to me of mere secondary rank, inasmuch as either their effects were limited in area, or they themselves merely confirmed some great tendency or bias which an earlier battle had originated." Consider Hannibal's victory over the Romans at Cannae (216 BC) and Frederick the Great's crushing of Austrian forces at Leuthen (1757). In Creasy's view these battles did not alter the course of history and thus do not merit inclusion on his list. While Hannibal won spectacularly at Cannae,

Rome would eventually expel him from Europe and destroy Carthage itself. The long-term historical impact of Cannae is thus negligible in Creasy's view. And while Frederick the Great displayed great tactical virtuosity and consistently won against superior numbers, Prussia never substantially altered the world's social or political order during Creasy's lifetime. Frederick's battles are thus for Creasy little more than a historical curiosity. Other omissions, however, are more puzzling. At Actium in 31 BC, Octavian defeated Mark Antony's forces and established the Roman empireEmpire in the eastern Mediterranean. This battle paved the way for a series of Roman emperors (including Claudius and Marcus Aurelius) who would influence history for generations. Had Antony won that day, world history might indeed have looked quite different.

But Creasy's choice of battles also reflects social and personal prejudices. No less than six of the most decisive battles involve England. This preference for the "home team" (even when it lost) obviously played well to a Victorian readership and accounts in part for the book's record sales. Creasy's history also gives pride of place to war on land over battles at sea. Among the fifteen, only England's 1588 victory over the Spanish armada counts as a pure naval contest (although sea power played an ancillary role in three others). This is somewhat surprising given England's long tradition as a naval power. Why not Trafalgar instead of Waterloo and Nelson instead of Wellington? Certainly Waterloo was the more recent and famous of the two battles. And one should not overlook Creasy's affinity for Wellington, that Old Etonian, in choosing Waterloo over Trafalgar.

Creasy's other academic writing focused almost exclusively on English history, or what historians have called "Little England.". How did invasions and war mold the country's national character? How did a small island nation on Europe's fringes grow so prosperous? Why did the country enjoy a high degree of political stability? Creasy returned to these themes time and again in his published work. But looming over Creasy's career, and indeed over *Fifteen Decisive Battles,* is not Little England but the British Empire. Creasy lived and wrote at the zenith of British imperial power, when Victorian England held sway over a quarter of the world's landmass, and its navy reigned supreme on the high seas. The empire would ultimately determine the trajectory of Creasy's legal career. As a knighted chief justice serving in Ceylon, Creasy would experience firsthand the splendor and hardships of life as a functionary serving in a far corner of the empire.

The centrality of empire in *Fifteen Decisive Battles* of the World reflects a worldview and sensibility of what might be termed an internationalized version of "Whig history." A number of prominent 18theighteenth- and 19thnineteenth-century historians — including William Blackstone, Henry Hallam, and Thomas Babington Macaulay—interpreted English history as a sequence of events promoting greater political stability, economic prosperity, and acceptance of liberal values. In keeping with this intellectual climate, Creasy views the relationship between battle and political change as the steady march of progress. His historical sequencing places Britain as the successor to and promoter of a western Western civilization that inevitably makes the world a better place. Creasy depicts history as a progression from ancient Greece and Rome through to Christendom and then culminating in Britain and her global empire. As he writes at the close of his book, England "is now teaching the peoples of the earth to achieve [victory] over selfish prejudices and international feuds, in the great cause of the general promotion of the industry and welfare of mankind."

But even in Creasy's time such a vision would be hard to sustain. Consider another series of omissions in his military history. The Ottoman Empire seized Constantinople in the fifteenth century, nearly grabbed Vienna in the sixteenth century, and occupied a large swathe of southeastern Europe well into the nineteenth century. Despite being well versed in Ottoman history, Creasy gave these episodes scant attention in *Fifteen Decisive Battles.* Non-western and non-Christian forces must inevitably fall by the wayside, and Creasy does not recognize contingency in history as such. While history might have turned out differently had Hannibal or Napoleon won, Creasy cannot accept such outcomes as plausible precisely because they were not desirable. Historians following Creasy's path-breaking work are uncomfortable with the idea that history inexorably moves in a single direction. Thinking more critically about alternative paths in history, they have carefully combed the detritus of time, sifting out with greater precision how events on the battlefield have influenced contests for world supremacy. But none of this invalidates the enduring significance of Fifteen Decisive Battles. Creasy's book, like many great works, continues to be read because it raises more intriguing questions than any author could possibly answer in a single volume.

Erik Yesson holds a Ph.D. in politics from Princeton University and specializes in international security and military affairs. He has taught at Brown University, Harvard University, and the Johannes-Guttenberg University in Mainz, Germany.

THE AUTHOR'S PREFACE

IT is an honorable characteristic of the spirit of this age, that projects of violence and warfare are regarded among civilized states with gradually increasing aversion. The Universal Peace Society certainly does not, and probably never will, enroll the majority of statesmen among its members. But even those who look upon the appeal of battle as occasionally unavoidable in international controversies, concur in thinking it a deplorable necessity, only to be resorted to when all peaceful modes of arrangement have been vainly tried, and when the law of self-defence justifies a state, like an individual, in using force to protect itself from imminent and serious injury. For a writer, therefore, of the present day to choose battles for his favorite topic, merely because they were battles; merely because so many myriads of troops were arrayed in them, and so many hundreds or thousands of human beings stabbed, hewed, or shot each other to death during them, would argue strange weakness or depravity of mind. Yet it cannot be denied that a fearful and wonderful interest is attached to these scenes of carnage. There is undeniable greatness in the disciplined courage, and in the love of honor, which makes the combatants confront agony and destruction. And the powers of the human intellect are rarely more strongly displayed than they are in the commander who regulates, arrays, and wields at his will these masses of armed, disputants; who, cool, yet daring in the midst of peril, reflects on all, and provides for all, ever ready with fresh resources and designs, as the vicissitudes of the storm of slaughter require. But these qualities, however high they may appear, are to be found in the basest as well as in the noblest of mankind. Catiline was as brave a soldier as Leonidas, and a much better officer. Alva surpassed the Prince of Orange in the field; and Suwarrow was the military superior of Kosciusko. To adopt the emphatic words of Byron,

> "'Tis the cause makes all,
> Degrades or hallows courage in its fall."

There are some battles, also, which claim our attention, independently of the moral worth of the combatants, on account of their enduring importance, and by reason of the practical influence on our own social and political condition, which we can trace up to the results of those engagements. They have for us an abiding and actual interest, both while we investigate the chain of causes and effects by which they have helped to make us what we are, and also while we speculate on what we probably should have been, if any one of these battles had come to a different termination. Hallam has admirably expressed this in his remarks on the victory gained by Charles Martel, between Tours and Poictiers, over the invading Saracens.

He says of it that "it may justly be reckoned among those few battles of which a contrary event would have essentially varied the drama of the world in all its subsequent scenes; with Marathon, Arbela, the Metaurus, Châlons, and Leipsic." It was the perusal of this note of Hallam's that first led me to the consideration of my present subject. I certainly differ from that great historian as to the comparative importance of some of the battles which he thus enumerates, and also of some which he omits. It is probable, indeed, that no two historical inquirers would entirely agree in their lists of the Decisive Battles of the World. Different minds will naturally vary in the impressions which particular events make on them, and in the degree of interest with which they watch the career and reflect on the importance of different historical personages. But our concurring in our catalogues is of little moment, provided we learn to look on these great historical events in the spirit which Hallam's observations indicate. Those remarks should teach us to watch how the interests of many states are often involved in the collisions between a few; and how the effect of those collisions is not limited to a single age, but may give an impulse which will sway the fortunes of successive generations of mankind. Most valuable, also, is the mental discipline which is thus acquired, and by which we are trained not only to observe what has been and what is, but also to ponder on what might have been.[1]

We thus learn not to judge of the wisdom of measures too exclusively by the results. We learn to apply the juster standard of seeing what the circumstances and the probabilities were that surrounded a statesman or a general at the time when he decided on his plan: we value him, not by his fortune, but by his προαίρεσις to adopt the Greek expressive word of Polybius,[2] for which our language gives no equivalent.

The reasons why each of the following fifteen battles has been selected will, I trust, appear when it is described. But it may be well to premise a few remarks on the negative tests which have led me to reject others, which at first sight may appear equal in magnitude and importance to the chosen fifteen.

I need hardly remark that it is not the number of killed and wounded in a battle that determines its general historical importance.[3] It is not because only a few hundreds fell in the battle by which Joan of Arc captured the Tourelles and raised the siege of Orleans that the effect of that crisis is to be judged; nor would a full belief in the largest number which Eastern historians state to have been slaughtered in any of the numerous conflicts between Asiatic rulers make me regard the engagement in which they fell as one of paramount importance to mankind. But, besides battles of this kind, there are many of great consequence, and attended with circumstances which powerfully excite our feelings and rivet our attention, and yet which appear to me of mere secondary rank, inasmuch as either their effects were limited in area, or they themselves merely confirmed some great tendency or bias which an earlier battle had originated. For example, the encounters between the Greeks and Persians, which followed Marathon, seem to me not to have been phenomena of primary impulse. Greek superiority had been already asserted, Asiatic ambition had already been checked, before Salamis and Platæa confirmed the superiority of European free states over Oriental despotism. So Ægospotamos, which finally crushed the maritime power of Athens, seems to me inferior in interest to the defeat before Syracuse, where Athens received her first fatal check, and after which she only struggled to retard her downfall. I think similarly of Zama with respect to Carthage, as compared with the Metaurus; and, on the same principle, the subsequent great battles of the Revolutionary war appear to me inferior in their importance to Valmy, which first determined the military character and career of the French Revolution.

I am aware that a little activity of imagination and a slight exercise of metaphysical ingenuity may amuse us by showing how the chain of circumstances is so linked together, that the smallest skirmish, or the slightest occurrence of any kind, that ever occurred, may be said to have been essential in its actual termination to the whole order of subsequent events. But when I speak of causes and effects, I speak of the obvious and important agency of one fact upon another, and not of remote and fancifully infinitesimal influences. I am aware that, on the other hand, the reproach of fatalism is justly incurred by those who, like the writers of a certain school in a neighboring country, recognize in history nothing more than a series of necessary phenomena, which follow inevitably one upon the other. But when, in this work, I speak of probabilities, I speak of human probabilities only. When I speak of cause and effect, I speak of those general laws only by which we perceive the sequence of human affairs to be usually regulated, and in which we recognize emphatically the wisdom and power of the supreme Lawgiver, the design of the Designer.

MITRE COURT CHAMBERS, TEMPLE,
June 26, 1851.

FIFTEEN DECISIVE BATTLES
OF THE WESTERN WORLD

CHAPTER I

THE BATTLE OF MARATHON

"Quibus actus uterque
Europæ atque Asiæ fatis concurrerit orbis."

Two thousand three hundred and forty years ago, a council of Athenian officers was summoned on the slope of one of the mountains that look over the plain of Marathon, on the eastern coast of Attica. The immediate subject of their meeting was to consider whether they should give battle to an enemy that lay encamped on the shore beneath them; but on the result of their deliberations depended, not merely the fate of two armies, but the whole future progress of human civilization.

There were eleven members of that council of war. Ten were the generals who were then annually elected at Athens, one for each of the local tribes into which the Athenians were divided. Each general led the men of his own tribe, and each was invested with equal military authority. But one of the archons was also associated with them in the general command of the army. This magistrate was termed the Pole-march or War-ruler; he had the privilege of leading the right wing of the army in battle, and his vote in a council of war was equal to that of any of the generals. A noble Athenian named Callimachus was the War-ruler of this year; and as such stood listening to the earnest discussion of the ten generals. They had, indeed, deep matter for anxiety, though little aware how momentous to mankind were the votes they were about

1

to give, or how the generations to come would read with interest the record of their discussions. They saw before them the invading forces of a mighty empire, which had in the last fifty years shattered and enslaved nearly all the kingdoms and principalities of the then known world. They knew that all the resources of their own country were comprised in the little army intrusted to their guidance. They saw before them a chosen host of the great King, sent to wreak his special wrath on that country and on the other insolent little Greek community, which had dared to aid his rebels and burn the capital of one of his provinces. That victorious host had already fulfilled half its mission of vengeance. Eretria, the confederate of Athens in the bold march against Sardis nine years before, had fallen in the last few days; and the Athenian generals could discern from the heights the island of Ægilia, in which the Persians had deposited their Eretrian prisoners, whom they had reserved to be led away captives into Upper Asia, there to hear their doom from the lips of King Darius himself. Moreover, the men of Athens knew that in the camp before them was their own banished tyrant, who was seeking to be reinstated by foreign cimeters in despotic sway over any remnant of his countrymen that might survive the sack of their town, and might be left behind as too worthless for leading away into Median bondage.

The numerical disparity between the force which the Athenian commanders had under them, and that which they were called on to encounter, was hopelessly apparent to some of the council. The historians who wrote nearest to the time of the battle do not pretend to give any detailed statements of the numbers engaged, but there are sufficient data for our making a general estimate. Every free Greek was trained to military duty; and, from the incessant border wars between the different states, few Greeks reached the age of manhood without having seen some service. But the muster-roll of free Athenian citizens of an age fit for military duty never exceeded thirty thousand, and at this epoch probably did not amount to two-thirds of that number. Moreover, the poorer portion of these were unprovided with the equipments, and

untrained to the operations of the regular infantry. Some detachments of the best-armed troops would be required to garrison the
city itself and man the various fortified posts in the territory; so
that it is impossible to reckon the fully equipped force that
marched from Athens to Marathon, when the news of the Persian
landing arrived, at higher than ten thousand men.[1]

With one exception, the other Greeks held back from aiding
them. Sparta had promised assistance, but the Persians had landed
on the sixth day of the moon, and a religious scruple delayed the
march of Spartan troops till the moon should have reached its full.
From one quarter only, and that from a most unexpected one, did
Athens receive aid at the moment of her great peril.

Some years before this time the little state of Platæa in Bœotia,
being hard pressed by her powerful neighbor. Thebes, had asked
the protection of Athens, and had owed to an Athenian army the
rescue of her independence. Now when it was noised over Greece
that the Mede had come from the uttermost parts of the earth to
destroy Athens, the brave Platæans, unsolicited, marched with
their whole force to assist the defense, and to share the fortunes of
their benefactors. The general levy of the Platæans only amounted
to a thousand men; and this little column, marching from their city
along the southern ridge of Mount Cithæron, and thence across
the Attic territory, joined the Athenian forces above Marathon
almost immediately before the battle. The re-enforcement was
numerically small, but the gallant spirit of the men who composed
it must have made it of ten-fold value to the Athenians; and its presence must have gone far to dispel the cheerless feeling of being
deserted and friendless, which the delay of the Spartan succors was
calculated to create among the Athenian ranks.[2]

This generous daring of their weak but true-hearted ally was
never forgotten at Athens. The Platæans were made the civil fellow-
countrymen of the Athenians, except the right of exercising certain political functions; and from that time forth, in the solemn
sacrifices at Athens, the public prayers were offered up for a joint
blessing from Heaven upon the Athenians, and the Platæans also.

After the junction of the column from Platæa, the Athenian commanders must have had under them about eleven thousand fully armed and disciplined infantry, and probably a larger number of irregular light-armed troops; as, besides the poorer citizens who went to the field armed with javelins, cutlasses, and targets, each regular heavy-armed soldier was attended in the camp by one or more slaves, who were armed like the inferior freemen.[3] Cavalry or archers the Athenians (on this occasion) had none; and the use in the field of military engines was not at that period introduced into ancient warfare.

Contrasted with their own scanty forces, the Greek commanders saw stretched before them, along the shores of the winding bay, the tents and shipping of the varied nations who marched to do the bidding of the king of the Eastern world. The difficulty of finding transports and of securing provisions would form the only limit to the numbers of a Persian army. Nor is there any reason to suppose the estimate of Justin exaggerated, who rates at a hundred thousand the force which on this occasion had sailed, under the satraps Datis and Artaphernes, from the Cilician shores against the devoted coasts of Eubœa and Attica. And after largely deducting from this total, so as to allow for mere mariners and camp followers, there must still have remained fearful odds against the national levies of the Athenians. Nor could Greek generals then feel that confidence in the superior quality of their troops, which ever since the battle of Marathon has animated Europeans in conflicts with Asiatics; as, for instance, in the after struggles between Greece and Persia, or when the Roman legions encountered the myriads of Mithridates and Tigranes, or as is the case in the Indian campaigns of our own regiments. On the contrary, up to the day of Marathon the Medes and Persians were reputed invincible. They had more than once met Greek troops in Asia Minor, in Cyprus, in Egypt, and had invariably beaten them. Nothing can be stronger than the expressions used by the early Greek writers respecting the terror which the name of the Medes inspired, and the prostration of men's spirits before the apparently resistless career of the Persian arms.[4] It is, therefore, little to be wondered at, that five of the ten Athenian generals shrank from the prospect of fighting a pitched battle against an enemy so superior in numbers and so formidable in military renown. Their own position on the heights was strong, and offered great advantages to a small defending force against assailing masses. They deemed it mere foolhardiness to descend into the plain to be trampled down by the Asiatic horse, overwhelmed with the archery, or cut to pieces by the invincible veterans of Cambyses and Cyrus. Moreover, Sparta, the great war-state of Greece, had been applied to, and had promised succor to Athens, though the religious observance which the Dorians paid to certain times and seasons had for the present delayed their march. Was it not wise, at any rate, to wait till the Spartans came up, and to have the help of the best troops in Greece, before they exposed themselves to the shock of the dreaded Medes?

Specious as these reasons might appear, the other five generals were for speedier and bolder operations. And, fortunately for Athens and for the world, one of them was a man, not only of the highest military genius, but also of that energetic character which impresses its own type and ideas upon spirits feebler in conception.

Miltiades was the head of one of the noblest houses at Athens; he ranked the Æacidæ among his ancestry, and the blood of Achilles flowed in the veins of the hero of Marathon. One of his immediate ancestors had acquired the dominion of the Thracian Chersonese, and thus the family became at the same time Athenian citizens and Thracian princes. This occurred at the time when Pisistratus was tyrant of Athens. Two of the relatives of Miltiades — an uncle of the same name, and a brother named Stesagoras — had ruled the Chersonese before Miltiades became its prince. He had been brought up at Athens in the house of his father, Cimon,[5] who was renowned throughout Greece for his victories in the Olympic chariot-races, and who must have been possessed of great wealth. The sons of Pisistratus, who succeeded their father in the tyranny at Athens, caused Cimon to be assassinated;[6]

but they treated the young Miltiades with favor and kindness, and when his brother Stesagoras died in the Chersonese, they sent him out there as lord of the principality. This was about twenty-eight years before the battle of Marathon, and it is with his arrival in the Chersonese that our first knowledge of the career and character of Miltiades commences. We find, in the first act recorded of him, the proof of the same resolute and unscrupulous spirit that marked his mature age. His brother's authority in the principality had been shaken by war and revolt: Miltiades determined to rule more securely. On his arrival he kept close within his house, as if he was mourning for his brother. The principal men of the Chersonese, hearing of this, assembled from all the towns and districts, and went together to the house of Miltiades, on a visit of condolence. As soon as he had thus got them in his power, he made them all prisoners. He then asserted and maintained his own absolute authority in the peninsula, taking into his pay a body of five hundred regular troops, and strengthening his interest by marrying the daughter of the king of the neighboring Thracians.

When the Persian power was extended to the Hellespont and its neighborhood, Miltiades, as prince of the Chersonese, submitted to King Darius; and he was one of the numerous tributary rulers who led their contingents of men to serve in the Persian army, in the expedition against Scythia. Miltiades and the vassal Greeks of Asia Minor were left by the Persian king in charge of the bridge across the Danube, when the invading army crossed that river, and plunged into the wilds of the country that now is Russia, in vain pursuit of the ancestors of the modern Cossacks. On learning the reverses that Darius met with in the Scythian wilderness, Miltiades proposed to his companions that they should break the bridge down, and leave the Persian king and his army to perish by famine and the Scythian arrows. The rulers of the Asiatic Greek cities, whom Miltiades addressed, shrank from this bold but ruthless stroke against the Persian power, and Darius returned in safety. But it was known what advice Miltiades had given, and the vengeance of Darius was thenceforth specially directed against the man who had counseled such a deadly blow against his empire and his person. The occupation of the Persian arms in other quarters left Miltiades for some years after this in possession of the Chersonese; but it was precarious and interrupted. He, however, availed himself of the opportunity which his position gave him of conciliating the good will of his fellow-countrymen at Athens, by conquering and placing under the Athenian authority the islands of Lemnos and Imbros, to which Athens had ancient claims, but which she had never previously been able to bring into complete subjection. At length, in 494 B. C., the complete suppression of the Ionian revolt by the Persians left their armies and fleets at liberty to act against the enemies of the Great King to the west of the Hellespont. A strong squadron of Phœnician galleys was sent against the Chersonese. Miltiades knew that resistance was hopeless; and while the Phœnicians were at Tenedos, he loaded five galleys with all the treasure that he could collect, and sailed away for Athens. The Phœnicians fell in with him, and chased him hard along the north of the Ægæan. One of his galleys, on board of which was his eldest son Metiochus, was actually captured. But Miltiades, with the other four, succeeded in reaching the friendly coast of Imbros in safety. Thence he afterward proceeded to Athens, and resumed his station as a free citizen of the Athenian commonwealth.

The Athenians, at this time, had recently expelled Hippias, the son of Pisistratus, the last of their tyrants. They were in the full glow of their newly-recovered liberty and equality; and the constitutional changes of Cleisthenes had inflamed their republican zeal to the utmost. Miltiades had enemies at Athens; and these, availing themselves of the state of popular feeling, brought him to trial for his life for having been tyrant of the Chersonese. The charge did not necessarily import any acts of cruelty or wrong to individuals: it was founded on no specific law; but it was based on the horror with which the Greeks of that age regarded every man who made himself arbitrary master of his fellow-men, and exercised irresponsible dominion over them. The fact of Miltiades having so ruled in the Chersonese was undeniable; but the question which the Athenians assembled in judgment must have tried, was whether Miltiades, although tyrant of the Chersonese, deserved punishment as an Athenian citizen. The eminent service that he had done the state in conquering Lemnos and Imbros for it pleaded strongly in his favor. The people refused to convict him. He stood high in public opinion. And when the coming invasion of the Persians was known, the people wisely elected him one of their generals for the year.

Two other men of high eminence in history, though their renown was achieved at a later period than that of Miltiades, were also among the ten Athenian generals at Marathon. One was Themistocles, the future founder of the Athenian navy, and the destined victor of Salamis. The other was Aristides, who afterward led the Athenian troops at Platæa, and whose integrity and just popularity acquired for his country, when the Persians had finally been repulsed, the advantageous preeminence of being acknowledged by half of the Greeks as their imperial leader and protector. It is not recorded what part either Themistocles or Aristides took in the debate of the council of war at Marathon. But, from the character of Themistocles, his boldness, and his intuitive genius for extemporizing the best measures in every emergency[7] (a quality which the greatest of historians ascribes to him beyond all his contemporaries), we may well believe that the vote of Themistocles was for prompt and decisive action. On the vote of Aristides it may be more difficult to speculate. His predilection for the Spartans may have made him wish to wait till they came up; but, though circumspect, he was neither timid as a soldier nor as a politician, and the bold advice of Miltiades may probably have found in Aristides a willing—most assuredly it found in him a candid—hearer.

Miltiades felt no hesitation as to the course which the Athenian army ought to pursue; and earnestly did he press his opinion on his brother-generals. Practically acquainted with the organization of the Persian armies, Miltiades felt convinced of the superiority of the Greek troops, if properly handled; he saw with the military eye of a great general the advantage which the position of the forces gave him for a sudden attack, and as a profound politician he felt the perils of remaining inactive, and of giving treachery time to ruin the Athenian cause.

One officer in the council of war had not yet voted. This was Callimachus, the War-ruler. The votes of the generals were five and five, so that the voice of Callimachus would be decisive.

On that vote, in all human probability, the destiny of all the nations of the world depended. Miltiades turned to him, and in simple soldierly eloquence, the substance of which we may read faithfully reported in Herodotus, who had conversed with the veterans of Marathon, the great Athenian thus adjured his countrymen to vote for giving battle:

"It now rests with you, Callimachus, either to enslave Athens, or, by assuring her freedom, to win yourself an immortality of fame, such as not even Harmodius and Aristogiton have acquired; for never, since the Athenians were a people, were they in such danger as they are in at this moment. If they bow the knee to these Medes, they are to be given up to Hippias, and you know what they then will have to suffer. But if Athens comes victorious out of this contest, she has it in her to become the first city of Greece. Your vote is to decide whether we are to join battle or not. If we do not bring on a battle presently, some factious intrigue will disunite the Athenians, and the city will be betrayed to the Medes. But if we fight, before there is anything rotten in the state of Athens, I believe that, provided the gods will give fair play and no favor, we are able to get the best of it in an engagement."[8]

The vote of the brave War-ruler was gained, the council determined to give battle; and such was the ascendancy and acknowledged military eminence of Miltiades, that his brother-generals one and all gave up their days of command to him, and cheerfully acted under his orders. Fearful, however, of creating any jealousy, and of so failing to obtain the vigorous co-operation of all parts of his small army, Miltiades waited till the day when the chief command would have come round to him in regular rotation before he led the troops against the enemy.

9

The inaction of the Asiatic commanders during this interval appears strange at first sight; but Hippias was with them, and they and he were aware of their chance of a bloodless conquest through the machinations of his partisans among the Athenians. The nature of the ground also explains in many points the tactics of the opposite generals before the battle, as well as the operations of the troops during the engagement.

The plain of Marathon, which is about twenty-two miles distant from Athens, lies along the bay of the same name on the northeastern coast of Attica. The plain is nearly in the form of a crescent, and about six miles in length. It is about two miles broad in the centre, where the space between the mountains and the sea is greatest, but it narrows toward either extremity, the mountains coming close down to the water at the horns of the bay. There is a valley trending inward from the middle of the plain, and a ravine comes down to it to the southward. Elsewhere it is closely girt round on the land side by rugged limestone mountains, which are thickly studded with pines, olive-trees and cedars, and overgrown with the myrtle, arbutus, and the other low odoriferous shrubs that everywhere perfume the Attic air. The level of the ground is now varied by the mound raised over those who fell in the battle, but it was an unbroken plain when the Persians encamped on it. There are marshes at each end, which are dry in spring and summer and then offer no obstruction to the horseman, but are commonly flooded with rain and so rendered impracticable for cavalry in the autumn, the time of year at which the action took place.

The Greeks, lying encamped on the mountains, could watch every movement of the Persians on the plain below, while they were enabled completely to mask their own. Miltiades also had, from his position, the power of giving battle whenever he pleased, or of delaying it at his discretion, unless Datis were to attempt the perilous operation of storming the heights.

If we turn to the map of the Old World, to test the comparative territorial resources of the two states whose armies were now about to come into conflict, the immense preponderance of the material power of the Persian king over that of the Athenian republic is more striking than any similar contrast which history can supply. It has been truly remarked that, in estimating mere areas, Attica, containing on its whole surface only seven hundred square miles, shrinks into insignificance if compared with many a baronial fief of the Middle Ages, or many a colonial allotment of modern times. Its antagonist, the Persian empire, comprised the whole of modern Asiatic and much of modern European Turkey, the modern kingdom of Persia, and the countries of modern Georgia, Armenia, Balkh, the Punjaub, Afghanistan, Beloochistan, Egypt, and Tripoli.

Nor could a European, in the beginning of the fifth century before our era, look upon this huge accumulation of power beneath the sceptre of a single Asiatic ruler with the indifference with which we now observe on the map the extensive dominions of modern Oriental sovereigns; for, as has been already remarked, before Marathon was fought, the prestige of success and of supposed superiority of race was on the side of the Asiatic against the European. Asia was the original seat of human societies, and long before any trace can be found of the inhabitants of the rest of the world having emerged from the rudest barbarism, we can perceive that mighty and brilliant empires flourished in the Asiatic continent. They appear before us through the twilight of primeval history, dim and indistinct, but massive and majestic, like mountains in the early dawn.

Instead, however, of the infinite variety and restless change which has characterized the institutions and fortunes of European states ever since the commencement of the civilization of our continent, a monotonous uniformity pervades the histories of nearly all Oriental empires, from the most ancient down to the most recent times. They are characterized by the rapidity of their early conquests, by the immense extent of the dominions comprised in them, by the establishment of a satrap or pashaw system of governing the provinces, by an invariable and speedy degeneracy in the princes of the royal house, the effeminate nurslings of the seraglio succeeding to the warrior sovereigns reared in the camp, and by the internal anarchy and insurrections which indicate and accelerate the decline and fall of these unwieldy and ill-organized fabrics of power. It is also a striking fact that the governments of all the great Asiatic empires have in all ages been absolute despotisms. And Heeren is right in connecting this with another great fact, which is important from its influence both on the political and the social life of Asiatics. "Among all the considerable nations of Inner Asia, the paternal government of every household was corrupted by polygamy: where that custom exists, a good political constitution is impossible. Fathers, being converted into domestic despots, are ready to pay the same abject obedience to their sovereign which they exact from their family and dependents in their domestic economy." We should bear in mind, also, the inseparable connection between the state religion and all legislation which has always prevailed in the East, and the constant existence of a powerful sacerdotal body, exercising some check, though precarious and irregular, over the throne itself, grasping at all civil administration, claiming the supreme control of education, stereotyping the lines in which literature and science must move, and limiting the extent to which it shall be lawful for the human mind to prosecute its inquiries.

With these general characteristics rightly felt and understood it becomes a comparatively easy task to investigate and appreciate the origin, progress and principles of Oriental empires in general, as well as of the Persian monarchy in particular. And we are thus better enabled to appreciate the repulse which Greece gave to the arms of the East, and to judge of the probable consequences to human civilization, if the Persians had succeeded in bringing Europe under their yoke, as they had already subjugated the fairest portions of the rest of the then known world.

The Greeks, from their geographical position, formed the natural vanguard of European liberty against Persian ambition; and they pre-eminently displayed the salient points of distinctive national character which have rendered European civilization so far superior to Asiatic. The nations that dwelt in ancient times

around and near the northern shores of the Mediterranean Sea
were the first in our continent to receive from the East the rudi-
ments of art and literature, and the germs of social and political
organizations. Of these nations the Greeks, through their vicinity
to Asia Minor, Phœnicia, and Egypt, were among the very foremost in acquiring the principles and habits of civilized life; and
they also at once imparted a new and wholly original stamp on all
which they received. Thus, in their religion, they received from
foreign settlers the names of all their deities and many of their
rites, but they discarded the loathsome monstrosities of the Nile,
the Orontes, and the Ganges; they nationalized their creed; and
their own poets created their beautiful mythology. No sacerdotal
caste ever existed in Greece. So, in their governments, they lived
long under hereditary kings, but never endured the permanent
establishment of absolute monarchy. Their early kings were constitutional rulers, governing with defined prerogatives.[9] And long
before the Persian invasion, the kingly form of government had
given way in almost all the Greek states to republican institutions,
presenting infinite varieties of the blending or the alternate predominance of the oligarchical and democratical principles. In literature and science the Greek intellect followed no beaten track,
and acknowledged no limitary rules. The Greeks thought their
subjects boldly out; and the novelty of a speculation invested it in
their minds with interest, and not with criminality. Versatile, restless, enterprising, and self-confident, the Greeks presented the
most striking contrast to the habitual quietude and submissiveness
of the Orientals; and, of all the Greeks, the Athenians exhibited
these national characteristics in the strongest degree. This spirit of
activity and daring, joined to a generous sympathy for the fate of
their fellow-Greeks in Asia, had led them to join in the last Ionian
war, and now mingling with their abhorrence of the usurping family of their own citizens, which for a period had forcibly seized on
and exercised despotic power at Athens, nerved them to defy the
wrath of King Darius, and to refuse to receive back at his bidding
the tyrant whom they had some years before driven out.

The enterprise and genius of an Englishman have lately confirmed by fresh evidence, and invested with fresh interest, the might of the Persian monarch who sent his troops to combat at Marathon. Inscriptions in a character termed the Arrow-headed or Cuneiform, had long been known to exist on the marble monuments at Persepolis, near the site of the ancient Susa, and on the faces of rocks in other places formerly ruled over by the early Persian kings. But for thousands of years they had been mere unintelligible enigmas to the curious but baffled beholder; and they were often referred to as instances of the folly of human pride, which could indeed write its own praises in the solid rock, but only for the rock to outlive the language as well as the memory of the vainglorious inscribers. The elder Niebuhr, Grotefend, and Lassen, had made some guesses at the meaning of the Cuneiform letters; but Major Rawlinson, of the East India Company's service, after years of labor, has at last accomplished the glorious achievement of fully revealing the alphabet and the grammar of this long unknown tongue. He has, in particular, fully deciphered and expounded the inscription on the sacred rock of Behistun, on the western frontiers of Media. These records of the Achæmenidæ have at length found their interpreter; and Darius himself speaks to us from the consecrated mountain, and tells us the names of the nations that obeyed him, the revolts that he suppressed, his victories, his piety, and his glory.[10]

Kings who thus seek the admiration of posterity are little likely to dim the record of their successes by the mention of their occasional defeats; and it throws no suspicion on the narrative of the Greek historians that we find these inscriptions silent respecting the overthrow of Datis and Artaphernes, as well as respecting the reverses which Darius sustained in person during his Scythian campaigns. But these indisputable monuments of Persian fame confirm, and even increase the opinion with which Herodotus inspires us of the vast power which Cyrus founded and Cambyses increased; which Darius augmented by Indian and Arabian conquests, and seemed likely, when he directed his arms against Europe, to make the predominant monarchy of the world.

With the exception of the Chinese empire, in which, throughout all ages down to the last few years, one-third of the human race has dwelt almost unconnected with the other portions, all the great kingdoms, which we know to have existed in ancient Asia, were, in Darius' time, blended into the Persian. The northern Indians, the Assyrians, the Syrians, the Babylonians, the Chaldees, the Phœnicians, the nations of Palestine, the Armenians, the Bactrians, the Lydians, the Phrygians, the Parthians, and the Medes, all obeyed the sceptre of the Great King: the Medes standing next to the native Persians in honor, and the empire being frequently spoken of as that of the Medes, or as that of the Medes and Persians. Egypt and Cyrene were Persian provinces; the Greek colonists in Asia Minor and the islands of the Ægæan were Darius' subjects; and their gallant but unsuccessful attempts to throw off the Persian yoke had only served to rivet it more strongly, and to increase the general belief that the Greeks could not stand before the Persians in a field of battle. Darius' Scythian war, though unsuccessful in its immediate object, had brought about the subjugation of Thrace and the submission of Macedonia. From the Indus to the Peneus, all was his.

We may imagine the wrath with which the lord of so many nations must have heard, nine years before the battle of Marathon, that a strange nation toward the setting sun, called the Athenians, had dared to help his rebels in Ionia against him, and that they had plundered and burned the capital of one of his provinces. Before the burning of Sardis, Darius seems never to have heard of the existence of Athens; but his satraps in Asia Minor had for some time seen Athenian refugees at their provincial courts imploring assistance against their fellow-countrymen. When Hippias was driven away from Athens, and the tyrannic dynasty of the Pisistratidæ finally overthrown in 510 BC, the banished tyrant and his adherents, after vainly seeking to be restored by Spartan intervention, had betaken themselves to Sardis, the capital city of the satrapy of Artaphernes. There Hippias (in the expressive words of Herodotus[11]) began every kind of agitation, slandering the Athenians before Artaphernes, and doing all he could to induce the satrap to place Athens in subjection to him, as the tributary vassal of King Darius. When the Athenians heard of his practices, they sent envoys to Sardis to remonstrate with the Persians against taking up the quarrel of the Athenian refugees.

But Artaphernes gave them in reply a menacing command to receive Hippias back again if they looked for safety. The Athenians were resolved not to purchase safety at such a price, and after rejecting the satrap's terms, they considered that they and the Persians were declared enemies. At this very crisis the Ionian Greeks implored the assistance of their European brethren, to enable them to recover their independence from Persia. Athens, and the city of Eretria in Euboea, alone consented. Twenty Athenian galleys, and five Eretrian, crossed the Ægæan Sea, and by a bold and sudden march upon Sardis, the Athenians and their allies succeeded in capturing the capital city of the haughty satrap, who had recently menaced them with servitude or destruction. They were pursued, and defeated on their return to the coast, and Athens took no further part in the Ionian war; but the insult that she had put upon the Persian power was speedily made known throughout the empire, and was never to be forgiven or forgotten. In the emphatic simplicity of the narrative of Herodotus, the wrath of the Great King is thus described: "Now when it was told to King Darius that Sardis had been taken and burned by the Athenians and Ionians, he took small heed of the Ionians, well knowing who they were, and that their revolt would soon be put down; but he asked who, and what manner of men, the Athenians were. And when he had been told, he called for his bow; and, having taken it, and placed an arrow on the string, he let the arrow fly toward heaven; and as he shot it into the air, he said, 'O supreme God, grant me that I may avenge myself on the Athenians.' And when he had said this, he appointed one of his servants to say to him every day as he sat at meat,' Sire, remember the Athenians.' "

Some years were occupied in the complete reduction of Ionia. But when this was effected, Darius ordered his victorious forces to proceed to punish Athens and Eretria, and to conquer European Greece. The first armanent sent for this purpose was shattered by shipwreck, and nearly destroyed off Mount Athos. But the purpose of King Darius was not easily shaken. A larger army was ordered to be collected in Cilicia, and requisitions were sent to all the maritime cities of the Persian empire for ships of war, and for transports of sufficient size for carrying cavalry as well as infantry across the Ægæan. While these preparations were being made, Darius sent heralds round to the Grecian cities demanding their submission to Persia. It was proclaimed in the market-place of each little Hellenic state (some with territories not larger than the Isle of Wight), that King Darius, the lord of all men, from the rising to the setting sun,[12] required earth and water to be delivered to his heralds, as a symbolical acknowledgment that he was head and master of the country. Terror-stricken at the power of Persia and at the severe punishment that had recently been inflicted on the refractory Ionians, many of the continental Greeks and nearly all the islanders submitted, and gave the required tokens of vassalage. At Sparta and Athens an indignant refusal was returned—a refusal which was disgraced by outrage and violence against the persons of the Asiatic heralds.

Fresh fuel was thus added to the anger of Darius against Athens, and the Persian preparations went on with renewed vigor. In the summer of 490 B. C., the army destined for the invasion was assembled in the Aleian plain of Cilicia, near the sea. A fleet of six hundred galleys and numerous transports was collected on the coast for the embarkation of troops, horse as well as foot. A Median general named Datis, and Artaphernes, the son of the satrap of Sardis, and who was also nephew of Darius, were placed in titular joint command of the expedition. The real supreme authority was probably given to Datis alone, from the way in which the Greek writers speak of him. We know no details of the previous career of this officer; but there is every reason to believe that his abilities and bravery had been proved by experience, or his Median birth would have prevented his being placed in high command by Darius. He appears to have been the first Mede who was thus trusted by the Persian kings after the overthrow of the conspiracy of the Median magi against the Persians immediately before Darius obtained the throne. Datis received instructions to complete the subjugation of Greece, and especial orders were given him with regard to Eretria and Athens. He was to take these two cities, and he was to lead the inhabitants away captive, and bring them as slaves into the presence of the Great King.

Datis embarked his forces in the fleet that awaited them, and coasting along the shores of Asia Minor till he was off Samos, he thence sailed due westward through the Ægæan Sea for Greece, taking the islands in his way. The Naxians had, ten years before, successfully stood a siege against a Persian armament, but they now were too terrified to offer any resistance, and fled to the mountain tops, while the enemy burned their town and laid waste their lands. Thence Datis, compelling the Greek islanders to join him with their ships and men, sailed onward to the coast of Eubœa. The little town of Carystus essayed resistance, but was quickly overpowered. He next attacked Eretria. The Athenians sent four thousand men to its aid; but treachery was at work among the Eretrians; and the Athenian force received timely warning from one of the leading men of the city to retire to aid in saving their own country, instead of remaining to share in the inevitable destruction of Eretria. Left to themselves, the Eretrians repulsed the assaults of the Persians against their walls for six days; on the seventh they were betrayed by two of their chiefs, and the Persians occupied the city. The temples were burned in revenge for the firing of Sardis, and the inhabitants were bound, and placed as prisoners in the neighboring islet of Ægilia, to wait there till Datis should bring the Athenians to join them in captivity, when both populations were to be led into Upper Asia, there to learn their doom from the lips of King Darius himself.

Flushed with success, and with half his mission thus accomplished, Datis re-embarked his troops, and, crossing the little channel that separates Euboea from the mainland, he encamped his troops on the Attic coast at Marathon, drawing up his galleys on the shelving beach, as was the custom with the navies of antiquity. The conquered islands behind him served as places of deposit for his provisions and military stores. His position at Marathon seemed to him in every respect advantageous, and the level nature of the ground on which he camped was favorable for the employment of his cavalry, if the Athenians should venture to engage him. Hippias, who accompanied him, and acted as the guide of the invaders, had pointed out Marathon as the best place for a landing, for this very reason. Probably Hippias was also influenced by the recollection that forty-seven years previously, he, with his father Pisistratus, had crossed with an army from Eretria to Marathon, and had won an easy victory over their Athenian enemies on that very plain, which had restored them to tyrannic power. The omen seemed cheering. The place was the same, but Hippias soon learned to his cost how great a change had come over the spirit of the Athenians.

But though "the fierce democracy" of Athens was zealous and true against foreign invader and domestic tyrant, a faction existed in Athens, as at Eretria, who were willing to purchase a party triumph over their fellow-citizens at the price of their country's ruin. Communications were opened between these men and the Persian camp, which would have led to a catastrophe like that of Eretria, if Miltiades had not resolved and persuaded his colleagues to resolve on fighting at all hazards.

When Miltiades arrayed his men for action, he staked on the arbitrament of one battle not only the fate of Athens, but that of all Greece; for if Athens had fallen, no other Greek state, except Lacedæmon, would have had the courage to resist; and the Lacedæmonians, though they would probably have died in their ranks to the last man, never could have successfully resisted the victorious Persians and the numerous Greek troops which would have soon marched under the Persian satraps, had they prevailed over Athens.

Nor was there any power to the westward of Greece that could have offered an effectual opposition to Persia, had she once conquered Greece, and made that country a basis for future military operations. Rome was at this time in her season of utmost weakness. Her dynasty of powerful Etruscan kings had been driven out; and her infant commonwealth was reeling under the attacks of the Etruscans and Volscians from without, and the fierce dissensions between the patricians and plebeians within. Etruria, with her Lucumos and serfs, was no match for Persia. Samnium had not grown into the might which she afterward put forth; nor could the Greek colonies in South Italy and Sicily hope to conquer when their parent states had perished. Carthage had escaped the Persian yoke in the time of Cambyses, through the reluctance of the Phœnician mariners to serve against their kinsmen. But such forbearance could not long have been relied on, and the future rival of Rome would have become as submissive a minister of the Persian power as were the Phœnician cities themselves. If we turn to Spain; or if we pass the great mountain chain, which, prolonged through the Pyrenees, the Cevennes, the Alps, and the Balkan, divides Northern from Southern Europe, we shall find nothing at that period but mere savage Finns, Celts, Slavs, and Teutons. Had Persia beaten Athens at Marathon, she could have found no obstacle to prevent Darius, the chosen servant of Ormuzd, from advancing his sway over all the known Western races of mankind. The infant energies of Europe would have been trodden out beneath universal conquest, and the history of the world, like the history of Asia, have become a mere record of the rise and fall of despotic dynasties, of the incursions of barbarous hordes, and of the mental and political prostration of millions beneath the diadem, the tiara, and the sword.

Great as the preponderance of the Persian over the Athenian power at that crisis seems to have been, it would be unjust to impute wild rashness to the policy of Miltiades, and those who voted with him in the Athenian council of war, or to look on the after-current of events as the mere fortunate result of successful folly. As before has been remarked, Miltiades, while prince of the Chersonese, had seen service in the Persian armies; and he knew by personal observation how many elements of weakness lurked beneath their imposing aspect of strength. He knew that the bulk of their troops no longer consisted of the hardy shepherds and mountaineers from Persia proper and Kurdistan, who won Cyrus's battles; but that unwilling contingents from conquered nations now filled up the Persian muster-rolls, fighting more from compulsion than from any zeal in the cause of their masters. He had also the sagacity and the spirit to appreciate the superiority of the Greek armor and organization over the Asiatic, notwithstanding former reverses. Above all, he felt and worthily-trusted the enthusiasm of those whom he led.

The Athenians whom he led had proved by their newborn valor in recent wars against the neighboring states that "liberty and equality of civic rights are brave spirit-stirring things, and they, who, while under the yoke of a despot, had been no better men of war than any of their neighbors, as soon as they were free, became the foremost men of all; for each felt that in fighting for a free commonwealth, he fought for himself, and whatever he took in hand, he was zealous to do the work thoroughly." So the nearly contemporaneous historian describes the change of spirit that was seen in the Athenians after their tyrants were expelled;[13] and Miltiades knew that in leading them against the invading army, where they had Hippias, the foe they most hated, before them, he was bringing into battle no ordinary men, and could calculate on no ordinary heroism. As for traitors, he was sure that, whatever treachery might lurk among some of the higher-born and wealthier Athenians, the rank and file whom he commanded were ready to do their utmost in his and their own cause. With regard to future attacks from Asia, he might reasonably hope that one victory would inspirit all Greece to combine against the common foe; and that the latent seeds of revolt and disunion in the Persian empire would soon burst forth and paralyze its energies, so as to leave Greek independence secure.

With these hopes and risks, Miltiades, on the afternoon of a September day, 490 BC, gave the word for the Athenian army to prepare the battle. There were many local associations connected with those mountain heights which were calculated powerfully to excite the spirits of the men, and of which the commanders well knew how to avail themselves in their exhortations to their troops before the encounter. Marathon itself was a region sacred to Hercules. Close to them was the fountain of Macaria, who had in days of yore devoted herself to death for the liberty of her people. The very plain on which they were to fight was the scene of the exploits of their national hero, Theseus; and there, too, as old legends told, the Athenians and the Heraclidæ had routed the invader, Eurystheus. These traditions were not mere cloudy myths or idle fictions, but matters of implicit earnest faith to the men of that day, and many a fervent prayer arose from the Athenian ranks to the heroic spirits who, while on earth, had striven and suffered on that very spot, and who were believed to be now heavenly powers, looking down with interest on their, still beloved country, and capable of interposing with superhuman aid in its behalf.

According to old national custom, the warriors of each tribe were arrayed together; neighbor thus fighting by the side of neighbor, friend by friend, and the spirit of emulation and the consciousness of responsibility excited to the very utmost. The War-ruler, Callimachus, had the leading of the right wing; the Platæans formed the extreme left; and Themistocles and Aristides commanded the centre. The line consisted of the heavy armed spearmen only; for the Greeks (until the time of Iphicrates) took little or no account of light-armed soldiers in a pitched battle, using them only in skirmishes, or for the pursuit of a defeated enemy. The panoply of the regular infantry consisted of a long spear, of a shield, helmet, breast-plate, greaves, and short sword. Thus equipped, they usually advanced slowly and steadily into action in a uniform phalanx of about eight spears deep. But the military genius of Miltiades led him to deviate on this occasion from the commonplace tactics of his countrymen. It was essential for him to extend his line so as to cover all the practicable ground, and to secure himself from being outflanked and charged in the rear by the Persian horse. This extension involved the weakening of his line. Instead of a uniform reduction of its strength, he determined on detaching principally from his centre, which, from the nature of the ground, would have the best opportunities for rallying, if broken; and on strengthening his wings so as to insure advantage at those points; and he trusted to his own skill and to his soldiers' discipline for the improvement of that advantage into decisive victory.[14]

In this order, and availing himself probably of the inequalities of the ground, so as to conceal his preparations from the enemy till the last possible moment, Miltiades drew up the eleven thousand infantry whose spears were to decide this crisis in the struggle between the European and the Asiatic worlds. The sacrifices by which the favor of heaven was sought, and its will consulted, were announced to show propitious omens. The trumpet sounded for action, and, chanting the hymn of battle, the little army bore down upon the host of the foe. Then, too, along the mountain slopes of Marathon must have resounded the mutual exhortation, which Æschylus, who fought in both battles, tells us was afterward heard over the waves of Salamis: "On, sons of the Greeks! Strike for the freedom of your country! strike for the freedom of your children and of your wives—for the shrines of your fathers' gods, and for the sepulchres of your sires. All—all are now staked upon the strife."

Ὦ παῖδης Ἑλλήνων ἴτε.
Ἐλευθεροῦτε πατρίδ᾽, ἐλευθεροῦτε δὲ
Παῖδας, γυναῖκας, θεῶν τε πατρώων ἕδη,
Θήκας τε προγόνων. Νῦν ὑπὲρ πάντων ἀγών.[15]

Instead of advancing at the usual slow pace of the phalanx, Miltiades brought his men on at a run. They were all trained in the exercise of the palæstra, so that there was no fear of their ending the charge in breathless exhaustion; and it was of the deepest importance for him to traverse as rapidly as possible the mile or so of level ground that lay between the mountain foot and the Persian outposts, and so to get his troops into close action before the Asiatic cavalry could mount, form and manoeuvre against him, or their archers keep him long under fire, and before the enemy's generals could fairly deploy their masses. "When the Persians," says Herodotus, "saw the Athenians running down on them, without horse or bowmen, and scanty in numbers, they thought them a set of madmen rushing upon certain destruction." They began, however, to prepare to receive them, and the Eastern chiefs arrayed, as quickly as time and place allowed, the varied races who served in their motley ranks. Mountaineers from Hyrcania and Afghanistan, wild horsemen from the steppes of Khorassan, the black archers of Ethiopia, swordsmen from the banks of the Indus, the Oxus, the Euphrates and the Nile, made ready against the enemies of the Great King. But no national cause inspired them except the division of native Persians; and in the large host there was no uniformity of language, creed, race or military system. Still, among them there were many gallant men, under a veteran general; they were familiarized with victory, and in contemptuous confidence, their infantry, which alone had time to form, awaited the Athenian charge. On came the Greeks, with one unwavering line of levelled spears, against which the light targets, the short lances and cimeters of the Orientals, offered weak defence. The front rank of the Asiatics must have gone down to a man at the first shock. Still they recoiled not, but strove by individual gallantry and by the weight of numbers to make up for the disadvantages of weapons and tactics, and to bear back the shallow line of the Europeans. In the centre, where the native Persians and the Sacæ fought, they succeeded in breaking through the weakened part of the Athenian phalanx; and the tribes led by Aristides and Themistocles were, after a brave resistance, driven back over the plain, and chased by the Persians up the valley toward the inner country. There the nature of the ground gave the opportunity of rallying and renewing the struggle. Meanwhile, the Greek wings, where Miltiades had concentrated his chief strength, had routed the Asiatics opposed to them; and the Athenian and Platæan officers, instead of pursuing the fugitives, kept their troops well in hand, and, wheeling round, they formed the two wings together. Miltiades instantly led them against the Persian centre, which had hitherto been triumphant, but which now fell back, and prepared to encounter these new and unexpected assailants. Aristides and Themistocles renewed the fight with their reorganized troops, and the full force of the Greeks was brought into close action with the Persian and Sacian divisions of the enemy. Datis' veterans strove hard to keep their ground, and evening[16] was approaching before the stern encounter was decided.

But the Persians, with their slight wicker shields, destitute of body-armor, and never taught by training to keep the even front and act with the regular movement of the Greek infantry, fought at heavy disadvantage with their shorter and feebler weapons against the compact array of well-armed Athenian and Platæan spearmen, all perfectly drilled to perform each necessary evolution in concert, and to preserve a uniform and unwavering line in battle. In personal courage and in bodily activity the Persians were not inferior to their adversaries. Their spirits were not yet cowed by the recollection of former defeats; and they lavished their lives freely, rather than forfeit the fame which they had won by so many victories. While their rear ranks poured an incessant shower of arrows[17] over the heads of their comrades, the foremost Persians kept rushing forward, sometimes singly, sometimes in desperate groups of twelve or ten upon the projecting spears of the Greeks, striving to force a lane into the phalanx, and to bring their cimeters and daggers into play.[18] But the Greeks felt their superiority, and though the fatigue of the long-continued action told heavily on their inferior numbers, the sight of the carnage that they dealt upon their assailants nerved them to fight still more fiercely on.

At last the previously unvanquished lords of Asia turned their backs and fled, and the Greeks followed, striking them down, to the water's edge,[19] where the invaders were now hastily launching their galleys, and seeking to embark and fly. Flushed with success, the Athenians attacked and strove to fire the fleet. But here the Asiatics resisted desperately, and the principal loss sustained by the Greeks was in the assault on the ships. Here fell the brave War-ruler Callimachus, the general Stesilaus, and other Athenians of note. Seven galleys were fired; but the Persians succeeded in saving the rest. They pushed off from the fatal shore; but even here the skill of Datis did not desert him, and he sailed round to the western coast of Attica, in hopes to find the city unprotected, and to gain possession of it from some of the partisans of Hippias. Miltiades, however, saw and counteracted his manoeuvre. Leaving Aristides, and the troops of his tribe, to guard the spoil and the slain, the Athenian commander led his conquering army by a rapid night-march back across the country to Athens. And when the Persian fleet had doubled the Cape of Sunium and sailed up to the Athenian harbor in the morning, Datis saw arrayed on the heights above the city the troops before whom his men had fled on the preceding evening. All hope of further conquest in Europe for the time was abandoned, and the baffled armada returned to the Asiatic coasts.

After the battle had been fought, but while the dead bodies were yet on the ground, the promised re-enforcement from Sparta arrived. Two thousand Lacedæmonian spearmen, starting immediately after the full moon, had marched the hundred and fifty miles between Athens and Sparta in the wonderfully short time of three days. Though too late to share in the glory of the action, they requested to be allowed to march to the battle-field to behold the Medes. They proceeded thither, gazed on the dead bodies of the invaders, and then praising the Athenians and what they had done, they returned to Lace-dæmon.

The number of the Persian dead was 6,400; of the Athenians, 192. The number of the Platæans who fell is not mentioned; but, as they fought in the part of the army which was not broken, it cannot have been large.

The apparent disproportion between the losses of the two armies is not surprising when we remember the armor of the Greek spearmen, and the impossibility of heavy slaughter being inflicted by sword or lance on troops so armed, as long as they kept firm in their ranks.[20] The Athenian slain were buried on the field of battle. This was contrary to the usual custom, according to which the bones o[all who fell fighting for their country in each year were deposited in a public sepulchre in the suburb of Athens called the Cerameicus. But it was felt that a distinction ought to be made in the funeral honors paid to the men of Marathon, even as their merit had been distinguished over that of all other Athenians. A lofty mound was raised on the plain of Marathon, beneath which the remains of the men of Athens who fell in the battle were deposited. Ten columns were erected on the spot, one for each of the Athenian tribes; and on the monumental column of each tribe were graven the names of those of its members whose glory it was to have fallen in the great battle of liberation. The antiquarian Pausanias read those names there six hundred years after the time when they were first graven.[21] The columns have long perished, but the mound still marks the spot where the noblest heroes of antiquity, the Μαραθωνόμαχοι, repose.

A separate tumulus was raised over the bodies of the slain Platæans, and another over the light-armed slaves who had taken part and had fallen in the battle.[22] There was also a separate funeral monument to the general to whose genius the victory was mainly due. Miltiades did not live long after his achievement at Marathon, but he lived long enough to experience a lamentable reverse of his popularity and success. As soon as the Persians had quitted the western coasts of the Ægæan, he proposed to an assembly of the Athenian people that they should fit out seventy galleys, with a proportionate force of soldiers and military stores, and place it at his disposal; not telling them whither he meant to lead it, but promising them that if they would equip the force he asked for, and give him discretionary powers, he would lead it to a land where there was gold in abundance to be won with ease. The Greeks of that time believed in the existence of Eastern realms teeming with gold, as firmly as the Europeans of the sixteenth century believed in El Dorado of the West. The Athenians probably thought that the recent victor of Marathon, and former officer of Darius, was about to lead them on a secret expedition against some wealthy and unprotected cities of treasure in the Persian dominions. The armament was voted and equipped, and sailed eastward from Attica, no one but Miltiades knowing its destination until the Greek isle of Paros was reached, when his true object appeared. In former years, while connected with the Persians as prince of the Chersonese, Miltiades had been involved in a quarrel with one of the leading men among the Parians, who had injured his credit and caused some slights to be put upon him at the court of the Persian satrap Hydarnes. The feud had ever since rankled in the heart of the Athenian chief, and he now attacked Paros for the sake of avenging himself on his ancient enemy. His pretext, as general of the Athenians, was, that the Parians had aided the armament of Datis with a war-galley. The Parians pretended to treat about terms of surrender, but used the time which they thus gained in repairing the defective parts of the fortifications of their city, and they then set the Athenians at defiance. So far, says Herodotus, the accounts of all the Greeks agree. But the Parians in after years told also a wild legend, how a captive priestess of a Parian temple of the Deities of the Earth promised Miltiades to give him the means of capturing Paros; how, at her bidding, the Athenian general went alone at night and forced his way into a holy shrine, near the city gate, but with what purpose it was not known; how a supernatural awe came over him, and in his flight he fell and fractured his leg; how an oracle afterward forbade the Parians to punish the sacrilegious and traitorous priestess, "because it was fated that Miltiades should come to an ill end, and she was only the instrument to lead him to evil." Such was the tale that Herodotus heard at Paros. Certain it was that Miltiades either dislocated or broke his leg during an unsuccessful siege of the city, and returned home in evil plight with his baffled and defeated forces.

The indignation of the Athenians was proportionate to the hope and excitement which his promises had raised. Xanthippus, the head of one of the first families in Athens, indicted him before the supreme popular tribunal for the capital offense of having deceived the people. His guilt was undeniable, and the Athenians passed their verdict accordingly. But the recollections of Lemnos and Marathon, and the sight of the fallen general, who lay stretched on a couch before them, pleaded successfully in mitigation of punishment, and the sentence was commuted from death to a fine of fifty talents. This was paid by his son, the afterward illustrious Cimon, Miltiades dying, soon after the trial, of the injury which he had received at Paros.[23]

The melancholy end of Miltiades, after his elevation to such a height of power and glory, must often have been recalled to the minds of the ancient Greeks by the sight of one in particular of the memorials of the great battle which he won. This was the remarkable statue (minutely described by Pausanias) which the Athenians, in the time of Pericles, caused to be hewn out of a huge block of marble, which, it was believed, had been provided by Datis, to form a trophy of the anticipated victory of the Persians. Phidias fashioned out of this a colossal image of the goddess Nemesis, the deity whose peculiar function was to visit the exuberant prosperity both of nations and individuals with sudden and awful reverses. This statue was placed in a temple of the goddess at Rhamnus, about eight miles from Marathon. Athens itself contained numerous memorials of her primary great victory. Panenus, the cousin of Phidias, represented it in fresco on the walls of the painted porch; and, centuries afterward, the figures of Miltiades and Callimachus at the head of the Athenians were conspicuous in the fresco. The tutelary deities were exhibited taking part in the fray. In the background were seen the Phœnician galleys, and, nearer to the spectator, the Athenians and the Platæans (distinguished by their leather helmets) were chasing routed Asiatics into the marshes and the sea. The battle was sculptured also on the Temple of Victory in the Acropolis, and even now there may be traced on the freize the figures of the Persian combatants with their lunar shields, their bows and quivers, their curved cimeters, their loose trousers, and Phrygian tiaras.[24]

These and other memorials of Marathon were the produce of the meridian age of Athenian intellectual splendor, of the age of Phidias and Pericles; for it was not merely by the generation whom the battle liberated from Hippias and the Medes that the transcendent importance of their victory was gratefully recognized. Through the whole epoch of her prosperity, through the long Olympiads of her decay, through centuries after her fall, Athens looked back on the day of Marathon as the brightest of her national existence.

By a natural blending of patriotic pride with grateful piety, the very spirits of the Athenians who fell at Marathon were deified by their countrymen. The inhabitants of the district of Marathon paid religious rites to them, and orators solemnly invoked them in their most impassioned adjurations before the assembled men of Athens. "Nothing was omitted that could keep alive the remembrance of a deed which had first taught the Athenian people to know its own strength, by measuring it with the power which had subdued the greater part of the known world. The consciousness thus awakened fixed its character, its station, and its destiny; it was the spring of its later great actions and ambitious enterprises."[25]

It was not indeed by one defeat, however signal, that the pride of Persia could be broken, and her dreams of universal empire dispelled. Ten years afterward she renewed her attempts upon Europe on a grander scale of enterprise, and was repulsed by Greece with greater and reiterated loss. Larger forces and heavier slaughter than had been seen at Marathon signalized the conflicts of Greeks and Persians at Artemisium, Salamis, Platæa, and the Eurymedon. But, mighty and momentous as these battles were, they rank not with Marathon in importance. They originated no new impulse. They turned back no current of fate. They were merely confirmatory of the already existing bias which Marathon had created. The day of

Marathon is the critical epoch in the history of the two nations. It broke forever the spell of Persian invincibility, which had previously paralyzed men's minds. It generated among the Greeks the spirit which beat back Xerxes, and afterward led on Xenophon, Agesilaus, and Alexander, in terrible retaliation through their Asiatic campaigns. It secured for mankind the intellectual treasures of Athens, the growth of free institutions, the liberal enlightenment of the Western world, and the gradual ascendancy for many ages of the great principles of European civilization.

Explanatory Remarks on Some of the Circumstances of the Battle of Marathon.

Nothing is said by Herodotus of the Persian cavalry taking any part in the battle, although he mentions that Hippias recommended the Persians to land at Marathon, because the plain was favorable for cavalry evolutions. In the life of Miltiades which is usually cited as the production of Cornelius Nepos, but which I believe to be of no authority whatever, it is said that Miltiades protected his flanks from the enemy's horse by an abatis of felled trees. While he was on the high ground he would not have required this defence, and it is not likely that the Persians would have allowed him to erect it on the plain.

Bishop Thirlwall calls our attention to a passage in Suidas, where the proverb Χωρὶς ἱππεις is said to have originated from some Ionian Greeks, who were serving compulsorily in the army of Datis, contriving to inform Miltiades that the Persian cavalry had gone away, whereupon Miltiades immediately joined battle and gained the victory. There may probably be a gleam of truth in this legend. If Datis' cavalry was numerous, as the abundant pastures of Euboea were close at hand, the Persian general, when he thought, from the inaction of his enemy, that they did not mean to come down from the heights and give battle, might naturally send the larger part of his horse back across the channel to the neighborhood of Eretria, where he had already left a detachment, and where his military stores must have been deposited. The knowledge of such a movement would of course confirm Miltiades in his resolution to bring on a speedy engagement.

But, in truth, whatever amount of cavalry we suppose Datis to have had with him on the day of Marathon, their inaction in the battle is intelligible, if we believe the attack of the Athenian spearmen to have been as sudden as it was rapid. The Persian horse-soldier, on an alarm being given, had to take the shackles off his horse, to strap the saddle on, and bridle him, besides equipping himself (see Xenophon, "Anabasis," lib. iii., c. 4); and when each individual horseman was ready, the line had to be formed; and the time that it takes to form the Oriental cavalry in line for a charge has, in all ages, been observed by Europeans.

The wet state of the marshes at each end of the plain, in the time of year when the battle was fought, has been adverted to by Mr. Wordsworth, and this would hinder the Persian general from arranging and employing his horsemen on his extreme wings, while it also enabled the Greeks, as they came forward, to occupy the whole breadth of the practicable ground with an unbroken line of levelled spears, against which, if any Persian horse advanced, they would be driven back in confusion upon their own foot.

Even numerous and fully arrayed bodies of cavalry have been repeatedly broken, both in ancient and modern warfare, by resolute charges of infantry. For instance, it was by an attack of some picked cohorts that Cæsar routed the Pompeian cavalry (which had previously defeated his own), and won the battle of Pharsalia.

I have represented the battle of Marathon as beginning in the afternoon and ending toward evening. If it had lasted all day, Herodotus would have probably mentioned that fact. That it ended toward evening is, I think, proved by the line from the "Vespæ," which I have already quoted, and to which my attention was called by Sir Edward Bulwer's account of the battle. I think that the succeeding lines in Aristophanes, also already quoted, justify the description which I have given of the rear ranks of the Persians keeping up a fire of arrows over the heads of their comrades, as the Normans did at Hastings.

SYNOPSIS OF EVENTS BETWEEN THE BATTLE OF MARATHON, BC 490, AND THE DEFEAT OF THE ATHENIANS AT SYRACUSE, BC 413

BC 490 to 487. All Asia filled with the preparations made by King Darius for a new expedition against Greece. Themistocles persuades the Athenians to leave off dividing the proceeds of their silver mines among themselves, and to employ the money in strengthening their navy.

487. Egypt revolts from the Persians, and delays the expedition against Greece.

485. Darius dies, and Xerxes his son becomes King of Persia in his stead.

484. The Persians recover Egypt.

480. Xerxes invades Greece. Indecisive actions between the Persian and Greek fleets at Artemisium. Destruction of the three hundred Spartans at Thermopylæ. The Athenians abandon Attica and go on shipboard. Great naval victory of the Greeks at Salamis. Xerxes returns to Asia, leaving a chosen army under Mardonius to carry on the war against the Greeks.

478. Mardonius and his army destroyed by the Greeks at Platæa. The Greeks land in Asia Minor, and defeat a Persian force at Mycale. In this and the following years the Persians lose all their conquests in Europe, and many on the coast of Asia.

477. Many of the Greek maritime states take Athens as their leader instead of Sparta.

466. Victories of Cimon over the Persians at the Eurymedon.

464. Revolt of the Helots against Sparta. Third Messenian war.

460. Egypt again revolts against Persia. The Athenians send a powerful armament to aid the Egyptians, which, after gaining some successes, is destroyed; and Egypt submits. This war lasted six years.

457. Wars in Greece between the Athenian and several Peloponnesian states. Immense exertions of Athens at this time. "There is an original inscription still preserved in the Louvre which

attests the energies of Athens at this crisis, when Athens, like England in modern wars, at once sought conquests abroad and repelled enemies at home. At the period we now advert to (B. C. 457), an Athenian armament of two hundred galleys was engaged in a bold though unsuccessful expedition against Egypt. The Athenian crews had landed, had won a battle; they had then re-embarked and sailed up the Nile, and were busily besieging the Persian garrison in Memphis. As the complement of a trireme galley was at least two hundred men, we can not estimate the forces then employed by Athens against Egypt at less than forty thousand men. At the same time, she kept squadrons on the coasts of Phœnicia and Cyprus, and yet maintained a home fleet that enabled her to defeat her Peloponnesian enemies at Cecryphalæ and Ægina, capturing in the last engagement seventy galleys. This last fact may give us some idea of the strength of the Athenian home fleet that gained the victory, and by adopting the same ratio of multiplying whatever number of galleys we suppose to have been employed by two hundred, so as to gain the aggregate number of the crews, we may form some estimate of the forces which this little Greek state then kept on foot. Between sixty and seventy thousand men must have served in her fleets during that year. Her tenacity of purpose was equal to her boldness of enterprise. Sooner than yield or withdraw from any of their expeditions, the Athenians at this very time, when Corinth sent an army to attack their garrison at Megara, did not recall a single crew or a single soldier from Ægina or from abroad; but the lads and old men, who had been left to guard the city, fought and won a battle against these new assailants. The inscription which we have referred to is graven on a votive tablet to the memory of the dead, erected in that year by the Erechthean tribe, one of the ten into which the Athenians were divided. It shows, as Thirlwall has remarked, 'that the Athenians were conscious of the greatness of their own effort;' and in it this little civic community of the ancient world still' records to us with emphatic simplicity, that its slain fell in Cyprus, in Egypt, in Phœnicia, at Haliæ, in Ægina, and in Megara, *in the same year.*' "[26]

445. A thirty years' truce concluded between Athens and Lacedæmon.

440. The Samians endeavor to throw off the supremacy of Athens. Samos completely reduced to subjection. Pericles is now sole director of the Athenian councils.

431. Commencement of the great Peloponnesian war, in which Sparta, at the head of nearly all the Peloponnesian states, and aided by the Bœotians and some of the other Greeks beyond the Isthmus, endeavors to reduce the power of Athens, and to restore independence to the Greek maritime states who were the subject allies of Athens. At the commencement of the war the Peloponnesian armies repeatedly invade and ravage Attica, but Athens herself is impregnable, and her fleets secure her the dominion of the sea.

430. Athens visited by a pestilence, which sweeps off large numbers of her population.

425. The Athenians gain great advantages over the Spartans at Sphacteria, and by occupying Cythera; but they suffer a severe defeat in Bœotia, and the Spartan general, Brasidas, leads an expedition to the Thracian coasts, and conquers many of the most valuable Athenian possessions in those regions.

421. Nominal truce for thirty years between Athens and Sparta, but hostilities continue on the Thracian coast and in other quarters.

415. The Athenians send an expedition to conquer Sicily.

CHAPTER II

DEFEAT OF THE ATHENIANS
AT SYRACUSE, B. C. 413

"The Romans knew not, and could not know, how deeply the greatness of their own posterity, and the fate of the whole Western world, were involved in the destruction of the fleet of Athens in the harbor of Syracuse. Had that great expedition proved victorious, the energies of Greece during the next eventful century would have found their field in the West no less than in the East; Greece, and not Rome, might have conquered Carthage; Greek instead of Latin might have been at this day the principal element of the language of Spain, of France, and of Italy; and the laws of Athens, rather than of Rome, might be the foundation of the law of the civilized world."

—Arnold.

FEW cities have undergone more memorable sieges during ancient and mediæval times than has the city of Syracuse. Athenian, Carthaginian, Roman, Vandal, Byzantine, Saracen, and Norman, have in turns beleaguered her walls; and the resistance which she successfully opposed to some of her early assailants was of the deepest importance, not only to the fortunes of the generations then in being, but to all the subsequent current of human events. To adopt the eloquent expressions of Arnold respecting the check which she gave to the Carthaginian arms, "Syracuse was a break-water which God's providence raised up to protect the yet immature strength of Rome." And her triumphant repulse of the great Athenian expedition against her was of even more wide-spread and enduring importance. It forms a decisive epoch in the strife for universal empire, in which all the great states of antiquity successively engaged and failed.

The present city of Syracuse is a place of little or no military strength, as the fire of artillery from the neighboring heights would almost completely command it. But in ancient warfare, its position, and the care bestowed on its walls, rendered it formidably strong against the means of offence which then were employed by besieging armies.

The ancient city, in its most prosperous times, was chiefly built on the knob of land which projects into the sea on the eastern coast of Sicily, between two bays; one of which, to the north, was called the Bay of Thapsus, while the southern one formed the great harbor of the city of Syracuse itself. A small island, or peninsula (for such it soon was rendered), lies at the southeastern extremity of this knob of land, stretching almost entirely across the mouth of the great harbor, and rendering it nearly land-locked. This island comprised the original settlement of the first Greek colonists from Corinth, who founded Syracuse two thousand five hundred years ago; and the modern city has shrunk again into these primary limits. But, in the fifth century before our era, the growing wealth and population of the Syracusans had led them to occupy and include within their city walls portion after portion of the mainland lying next to the little isle, so that at the time of the Athenian expedition the seaward part of the land between the two bays already spoken of was built over, and fortified from bay to bay, and constituted the larger part of Syracuse.

The landward wall, therefore, of this district of the city traversed this knob of land, which continues to slope upward from the sea, and which, to the west of the old fortifications (that is, towards the interior of Sicily), rises rapidly for a mile or two, but diminishes in width, and finally terminates in a long narrow ridge, between which and Mount Hybla a succession of chasms and uneven low ground extends. On each flank of this ridge the descent is steep and precipitous from its summits to the strips of level land that lie immediately below it, both to the southwest and northwest.

The usual mode of assailing fortified towns in the time of the Peloponnesian war was to build a double wall round them, sufficiently strong to check any sally of the garrison from within, or any attack of a relieving force from without. The interval within the two walls of the circumvallation was roofed over, and formed barracks, in which the besiegers posted themselves, and awaited the effects of want or treachery among the besieged in producing a surrender; and, in every Greek city of those days, as in every Italian republic of the Middle Ages, the rage of domestic sedition between aristocrats and democrats ran high. Rancorous refugees swarmed in the camp of every invading enemy; and every blockaded city was sure to contain within its walls a body of intriguing malcontents, who were eager to purchase a party triumph at the expense of a national disaster. Famine and faction were the allies on whom besiegers relied. The generals of that time trusted to the operation of these sure confederates as soon as they could establish a complete blockade. They rarely ventured on the attempt to storm any fortified post, for the military engines of antiquity were feeble in breaching masonry before the improvements which the first Dionysius effected in the mechanics of destruction; and the lives of spearmen the boldest and most high-trained would, of course, have been idly spent in charges against unshattered walls.

A city built close to the sea, like Syracuse, was impregnable, save by the combined operations of a superior hostile fleet and a superior hostile army; and Syracuse, from her size, her population, and her military and naval resources, not unnaturally thought herself secure from finding in another Greek city a foe capable of sending a sufficient armament to menace her with capture and subjection. But in the spring of 414 B. C., the Athenian navy was mistress of her harbor and the adjacent seas; an Athenian army had defeated her troops, and cooped them within the town; and from bay to bay a blockading wall was being rapidly carried across the strips of level ground and the high ridge outside the city (then termed Epipolæ), which, if completed, would have cut the Syracusans off from all succor from the interior of Sicily, and have left them at the mercy of the Athenian generals. The besiegers' works were, indeed, unfinished; but every day the unfortified interval in their lines grew narrower, and with it diminished all apparent hope of safety for the beleaguered town.

Athens was now staking the flower of her forces, and the accumulated fruits of seventy years of glory, on one bold throw for the dominion of the Western world. As Napoleon from Mount Cœur de Lion pointed to St. Jean d'Acre, and told his staff that the capture of that town would decide his destiny and would change the face of the world, so the Athenian officers, from the heights of Epipolæ, must have looked on Syracuse, and felt that with its fall all the known powers of the earth would fall beneath them. They must have felt also that Athens, if repulsed there, must pause forever from her career of conquest, and sink from an imperial republic into a ruined and subservient community.

At Marathon, the first in date of the great battles of the world, we beheld Athens struggling for self-preservation against the invading armies of the East. At Syracuse she appears as the ambitious and oppressive invader of others. In her, as in other republics of old and of modern times, the same energy that had inspired the most heroic efforts in defence of the national independence, soon learned to employ itself in daring and unscrupulous schemes of self-aggrandizement at the expense of neighboring nations. In the interval between the Persian and the Peloponnesian wars she had rapidly grown into a conquering and dominant state, the chief of a thousand tributary cities, and the mistress of the largest and best-manned navy that the Mediterranean had yet beheld. The occupations of her territory by Xerxes and Mardonius, in the second Persian war, had forced her whole population to become mariners; and the glorious results of that struggle confirmed them in their zeal for their country's service at sea. The voluntary suffrage of the Greek cities of the coasts and islands of the Ægæan first placed Athens at the head of the confederation formed for the further prosecution of the war against Persia. But this titular ascendancy was soon converted by her into practical and arbitrary dominion. She protected them from piracy and the Persian power, which soon fell into decrepitude and decay, but she exacted in return implicit obedience to her self. She claimed and enforced a prerogative of taxing them at her discretion, and proudly refused to be accountable for her mode of expending their supplies. Remonstrance against her assessments was treated as factious disloyalty, and refusal to pay was promptly punished as revolt. Permitting and encouraging her subject allies to furnish all their contingents in money, instead of part consisting of ships and men, the sovereign republic gained the double object of training her own citizens by constant and well-paid service in her fleets, and of seeing her confederates lose their skill and discipline by inaction, and become more and more passive and powerless under her yoke. Their towns were generally dismantled, while the imperial city herself was fortified with the greatest care and sumptuousness; the accumulated revenues from her tributaries serving to strengthen and adorn to the utmost her havens, her docks, her arsenals, her theatres, and her shrines, and to array her in that plenitude of architectural magnificence, the ruins of which still attest the intellectual grandeur of the age and people which produced a Pericles to plan and a Phidias to execute.

All republics that acquire supremacy over other nations rule them selfishly and oppressively. There is no exception to this in either ancient or modern times. Carthage, Rome, Venice, Genoa, Florence, Pisa, Holland, and republican France, all tyrannized over every province and subject state where they gained authority. But none of them openly avowed their system of doing so upon principle with the candor which the Athenian republicans displayed when any remonstrance was made against the severe exactions which they imposed upon their vassal allies. They avowed that their empire was a tyranny, and frankly stated that they solely trusted to force and terror to uphold it. They appealed to what they called "the eternal law of nature, that the weak should be coerced by the strong."[1] Sometimes they stated, and not without some truth, that the unjust hatred of Sparta against themselves forced them to be unjust to others in self-defence. To be safe, they must be powerful; and to be powerful, they must plunder and coerce their neighbors. They never dreamed of communicating any franchise, or share in office, to their dependents, but jealously monopolized every post of command, and all political and judicial power; exposing themselves to every risk with unflinching gallantry; embarking readily in every ambitious scheme; and never suffering difficulty or disaster to shake their tenacity of purpose: in the hope of acquiring unbounded empire for their country, and the means of maintaining each of the thirty thousand citizens who made up the sovereign republic, in exclusive devotion to military occupations, and to those brilliant sciences and arts in which Athens already had reached the meridian of intellectual splendor.

Her great political dramatist speaks of the Athenian empire as comprehending a thousand states. The language of the stage must not be taken too literally; but the number of the dependencies of Athens, at the time when the Peloponnesian confederacy attacked her, was undoubtedly very great. With a few trifling exceptions, all the islands of the Ægæan, and all the Greek cities, which in that age fringed the coasts of Asia Minor, the Hellespont, and Thrace, paid tribute to Athens, and implicitly obeyed her orders. The Ægæan Sea was an Attic lake. Westward of Greece, her influence, though strong, was not equally predominant. She had colonies and allies among the wealthy and populous Greek settlements in Sicily and South Italy, but she had no organized system of confederates in those regions; and her galleys brought her no tribute from the Western seas. The extension of her empire over Sicily was the favorite project of her ambitious orators and generals. While her great statesman, Pericles, lived, his commanding genius kept his countrymen under control, and forbade them to risk the fortunes of Athens in distant enterprises, while they had unsubdued and powerful enemies at their own doors. He taught Athens this maxim; but he also taught her to know and to use her own strength, and when Pericles had departed, the bold spirit which he had fostered overleaped the salutary limits which he had prescribed. When her bitter enemies, the Corinthians, succeeded, in 431 BC, in inducing Sparta to attack her, and a confederacy was formed of five-sixths of the continental Greeks, all animated by anxious jealousy and bitter hatred of Athens; when armies far superior in numbers and equipment to those which had marched against the Persians were poured into the Athenian territory, and laid it waste to the city walls, the general opinion was that Athens would be reduced, in two or three years at the farthest, to submit to the requisitions of her invaders. But her strong fortifications, by which she was girt and linked to her principal haven, gave her, in those ages, almost all the advantages of an insular position. Pericles had made her trust to her empire of the seas. Every Athenian in those days was a practised seaman. A state, indeed, whose members, of an age fit for service, at no time exceeded thirty thousand, and whose territorial extent did not equal half Sussex, could only have acquired such a naval dominion as Athens once held, by devoting and zealously training all its sons to service in its fleets. In order to man the numerous galleys which she sent out, she necessarily employed large numbers of hired mariners and slaves at the oar; but the staple of her crews was Athenian, and all posts of command were held by native citizens. It was by reminding them of this, of their long practice in seamanship, and the certain superiority which their discipline gave them over the enemy's marine, that their great minister mainly encouraged them to resist the combined power of Lacedæmon and her allies. He taught them that Athens might thus reap the fruit of her zealous devotion to maritime affairs ever since the invasion of the Medes; "she had not, indeed, perfected herself; but the reward of her superior training was the rule of the sea—a mighty dominion, for it gave her the rule of much fair land beyond its waves, safe from the idle ravages with which the Lacedæmonians might harass Attica, but never could subdue Athens."[2]

Athens accepted the war with which her enemies threatened her rather than descend from her pride of place; and though the awful visitation of the plague came upon her, and swept away more of her citizens than the Dorian spear laid low, she held her own gallantly against her enemies. If the Peloponnesian armies in irresistible strength wasted every spring her corn-lands, her vine-yards and her olive groves with fire and sword, she retaliated on their coasts with her fleets; which, if resisted, were only resisted to display the pre-eminent skill and bravery of her seamen. Some of her subject allies revolted, but the revolts were in general sternly and promptly quelled. The genius of one enemy had indeed inflicted blows on her power in Thrace which she was unable to remedy; but he fell in battle in the tenth year of the war, and with the loss of Brasidas the Lacedæmonians seemed to have lost all energy and judgment. Both sides at length grew weary of the war, and in 421 a truce for fifty years was concluded, which, though ill kept, and though many of the confederates of Sparta refused to recognize it, and hostilities still continued in many parts of Greece, protected the Athenian territory from the ravages of ene-mies, and enabled Athens to accumulate large sums out of the proceeds of her annual revenues. So also, as a few years passed by, the havoc which the pestilence and the sword had made in her population was repaired; and in 415 BC Athens was full of bold and restless spirits, who longed for some field of distant enter-prise wherein they might signalize themselves and aggrandize the state, and who looked on the alarm of Spartan hostility as a mere old woman's tale. When Sparta had wasted their territory she had done her worst; and the fact of its always being in her power to do so seemed a strong reason for seeking to increase the trans-marine dominion of Athens.

The West was now the quarter toward which the thoughts of every aspiring Athenian were directed. From the very beginning of the war Athens had kept up an interest in Sicily, and her squadron had, from time to time, appeared on its coasts and taken part in the dissensions in which the Sicilian Greeks were universally engaged one against each other. There were plausible grounds for a direct quarrel, and an open attack by the Athenians upon Syracuse.

With the capture of Syracuse, all Sicily, it was hoped, would be secured. Carthage and Italy were next to be attacked. With large levies of Iberian mercenaries she then meant to overwhelm her Peloponnesian enemies. The Persian monarchy lay in hopeless imbecility, inviting Greek invasion; nor did the known world contain the power that seemed capable of checking the growing might of Athens, if Syracuse once could be hers.

The national historian of Rome has left us an episode of his great work, a disquisition on the probable effects that would have followed if Alexander the Great had invaded Italy. Posterity has generally regarded that disquisition as proving Livy's patriotism more strongly than his impartiality or acuteness. Yet right or wrong, the speculations of the Roman writer were directed to the consideration of a very remote possibility. To whatever age Alexander's life might have been prolonged, the East would have furnished full occupation for his martial ambition, as well as for those schemes of commercial grandeur and imperial amalgamation of nations in which the truly great qualities of his mind loved to display themselves. With his death the dismemberment of his empire among his generals was certain, even as the dismemberment of Napoleon's empire among his marshals would certainly have ensued if he had been cut off in the zenith of his power. Rome, also, was far weaker when the Athenians were in Sicily than she was a century after-ward in Alexander's time. There can be little doubt but that Rome would have been blotted out from the independent powers of the West, had she been attacked at the end of the fifth century BC by an Athenian army, largely aided by Spanish mercenaries, and flushed with triumphs over Sicily and Africa, instead of the collision between her and Greece having been deferred until the latter had sunk into decrepitude, and the Roman Mars had grown into full vigor.

The armament which the Athenians equipped against Syracuse was in every way worthy of the state which formed such projects of universal empire, and it has been truly termed "the noblest that ever yet had been sent forth by a free and civilized commonwealth."[3] The fleet consisted of one hundred and thirty-four war-galleys, with a multitude of store-ships. A powerful force of the best heavy-armed infantry that Athens and her allies could furnish was sent on board it, together with a smaller number of slingers and bowmen. The quality of the forces was even more remarkable than the number. The zeal of individuals vied with that of the republic in giving every galley the best possible crew, and every troop the most perfect accoutrements. And with private as well as public wealth eagerly lavished on all that could give splendor as well as efficiency to the expedition, the fated fleet began its voyage for the Sicilian shores in the summer of 415.

The Syracusans themselves, at the time of the Peloponnesian war, were a bold and turbulent democracy, tyrannizing over the weaker Greek cities in Sicily, and trying to gain in that island the same arbitrary supremacy which Athens maintained along the eastern coast of the Mediterranean. In numbers and in spirit they were fully equal to the Athenians, but far inferior to them in military and naval discipline. When the probability of an Athenian invasion was first publicly discussed at Syracuse, and efforts were made by some of the wiser citizens to improve the state of the national defences, and prepare for the impending danger, the rumors of coming war and the proposal for preparation were received by the mass of the Syracusans with scornful incredulity. The speech of one of their popular orators is preserved to us in Thucydides,[4] and many of its topics might, by a slight alteration of names and details, serve admirably for the party among ourselves at present,[5] which opposes the augmentation of our forces, and derides the idea of our being in any peril from the sudden attack of a French expedition. The Syracusan orator told his countrymen to dismiss with scorn the visionary terrors which a set of designing men among themselves strove to excite, in order to get power and influence thrown into their own hands. He told them that Athens knew her own interest too well to think of wantonly provoking their hostility: *"Even if the enemies were to come,"* said he, *"so distant from their resources, and opposed to such a power as ours, their destruction would be easy and inevitable. Their ships will have enough to do to get to our island at all, and to carry such stores of all sorts as will be needed. They cannot therefore carry, besides, an army large enough to cope with such a population as ours. They will have no fortified place from which to commence their operations, but must rest them on no better base than a set of wretched tents, and such means as the necessities of the moment will allow them. But, in truth, I do not believe that they would even be able to effect a disembarkation. Let us, therefore, set at naught these reports as altogether of home manufacture; and be sure that if any enemy does come, the state will know how to defend itself in a manner worthy of the national honor."*

Such assertions pleased the Syracusan assembly, and their counterparts find favor now among some portion of the English public. But the invaders of Syracuse came; made good their landing in Sicily; and, if they had promptly attacked the city itself, instead of wasting nearly a year in desultory operations in other parts of Sicily, the Syracusans must have paid the penalty of their self-sufficient carelessness in submission to the Athenian yoke. But, of the three generals who led the Athenian expedition, two only were men of ability, and one was most weak and incompetent. Fortunately for Syracuse, Alcibiades, the most skilful of the three, was soon deposed from his command by a fractious and fanatic vote of his fellow countrymen, and the other competent one, Lamachus, fell early in a skirmish; while, more fortunately still for her, the feeble and vacillating Nicias remained unrecalled and unhurt, to assume the undivided leadership of the Athenian army and fleet, and to mar, by alternate over-caution and over-carelessness, every chance of success which the early part of the operations offered. Still, even under him, the Athenians nearly won the town. They defeated the raw levies of the Syracusans, cooped them within the walls, and, as before mentioned, almost effected a continuous fortification from bay to bay over Epipolæ, the completion of which would certainly have been followed by a capitulation.

Alcibiades, the most complete example of genius without principle that history produces, the Bolingbroke of antiquity, but with high military talents superadded to diplomatic and oratorical powers, on being summoned home from his command in Sicily to take his trial before the Athenian tribunal, had escaped to Sparta, and had exerted himself there with all the selfish rancor of a renegade to renew the war with Athens, and to send instant assistance to Syracuse.

When we read his words in the pages of Thucydides (who was himself an exile from Athens at this period, and may probably have been at Sparta, and heard Alcibiades speak), we are at a loss whether most to admire or abhor his subtile counsels. After an artful exordium, in which he tried to disarm the suspicions which he felt must be entertained of him, and to point out to the Spartans how completely his interests and theirs were identified, through hatred of the Athenian democracy, he thus proceeded:

"Hear me, at any rate, on the matters which require your grave attention, and which I, from the personal knowledge that I have of them, can and ought to bring before you. We Athenians sailed to Sicily with the design of subduing, first the Greek cities there, and next those in Italy. Then we intended to make an attempt on the dominions of Carthage, and on Carthage itself.[6] If all these projects succeeded (nor did we limit ourselves to them in these quarters), we intended to increase our fleet with the inexhaustible supplies of ship timber which Italy affords, to put in requisition the whole military force of the conquered Greek states, and also to hire large armies of the barbarians, of the Iberians,[7] and others in those regions, who are allowed to make the best possible soldiers. *Then*, when we had done all this, we intended to assail Peloponnesus with our collected force. Our fleets would blockade you by sea, and desolate your coasts, our armies would be landed at different points and assail your cities. Some of these we expected to storm,[8] and others we meant to take by surrounding them with fortified lines. We thought that it would thus be an easy matter thoroughly to wear you down; and then we should become the masters of the whole Greek race. As for expense, we reckoned that each conquered state would give us supplies of money and provisions sufficient to pay for its own conquest, and furnish the means for the conquest of its neighbors.

"Such are the designs of the present Athenian expedition to Sicily, and you have heard them from the lips of the man who, of all men living, is most accurately acquainted with them. The other Athenian generals, who remain with the expedition, will endeavor to carry out these plans. And be sure that without your speedy interference they will all be accomplished. The Sicilian Greeks are deficient in military training; but still, if they could at once be brought to combine in an organized resistance to Athens, they might even now be saved. But as for the Syracusans resisting Athens by themselves, they have already, with the whole strength of their population, fought a battle and been beaten; they cannot face the Athenians at sea; and it is quite impossible for them to hold out against the force of their invaders. And if this city falls into the hands of the Athenians, all Sicily is theirs, and presently Italy also; and the danger, which I warned you of from that quarter, will soon fall upon yourselves. You must, therefore, in Sicily, fight for the safety of Peloponnesus. Send some galleys thither instantly. Put men on board who can work their own way over, and who, as soon as they land, can do duty as regular troops. But, above all, let one of yourselves, let a man of Sparta, go over to take the chief command, to bring into order and effective discipline the forces that are in Syracuse, and urge those who at present hang back to come forward and aid the Syracusans. The presence of a Spartan general at this crisis will do more to save the city than a whole army."[9] The renegade then proceeded to urge on them the necessity of encouraging their friends in Sicily, by showing that they themselves were in earnest in hostility to Athens. He exhorted them not only to march their armies into Attica again, but to take up a permanent fortified position in the country; and he gave them in detail information of all that the Athenians most dreaded, and how his country might receive the most distressing and enduring injury at their hands.

The Spartans resolved to act on his advice, and appointed Gylippus to the Sicilian command. Gylippus was a man who, to the national bravery and military skill of a Spartan, united political sagacity that was worthy of his great fellow-countryman Brasidas; but his merits were debased by mean and sordid vices; and his is one of the cases in which history has been austerely just, and where little or no fame has been accorded to the successful but venal soldier. But for the purpose for which he was required in Sicily, an abler man could not have been found in Lacedæmon. His country gave him neither men nor money, but she gave him her authority; and the influence of her name and of his own talents was speedily seen in the zeal with which the Corinthians and other Peloponnesian Greeks began to equip a squadron to act under him for the rescue of Sicily. As soon as four galleys were ready, he hurried over with them to the southern coast of Italy, and there, though he received such evil tidings of the state of Syracuse that he abandoned all hope of saving that city, he determined to remain on the coast, and do what he could in preserving the Italian cities from the Athenians.

So nearly, indeed, had Nicias completed his beleaguering lines, and so utterly desperate had the state of Syracuse seemingly become, that an assembly of the Syracusans was actually convened, and was discussing the terms on which they should offer to capitulate, when a galley was seen dashing into the great harbor, and making her way toward the town with all the speed which her rowers could supply. From her shunning the part of the harbor where the Athenian fleet lay, and making straight for the Syracusan side, it was clear that she was a friend; the enemy's cruisers, careless through confidence of success, made no attempt to cut her off; she touched the beach, and a Corinthian captain, springing on shore from her, was eagerly conducted to the assembly of the Syracusan people just in time to prevent the fatal vote being put for a surrender.

Providentially for Syracuse, Gongylus the commander of the galley, had been prevented by an Athenian squadron from following Gylippus to South Italy, and he had been obliged to push direct for Syracuse from Greece.

The sight of actual succor, and the promise of more, revived the drooping spirits of the Syracusans. They felt that they were not left desolate to perish, and the tidings that a Spartan was coming to command them confirmed their resolution to continue their resistance. Gylippus was already near the city. He had learned at Locri that the first report which had reached him of the state of Syracuse was exaggerated, and that there was unfinished space in the besiegers' lines through which it was barely possible to introduce re-enforcements into the town. Crossing the Straits of Messina, which the culpable negligence of Nicias had left unguarded, Gylippus landed on the northern coast of Sicily, and there began to collect from the Greek cities an army, of which the regular troops that he brought from Peloponnesus formed the nucleus. Such was the influence of the name of Sparta,[10] and such were his own abilities and activity that he succeeded in raising a force of about two thousand fully-armed infantry, with a larger number of irregular troops. Nicias, as if infatuated, made no attempt to counteract his operations, nor, when Gylippus marched his little army toward Syracuse, did the Athenian commander endeavor to check him. The Syracusans marched out to meet him; and while the Athenians were solely intent on completing their fortifications on the southern side toward the harbor, Gylippus turned their position by occupying the high ground in the extreme rear of Epipolæ. He then marched through the unfortified interval of Nicias' lines into the besieged town, and joining his troops with the Syracusan forces, after some engagements with varying success, gained the mastery over Nicias, drove the Athenians from Epipolæ, and hemmed them into a disadvantageous position in the low grounds near the great harbor.

The attention of all Greece was now fixed on Syracuse, and every enemy of Athens felt the importance of the opportunity now offered of checking her ambition, and, perhaps, of striking a deadly blow at her power. Large re-enforcements from Corinth, Thebes and other cities now reached the Syracusans, while the baffled and dispirited Athenian general earnestly besought his countrymen to recall him, and represented the further prosecution of the siege as hopeless.

But Athens had made it a maxim never to let difficulty or disaster drive her back from any enterprise once undertaken, so long as she possessed the means of making any effort, however desperate, for its accomplishment. With indomitable pertinacity, she now decreed, instead of recalling her first armament from before Syracuse, to send out a second, though her enemies near home had now renewed open warfare against her, and by occupying a permanent fortification in her territory had severely distressed her population, and were pressing her with almost all the hardships of an actual siege. She still was mistress of the sea, and she sent forth another fleet of seventy galleys, and another army, which seemed to drain almost the last reserves of her military population, to try if Syracuse could not yet be won, and the honor of the Athenian arms be preserved from the stigma of a retreat. Hers was, indeed, a spirit that might be broken, but never would bend. At the head of this second expedition she wisely placed her best general, Demosthenes, one of the most distinguished officers that the long Peloponnesian war had produced, and who, if he had originally held the Sicilian command, would soon have brought Syracuse to submission.

The fame of Demosthenes the general has been dimmed by the superior lustre of his great countryman, Demosthenes the orator. When the name of Demosthenes is mentioned, it is the latter alone that is thought of. The soldier has found no biographer. Yet out of the long list of great men whom the Athenian republic produced, there are few that deserve to stand higher than this brave, though finally unsuccessful, leader of her fleets and armies in the first half of the Peloponnesian war. In his first campaign in Ætolia he had shown some of the rashness of youth, and had received a lesson of caution by which he profited throughout the rest of his career, but without losing any of his natural energy in enterprise or in execution. He had performed the distinguished service of rescuing Naupactus from a powerful hostile armament in the seventh year of the war; he had then, at the request of the Acarnanian republics, taken on himself the office of commander-in-chief of all their forces, and at their head he had gained some important advantages over the enemies of Athens in Western Greece. His most celebrated exploits had been the occupation of Pylos on the Messenian coast, the successful defence of that place against the fleet and armies of Lacedæmon, and the subsequent capture of the Spartan forces on the isle of Sphacteria, which was the severest blow dealt to Sparta throughout the war, and which had mainly caused her to humble herself to make the truce with Athens. Demosthenes was as honorably unknown in the war of party politics at Athens as he was eminent in the war against the foreign enemy. We read of no intrigues of his on either the aristocratic or democratic side. He was neither in the interest of Nicias nor of Cleon. His private character was free from any of the stains which polluted that of Alcibiades. On all these points the silence of the comic dramatist is decisive evidence in his favor. He had also the moral courage, not always combined with physical, of seeking to do his duty to his country, irrespective of any odium that he himself might incur, and unhampered by any petty jealousy of those who were associated with him in command. There are few men named in ancient history of whom posterity would gladly know more, or whom we sympathize with more deeply in the calamities that befell them, than Demosthenes, the son of Alcisthenes, who, in the spring of the year 413 BC, left Piræus at the head of the second Athenian expedition against Sicily.

His arrival was critically timed; for Gylippus had encouraged the Syracusans to attack the Athenians under Nicias by sea as well as by land, and by one able stratagem of Ariston, one of the admirals of the Corinthian auxiliary squadron, the Syracusans and their confederates had inflicted on the fleet of Nicias the first defeat that the Athenian navy had ever sustained from a numerically inferior enemy. Gylippus was preparing to follow up his advantage by fresh attacks on the Athenians on both elements, when the arrival of Demosthenes completely changed the aspect of affairs, and restored the superiority to the invaders. With seventy-three war-galleys in the highest state of efficiency, and brilliantly equipped, with a force of five thousand picked men of the regular infantry of Athens and her allies, and a still larger number of bow-men, javelin-men, and slingers on board, Demosthenes rowed round the great harbor with loud cheers and martial music, as if in defiance of the Syracusans and their confederates. His arrival had indeed changed their newly-born hopes into the deepest consternation. The resources of Athens seemed inexhaustible, and resistance to her hopeless. They had been told that she was reduced to the last extremities, and that her territory was occupied by an enemy; and yet here they saw her sending forth, as if in prodigality of power, a second armament to make foreign conquests, not inferior to that with which Nicias had first landed on the Sicilian shores.

With the intuitive decision of a great commander, Demosthenes at once saw that the possession of Epipolæ was the key to the possession of Syracuse, and he resolved to made a prompt and vigorous attempt to recover that position, while his force was unimpaired, and the consternation which its arrival had produced among the besieged remained unabated. The Syracusans and their allies had run out an outwork along Epipolæ from the city walls, intersecting the fortified lines of circumvallation which Nicias had commenced, but from which he had been driven by Gylippus. Could Demosthenes succeed in storming this outwork, and in re-establishing the Athenian troops on the high ground, he might fairly hope to be able to resume the circumvallation of the city, and become the conqueror of Syracuse; for when once the besiegers' lines were completed, the number of the troops with which Gylippus had garrisoned the place would only tend to exhaust the stores of provisions and accelerate its downfall.

An easily-repelled attack was first made on the outwork in the day-time, probably more with the view of blinding the besieged to the nature of the main operations than with any expectation of succeeding in an open assault, with every disadvantage of the ground to contend against. But, when the darkness had set in, Demosthenes formed his men in columns, each soldier taking with him five days' provisions, and the engineers and workmen of the camp following the troops with their tools, and all portable implements of fortification, so as at once to secure any advantage of ground that the army might gain. Thus equipped and prepared, he led his men along by the foot of the southern flank of Epipolæ, in a direction toward the interior of the island, till he came immediately below the narrow ridge that forms the extremity of the high ground looking westward. He then wheeled his vanguard to the right, sent them rapidly up the paths that wind along the face of the cliff, and succeeded in completely surprising the Syracusan outposts, and in placing his troops fairly on the extreme summit of the all-important Epipolæ. Thence the Athenians marched eagerly down the slope toward the town, routing some Syracusan detachments that were quartered in their way, and vigorously assailing the unprotected side of the outwork. All at first favored them. The outwork was abandoned by its garrison, and the Athenian engineers began to dismantle it. In vain Gylippus brought up fresh troops to check the assault; the Athenians broke and drove them back, and continued to press hotly forward, in the full confidence of victory. But, amid the general consternation of the Syracusans and their confederates, one body of infantry stood firm. This was a brigade of their Boeotian allies, which was posted low down the slope of Epipolæ, outside the city walls. Coolly and steadily the Bœotian infantry formed their line, and, undismayed by the current of flight around them, advanced against the advancing Athenians. This was the crisis of the battle. But the Athenian van was disorganized by its own previous successes; and, yielding to the unexpected charge thus made on it by troops in perfect order, and of the most obstinate courage, it was driven back in confusion upon the other divisions of the army, that still continued to press forward. When once the tide was thus turned, the Syracusans passed rapidly from the extreme of panic to the extreme of vengeful daring, and with all their forces they now fiercely assailed the embarrassed and receding Athenians. In vain did the officers of the latter strive to re-form their line. Amid the din and the shouting of the fight, and the confusion inseparable upon a night engagement, especially one where many thousand combatants were pent and whirled together in a narrow and uneven area, the necessary manœuvres were impracticable; and though many companies still fought on desperately, wherever the moonlight showed them the semblance of a foe,[11] they fought without concert or subordination; and not unfrequently, amid the deadly chaos, Athenian troops sailed each other. Keeping their ranks close, the Syracusans and their allies pressed on against the disorganized masses of the besiegers, and at length drove them, with heavy slaughter, over the cliffs, which an hour or two before they had scaled full of hope, and apparently certain of success.

This defeat was decisive of the event of the siege. The Athenians afterward struggled only to protect themselves from the vengeance which the Syracusans sought to wreak in the complete destruction of their invaders. Never, however, was vengeance more complete and terrible. A series of sea-fights followed, in which the Athenian galleys were utterly destroyed or captured. The mariners and soldiers who escaped death in disastrous engagements, and in a vain attempt to force a retreat into the interior of the island, became prisoners of war. Nicias and Demosthenes were put to death in cold blood, and their men either perished miserably in the Syracusan dungeons, or were sold into slavery to the very persons whom, in their pride of power, they had crossed the seas to enslave.

All danger from Athens to the independent nations of the West was now forever at an end. She, indeed, continued to struggle against her combined enemies and revolted allies with unparalleled gallantry, and many more years of varying warfare passed away before she surrendered to their arms. But no success in subsequent contests could ever have restored her to the pre-eminence in enterprise, resources, and maritime skill which she had acquired before her fatal reverses in Sicily. Nor among the rival Greek republics, whom her own rashness aided to crush her, was there any capable of reorganizing her empire, or resuming her schemes of conquest. The dominion of Western Europe was left for Rome and Carthage to dispute two centuries later, in conflicts still more terrible, and with even higher displays of military daring and genius than Athens had witnessed either in her rise, her meridian, or her fall.

Synopsis of Events Between the Defeat of the Athenians at Syracuse and the Battle of Arbela.

412 BC Many of the subject allies of Athens revolt from her on her disasters before Syracuse being known; the seat of war is transferred to the Hellespont and eastern side of the Ægæan.

410. The Carthaginians attempt to make conquests in Sicily.

407. Cyrus the Younger is sent by the King of Persia to take the government of all the maritime parts of Asia Minor, and with orders to help the Lacedæmonian fleet against the Athenian.

406. Agrigentum taken by the Carthaginians.

405. The last Athenian fleet destroyed by Lysander at Ægospotami. Athens closely besieged. Rise of the power of Dionysius at Syracuse.

404. Athens surrenders. End of the Peloponnesian war. The ascendancy of Sparta complete throughout Greece.

403. Thrasybulus, aided by the Thebans and with the connivance of one of the Spartan kings, liberates Athens from the Thirty Tyrants and restores the democracy.

401. Cyrus the Younger commences his expedition into Upper Asia to dethrone his brother, Artaxerxes Mnemon. He takes with him an auxiliary force of ten thousand Greeks. He is killed in battle at Cunaxa, and the Ten Thousand, led by Xenophon, effect their retreat in spite of the Persian armies and the natural obstacles of their march.

399. In this and the five following years, the Lacedæmonians, under Agesilaus and other commanders, carry on war against the Persian satraps in Asia Minor.

396. Syracuse besieged by the Carthaginians, and successfully defended by Dionysius.

394. Rome makes her first great stride in the career of conquest by the capture of Veii.

393. The Athenian admiral, Conon, in conjunction with the Persian satrap Pharnabazus, defeats the Lacedæmonian fleet off Cnidus, and restores the fortifications of Athens. Several of the former allies of Sparta in Greece carry on hostilities against her.

388. The nations of Northern Europe now first appear in authentic history. The Gauls overrun great part of Italy and burn Rome. Rome recovers from the blow, but her old enemies the Æquians and Volscians are left completely crushed by the Gallic invaders.

387. The peace of Antalcidas is concluded among the Greeks by the mediation, and under the sanction, of the Persian king.

378 to 361. Fresh wars in Greece. Epaminondas raises Thebes to be the leading state of Greece, and the supremacy of Sparta is destroyed at the battle of Leuctra. Epaminondas is killed in gaining the victory of Mantinea, and the power of Thebes falls with him. The Athenians attempt a balancing system between Sparta and Thebes.

359. Philip becomes king of Macedon.

357. The Social War breaks out in Greece and lasts three years. Its result checks the attempt of Athens to regain her old maritime empire.

356. Alexander the Great is born.

343. Rome begins her wars with the Samnites; they extend over a period of fifty years. The end of this obstinate contest is to secure for her the dominion of Italy.

340. Fresh attempts of the Carthaginians upon Syracuse. Timoleon defeats them with great slaughter.

338. Philip defeats the confederate armies of Athens and Thebes at Chæronea, and the Macedonian supremacy over Greece is firmly established.

336. Philip is assassinated, and Alexander the Great becomes king of Macedon. He gains several victories over the northern barbarians who had attacked Macedonia, and destroys Thebes, which, in conjunction with Athens, had taken up arms against the Macedonians.

334. Alexander passes the Hellespont.

CHAPTER III

THE BATTLE OF ARBELA, BC 331

"Alexander deserves the glory which he has enjoyed for so many centuries and among all nations: but what if he had been beaten at Arbela, having the Euphrates, the Tigris, and the deserts in his rear, without any strong places of refuge, nine hundred leagues from Macedonia!"

—Napoleon.

"Asia beheld with astonishment and awe the uninterrupted progress of a hero, the sweep of whose conquests was as wide and rapid as that of her own barbaric kings, or of the Scythian or Chaldæan hordes; but, far unlike the transient whirlwinds of Asiatic warfare, the advance of the Macedonian leader was no less deliberate than rapid: at every step the Greek power took root, and the language and the civilization of Greece were planted from the shores of the Ægæan to the banks of the Indus, from the Caspian and the great Hyrcanian plain to the cataracts of the Nile; to exist actually for nearly a thousand years, and in their effects to endure forever."

—Arnold.

A long and not uninstructive list might be made out of illustrious men whose characters have been vindicated during recent times from aspersions which for centuries had been thrown on them. The spirit of modern inquiry, and the tendency of modern scholarship, both of which are often said to be solely negative and destructive, have, in truth, restored to splendor, and almost created anew, far more than they have assailed with censure, or dismissed from consideration as unreal. The truth of many a brilliant narrative of brilliant exploits has of late years been triumphantly demonstrated, and the shallowness of the skeptical scoffs with which little minds have carped at the great minds of antiquity has been in many instances decisively exposed. The laws, the politics, and the lines of action adopted or recommended by eminent men and powerful nations have been examined with keener investigation, and considered with more comprehensive judgment than formerly were brought to bear on these subjects. The result has been at least as often favorable as unfavorable to the persons and the states so scrutinized, and many an oft-repeated slander against both measures and men has thus been silenced, we may hope forever.

The veracity of Herodotus, the pure patriotism of Pericles, of Demosthenes, and of the Gracchi, the wisdom of Clisthenes and of Licinius as constitutional reformers, may be mentioned as facts which recent writers have cleared from unjust suspicion and censure. And it might be easily shown that the defensive tendency, which distinguishes the present and recent great writers of Germany, France, and England, has been equally manifested in the spirit in which they have treated the heroes of thought and heroes of action who lived during what we term the Middle Ages, and whom it was so long the fashion to sneer at or neglect.

The name of the victor of Arbela has led to these reflections; for, although the rapidity and extent of Alexander's conquests have through all ages challenged admiration and amazement, the grandeur of genius which he displayed in his schemes of commerce, civilization, and of comprehensive union and unity among nations, has, until lately, been comparatively unhonored. This long-continued depreciation was of early date. The ancient rhetoricians—a class of babblers, a school for lies and scandal, as Niebuhr justly termed them—chose, among the stock themes for their commonplaces, the character and exploits of Alexander. They had their followers in every age; and, until a very recent period, all who wished to "point a moral or adorn a tale," about unreasoning ambition, extravagant pride, and the formidable frenzies of free will when leagued with free power, have never failed to blazon forth the so-called madman of Macedonia as one of the most glaring examples. Without doubt, many of these writers adopted with implicit credence, traditional ideas, and supposed, with uninquiring philanthropy, that in blackening Alexander they were doing humanity good service. But also, without doubt, many of his assailants, like those of other great men, have been mainly instigated by "that strongest of all antipathies, the antipathy of a second-rate mind to a first-rate one,"[1] and by the envy which talent too often bears to genius.

Arrian, who wrote his history of Alexander when Hadrian was emperor of the Roman world, and when the spirit of declamation and dogmatism was at its full height, but who was himself, unlike the dreaming pedants of the schools, a statesman and a soldier of practical and proved ability, well rebuked the malevolent aspersions which he heard continually thrown upon the memory of the great conqueror of the East. He truly says, "Let the man who speaks evil of Alexander not merely bring forward those passages of Alexander's life which were really evil, but let him collect and review *all* the actions of Alexander, and then let him thoroughly consider first who and what manner of man he himself is, and what has been his own career; and then let him consider who and what manner of man Alexander was, and to what an eminence of human grandeur *he* arrived. Let him consider that Alexander was a king, and the undisputed lord of the two continents, and that his name is renowned throughout the whole earth. Let the evil-speaker against Alexander bear all this in mind, and then let him reflect on his own insignificance, the pettiness of his own circumstances and affairs, and the blunders that he makes about these, paltry and trifling as they are. Let him then ask himself whether he is a fit person to censure and revile such a man as Alexander. I believe that there was in his time no nation of men, no city, nay, no single individual, with whom Alexander's name had not become a familiar word. I therefore hold that such a man, who was like no ordinary mortal, was not born into the world without some special providence."[2]

And one of the most distinguished soldiers and writers of our own nation. Sir Walter Raleigh, though he failed to estimate justly the full merits of Alexander, has expressed his sense of the grandeur of the part played in the world by "the great Emathian conqueror" in language that well deserves quotation:

"So much hath the spirit of some one man excelled as it hath undertaken and effected the alteration of the greatest states and commonweals, the erection of monarchies, the conquest of kingdoms and empires, guided handfuls of men against multitudes of equal bodily strength, contrived victories beyond all hope and discourse of reason, converted the fearful passions of his own followers into magnanimity, and the valor of his enemies into cowardice; such spirits have been stirred up in sundry ages of the world, and in divers parts thereof, to erect and cast down again, to establish and to destroy, and to bring all things, persons, and states to the same certain ends, which the infinite spirit of the *Universal*, piercing, moving and governing all things, hath ordained. Certainly, the things that this king did were marvelous, and would hardly have been undertaken by any one else; and though his father had determined to have invaded the Lesser Asia, it is like enough that he would have contented himself with some part thereof, and not have discovered the river of Indus, as this man did."[3]

A higher authority than either Arrian or Raleigh may now be referred to by those who wish to know the real merit of Alexander as a general, and how far the commonplace assertions are true that his successes were the mere results of fortunate rashness and unreasoning pugnacity. Napoleon selected Alexander as one of the seven greatest generals whose noble deeds history has handed down to us, and from the study of whose campaigns the principles of war are to be learned. The critique of the greatest conqueror of modern times on the military career of the great conqueror of the Old World is no less graphic than true:

"Alexander crossed the Dardanelles 334 BC, with an army of about forty thousand men, of which one-eighth was cavalry; he forced the passage of the Granicus in opposition to an army under Memnon, the Greek, who commanded for Darius on the coast of Asia, and he spent the whole of the year 333 in establishing his power in Asia Minor. He was seconded by the Greek colonies, who dwelt on the borders of the Black Sea and on the Mediterranean, and in Sardis, Ephesus, Tarsus, Miletus, etc. The kings of Persia left their provinces and towns to be governed according to their own particular laws. Their empire was a union of confederated states, and did not form one nation; this facilitated its conquest. As Alexander only wished for the throne of the monarch, he easily effected the change by respecting the customs, manners, and laws of the people, who experienced no change in their condition.

"In the year 332 he met with Darius at the head of sixty thousand men, who had taken up a position near Tarsus, on the banks of the Issus, in the province of Cilicia. He defeated him, entered Syria, took Damascus, which contained all the riches of the Great King, and laid siege to Tyre. This superb metropolis of the commerce of the world detained him nine months. He took Gaza after a siege of two months; crossed the Desert in seven days; entered Pelusium and Memphis, and founded Alexandria. In less than two years, after two battles and four or five sieges, the coasts of the Black Sea, from Phasis to Byzantium, those of the Mediterranean as far as Alexandria, all Asia Minor, Syria, and Egypt, had submitted to his arms.

"In 331 he repassed the Desert, encamped in Tyre, recrossed Syria, entered Damascus, passed the Euphrates and Tigris, and defeated Darius on the field of Arbela when he was at the head of a still stronger army than that which he commanded on the Issus, and Babylon opened her gates to him. In 330 he overran Susa and took that city, Persepolis, and Pasargada, which contained the tomb of Cyrus. In 329 he directed his course northward, entered Ecbatana, and extended his conquests to the coasts of the Caspian, punished Bessus, the cowardly assassin of Darius, penetrated into

Scythia, and subdued the Scythians. In 328 he forced the passage of the Oxus, received sixteen thousand recruits from Macedonia, and reduced the neighboring people to subjection. In 327 he crossed the Indus, vanquished Porus in a pitched battle, took him prisoner, and treated him as a king. He contemplated passing the Ganges, but his army refused. He sailed down the Indus, in the year 326, with eight hundred vessels; having arrived at the ocean, he sent Nearchus with a fleet to run along the coasts of the Indian Ocean and the Persian Gulf as far as the mouth of the Euphrates. In 325 he took sixty days in crossing from Gedrosia, entered Keramania, returned to Pasargada, Persepolis, and Susa, and married Statira, the daughter of Darius. In 324 he marched once more to the north, passed Ecbatana, and terminated his career at Babylon."[4]

The enduring importance of Alexander's conquests is to be estimated, not by the duration of his own life and empire, or even by the duration of the kingdoms which his generals after his death formed out of the fragments of that mighty dominion. In every region of the world that he traversed, Alexander planted Greek settlements and founded cities, in the populations of which the Greek element at once asserted its predominance. Among his successors, the Seleucidæ and the Ptolemies imitated their great captain in blending schemes of civilization, of commercial intercourse, and of literary and scientific research with all their enterprises of military aggrandizement and with all their systems of civil administration. Such was the ascendancy of the Greek genius, so wonderfully comprehensive and assimilating was the cultivation which it introduced, that, within thirty years after Alexander crossed the Hellespont, the Greek language was spoken in every country from the shores of the Ægæan to the Indus, and also throughout Egypt—not, indeed, wholly to the extirpation of the native dialects, but it became the language of every court, of all literature, of every judicial and political function, and formed a medium of communication among the many myriads of mankind inhabiting these large portions of the Old World.[5] Throughout

Asia Minor, Syria, and Egypt, the Hellenic character that was thus imparted remained in full vigor down to the time of the Mohammedan conquests. The infinite value of this to humanity in the highest and holiest point of view has often been pointed out, and the workings of the finger of Providence have been gratefully recognized by those who have observed how the early growth and progress of Christianity were aided by that diffusion of the Greek language and civilization throughout Asia Minor, Syria, and Egypt, which had been caused by the Macedonian conquest of the East.

In upper Asia, beyond the Euphrates, the direct and material influence of Greek ascendancy was more short-lived. Yet, during the existence of the Hellenic kingdoms in these regions, especially of the Greek kingdom of Bactria, the modern Bokhara, very important effects were produced on the intellectual tendencies and tastes of the inhabitants of those countries, and of the adjacent ones, by the animating contact of the Grecian spirit. Much of Hindoo science and philosophy, much of the literature of the later Persian kingdom of the Arsacidæ, either originated from, or was largely modified by, Grecian influences. So, also, the learning and science of the Arabians were in a far less degree the result of original invention and genius, than the reproduction, in an altered form, of the Greek philosophy and the Greek lore acquired by the Saracenic conquerors, together with their acquisition of the provinces which Alexander had subjugated, nearly a thousand years before the armed disciples of Mohammed commenced their career in the East. It is well known that Western Europe in the Middle Ages drew its philosophy, its arts, and its science principally from Arabian teachers. And thus we see how the intellectual influence of ancient Greece, poured on the Eastern world by Alexander's victories, and then brought back to bear on Mediæval Europe by the spread of the Saracenic powers, has exerted its action on the elements of modern civilization by this powerful, though indirect, channel, as well as by the more obvious effects of the remnants of classic civilization which survived in Italy, Gaul, Britain, and Spain, after the irruption of the Germanic nations.[6]

These considerations invest the Macedonian triumphs in the East with never-dying interest, such as the most showy and sanguinary successes of mere "low ambition and the pride of kings," however they may dazzle for a moment, can never retain with posterity. Whether the old Persian empire which Cyrus founded could have survived much longer than it did, even if Darius had been victorious at Arbela, may safely be disputed. That ancient dominion, like the Turkish at the present time, labored under every cause of decay and dissolution. The satraps, like the modern pashaws, continually rebelled against the central power, and Egypt in particular was almost always in a state of insurrection against its nominal sovereign. There was no longer any effective central control, or any internal principle of unity fused through the huge mass of the empire, and binding it together. Persia was evidently about to fall; but, had it not been for Alexander's invasion of Asia, she would most probably have fallen beneath some other Oriental power, as Media and Babylon had formerly fallen before herself, and as, in after times, the Parthian supremacy gave way to the revived ascendancy of Persia in the East, under the sceptres of the Arsacidæ. A revolution that merely substituted one Eastern power for another would have been utterly barren and unprofitable to mankind.

Alexander's victory at Arbela not only overthrew an Oriental dynasty, but established European rulers in its stead. It broke the monotony of the Eastern world by the impression of Western energy and superior civilization, even as England's present mission is to break up the mental and moral stagnation of India and Cathay by pouring upon and through them the impulsive current of Anglo-Saxon commerce and conquest.

Arbela, the city which has furnished its name to the decisive battle which gave Asia to Alexander, lies more than twenty miles from the actual scene of the conflict. The little village, then named Gaugamela, is close to the spot where the armies met, but has ceded the honor of naming the battle to its more euphonious neighbor. Gaugamela is situate in one of the wide plains that lie between the Tigris and the mountains of Kurdistan. A few undulating hillocks diversify the surface of this sandy tract; but the ground is generally level, and admirably qualified for the evolutions of cavalry, and also calculated to give the larger of two armies the full advantage of numerical superiority. The Persian king (who, before he came to the throne, had proved his personal valor as a soldier and his skill as a general) had wisely selected this region for the third and decisive encounter between his forces and the invader. The previous defeats of his troops, however severe they had been, were not looked on as irreparable. The Granicus had been fought by his generals rashly and without mutual concert; and, though Darius himself had commanded and been beaten at Issus, that defeat might be attributed to the disadvantageous nature of the ground, where, cooped up between the mountains, the river, and the sea, the numbers of the Persians confused and clogged alike the general's skill and the soldiers' prowess, and their very strength had been made their weakness. Here, on the broad plains of Kurdistan, there was scope for Asia's largest host to array its lines, to wheel, to skirmish, to condense or expand its squadrons, to manoeuvre, and to charge at will. Should Alexander and his scanty band dare to plunge into that living sea of war, their destruction seemed inevitable.

Darius felt, however, the critical nature to himself, as well as to his adversary, of the coming encounter. He could not hope to retrieve the consequences of a third overthrow. The great cities of Mesopotamia and Upper Asia, the central provinces of the Persian empire, were certain to be at the mercy of the victor. Darius knew also the Asiatic character well enough to be aware how it yields to the *prestige* of success and the apparent career of destiny. He felt that the diadem was now either to be firmly replaced on his own brow, or to be irrevocably transferred to the head of his European conqueror. He, therefore, during the long interval left him after the battle of Issus, while Alexander was subjugating Syria and Egypt, assiduously busied himself in selecting the best troops which his vast empire supplied, and in training his varied forces to act together with some uniformity of discipline and system.

The hardy mountaineers of Afghanistan, Bokhara, Khiva, and Thibet were then, as at present, far different to the generality of Asiatics in warlike spirit and endurance. From these districts Darius collected large bodies of admirable infantry; and the countries of the modern Kurds and Turkomans supplied, as they do now, squadrons of horsemen, hardy, skilful, bold, and trained to a life of constant activity and warfare. It is not uninteresting to notice that the ancestors of our own late enemies, the Sikhs, served as allies of Darius against the Macedonians. They are spoken of in Arrian as Indians who dwelt near Bactria. They were attached to the troops of that satrapy, and their cavalry was one of the most formidable forces in the whole Persian army.

Besides these picked troops, contingents also came in from the numerous other provinces that yet obeyed the Great King. Altogether, the horse are said to have been forty thousand, the scythe-bearing chariots two hundred, and the armed elephants fifteen in number. The amount of the infantry is uncertain; but the knowledge which both ancient and modern times supply of the usual character of Oriental armies, and of ffieir populations of camp-followers, may warrant us in believing that many myriads were prepared to fight, or to encumber those who fought for the last Darius.

The position of the Persian king near Mesopotamia was chosen with great military skill. It was certain that Alexander, on his return from Egypt, must march northward along the Syrian coast before he attacked the central provinces of the Persian empire. A direct eastward march from the lower part of Palestine across the great Syrian Desert was then, as ever, utterly impracticable. Marching eastward from Syria, Alexander would, on crossing the Euphrates, arrive at the vast Mesopotamian plains. The wealthy capitals of the empire, Babylon, Susa, and Persepolis, would then lie to the south; and if he marched down through Mesopotamia to attack them, Darius might reasonably hope to follow the Macedonians with his immense force of cavalry, and, without even risking a pitched battle, to harass and finally overwhelm them. We may remember that three centuries afterwards a Roman army under Crassus was thus actually destroyed by the Oriental archers and horsemen in these very plains,[7] and that the ancestors of the Parthians who thus vanquished the Roman legions served by thousands under King Darius. If, on the contrary, Alexander should defer his march against Babylon, and first seek an encounter with the Persian army, the country on each side of the Tigris in this latitude was highly advantageous for such an army as Darius commanded, and he had close in his rear the mountainous districts of Northern Media, where he himself had in early life been satrap, where he had acquired reputation as a soldier and a general, and where he justly expected to find loyalty to his person, and a safe refuge in case of defeat.[8]

His great antagonist came on across the Euphrates against him, at the head of an army which Arrian, copying from the journals of Macedonian officers, states to have consisted of forty thousand foot and seven thousand horse. In studying the campaigns of Alexander, we possess the peculiar advantage of deriving our information from two of Alexander's generals of division, who bore an important part in all his enterprises. Aristobulus and Ptolemy (who afterward became king of Egypt) kept regular journals of the military events which they witnessed, and these journals were in the possession of Arrian when he drew up his history of Alexander's expedition. The high character of Arrian for integrity makes us confident that he used them fairly, and his comments on the occasional discrepancies between the two Macedonian narratives prove that he used them sensibly. He frequently quotes the very words of his authorities; and his history thus acquires a charm such as very few ancient or modern military narratives possess. The anecdotes and expressions which he records we fairly believe to be genuine, and not to be the coinage of a rhetorician, like those in Curtius. In fact, in reading Arrian, we read General Aristobulus and General Ptolemy on the campaigns of the Macedonians, and it is like reading General Jomini or General Foy on the campaigns of the French.

The estimate which we find in Arrian of the strength of Alexander's army seems reasonable enough, when we take into account both the losses which he had sustained and the re-enforcements which he had received since he left Europe. Indeed, to Englishmen, who know with what mere handfuls of men our own generals have, at Plassy, at Assaye, at Meeanee, and other Indian battles, routed large hosts of Asiatics, the disparity of numbers that we read of in the victories won by the Macedonians over the Persians presents nothing incredible. The army which Alexander now led was wholly composed of veteran troops in the highest possible state of equipment and discipline, enthusiastically devoted to their leader, and full of confidence in his military genius and his victorious destiny.

The celebrated Macedonian phalanx formed the main strength of his infantry. This force had been raised and organized by his father Philip, who, on his accession to the Macedonian throne, needed a numerous and quickly-formed army, and who, by lengthening the spear of the ordinary Greek phalanx, and increasing the depth of the files, brought the tactic of armed masses to the highest extent of which it was capable with such materials as he possessed.[9] He formed his men sixteen deep, and placed in their grasp the *sarissa*, as the Macedonian pike was called, which was four-and-twenty feet in length, and when couched for action, reached eighteen feet in front of the soldier; so that, as a space of about two feet was allowed between the ranks, the spears of the five files behind him projected in front of each front-rank man. The phalangite soldier was fully equipped in the defensive armor of the regular Greek infantry. And thus the phalanx presented a ponderous and bristling mass, which, as long as its order was kept compact, was sure to bear down all opposition. The defects of such an organization are obvious, and were proved in after years, when the Macedonians were opposed to the Roman legions. But it is clear that under Alexander the phalanx was not the cumbrous, unwieldy body which it was at Cynoscephalæ and Pydna. His men were veterans; and he could obtain from them an accuracy of movement and steadiness of evolution such as probably the recruits of his father would only have floundered in attempting, and such as certainly were impracticable in the phalanx when handled by his successors, especially as under them it ceased to be a standing force, and became only a militia.[10] Under Alexander the phalanx consisted of an aggregate of eighteen thousand men, who were divided into six brigades of three thousand each. These were again subdivided into regiments and companies; and the men were carefully trained to wheel, to face about, to take more ground, or to close up, as the emergencies of the battle required. Alexander also arrayed troops armed in a different manner in the intervals of the regiments of his phalangites, who could prevent their line from being pierced and their companies taken in flank, when the nature of the ground prevented a close formation, and who could be withdrawn when a favorable opportunity arrived for closing up the phalanx or any of its brigades for a charge, or when it was necessary to prepare to receive cavalry.

Besides the phalanx, Alexander had a considerable force of infantry who were called shield-bearers: they were not so heavily armed as the phalangites, or as was the case with the Greek regular infantry in general, but they were equipped for close fight as well as for skirmishing, and were far superior to the ordinary irregular troops of Greek warfare. They were about six thousand strong. Besides these, he had several bodies of Greek regular infantry; and he had archers, slingers, and javelin-men, who fought also with broadsword and target, and who were principally supplied him by the highlanders of Illyria and Thracia. The main strength of his cavalry consisted in two chosen regiments of cuirassiers, one Macedonian and one Thessalian, each of which was about fifteen hundred strong. They were provided with long lances and heavy swords, and horse as well as man was fully equipped with defensive armor. Other regiments of regular cavalry were less heavily armed, and there were several bodies of light horsemen, whom Alexander's conquests in Egypt and Syria had enabled him to mount superbly.

A little before the end of August, Alexander crossed the Euphrates at Thapsacus, a small corps of Persian cavalry under Mazæus retiring before him. Alexander was too prudent to march down through the Mesopotamian deserts, and continued to advance eastward with the intention of passing the Tigris, and then, if he was unable to find Darius and bring him to action, of marching southward on the left side of that river along the skirts of a mountainous district where his men would suffer less from heat and thirst, and where provisions would be more abundant.

Darius, finding that his adversary was not to be enticed into the march through Mesopotamia against his capital, determined to remain on the battle-ground, which he had chosen on the left of the Tigris; where, if his enemy met a defeat or a check, the destruction of the invaders would be certain with two such rivers as the Euphrates and the Tigris in their rear. The Persian king availed himself to the utmost of every advantage in his power. He caused a large space of ground to be carefully levelled for the operation of his scythe-armed chariots; and he deposited his military stores in the strong town of Arbela, about twenty miles in his rear. The rhetoricians of after ages have loved to describe Darius Codomanus as a second Xerxes in ostentation and imbecility; but a fair examination of his generalship in this his last campaign shows that he was worthy of bearing the same name as his great predecessor, the royal son of Hystaspes.

On learning that Darius was with a large army on the left of the Tigris, Alexander hurried forward and crossed that river without opposition. He was at first unable to procure any certain intelligence of the precise position of the enemy, and after giving his army a short interval of rest, he marched for four days down the left bank of the river. A moralist may pause upon the fact that Alexander must in this march have passed within a few miles of the ruins of Nineveh, the great city of the primeval conquerors of the human race. Neither the Macedonian king nor any of his followers knew what those vast mounds had once been. They had already sunk into utter destruction; and it is only within the last few years that the intellectual energy of one of our own countrymen has rescued Nineveh from its long centuries of oblivion.[11]

On the fourth day of Alexander's southward march, his advanced guard reported that a body of the enemy's cavalry was in sight. He instantly formed his army in order for battle, and directing them to advance steadily, he rode forward at the head of some squadrons of cavalry, and charged the Persian horse, whom he found before him. This was a mere reconnoitring party, and they broke and fled immediately; but the Macedonians made some prisoners, and from them Alexander found that Darius was posted only a few miles off, and learned the strength of the army that he had with him. On receiving this news Alexander halted, and gave his men repose for four days, so that they should go into action fresh and vigorous. He also fortified his camp and deposited in it all his military stores, and all his sick and disabled soldiers, intending to advance upon the enemy with the serviceable part of his army perfectly unencumbered. After this halt, he moved forward, while it was yet dark, with the intention of reaching the enemy, and attacking them at break of day. About half way between the camps there were some undulations of the ground, which concealed the two armies from each other's view; but, on Alexander arriving at their summit, he saw, by the early light, the Persian host arrayed before him, and he probably also observed traces of some engineering operation having been carried on along part of the ground in front of them. Not knowing that these marks had been caused by the Persians having levelled the ground for the free use of their war-chariots, Alexander suspected that hidden pitfalls had been prepared with a view of disordering the approach of his cavalry. He summoned a council of war forthwith. Some of the officers were for attacking instantly, at all hazards; but the more prudent opinion of Parmenio prevailed, and it was determined not to advance further till the battle-ground had been carefully surveyed.

Alexander halted his army on the heights, and, taking with him some light-armed infantry and some cavalry, he passed part of the day in reconnoitring the enemy, and observing the nature of the ground which he had to fight on. Darius wisely refrained from moving from his position to attack the Macedonians on the eminences which they occupied, and the two armies remained until night without molesting each other. On Alexander's return to his headquarters, he summoned his generals and superior officers together, and telling them that he knew well that *their* zeal wanted no exhortation, he besought them to do their utmost in encouraging and instructing those whom each commanded, to do their best in the next day's battle. They were to remind them that they were now not going to fight for a province as they had hitherto fought, but they were about to decide by their swords the dominion of all Asia. Each officer ought to impress this upon his subalterns, and they should urge it on their men. Their natural courage required no long words to excite its ardor; but they should be reminded of the paramount importance of steadiness in action. The silence in the ranks must be unbroken as long as silence was proper; but when the time came for the charge, the shout and the cheer must be full of terror for the foe. The officers were to be alert in receiving and communicating orders; and every one was to act as if he felt that the whole result of the battle depended on his own single good conduct.

Having thus briefly instructed his generals, Alexander ordered that the army should sup, and take their rest for the night.

Darkness had closed over the tents of the Macedonians, when Alexander's veteran general, Parmenio, came to him, and proposed that they should make a night attack on the Persians. The king is said to have answered that he scorned to filch a victory, and that Alexander must conquer openly and fairly. Arrian justly remarks that Alexander's resolution was as wise as it was spirited. Besides the confusion and uncertainty which are inseparable from night engagements, the value of Alexander's victory would have been impaired, if gained under circumstances which might supply the enemy with any excuse for his defeat, and encouraged him to renew the contest. It was necessary for Alexander not only to beat Darius, but to gain such a victory as should leave his rival without apology and without hope of recovery.

The Persians, in fact, expected, and were prepared to meet, a night attack. Such was the apprehension that Darius entertained of it, that he formed his troops at evening in order of battle, and kept them under arms all night. The effect of this was, that the morning found them jaded and dispirited, while it brought their adversaries all fresh and vigorous against them.

The written order of battle which Darius himself caused to be drawn up, fell into the hands of the Macedonians after the engagement, and Aristobulus copied it into his journal. We thus possess, through Arrian, unusually authentic information as to the composition and arrangement of the Persian army. On the extreme left were the Bactrian, Daan, and Arachosian cavalry. Next to these Darius placed the troops from Persia proper, both horse and foot. Then came the Susians, and next to these the Cadusians. These forces made up the left wing. Darius' own station was in the centre. This was composed of the Indians, the Carians, the Mardian archers, and the division of Persians who were distinguished by the golden apples that formed the knobs of their spears. Here also were stationed the body-guard of the Persian nobility. Besides these, there were, in the centre, formed in deep order, the Uxian and Babylonian troops, and the soldiers from the Red Sea. The brigade of Greek mercenaries whom Darius had in his service, and who alone were considered fit to stand the charge of the Macedonian phalanx, was drawn up on either side of the royal chariot. The right wing was composed of the Cœlosyrians and Mesopotamians, the Medes, the Parthians, the Sacians, the Tapurians, Hyrcanians, Albanians, and Sacesinæ. In advance of the line on the left wing were placed the Scythian cavalry, with a thousand of the Bactrian horse, and a hundred scythe-armed chariots. The elephants and fifty scythe-armed chariots were ranged in front of the centre; and fifty more chariots, with the Armenian and Cappadocian cavalry, were drawn up in advance of the right wing.

Thus arrayed, the great host of King Darius passed the night, that to many thousands of them was the last of their existence. The morning of the first of October,[12] two thousand one hundred and eighty-two years ago, dawned slowly to their wearied watching, and they could hear the note of the Macedonian trumpet sounding to arms, and could see King Alexander's forces descend from their tents on the heights, and form in order of battle on the plain.

There was deep need of skill, as well as of valor, on Alexander's side; and few battle-fields have witnessed more consummate generalship than was now displayed by the Macedonian king. There were no natural barriers by which he could protect his flanks; and not only was he certain to be overlapped on either wing by the vast lines of the Persian army, hut there was imminent risk of their circling round him, and charging him in the rear, while he advanced against their centre. He formed, therefore, a second or reserve line, which was to wheel round, if required, or to detach troops to either flank, as the enemy's movements might necessitate; and thus, with their whole army ready at any moment to be thrown into one vast hollow square, the Macedonians advanced in two lines against the enemy, Alexander himself leading on the right wing, and the renowned phalanx forming the centre, while Parmenio commanded on the left.

Such was the general nature of the disposition which Alexander made of his army. But we have in Arrian the details of the position of each brigade and regiment; and as we know that these details were taken from the journals of Macedonian generals, it is interesting to examine them, and to read the names and stations of King Alexander's generals and colonels in this, the greatest of his battles.

The eight regiments of the royal horse-guards formed the right of Alexander's line. Their colonels were Cleitus (whose regiment was on the extreme right, the post of peculiar danger), Glaucias, Ariston, Sopolis, Heracleides, Demetrias, Meleager, and Hegelochus. Philotas was general of the whole division. Then came the shield-bearing infantry: Nicanor was their general. Then came the phalanx in six brigades. Cœnus' brigade was on the right, and nearest to the shield-bearers; next to this stood the brigade of Perdiccas, then Meleager's, then Polysperchon's; and then the brigade of Amynias, but which was now commanded by Simmias, as Amynias had been sent to Macedonia to levy recruits. Then came the infantry of the left wing, under the command of Craterus. Next to Craterus' infantry were placed the cavalry regiments of the allies, with Eriguius for their general. The Thessalian cavalry, commanded by Philippus, were next, and held the extreme left of the whole army. The whole left wing was intrusted to the command of Parmenio, who had round his person the Pharsalian regiment of cavalry, which was the strongest and best of all the Thessalian horse regiments.

The centre of the second line was occupied by a body of phalangite infantry, formed of companies which were dratted for this purpose from each of the brigades of their phalanx. The officers in command of this corps were ordered to be ready to face about, if the enemy should succeed in gaining the rear of the army. On the right of this reserve of infantry, in the second line, and behind the royal horse-guards, Alexander placed half the Agrian light-armed infantry under Attalus, and with them Brison's body of Macedonian archers and Cleander's regiment of foot. He also placed in this part of his army Menidas' squadron of calvary, and Aretes' and Ariston's light horse. Menidas was ordered to watch if the enemy's cavalry tried to turn their flank, and, if they did so, to charge them before they wheeled completely round, and so take them in flank themselves. A similar force was arranged on the left of the second line for the same purpose. The Thracian infantry of Sitalces were placed there, and Cœranus' regiment of the cavalry of the Greek allies, and Agathon's troops of the Odrysian irregular horse. The extreme left of the second line in this quarter was held by Andromachus' cavalry. A division of Thracian infantry was left in guard of the camp. In advance of the right wing and centre was scattered a number of light-armed troops, of javelin-men and bow-men, with the intention of warding off the charge of the armed chariots.[13]

Conspicuous by the brilliancy of his armor, and by the chosen band of officers who were round his person, Alexander took his own station, as his custom was, in the right wing, at the head of his cavalry; and when all the arrangements for the battle were complete, and his generals were fully instructed how to act in each probable emergency, he began to lead his men toward the enemy. It was ever his custom to expose his life freely in battle, and to emulate the personal prowess of his great ancestor, Achilles. Perhaps, in the bold enterprise of conquering Persia, it was politic for Alexander to raise his army's daring to the utmost by the example of his own heroic valor; and, in his subsequent campaigns, the love of the excitement, of "the raptures of the strife," may have made him, like Murat, continue from choice a custom which he commenced from duty. But he never suffered the ardor of the soldier to make him lose the coolness of the general, and at Arbela, in particular, he showed that he could act up to his favorite Homeric maxim of being

Ἀμφότερον, βασιλεύς τ' ἀγαθὸς κρατερός τ' αἰχμητής.

Great reliance had been placed by the Persian king on the effects of the scythe-bearing chariots. It was designed to launch these against the Macedonian phalanx, and to follow them up by a heavy charge of cavalry, which, it was hoped, would find the ranks of the spearmen disordered by the rush of the chariots, and easily destroy this most formidable part of Alexander's force. In front, therefore, of the Persian centre, where Darius took his station, and which it was supposed that the phalanx would attack, the ground had been carefully levelled and smoothed, so as to allow the chariots to charge over it with their full sweep and speed. As the Macedonian army approached the Persian, Alexander found that the front of his whole line barely equalled the front of the Persian centre, so that he was outflanked on his right by the entire left wing of the enemy, and by their entire right wing on his left. His tactics were to assail some one point of the hostile army, and gain a decisive advantage, while he refused, as far as possible, the encounter along the rest of the line. He therefore inclined his order of march to the right, so as to enable his right wing and centre to come into collision with the enemy on as favorable terms as possible, although the manœuvre might in some respect compromise his left.

The effect of this oblique movement was to bring the phalanx and his own wing nearly beyond the limits of the ground which the Persians had prepared for the operations of the chariots; and Darius, fearing to lose the benefit of this arm against the most important parts of the Macedonian force, ordered the Scythian and Bactrian cavalry, who were drawn up in advance on his extreme left, to charge round upon Alexander's right wing, and check its further lateral progress. Against these assailants Alexander sent from his second line Menidas' cavalry. As these proved too few to make head against the enemy, he ordered Ariston also from the second line with his right horse, and Cleander with his foot, in support of Menidas. The Bactrians and Scythians now began to give way; but Darius reinforced them by the mass of Bactrian cavalry from his main line, and an obstinate cavalry fight now took place. The Bactrians and Scythians were numerous, and were better armed than the horsemen under Menidas and Ariston; and the loss at first was heaviest on the Macedonian side. But still the European cavalry stood the charge of the Asiatics, and at last, by their superior discipline, and by acting in squadrons that supported each other,[14] instead of fighting in a confused mass like the barbarians, the Macedonians broke their adversaries, and drove them off the field.

Darius now directed the scythe-armed chariots to be driven against Alexander's horse-guards and the phalanx, and these formidable vehicles were accordingly sent rattling across the plain, against the Macedonian line. When we remember the alarm which the war-chariots of the Britons created among Cæsar's legions, we shall not be prone to deride this arm of ancient warfare as always useless. The object of the chariots was to create unsteadiness in the ranks against which they were driven, and squadrons of cavalry followed close upon them to profit by such rder. But the Asiatic chariots were rendered ineffective at ̲.̲.̲.̲:la by the light-armed troops, whom Alexander had specially appointed for the service, and who, wounding the horses and drivers with their missile weapons, and running alongside so as to cut the traces or seize the reins, marred the intended charge; and the few chariots that reached the phalanx passed harmlessly through the intervals which the spearmen opened for them, and were easily captured in the rear.

A mass of the Asiatic cavalry was now, for the second time, collected against Alexander's extreme right, and moved round it, with the view of gaining the flank of his army. At the critical moment, when their own flanks were exposed by this evolution, Aretes dashed on the Persian squadrons with his horsemen from Alexander's second line. While Alexander thus met and baffled all the flanking attacks of the enemy with troops brought up from his second line, he kept his own horse-guards and the rest of the front line of his wing fresh, and ready to take advantage of the first opportunity for striking a decisive blow. This soon came. A large body of horse, who were posted on the Persian left wing nearest to the centre, quitted their station, and rode off to help their comrades in the cavalry fight, that still was going on at the extreme right of Alexander's wing against the detachments from his second line. This made a huge gap in the Persian array, and into this space Alexander instantly charged with his guard and all the cavalry of his wing; and then pressing toward his left, he soon began to make havoc in the left flank of the Persian centre. The shield-bearing infantry now charged also among the reeling masses of the Asiatics; and five of the brigades of the phalanx, with the irresistible might of their sarissas, bore down the Greek mercenaries of Darius, and dug their way through the Persian centre. In the early part of the battle Darius had showed skill and energy; and he now, for some time, encouraged his men, by voice and example, to keep firm. But the lances of Alexander's cavalry and the pikes of the phalanx now pressed nearer and nearer to him. His charioteer was struck down by a javelin at his side; and at last Darius' nerve failed him, and, descending from his chariot, he mounted on a fleet horse and galloped from the plain, regardless of the state of the battle in other parts of the field, where matters were going on much more favorably for his cause, and where his presence might have done much toward gaining a victory.

Alexander's operations with his right and centre had exposed his left to an immensely preponderating force of the enemy. Parmenio kept out of action as long as possible; but Mazæus, who commanded the Persian right wing, advanced against him, completely outflanked him, and pressed him severely with reiterated charges by superior numbers. Seeing the distress of Parmenio's wing, Simmias, who commanded the sixth brigade of the phalanx, which was next to the left wing, did not advance with the other brigades in the great charge upon the Persian centre, but kept back to cover Parmenio's troops on *their* right flank, as otherwise they would have been completely surrounded and cut off from the rest of the Macedonian army. By so doing, Simmias had unavoidably opened a gap in the Macedonian left centre; and a large column of Indian and Persian horse, from the Persian right centre, had galloped forward through this interval, and right through the troops of the Macedonian second line. Instead of then wheeling round upon Parmenio, or upon the rear of Alexander's conquering wing, the Indian and Persian cavalry rode straight on to the Macedonian camp, overpowered the Thracians who were left in charge of it, and began to plunder. This was stopped by the phalangite troops of the second line, who, after the enemy's horsemen had rushed by them, faced about, counter-marched upon the camp, killed many of the Indians and Persians in the act of plundering, and forced the rest to ride off again. Just at this crisis, Alexander had been recalled from his pursuit of Darius by tidings of the distress of Parmenio and of his inability to bear up any longer against the hot attacks of Mazæus. Taking his horse-guards with him, Alexander rode toward the part of the field where his left wing was fighting; but on his way thither he encountered the Persian and Indian cavalry, on their return from his camp.

These men now saw that their only chance of safety was to cut their way through, and in one huge column they charged desperately upon the Macedonian regiments. There was here a close hand-to-hand fight, which lasted some time, and sixty of the royal horse-guards fell, and three generals, who fought close to Alexander's side, were wounded. At length the Macedonian discipline and valor again prevailed, and a large number of the Persian and Indian horsemen were cut down, some few only succeeding in breaking through and riding away. Relieved of these obstinate enemies, Alexander again formed his regiments of horse-guards, and led them toward Parmenio; but by this time that general also was victorious. Probably the news of Darius' flight had reached Mazæus, and had damped the ardor of the Persian right wing, while the tidings of their comrades' success must have proportionally encouraged the Macedonian forces under Parmenio. His Thessalian cavalry particularly distinguished themselves by their gallantry and persevering good conduct; and by the time that Alexander had ridden up to Parmenio, the whole Persian army was in full flight from the field.

It was of the deepest importance to Alexander to secure the person of Darius, and he now urged on the pursuit. The River Lycus was between the field of battle and the city of Arbela, whither the fugitives directed their course, and the passage of this river was even more destructive to the Persians than the swords and spears of the Macedonians had been in the engagement.[15] The narrow bridge was soon choked up by the flying thousands who rushed toward it, and vast numbers of the Persians threw themselves, or were hurried by others, into the rapid stream, and perished in its waters. Darius had crossed it, and had ridden on through Arbela without halting. Alexander reached the city on the next day, and made himself master of all Darius' treasure and stores; but the Persian king, unfortunately for himself, had fled too fast for his conqueror, but had only escaped to perish by the treachery of his Bactrian satrap, Bessus.

A few days after the battle Alexander entered Babylon, "the oldest seat of earthly empire" then in existence, as its acknowledged lord and master. There were yet some campaigns of his brief and bright career to be accomplished. Central Asia was yet to witness the march of his phalanx. He was yet to effect that conquest of Afghanistan in which England since has failed. His generalship, as well as his valor, was yet to be signalized on the banks of the Hydaspes and the field of Chillianwallah; and he was yet to precede the Queen of England in annexing the Punjaub to the dominions of a European sovereign. But the crisis of his career was reached; the great object of his mission was accomplished; and the ancient Persian empire, which once menaced all the nations of the earth with subjection, was irreparably crushed when Alexander had won his crowning victory at Arbela.

Synopsis of Events Between the Battle of Arbela and the Battle of the Metaurus.

BC 330. The Lacedaemonians endeavor to create a rising in Greece against the Macedonian power; they are defeated by Antipater, Alexander's viceroy; and their king, Agis, falls in the battle.

330 to 327. Alexander's campaigns in Upper Asia.

327, 326. Alexander marches through Afghanistan to the Punjaub. He defeats Porus. His troops refuse to march toward the Ganges and he commences the descent of the Indus. On his march he attacks and subdues several Indian tribes—among others, the Malli, in the storming of whose capital (Moortan) he is severely wounded. He directs his admiral, Nearchus, to sail round from the Indus to the Persian Gulf, and leads the army back across Scinde and Beloochistan.

324. Alexander returns to Babylon. "In the tenth year after he had crossed the Hellespont, Alexander, having won his vast dominion, entered Babylon; and resting from his career in that oldest seat of earthly empire, he steadily surveyed the mass of various nations which owned his sovereignty, and resolved in his mind the great work of breathing into this huge but inert body the living spirit of Greek civilization. In the bloom of youthful manhood, at the age of thirty-two, he paused from the fiery speed of his earlier

course, and for the first time gave the nations an opportunity of offering their homage before his throne. They came from all the extremities of the earth to propitiate his anger, to celebrate his greatness, or to solicit his protection. * * * History may allow us to think that Alexander and a Roman ambassador did meet at Babylon; that the greatest man of the ancient world saw and spoke with a citizen of that great nation which was destined to succeed him in his appointed work, and to found a wider and still more enduring empire. They met, too, in Babylon, almost beneath the shadow of the Temple of Bel, perhaps the earliest monument ever raised by human pride and power in a city, stricken, as it were, by the word of God's heaviest judgment, as the symbol of greatness apart from and opposed to goodness." — (ARNOLD.)

323. Alexander dies at Babylon. On his death being known at Greece, the Athenians, and others of the southern states, take up arms to shake off the domination of Macedon. They are at first successful; but the return of some of Alexander's veterans from Asia enables Antipater to prevail over them.

317 to 289. Agathocles is tyrant of Syracuse, and carries on repeated wars with the Carthaginians, in the course of which (311) he invades Africa, and reduces the Carthaginians to great distress.

306. After a long series of wars with each other, and after all the heirs of Alexander had been murdered, his principal surviving generals assume the title of king, each over the provinces which he has occupied. The four chief among them were Antigonus, Ptolemy, Lysimachus, and Seleucus. Antipater was now dead, but his son Cassander succeeded to his power in Macedonia and Greece.

301. Seleucus and Lysimachus defeat Antigonus at Ipsus. Antigonus is killed in the battle.

280. Seleucus, the last of Alexander's captains, is assassinated. Of all of Alexander's successors, Seleucus had formed the most powerful empire. He had acquired all the provinces between Phrygia and the Indus. He extended his dominion in India beyond the limits reached by Alexander. Seleucus had some sparks of his great master's genius in promoting civilization and

commerce, as well as in gaining victories. Under his successors, the Seleucidæ, this vast empire rapidly diminished: Bactria became independent, and a separate dynasty of Greek kings ruled there in the year 125, when it was overthrown by the Scythian tribe. Parthia threw off its allegiance to the Seleucidæ in 250 BC, and the powerful Parthian kingdom, which afterwards proved so formidable a foe to Rome, absorbed nearly all the provinces west of the Euphrates that had obeyed the first Seleucus. Before the battle of Ipsus, Mithridates, a Persian prince of the blood-royal of the Achæmenidæ, had escaped to Pontus and founded there the kingdom of that name.

Besides the kingdom of Seleucus, which, when limited to Syria, Palestine, and parts of Asia Minor, long survived, the most important kingdom formed by a general of Alexander was that of the Ptolemies in Egypt. The throne of Macedonia was long and obstinately contended for by Cassander, Polysperchon, Lysimachus, Pyrrhus, Antigonus, and others, but at last was secured by the dynasty of Antigonus Gonatas. The old republics of Southern Greece suffered severely during these tumults, and the only Greek states that showed any strength and spirit were the cities of the Achæan league, the Ætolians, and the islanders of Rhodes.

290. Rome had now thoroughly subdued the Samnites and the Etruscans, and had gained numerous victories over the Cisalpine Gauls. Wishing to confirm her dominion in Lower Italy, she became entangled in a war with Pyrrhus, fourth king of Epirus, who was called over by the Tarentines to aid them. Pyrrhus was at first victorious, but in the year 275 was defeated by the Roman legions in a pitched battle. He returned to Greece, remarking of Sicily, Οἵαν ἀπολείπομεν Καρχηδονίοις καὶ Ῥωμαίοις παλαίστραν, "Rome becomes mistress of all Italy from the Rubicon to the Straits of Messina."

264. The first Punic war begins. Its primary cause was the desire of both the Romans and the Carthaginians to possess themselves of Sicily. The Romans form a fleet, and successfully compete with the marine of Carthage.[16] During the latter half of the war

the military genius of Hamilcar Barca sustains the Carthaginian cause in Sicily. At the end of twenty-four years the Carthaginians sue for peace, though their aggregate loss in ships and men had been less than that sustained by the Romans since the beginning of the war. Sicily becomes a Roman province.

240 to 218. The Carthaginian mercenaries who had been brought back from Sicily to Africa mutiny against Carthage, and nearly succeed in destroying her. After a sanguinary and desperate struggle, Hamilcar Barca crushes them. During this season of weakness to Carthage, Rome takes from her the island of Sardinia. Hamilcar Barca forms the project of obtaining compensation by conquests in Spain, and thus enabling Carthage to renew the struggle with Rome. He takes Hannibal (then a child) to Spain with him. He, and, after his death, his brother win great part of Southern Spain to the Carthaginian interest. Hannibal obtains the command of the Carthaginian armies in Spain 221 BC, being then twenty-six years old. He attacks Saguntum, a city on the Ebro, in alliance with Rome, which is the immediate pretext for the second Punic war.

During this interval Rome had to sustain a storm from the North. The Cisalpine Gauls, in 226, formed an alliance with one of the fiercest tribes of their brethren north of the Alps, and began a furious war against the Romans, which lasted six years. The Romans gave them several severe defeats, and took from them part of their territories near the Po. It was on this occasion that the Roman colonies of Cremona and Placentia were founded, the latter of which did such essential service to Rome in the second Punic war by the resistance which it made to the army of Hasdrubal. A muster-roll was made in this war of the effective military force of the Romans themselves, and of those Italian states that were subject to them. The return showed a force of seven hundred thousand foot and seventy thousand horse. Polybius, who mentions this muster, remarks,

Εφ' οὕς Ἀννίβας ἐλάττους ἔχων δισμυρίων, ἐπέβαλεν εἰς τήν Ἰταλίαν.

218. Hannibal crosses the Alps and invades Italy.

CHAPTER IV

THE BATTLE OF THE METAURUS, BC 207

"Quid debeas, O Roma, Neronibus,
Testis Metaurum flumen, et Hasdrubal
Devictus, et pulcher fugatis
Ille dies Latio tenebris.

"Qui primus alma risit adorea;
Dirus per urbes Afer ut Italas,
Ceu flamma per taedas vel Eurus
Per Siculas equitavit undas."

—*Horatius, iv. od. 4."*

The consul Nero, who made the unequalled march which deceived
Hannibal and deceived Hasdrubal, thereby accomplishing an achieve-
ment almost unrivaled in military annals. The first intelligence of his
return, to Hannibal, was the sight of Hasdrubal's head thrown into
his camp. When Hannibal saw this, he exclaimed, with a sigh, that
Rome would now be the mistress of the world. To this victory of Nero's
it might be owing that his imperial namesake reigned at all. But the
infamy of the one has eclipsed the glory of the other. When the name of
Nero is heard, who thinks of the consul? But such are human things."

—*Byron.*

ABOUT midway between Rimini and Ancona a little river falls into
the Adriatic, after traversing one of those districts of Italy in which
a vain attempt has lately been made to revive, after long centuries
of servitude and shame, the spirit of Italian nationality and the

energy of free institutions. That stream is still called the Metauro, and wakens by its name the recollections of the resolute daring of ancient Rome, and of the slaughter that stained its current two thousand and sixty three years ago, when the combined consular armies of Livius and Nero encountered and crushed near its banks the varied hosts which Hannibal's brother was leading from the Pyrenees, the Rhone, the Alps, and the Po, to aid the great Carthaginian in his stern struggle to annihilate the growing might of the Roman republic, and make the Punic power supreme over all the nations of the world.

The Roman historian, who termed that struggle the most memorable of all wars that ever were carried on,[1] wrote in no spirit of exaggeration; for it is not in ancient, but in modern history, that parallels for its incidents and its heroes are to be found. The similitude between the contest which Rome maintained against Hannibal, and that which England was for many years engaged in against Napoleon, has not passed unobserved by recent historians. "Twice," says Arnold,[2] "has there been witnessed the struggle of the highest individual genius against the resources and institutions of a great nation, and in both cases the nation has been victorious. For seventeen years Hannibal strove against Rome; for sixteen years Napoleon Bonaparte strove against England: the efforts of the first ended in Zama; those of the second in Waterloo." One point, however, of the similitude between the two wars has scarcely been adequately dwelt on; that is, the remarkable parallel between the Roman general who finally defeated the great Carthaginian, and the English general who gave the last deadly overthrow to the French emperor. Scipio and Wellington both held for many years commands of high importance, but distant from the main theatres of warfare. The same country was the scene of the principal military career of each. It was in Spain that Scipio, like Wellington, successively encountered and overthrew nearly all the subordinate generals of the enemy before being opposed to the chief champion and conqueror himself. Both Scipio and Wellington restored their countrymen's confidence in arms when shaken by a series of reverses, and each of them closed a long and perilous war by a complete and overwhelming defeat of the chosen leader and the chosen veterans of the foe.

Nor is the parallel between them limited to their military characters and exploits. Scipio, like Wellington, became an important leader of the aristocratic party among his countrymen, and was exposed to the unmeasured invectives of the violent section of his political antagonists. When, early in the reign of William IV., an infuriated mob assaulted the Duke of Wellington in the streets of the English capital on the anniversary of Waterloo, England was even more disgraced by that outrage than Rome was by the factious accusations which demagogues brought against Scipio, but which he proudly repelled on the day of trial by reminding the assembled people that it was the anniversary of the battle of Zama. Happily, a wiser and a better spirit has now for years pervaded all classes of our community, and we shall be spared the ignominy of having worked out to the end the parallel of national ingratitude. Scipio died a voluntary exile from the malevolent turbulence of Rome. Englishmen of all ranks and politics have now long united in affectionate admiration of our modern Scipio; and even those who have most widely differed from the duke on legislative or administrative questions, forget what they deem the political errors of that time-honored head, while they gratefully call to mind the laurels that have wreathed it.

Scipio at Zama trampled in the dust the power of Carthage, but that power had been already irreparably shattered in another field, where neither Scipio nor Hannibal commanded. When the Metaurus witnessed the defeat and death of Hasdrubal, it witnessed the ruin of the scheme by which alone Carthage could hope to organize decisive success — the scheme of enveloping Rome at once from the north and the south of Italy by two chosen armies, led by two sons of Hamilcar.[3] That battle was the determining crisis of the contest, not merely between Rome and Carthage, but between the two great families of the world, which then made Italy the arena of their oft-renewed contest for pre-eminence.

The French historian, Michelet, whose "Histoire Romaine" would have been invaluable if the general industry and accuracy of the writer had in any degree equalled his originality and brilliancy, eloquently remarks, "It is not without reason that so universal and vivid a remembrance of the Punic wars has dwelt in the memories of men. They formed no mere struggle to determine the lot of two cities or two empires; but it was a strife, on the event of which depended the fate of two races of mankind, whether the dominion of the world should belong to the Indo-Germanic or to the Semitic family of nations. Bear in mind that the first of these comprises, besides the Indians and the Persians, the Greeks, the Romans, and the Germans. In the other are ranked the Jews and the Arabs, the Phœnicians and the Carthaginians. On the one side is the genius of heroism, of art, and legislation; on the other is the spirit of industry, of commerce, of navigation. The two opposite races have everywhere come into contact, everywhere into hostility. In the primitive history of Persia and Chaldea, the heroes are perpetually engaged in combat with their industrious and perfidious neighbors. The struggle is renewed between the Phœnicians and the Greeks on every coast of the Mediterranean. The Greek supplants the Phœnician in all his factories, all his colonies in the East: soon will the Roman come, and do likewise in the West. Alexander did far more against Tyre than Salmanasar or Nabuchodonosor had done. Not content with crushing her, he took care that she never should revive; for he founded Alexandria as her substitute, and changed forever the track of the commerce of the world. There remained Carthage—the great Carthage, and her mighty empire—mighty in a far different degree than Phœnicia's had been. Rome annihilated it. Then occurred that which has no parallel in history—an entire civilization perished at one blow—banished, like a falling star. The 'Periplus' of Hanno, a few coins, a score of lines in Plautus, and, lo, all that remains of the Carthaginian world!

"Many generations must needs pass away before the struggle between the two races could be renewed; and the Arabs, that formidable rear-guard of the Semitic world, dashed forth from their deserts. The conflict between the two races then became the conflict of two religions. Fortunate was it that those daring Saracenic cavaliers encountered in the East the impregnable walls of Constantinople, in the West the chivalrous valor of Charles Martel, and the sword of the Cid. The crusades were the natural reprisals for the Arab invasions, and form the last epoch of that great struggle between the two principal families of the human race."

It is difficult, amid the glimmering light supplied by the allusions of the classical writers, to gain a full idea of the character and institutions of Rome's great rival. But we can perceive how inferior Carthage was to her competitor in military resources, and how far less fitted than Rome she was to become the founder of centralized and centralizing dominion, that should endure for centuries, and fuse into imperial unity the narrow nationalities of the ancient races, that dwelt around and near the shores of the Mediterranean Sea.

Carthage was originally neither the most ancient nor the most powerful of the numerous colonies which the Phœnicians planted on the coast of Northern Africa. But her advantageous position, the excellence of her constitution (of which, though ill-informed as to its details, we know that it commanded the admiration of Aristotle), and the commercial and political energy of her citizens, gave her the ascendency over Hippo, Utica, Leptis, and her other sister Phœnician cities in those regions; and she finally reduced them to a condition of dependency, similar to that which the subject allies of Athens occupied relatively to that once imperial city. When Tyre and Sidon, and the other cities of Phœnicia itself sank from independent republics into mere vassal states of the great Asiatic monarchies, and obeyed by turns a Babylonian, a Persian, and a Macedonian master, their power and their traffic rapidly declined, and Carthage succeeded to the important maritime and commercial character which they had previously maintained. The Carthaginians did not seek to compete with the Greeks on the northeastern shores of the Mediterranean, or in the three inland seas which are connected with it; but they maintained an active intercourse with the Phœnicians, and through them with Lower and Central Asia; and they, and they alone, after the decline and fall of Tyre, navigated the waters of the Atlantic. They had the monopoly of all the commerce of the world that was carried on beyond the Straits of Gibraltar. We have yet extant (in a Greek translation) the narrative of the voyage of Hanno, one of their admirals, along the western coast of Africa as far as Sierra Leone; and in the Latin poem of Festus Avienus frequent references are made to the records of the voyages of another celebrated Carthaginian admiral, Himilco, who had explored the northwestern coast of Europe. Our own islands are mentioned by Himilco as the lands of the Hiberni and Albioni. It is indeed certain that the Carthaginians frequented the Cornish coast (as the Phœnicians had done before them) for the purpose of procuring tin; and there is every reason to believe that they sailed as far as the coasts of the Baltic for amber. When it is remembered that the mariner's compass was unknown in those ages, the boldness and skill of the seamen of Carthage, and the enterprise of her merchants, may be paralleled with any achievements that the history of modern navigation and commerce can produce.

In their Atlantic voyages along the African shores, the Carthaginians followed the double object of traffic and colonization. The numerous settlements that were planted by them along the coast from Morocco to Senegal provided for the needy members of the constantly increasing population of a great commercial capital, and also strengthened the influence which Carthage exercised among the tribes of the African coast. Besides her fleets, her caravans gave her a large and lucrative trade with the native Africans; nor must we limit our belief of the extent of the Carthaginian trade with the tribes of Central and Western Africa by the narrowness of the commercial intercourse which civilized nations of modern times have been able to create in those regions.

Although essentially a mercantile and seafaring people, the Carthaginians by no means neglected agriculture. On the contrary, the whole of their territory was cultivated like a garden. The fertility of the soil repaid the skill and toil bestowed on it; and every invader, from Agathocles to Scipio Æmilianus, was struck with admiration at the rich pasture lands carefully irrigated, the abundant harvests, the luxuriant vineyards, the plantations of fig and olive trees, the thriving villages, the populous towns, and the splendid villas of the wealthy Carthaginians, through which his march lay, as long as he was on Carthaginian ground.

Although the Carthaginians abandoned the Ægæan and the Pontus to the Greek, they were by no means disposed to relinquish to those rivals the commerce and the dominion of the coasts of the Mediterranean westward of Italy. For centuries the Carthaginians strove to make themselves masters of the islands that lie between Italy and Spain. They acquired the Balearic Islands, where the principal harbor, Port Mahon, still bears the name of a Carthaginian admiral. They succeeded in reducing the great part of Sardinia; but Sicily could never be brought into their power. They repeatedly invaded that island, and nearly overran it; but the resistance which was opposed to them by the Syracusans under Gelon, Dionysius, Timoleon, and Agathocles, preserved the island from becoming Punic, though many of its cities remained under the Carthaginian rule until Rome finally settled the question to whom Sicily was to belong by conquering it for herself.

With so many elements of success, with almost unbounded wealth, with commercial and maritime activity, with a fertile territory, with a capital city of almost impregnable strength, with a constitution that insured for centuries the blessing of social order, with an aristocracy singularly fertile in men of the highest genius, Carthage yet failed signally and calamitously in her contest for power with Rome. One of the immediate causes of this may seem to have been the want of firmness among her citizens, which made them terminate the first Punic war by begging peace, sooner than endure any longer the hardships and burdens caused by a state of warfare, although their antagonists had suffered far more severely than themselves. Another cause was the spirit of faction among their leading men, which prevented Hannibal in the second war from being properly re-enforced and supported. But there were also more general causes why Carthage proved inferior to Rome. These were her position relatively to the mass of the inhabitants of the country which she ruled, and her habit of trusting to mercenary armies in her wars.

Our clearest information as to the different races of men in and about Carthage is derived from Diodorus Siculus.[4] That historian enumerates four different races: first, he mentions the Phœnicians who dwelt in Carthage; next, he speaks of the Liby-Phœnicians: these, he tells us, dwelt in many of the maritime cities, and were connected by intermarriage with the Phœnicians, which was the cause of their compound name; thirdly, he mentions the Libyans, the bulk and the most ancient part of the population, hating the Carthaginians intensely on account of the oppressiveness of their domination; lastly, he names the Numidians, the nomade tribes of the frontier.

It is evident, from this description, that the native Libyans were a subject class, without franchise or political rights; and, accordingly, we find no instance specified in history of a Libyan holding political office or military command. The half-castes, the Liby-Phœnicians, seem to have been sometimes sent out as colonists;[5] but it may be inferred, from what Diodorus says of their residence, that they had not the right of the citizenship of Carthage; and only a single solitary case occurs of one of this race being intrusted with authority, and that, too, not emanating from the home government. This is the instance of the officer sent by Hannibal to Sicily after the fall of Syracuse, whom Polybius[6] calls Myttinus the Libyan, but whom, from the fuller accounts in Livy, we find to have been a Liby-Phœnician;[7] and it is expressly mentioned what indignation was felt by the Carthaginian commanders in the island that this half-caste should control their operations.

With respect to the composition of their armies, it is observable that, though thirsting for extended empire, and though some of their leading men became generals of the highest order, the Carthaginians, as a people, were anything but personally warlike.

As long as they could hire mercenaries to fight for them, they had little appetite for the irksome training and the loss of valuable time which military service would have entailed on themselves.

As Michelet remarks: "The life of an industrious merchant, of a Carthaginian, was too precious to be risked, as long as it was possible to substitute advantageously for it that of a barbarian from Spain or Gaul. Carthage knew, and could tell to a drachma, what the life of a man of each nation came to. A Greek was worth more than a Campanian, a Campanian worth more than a Gaul or a Spaniard. When once this tariff of blood was correctly made out, Carthage began a war as a mercantile speculation. She tried to make conquests in the hope of getting new mines to work, or to open fresh markets for her exports. In one venture she could afford to spend fifty thousand mercenaries, in another rather more. If the returns were good, there was no regret felt for the capital that had been sunk in the investment; more money got more men, and all went on well."[8]

Armies composed of foreign mercenaries have in all ages been as formidable to their employers as to the enemy against whom they were directed. We know of one occasion (between the first and second Punic wars) when Carthage was brought to the very brink of destruction by a revolt of her foreign troops. Other mutinies of the same kind must from time to time have occurred. Probably one of these was the cause of the comparative weakness of Carthage at the time of the Athenian expedition against Syracuse, so different from the energy with which she attacked Gelon half a century earlier, and Dionysius half a century later. And even when we consider her armies with reference only to their efficiency in warfare, we perceive at once the inferiority of such bands of *condottieri*, brought together without any common bond of origin, tactics, or cause, to the legions of Rome, which, at the time of the Punic wars, were raised from the very flower of a hardy agricultural population, trained in the strictest discipline, habituated to victory, and animated by the most resolute patriotism. And this shows, also, the transcendency of the genius of

Hannibal, which could form such discordant materials into a compact organized force, and inspire them with the spirit of patient discipline and loyalty to their chief, so that they were true to him in his adverse as well as in his prosperous fortunes; and throughout the checkered series of his campaigns no panic rout ever disgraced a division under his command, no mutiny, or even attempt at mutiny, was ever known in his camp; and, finally, after fifteen years of Italian warfare, his men followed their old leader to Zama, "with no fear and little hope,"[9] and there, on that disastrous field, stood firm around him, his Old Guard, till Scipio's Numidian allies came up on their flank, when at last, surrounded and overpowered, the veteran battalions sealed their devotion to their general by their blood!

"But if Hannibal's genius may be likened to the Homeric god, who, in his hatred to the Trojans, rises from the deep to rally the fainting Greeks and to lead them against the enemy, so the calm courage with which Hector met his more than human adversary in his country's cause is no unworthy image of the unyielding magnanimity displayed by the aristocracy of Rome. As Hannibal utterly eclipses Carthage, so, on the contrary, Fabius,Marcellus, Claudius Nero, even Scipio himself, are as nothing when compared to the spirit, and wisdom, and power of Rome. The Senate, which voted its thanks to its political enemy, Varro, after his disastrous defeat, 'because he had not despaired of the commonwealth,' and which disdained either to solicit, or to reprove, or to threaten, or in any way to notice the twelve colonies which had refused their accustomed supplies of men for the army, is far more to be honored than the conqueror of Zama. This we should the more carefully bear in mind, because our tendency is to admire individual greatness far more than national; and, as no single Roman will bear comparison to Hannibal, we are apt to murmur at the event of the contest, and to think that the victory was awarded to the least worthy of the combatants. On the contrary, never was the wisdom of God's providence more manifest than in the issue of the struggle between Rome and Carthage. It was clearly for the good of mankind that Hannibal should be conquered; his triumph would have stopped the progress of the world; for great men can only act permanently by forming great nations; and no one man, even though it were Hannibal himself, can in one generation effect such a work. But where the nation has been merely enkindled for a while by a great man's spirit, the light passes away with him who communicated it; and the nation, when he is gone, is like a dead body, to which magic power had for a moment given unnatural life: when the charm has ceased, the body is cold and stiff as before. He who grieves over the battle of Zama should carry on his thoughts to a period thirty years later, when Hannibal must, in the course of nature, have been dead, and consider how the isolated Phœnician city of Carthage was fitted to receive and to consolidate the civilization of Greece, or by its laws and institutions to bind together barbarians of every race and language into an organized empire, and prepare them for becoming, when that empire was dissolved, the free members of the commonwealth of Christian Europe."[10]

It was in the spring of 207 BC that Hasdrubal, after skilfully disentangling himself from the Roman forces in Spain, and after a march conducted with great judgment and little loss through the interior of Gaul and the passes of the Alps, appeared in the country that now is the north of Lombardy at the head of troops which he had partly brought out of Spain and partly levied among the Gauls and Ligurians on his way. At this time Hannibal, with his unconquered and seemingly unconquerable army, had been eight years in Italy, executing with strenuous ferocity the vow of hatred to Rome which had been sworn by him while yet a child at the bidding of his father, Hamilcar; who, as he boasted, had trained up his three sons, Hannibal, Hasdrubal, and Mago, like three lion's whelps, to prey upon the Romans. But Hannibal's latter campaigns had not been signalized by any such great victories as marked the first years of his invasion of Italy. The stern spirit of Roman resolution, ever highest in disaster and danger, had neither bent nor despaired beneath the merciless blows which "the dire African" dealt her in rapid succession at Trebia, at Thrasymene, and at Cannæ. Her population was thinned by repeated slaughter in the field; poverty and actual scarcity ground down the survivors, through the fearful ravages which Hannibal's cavalry spread through their corn-fields, their pasture lands, and their vineyards; many of her allies went over to the invader's side, and new clouds of foreign war threatened her from Macedonia and Gaul. But Rome receded not. Rich and poor among her citizens vied with each other in devotion to their country. The wealthy placed their stores, and all placed their lives, at the state's disposal. And, though Hannibal could not be driven out of Italy, though every year brought its sufferings and sacrifices, Rome felt that her constancy had not been exerted in vain. If she was weakened by the continued strife, so was Hannibal also; and it was clear that the unaided resources of his army were unequal to the task of her destruction. The single deer-hound could not pull down the quarry which he had so furiously assailed. Rome not only stood fiercely at bay, but had pressed back and gored her antagonist, that still, however, watched her in act to spring. She was weary, and bleeding at every pore; and there seemed to be little hope of her escape, if the other hound of old Hamilcar's race should come up in time to aid his brother in the death-grapple.

Hasdrubal had commanded the Carthaginian armies in Spain for some time with varying but generally unfavorable fortune. He had not the full authority over the Punic forces in that country which his brother and father had previously exercised. The faction at Carthage, which was at feud with his family, succeeded in fettering and interfering with his power; and other generals were from time to time sent into Spain, whose errors and misconduct caused the reverses that Hasdrubal met with. This is expressly attested by the Greek historian Polybius, who was the intimate friend of the younger Africanus, and drew his information respecting the second Punic war from the best possible authorities. Livy gives a long narrative of campaigns between the Roman commanders in Spain and Hasdrubal, which is so palpably deformed by fictions and exaggerations as to be hardly deserving of attention.[11]

It is clear that, in the year 208 BC, at least, Hasdrubal outma-noeuvred Publius Scipio, who held the command of the Roman forces in Spain, and whose object was to prevent him from passing the Pyrenees and marching upon Italy. Scipio expected that Hasdrubal would attempt the nearest route along the coast of the Mediterranean, and he therefore carefully fortified and guarded the passes of the eastern Pyrenees. But Hasdrubal passed these mountains near their western extremity; and then, with a consid-erable force of Spanish infantry, with a small number of African troops, with some elephants and much treasure, he marched, not directly towards the coast of the Mediterranean, but in a north-eastern line towards the centre of Gaul. He halted for the winter in the territory of the Arverni, the modern Auvergne, and concili-ated or purchased the good-will of the Gauls in that region so far that he not only found friendly winter quarters among them, but great numbers of them enlisted under him; and, on the approach of spring, marched with him to invade Italy.

By thus entering Gaul at the southwest, and avoiding its south-ern maritime districts, Hasdrubal kept the Romans in complete ignorance of his precise operations and movements in that coun-try; all that they knew was that Hasdrubal had baffled Scipio's attempts to detain him in Spain; that he had crossed the Pyrenees with soldiers, elephants, and money, and that he was raising fresh forces among the Gauls. The spring was sure to bring him into Italy, and then would come the real tempest of the war, when from the north and from the south the two Carthaginian armies, each under a son of the Thunderbolt,[12] were to gather together around the seven hills of Rome.

In this emergency the Romans looked among themselves earnestly and anxiously for leaders fit to meet the perils of the coming campaign.

The Senate recommended the people to elect, as one of their consuls, Caius Claudius Nero, a patrician of one of the families of the great Claudian house. Nero had served during the preceding years of the war both against Hannibal in Italy and against

Hasdrubal in Spain; but it is remarkable that the histories which we possess record no successes as having been achieved by him either before or after his great campaign of the Metaurus. It proves much for the sagacity of the leading men of the senate that they recognized in Nero the energy and spirit which were required at this crisis, and it is equally creditable to the patriotism of the people that they followed the advice of the senate by electing a general who had no showy exploits to recommend him to their choice.

It was a matter of greater difficulty to find a second consul; the laws required that one consul should be a plebeian; and the plebeian nobility had been fearfully thinned by the events of the war. While the senators anxiously deliberated among themselves what fit colleague for Nero could be nominated at the coming comitia, and sorrowfully recalled the names of Marcellus, Gracchus, and other plebeian generals who were no more, one taciturn and moody old man sat in sullen apathy among the conscript fathers. This was Marcus Livius, who had been consul in the year before the beginning of this war, and had then gained a victory over the Illyrians. After his consulship he had been impeached before the people on a charge of peculation and unfair division of the spoils among his soldiers; the verdict was unjustly given against him, and the sense of this wrong, and of the indignity thus put upon him, had rankled unceasingly in the bosom of Livius, so that for eight years after his trial he had lived in seclusion in his country seat, taking no part in any affairs of state. Latterly the censors had compelled him to come to Rome and resume his place in the senate, where he used to sit gloomily apart, giving only a silent vote. At last an unjust accusation against one of his near kinsmen made him break silence, and he harangued the house in words of weight and sense, which drew attention to him, and taught the senators that a strong spirit dwelt beneath that unimposing exterior. Now, while they were debating on what noble of a plebeian house was fit to assume the perilous honors of the consulate, some of the elder of them looked on Marcus Livius, and remembered that in the very last triumph which had been celebrated in the streets of Rome, this grim old man had sat in the car of victory, and that he had offered the last thanksgiving sacrifice for the success of the Roman arms which had bled before Capitoline Jove. There had been no triumphs since Hannibal came into Italy. The Illyrian campaign of Livius was the last that had been so honored; perhaps it might be destined for him now to renew the long-interrupted series. The senators resolved that Livius should be put in nomination as consul with Nero; the people were willing to elect him: the only opposition came from himself. He taunted them with their inconsistency in honoring the man whom they had convicted of a base crime. "If I am innocent," said he, "why did you place such a stain on me? If I am guilty, why am I more fit for a second consulship than I was for my first one?" The other senators remonstrated with him, urging the example of the great Camillus, who, after an unjust condemnation on a similar charge, both served and saved his country. At last Livius ceased to object; and Caius Claudius Nero and Marcus Livius were chosen consuls of Rome.

A quarrel had long existed between the two consuls, and the senators strove to effect a reconciliation between them before the campaign. Here, again, Livius for a long time obstinately resisted the wish of his fellow-senators. He said it was best for the state that he and Nero should continue to hate one another. Each would do his duty better when he knew that he was watched by an enemy in the person of his own colleague. At last the entreaties of the senate prevailed, and Livius consented to forego the feud, and to co-operate with Nero in preparing for the coming struggle.

As soon as the winter snows were thawed, Hasdrubal commenced his march from Auvergne to the Alps. He experienced none of the difficulties which his brother had met with from the mountain tribes. Hannibal's army had been the first body of regular troops that had ever traversed their regions; and, as wild animals assail a traveller, the natives rose against it instinctively, in imagined defence of their own habitations, which they supposed to be the objects of Carthaginian ambition. But the fame of the war, with which Italy had now been convulsed for twelve years, had penetrated into the Alpine passes, and the mountaineers now understood that a mighty city southward of the Alps was to be attacked by the troops whom they saw marching among them. They now not only opposed no resistance to the passage of Hasdrubal, but many of them, out of love of enterprise and plunder, or allured by the high pay that he offered, took service with him; and thus he advanced upon Italy with an army that gathered strength at every league. It is said, also, that some of the most important engineering works which Hannibal had constructed were found by Hasdrubal still in existence, and materially favored the speed of his advance. He thus emerged into Italy from the Alpine valleys much sooner than had been anticipated. Many warriors of the Ligurian tribes joined him; and, crossing the River Po, he marched down its southern bank to the city of Placentia, which he wished to secure as a base for his future operations. Placentia resisted him as bravely as it had resisted Hannibal twelve years before, and for some time Hasdrubal was occupied with a fruitless siege before its walls.

Six armies were levied for the defence of Italy when the long dreaded approach of Hasdrubal was announced. Seventy thousand Romans served in the fifteen legions, of which, with an equal number of Italian allies, those armies and the garrisons were composed. Upwards of thirty thousand more Romans were serving in Sicily, Sardinia, and Spain. The whole number of Roman citizens of an age fit for military duty scarcely exceeded a hundred and thirty thousand. The census taken before the commencement of the war had shown a total of two hundred and seventy thousand, which had been diminished by more than half during twelve years. These numbers are fearfully emphatic of the extremity to which Rome was reduced, and of her gigantic efforts in that great agony of her fate. Not merely men, but money and military stores, were drained to the utmost, and if the armies of that year should be swept off by a repetition of the slaughters of Thrasymene and Cannæ, all felt that Rome would cease to exist. Even if the campaign were to be marked by no decisive success on either side, her ruin seemed certain. In South Italy, Hannibal had either detached Rome's allies from her, or had impoverished them by the ravages of his army. If Hasdrubal could have done the same in Upper Italy; if Etruria, Umbria, and Northern Latium had either revolted or been laid waste, Rome must nave sunk beneath sheer starvation, for the hostile or desolated territory would have yielded no supplies of corn Ior her population, and money to purchase it from abroad there was none. Instant victory was a matter of life or death. Three of her six armies were ordered to the north, but the first of these was required to overawe the disaffected Etruscan. The second army of the north was pushed forward, under Porcius, the praetor, to meet and keep in check the advanced troops of Hasdrubal; while the third, the grand army of the north, which was to be under the immediate command of the consul Livius, who had the chief command in all North Italy, advanced more slowly in its support. There were similarly three armies in the south, under the orders of the other consul, Claudius Nero.

The lot had decided that Livius was to be opposed to Hasdrubal, and that Nero should face Hannibal. And "when all was ordered as themselves thought best, the two consuls went forth of the city, each his several way. The people of Rome were now quite otherwise affected than they had been when L. Æmilius Paulus and C. Terentius Varro were sent against Hannibal. They did no longer take upon them to direct their generals, or bid them despatch and win the victory betimes, but rather they stood in fear lest all diligence, wisdom, and valor should prove too little; for since few years had passed wherein some one of their generals had not been slain, and since it was manifest that, if either of these present consuls was defeated, or put to the worst, the two Carthaginians would forthwith join, and make short work with the other, it seemed a greater happiness than could be expected that each of them should return home victor, and come off with honor from such mighty opposition as he was like to find. With extreme difficulty had Rome held up her head ever since the battle of Cannæ; though it were so, that Hannibal alone, with little help from Carthage, had continued the war in Italy. But there was now arrived another son of Hamilcar, and one that, in his present expedition, had seemed a man of more sufficiency than Hannibal himself; for whereas, in that long and dangerous march through barbarous nations, over great rivers and mountains that were thought unpassable, Hannibal had lost a great part of his army, this Hasdrubal, in the same places, had multiplied his numbers, and gathering the people that he found in the way, descended from the Alps like a rolling snowball, far greater than he came over the Pyrenees at his first setting out of Spain. These considerations and the like, of which fear presented many unto them, caused the people of Rome to wait upon their consuls out of the town, like a pensive train of mourners, thinking upon Marcellus and Cnspinus, upon whom, in the like sort, they had given attendance the last year, but saw neither of them return alive from a less dangerous war. Particularly old Q. Fabius gave his accustomed advice to M. Livius, that he should abstain from giving or taking battle until he well understood the enemy's condition. But the consul made him a froward answer, and said that he would fight the very first day, for that he thought it long till he should either recover his honor by victory, or, by seeing the overthrow of his own unjust citizens, satisfy himself with the joy of a great though not an honest revenge. But his meaning was better than his words."[13]

Hannibal at this period occupied with his veteran but much-reduced forces the extreme south of Italy. It had not been expected either by friend or foe that Hasdrubal would effect his passage of the Alps so early in the year as actually occurred. And even when Hannibal learned that his brother was in Italy, and had advanced as far as Placentia, he was obliged to pause for further intelligence before he himself commenced active operations, as he could not tell whether his brother might not be invited into Etruria, to aid the party there that was disaffected to Rome, or whether he would march down by the Adriatic Sea. Hannibal led his troops out of their winter quarters in Bruttium, and marched northward as far as Canusium. Nero had his head-quarters near

Venusia, with an army which he had increased to forty thousand foot and two thousand five hundred horse, by incorporating under his own command some of the legions which had been intended to act under other generals in the south. There was another Roman army, twenty thousand strong, south of Hannibal, at Tarentum. The strength of that city secured this Roman force from any attack by Hannibal, and it was a serious matter to march northward and leave it in his rear, free to act against all his depots and allies in the friendly part of Italy, which for the two or three last campaigns had served him for a base of his operations. Moreover, Nero's army was so strong that Hannibal could not concentrate troops enough to assume the offensive against it without weakening his garrisons, and relinquishing, at least for a time, his grasp upon the southern provinces. To do this before he was certainly informed of his brother's operations would have been a useless sacrifice, as Nero could retreat before him upon the other Roman armies near the capital, and Hannibal knew by experience that a mere advance of his army upon the walls of Rome would have no effect on the fortunes of the war. In the hope, probably, of inducing Nero to follow him and of gaining an opportunity of out-manoeuvring the Roman consul and attacking him on his march, Hannibal moved into Lucania, and then back into Apulia; he again marched down into Bruttium, and strengthened his army by a levy of recruits in that district. Nero followed him, but gave him no chance of assailing him at a disadvantage. Some partial encounters seem to have taken place; but the consul could not prevent Hannibal's junction with his Bruttian levies, nor could Hannibal gain an opportunity of surprising and crushing the consul.[14] Hannibal returned to his former head-quarters at Canusium, and halted there in expectation of further tidings of his brother's movements. Nero also resumed his former position in observation of the Carthaginian army.

Meanwhile, Hasdrubal had raised the siege of Placentia, and was advancing towards Ariminum on the Adriatic, and driving before him the Roman army under Porcius. Nor when the consul

Livius had come up, and united the second and third armies of the north, could he make head against the invaders. The Romans still fell back before Hasdrubal beyond Ariminum, beyond the Metaurus, and as far as the little town of Sena, to the southeast of that river. Hasdrubal was not unmindful of the necessity of acting in concert with his brother. He sent messengers to Hannibal to announce his own line of march, and to propose that they should unite their armies in South Umbria and then wheel round against Rome. Those messengers traversed the greater part of Italy in safety, but, when close to the object of their mission, were captured by a Roman detachment; and Hasdrubal's letter, detailing his whole plan of the campaign, was laid, not in his brother's hands, but in those of the commander of the Roman armies of the south. Nero saw at once the full importance of the crisis. The two sons of Hamilcar were now within two hundred miles of each other, and if Rome were to be saved, the brothers must never meet alive. Nero instantly ordered seven thousand picked men, a thousand being cavalry, to hold themselves in readiness for a secret expedition against one of Hannibal's garrisons, and as soon as night had set in, he hurried forward on his bold enterprise; but he quickly left the southern road towards Lucania, and, wheeling round, pressed northward with the utmost rapidity towards Picenum. He had, during the preceding afternoon, sent messengers to Rome, who were to lay Hasdrubal's letters before the senate. There was a law forbidding a consul to make war or march his army beyond the limits of the province assigned to him; but in such an emergency, Nero did not wait for the permission of the senate to execute his project, but informed them that he was already on his march to join Livius against Hasdrubal. He advised them to send the two legions which formed the home garrison on to Narnia, so as to defend that pass of the Flaminian road against Hasdrubal, in case he should march upon Rome before the consular armies could attack him. They were to supply the place of these two legions at Rome by a levy *en masse* in the city, and by ordering up the reserve legion from Capua. These were his communications to the senate. He also sent horsemen forward along his line of march, with orders to the local authorities to bring stores of provisions and refreshment of every kind to the roadside, and to have relays of carriages ready for the conveyance of the wearied soldiers. Such were the precautions which he took for accelerating his march; and when he had advanced some little distance from his camp, he briefly informed his soldiers of the real object of their expedition. He told them that never was there a design more seemingly audacious and more really safe. He said he was leading them to a certain victory, for his colleague had an army large enough to balance the enemy already, so that *their* swords would decisively turn the scale. The very rumor that a fresh consul and a fresh army had come up, when heard on the battlefield (and he would take care that they should not be heard of before they were seen and felt), would settle the business. They would have all the credit of the victory, and of having dealt the final decisive blow. He appealed to the enthusiastic reception which they already met with on their line of march as a proof and an omen of their good fortune.[15] And, indeed, their whole path was amid the vows, and prayers, and praises of their countrymen. The entire population of the districts through which they passed flocked to the road-side to see and bless the deliverers of their country. Food, drink, and refreshments of every kind were eagerly pressed on their acceptance. Each peasant thought a favor was conferred on him if one of Nero's chosen band would accept aught at his hands. The soldiers caught the full spirit of their leader. Night and day they marched forward, taking their hurried meals in the ranks, and resting by relays in the wagons which the zeal of the country people provided, and which followed in the rear of the column.

Meanwhile, at Rome, the news of Nero's expedition had caused the greatest excitement and alarm. All men felt the full audacity of the enterprise, but hesitated what epithet to apply to it. It was evident that Nero's conduct would be judged of by the event, that most unfair criterion, as the Roman historian truly terms it.[16] People reasoned on the perilous state in which Nero had left the rest of his army, without a general, and deprived of the core of its strength, in the vicinity of the terrible Hannibal. They speculated on how long it would take Hannibal to pursue and overtake Nero himself, and his expeditionary force. They talked over the former disasters of the war, and the fall of both the consuls of the last year. All these calamities had come on them while they had only one Carthaginian general and army to deal with in Italy. Now they had two Punic wars at a time. They had two Carthaginian armies, they had almost two Hannibals in Italy. Hasdrubal was sprung from the same father; trained up in the same hostility to Rome; equally practised in battle against their legions; and, if the comparative speed and success with which he had crossed the Alps was a fair test, he was even a better general than his brother. With fear for their interpreter of every rumor, they exaggerated the strength of their enemy's forces in every quarter, and criticised and distrusted their own.

Fortunately for Rome, while she was thus a prey to terror and anxiety, her consul's nerves were stout and strong, and he resolutely urged on his march towards Sena, where his colleague Livius and the praetor Porcius were encamped, Hasdrubal's army being in position about half a mile to their north. Nero had sent couriers forward to apprise his colleague of his project and of his approach; and by the advice of Livius, Nero so timed his final march as to reach the camp at Sena by night. According to a previous arrangement, Nero's men were received silently into the tents of their comrades, each according to his rank. By these means there was no enlargement of the camp that could betray to Hasdrubal the accession of force which the Romans had received. This was considerable, as Nero's numbers had been increased on the march by the volunteers, who offered themselves in crowds, and from whom he selected the most promising men, and especially the veterans of former campaigns. A council of war was held on the morning after his arrival, in which some advised that time should be given for Nero's men to refresh themselves after the fatigue of such a march. But Nero vehemently opposed all delay. "The officer," said he, "who is for giving time to my men here to rest themselves, is for giving time to Hannibal to attack my men whom I have left in the camp in Apulia. He is for giving time to Hannibal and Hasdrubal to discover my march, and to manoeuvre for a junction with each other in Cisalpine Gaul at their leisure. We must fight instantly, while both the foe here and the foe in the south are ignorant of our movements. We must destroy this Hasdrubal, and I must be back in Apulia before Hannibal awakes from his torpor."[17] Nero's advice prevailed. It was resolved to fight directly; and before the consuls and prætor left the tent of Livius, the red ensign, which was the signal to prepare for immediate, action, was hoisted, and the Romans forthwith drew up in battle array outside the camp.

Hasdrubal had been anxious to bring Livius and Porcius to battle, though he had not judged it expedient to attack them in their lines. And now, on hearing that the Romans offered battle, he also drew up his men, and advanced towards them. No spy or deserter had informed him of Nero's arrival, nor had he received any direct information that he had more than his old enemies to deal with. But as he rode forward to reconnoitre the Roman line, he thought that their numbers seemed to have increased, and that the armor of some of them was unusually dull and stained. He noticed, also, that the horses of some of the cavalry appeared to be rough and out of condition, as if they had just come from a succession of forced marches. So also, though, owing to the precaution of Livius, the Roman camp showed no change of size, it had not escaped the quick ear of the Carthaginian general that the trumpet which gave the signal to the Roman legions sounded that morning once oftener than usual, as if directing the troops of some additional superior officer. Hasdrubal, from his Spanish campaigns, was well acquainted with all the sounds and signals of Roman war, and from all that he heard and saw, he felt convinced that both the Roman consuls were before him. In doubt and difficulty as to what might have taken place between the armies of the south, and probably hoping that Hannibal also was approaching, Hasdrubal determined to avoid an encounter with the combined Roman forces, and to endeavor to retreat upon Insubrian Gaul, where he would be in a friendly country, and could endeavor to reopen his communication with his brother. He therefore led his troops back into their camp; and as the Romans did not venture on an assault upon his intrenchments, and Hasdrubal did not choose to commence his retreat in their sight, the day passed away in inaction. At the first watch of the night, Hasdrubal led his men silently out of their camp, and moved northward towards the Metaurus, in the hope of placing that river between himself and the Romans before his retreat was discovered. His guides betrayed him; and having purposely led him away from the part of the river that was ford-able, they made their escape in the dark, and left Hasdrubal and his army wandering in confusion along the steep bank, and seeking in vain for a spot where the stream could be safely crossed. At last they halted; and when day dawned on them, Hasdrubal found that great numbers of his men, in their fatigue and impatience, had lost all discipline and subordination, and that many of his Gallic auxiliaries had got drunk, and were lying helpless in their quarters. The Roman cavalry was soon seen coming up in pursuit, followed at no great distance by the legions, which marched in readiness for an instant engagement. It was hopeless for Hasdrubal to think of continuing his retreat before them. The prospect of immediate battle might recall the disordered part of his troops to a sense of duty, and revive the instinct of discipline. He therefore ordered his men to prepare for action instantly, and made the best arrangement of them that the nature of the ground would permit.

Heeren has well described the general appearance of a Carthaginian army. He says, "It was an assemblage of the most opposite races of the human species from the farthest parts of the globe. Hordes of half-naked Gauls were ranged next to companies of white-clothed Iberians, and savage Ligurians next to the far-travelled Nasamones and Lotophagi. Carthaginians and

Phœnici-Africans formed the centre, while innumerable troops of Numidian horsemen, taken from all the tribes of the Desert, swarmed about on unsaddled horses, and formed the wings; the van was composed of Balearic slingers; and a line of colossal elephants, with their Ethiopian guides, formed, as it were, a chain of moving fortresses before the whole army." Such were the usual materials and arrangements of the hosts that fought for Carthage; but the troops under Hasdrubal were not in all respects thus constituted or thus stationed. He seems to have been especially deficient in cavalry, and he had few African troops, though some Carthaginians of high rank were with him. His veteran Spanish infantry, armed with helmets and shields, and short cut-and-thrust swords, were the best part of his army. These, and his few Africans, he drew up on his right wing, under his own personal command. In the centre he placed his Ligurian infantry, and on the left wing he placed or retained the Gauls, who were armed with long javelins and with huge broad-swords and targets. The rugged nature of the ground in front and on the flank of this part of his line made him hope that the Roman right wing would be unable to come to close quarters with these unserviceable barbarians before he could make some impression with his Spanish veterans on the Roman left. This was the only chance that he had of victory or safety, and he seems to have done everything that good generalship could do to secure it. He placed his elephants in advance of his centre and right wing. He had caused the driver of each of them to be provided with a sharp iron spike and a mallet, and had given orders that every beast that became unmanageable, and ran back upon his own ranks, should be instantly killed, by driving the spike into the vertebra at the junction of the head and the spine. Hasdrubal's elephants were ten in number. We have no trustworthy information as to the amount of his infantry, but it is quite clear that he was greatly outnumbered by the combined Roman forces.

The tactics of the Roman legions had not yet acquired that perfection which it received from the military genius of Marius,[18] and which we read of in the first chapter of Gibbon. We possess, in that great work, an account of the Roman legions at the end of the commonwealth, and during the early ages of the empire, which those alone can adequately admire who have attempted a similar description. We have also, in the sixth and seventeenth books of Polybius, an elaborate discussion on the military system of the Romans in his time, which was not far distant from the time of the battle of the Metaurus. But the subject is beset with difficulties; and instead of entering into minute but inconclusive details, I would refer to Gibbon's first chapter as serving for a general description of the Roman army in its period of perfection, and remark, that the training and armor which the whole legion received in the time of Augustus was, two centuries earlier, only partially introduced. Two divisions of troops, called Hastati and Principes, formed the bulk of each Roman legion in the second Punic war. Each of these divisions was twelve hundred strong. The Hastatus and the Princeps legionary bore a breastplate or coat of mail, brazen greaves, and a brazen helmet, with a lofty upright crest of scarlet or black feathers. He had a large oblong shield; and, as weapons of offence, two javelins, one of which was light and slender, but the other was a strong and massive weapon, with a shaft about four feet long, and an iron head of equal length. The sword was carried on the right thigh, and was a short cut-and-thrust weapon, like that which was used by the Spaniards. Thus armed, the Hastati formed the front division of the legion, and the Principes the second. Each division was drawn up about ten deep, a space of three feet being allowed between the files as well as the ranks, so as to give each legionary ample room for the use of his javelins, and of his sword and shield. The men in the second rank did not stand immediately behind those in the first rank, but the files were alternate, like the position of the men on a draught-board. This was termed the quincunx order. Niebuhr considers that this arrangement enabled the legion to keep up a shower of javelins on the enemy for some considerable time. He says, "When the first line had hurled its pila, it probably stepped back between those who stood behind it, and two steps forward restored the front nearly to its first position; a movement which, on account of the arrangement of the quincunx, could be executed without losing a moment. Thus one line succeeded the other in the front till it was time to draw the swords; nay, when it was found expedient, the lines which had already been in the front might repeat this change, since the stores of pila were surely not confined to the two which each soldier took with him into battle.

"The same change must have taken place in fighting with the sword, which when the same tactic was adopted on both sides, was anything but a confused *mêlée;* on the contrary, it was a series of single combats." He adds, that a military man of experience had been consulted by him on the subject, and had given it as his opinion "that the change of the lines as described above was by no means impracticable; but, in the absence of the deafening noise of gunpowder, it cannot have had even any difficulty with well-trained troops."

The third division of the legion was six hundred strong and acted as a reserve. It was always composed of veteran soldiers, who were called the Triarii. Their arms were the same as these of the Principes and Hastati, except that each Triarian carried a spear instead of javelins. The rest of the legion consisted of light-armed troops, who acted as skirmishers. The cavalry of each legion was at this period about three hundred strong. The Italian allies, who were attached to the legion, seem to have been similarly armed and equipped, but their numerical proportion of cavalry was much larger.

Such was the nature of the forces that advanced on the Roman side to the battle of the Metaurus. Nero commanded the right wing, Livius the left, and the prætor Porcius had the command of the centre. "Both Romans and Carthaginians well understood how much depended upon the fortune of this day, and how little hope of safety there was for the vanquished. Only the Romans herein seemed to have had the better in conceit and opinion that they were to fight with men desirous to have fled from them; and according to this presumption came Livius the consul, with a proud bravery, to give charge on the Spaniards and Africans, by whom he was so sharply entertained that the victory seemed very doubtful. The Africans and Spaniards were stout soldiers, and well acquainted with the manner of the Roman fight. The Ligurians, also, were a hardy nation, and not accustomed to give ground, which they needed the less, or were able now to do, being placed in the midst. Livius, therefore, and Porcius found great opposition; and with great slaughter on both sides prevailed little or nothing. Besides other difficulties, they were exceedingly troubled by the elephants, that break their first ranks, and put them in such disorder as the Roman ensigns were driven to fall back; all this while Claudius Nero, laboring in vain against a steep hill, was unable to come to blows with the Gauls that stood opposite him, but out of danger. This made Hasdrubal the more confident, who, seeing his own left wing safe, did the more boldly and fiercely make impression on the other side upon the left wing of the Romans."[19]

But at last Nero, who found that Hasdrubal refused his left wing, and who could not overcome the difficulties of the ground in the quarter assigned to him, decided the battle by another stroke of that military genius which had inspired his march. Wheeling a brigade of his best men round the rear of the rest of the Roman army, Nero fiercely charged the flank of the Spaniards and Africans. The charge was as successful as it was sudden. Rolled back in disorder upon each other, and overwhelmed by numbers, the Spaniards and Ligurians died, fighting gallantly to the last. The Gauls, who had taken little or no part in the strife of the day, were then surrounded, and butchered almost without resistance. Hasdrubal, after having, by the confession of his enemies, done all that a general could do, when he saw that the victory was irreparably lost, scorning to survive the gallant host which he had led, and to gratify, as a captive, Roman cruelty and pride, spurred his horse into the midst of a Roman cohort, and, sword in hand, met the death that was worthy of the son of Hamilcar and the brother of Hannibal.

Success the most complete had crowned Nero's enterprise. Returning as rapidly as he had advanced, he was again facing the inactive enemies in the south before they even knew of his march. But he brought with him a ghastly trophy of what he had done. In the true spirit of that savage brutality which deformed the Roman national character, Nero ordered Hasdrubal's head to be flung into his brother's camp. Ten years had passed since Hannibal had last gazed on those features. The sons of Hamilcar had then planned their system of warfare against Rome which they had so nearly brought to successful accomplishment. Year after year had Hannibal been struggling in Italy, in the hope of one day hailing the arrival of him whom he had left in Spain, and of seeing his brother's eye flash with affection and pride at the junction of their irresistible hosts. He now saw that eye glazed in death, and in the agony of his heart the great Carthaginian groaned aloud that he recognized his country's destiny.

With the revival of confidence came also the revival of activity in traffic and commerce, and in all the busy intercourse of daily life. Hannibal was, certainly, still in the land; but all felt that his power to destroy was broken, and that the crisis of the war fever was past. Hannibal did actually, with almost superhuman skill, retain his hold on Southern Italy for a few years longer; but the imperial city and her allies were no longer in danger from his arms, and, after Hannibal's downfall, the great military republic of the ancient world met in her career of conquest no other worthy competitor. Byron has termed Nero's march "unequalled," and in the magnitude of its consequences it is so. Viewed only as a military exploit, it remains unparalleled, save by Marlborough's bold march from Flanders to the Danube, in the campaign of Blenheim, and perhaps also by the Archduke Charles's lateral march in 1796, by which he overwhelmed the French under Jourdan, and then, driving Moreau through the Black Forest and across the Rhine, for a while freed Germany from her invaders.

SYNOPSIS OF EVENTS BETWEEN THE BATTLE OF THE METAURUS, BC 207, AND ARMINIUS' VICTORY OVER THE ROMAN LEGIONS UNDER VARUS, AD 9.

BC 205 to 201. Scipio is made consul, and carries the war into Africa. He gains several victories there, and the Carthaginians recall Hannibal from Italy to oppose him. Battle of Zama is 201. Hannibal is defeated, and Carthage sues for peace. End of the second Punic war, leaving Rome confirmed in the dominion of Italy, Sicily, Sardinia, and Corsica, and also mistress of great part of Spain, and virtually predominant in North Africa.

200. Rome makes war upon Philip, king of Macedonia. She pretends to take the Greek cities of the Achæan league and the Ætolians under her protection as allies. Philip is defeated by the proconsul Flaminius at Cynoscephalæ, 198, and begs for peace. The Macedonian influence is now completely destroyed in Greece, and the Roman established in its stead, though Rome pretends to acknowledge the independence of the Greek cities.

194. Rome makes war upon Antiochus, king of Syria. He is completely defeated at the battle of Magnesia, 192, and is glad to accept peace on conditions which leave him dependent upon Rome.

200–190. "Thus, within the short space of ten years, was laid the foundation of the Roman authority in the East, and the general state of affairs entirely changed. If Rome was not yet the ruler, she was at least the arbitress of the world from the Atlantic to the Euphrates. The power of the three principal states was so completely humbled, that they durst not, without the permission of Rome, begin any new war; the fourth, Egypt, had already, in the year 201, placed herself under the guardianship of Rome; and the lesser powers followed of themselves, esteeming it an honor to be called the *allies of Rome*. With this name the nations were lulled into security, and brought under the Roman yoke; the new political system of Rome was founded and strengthened, partly by exciting and supporting the weaker states against the stronger, however unjust the cause of the former might be, and partly by factions which she found means to raise in every state, even the smallest."— (HEEREN.)

172. War renewed between Macedon and Rome. Decisive defeat of Perses, the Macedonian king, by Paulus Æmilius at Pydna, 168. Destruction of the Macedonian monarchy.

150. Rome oppresses the Carthaginians till they are driven to take up arms, and the third Punic war begins. Carthage is taken and destroyed by Scipio Æmilianus, 146, and the Carthaginian territory is made a Roman province.

146. In the same year in which Carthage falls, Corinth is stormed by the Roman army under Mummius. The Achæan league had been goaded into hostilities with Rome by means similar to those employed against Carthage. The greater part of Southern Greece is made a Roman province under the name of Achaia.

133. Numantia is destroyed by Scipio Æmilianus. "The war against the Spaniards, who, of all the nations subdued by the Romans, defended their liberty with the greatest obstinacy, began in the year 200, six years after the total expulsion of the Carthaginians from their country, 206. It was exceedingly obstinate, partly from the natural state of the country, which was thickly populated, and where every place became a fortress; partly from the courage of the inhabitants; but above all, owing to the peculiar policy of the Romans, who were wont to employ their allies to subdue other nations. This war continued, almost without interruption, from the year 200 to 133, and was for the most part carried on at the same time in Hispania Citerior, where the Celtiberi were the most formidable adversaries, and in Hispania Ulterior, where the Lusitani were equally powerful. Hostilities were at the highest pitch in 195, under Cato, who reduced Hispania Citerior to a state of tranquillity in 185–179, when the Celtiberi were attacked in their native territory; and 155–150, when the Romans in both provinces were so often beaten, that nothing was more dreaded by the soldiers at home than to be sent there. The extortions and perfidy of Servius Galbis placed

Viriathus, in the year 146, at the head of his nation, the Lusitani: the war, however, soon extended itself to Hispania Citerior, where many nations, particularly the Numantines, took up arms against Rome, 143. Viriathus, sometimes victorious and sometimes defeated, was never more formidable than in the moment of defeat, because he knew how to take advantage of his knowledge of the country and of the dispositions of his countrymen. After his murder, caused by the treachery of Cæpio, 140, Lusitania was subdued; but the Numantine war became still more violent, and the Numantines compelled the consul Mancinus to a disadvantageous treaty, 137. When Scipio, in the year 133, put an end to this war, Spain was certainly tranquil; the northern parts, however, were still unsubdued, though the Romans penetrated as far as Galatia." — (HEEREN.)

134. Commencement of the revolutionary century at Rome, *i.e.*, from the time of the excitement produced by the attempts made by the Gracchi to reform the commonwealth, to the battle of Actium (BC 31), which established Octavianus Cæsar as sole master of the Roman world. Throughout this period Rome was engaged in important foreign wars, most of which procured large accessions to her territory.

118–106. The Jugurthine war. Numidia is conquered, and made a Roman conquest.

113–101. The great and terrible war of the Cimbri and Teutones against Rome. These nations of northern warriors slaughter several Roman armies in Gaul, and in 102 attempt to penetrate into Italy. The military genius of Marius here saves his country; he defeats the Teutones near Aix, in Provence; and in the following year he destroys the army of the Cimbri, who had passed the Alps, near Vercellæ.

91–88. The war of the Italian allies against Rome. This was caused by the refusal of Rome to concede to them the rights of Roman citizenship. After a sanguinary struggle, Rome gradually concedes it.

89–85. First war of the Romans against Mithridates the Great, king of Pontus, who had overrun Asia Minor, Macedonia, and

Greece. Sylla defeats his armies, and forces him to withdraw his forces from Europe. Sylla returns to Rome to carry on the civil war against the son and partisans of Marius. He makes himself dictator.

74–64. The last Mithridatic wars. Lucullus, and after him Pompeius, command against the great king of Pontus, who at last is poisoned by his son, while designing to raise the warlike tribes of the Danube against Rome, and to invade Italy from the northeast. Great Asiatic conquests of the Romans. Besides the ancient province of Pergamus, the maritime countries of Bithynia and nearly all Paphlagonia and Pontus, are formed into a Roman province under the name of Bithynia, while on the southern coast Cilicia and Pamphylia form another under the name of Cilicia; Phœnicia and Syria compose a third, under the name of Syria. On the other hand, Great Armenia is left to Tigranes; Cappadocia to Ariobarzanes; the Bosphorus to Pharnaces; Judæa to Hyrcanus; and some other small states are also given to petty princes, all of whom remain dependent on Rome.

58–50. Cæsar conquers Gaul.

54. Crassus attacks the Parthians with a Roman army, but is overthrown and killed at Carrhæ in Mesopotamia. His lieutenant Cassius collects the wrecks of the army, and prevents the Parthians from conquering Syria.

49–45. The civil war between Cæsar and the Pompeian party. Egypt, Mauritania, and Pontus are involved in the consequences of this war.

44. Cæsar is killed in the Capitol; the civil wars are soon renewed.

42. Death of Brutus and Cassius at Philippi.

31. Death of Antony and Cleopatra. Egypt becomes a Roman province, and Augustus Cæsar is left undisputed master of Rome, and all that is Rome's.

CHAPTER V

VICTORY OF ARMINIUS OVER THE ROMAN LEGIONS UNDER VARUS, A.D. 9

"Hac clade factum, ut Imperium quod in littore oceani non steterat, in ripâ Rheni fluminis staret."

—*Florus.*

To a truly illustrious Frenchman, whose reverses as a minister can never obscure his achievements in the world of letters, we are indebted for the most profound and most eloquent estimate that we possess of the importance of the Germanic element in European civilization, and of the extent to which the human race is indebted to those brave warriors who long were the unconquered antagonists, and finally became the conquerors, of imperial Rome.

Twenty-three eventful years have passed away since M. Guizot delivered from the chair of modern history at Paris his course of lectures on the history of civilization in Europe. During those years the spirit of earnest inquiry into the germs and primary developments of existing institutions has become more and more active and universal, and the merited celebrity of M. Guizot's work has proportionally increased. Its admirable analysis of the complex political and social organizations of which the modern civilized world is made up, must have led thousands to trace with keener interest the great crises of times past, by which the characteristics of the present were determined. The narrative of one of these great crises, of the epoch A.D. 9, when Germany took up arms for her independence against Roman invasion, has for us this special attraction—that it forms part of our own national history. Had Arminius been supine or unsuccessful, our Germanic ancestors would have been enslaved or exterminated in their original seats along the Eyder and the Elbe. This island would never have borne the name of England, and "we, this great English nation, whose race and language are now overrunning the earth, from one end of it to the other,"[1] would have been utterly cut off from existence.

Arnold may, indeed, go too far in holding that we are wholly unconnected in race with the Romans and Britons who inhabited this country before the coming over of the Saxons; that, "nationally speaking, the history of Cæsar's invasion has no more to do with us than the natural history of the animals which then inhabited our forests." There seems ample evidence to prove that the Romanized Celts whom our Teutonic forefathers found here influenced materially the character of our nation. But the main stream of our people was and is Germanic. Our language alone decisively proves this. Arminius is far more truly one of our national heroes than Caractacus; and it was our own primeval fatherland that the brave German rescued when he slaughtered the Roman legions eighteen centuries ago, in the marshy glens between the Lippe and the Ems.[2]

Dark and disheartening, even to heroic spirits, must have seemed the prospects of Germany when Arminius planned the general rising of his countrymen against Rome. Half the land was occupied by Roman garrisons; and, what was worse, many of the Germans seemed patiently acquiescent in their state of bondage. The braver portion, whose patriotism could be relied on, was ill armed and undisciplined, while the enemy's troops consisted of veterans in the highest state of equipment and training, familiarized with victory, and commanded by officers of proved skill and valor. The resources of Rome seemed boundless; her tenacity of purpose was believed to be invincible. There was no hope of foreign sympathy or aid; for "the self-governing powers that had filled the Old World had bent one after another before the rising power of Rome, and had vanished. The earth seemed left void of independent nations."[3]

The German chieftain knew well the gigantic power of the oppressor. Arminius was no rude savage, fighting out of mere animal instinct, or in ignorance of the might of his adversary. He was familiar with the Roman language and civilization; he had served in the Roman armies; he had been admitted to the Roman citizenship, and raised to the rank of the equestrian order. It was part of the subtle policy of Rome to confer rank and privileges on the youth of the leading families in the nations which she wished to enslave. Among other young German chieftains, Arminius and his brother, who were the heads of the noblest house in the tribe of the Cherusci, had been selected as fit objects for the exercise of this insidious system. Roman refinements and dignities succeeded in denationalizing the brother, who assumed the Roman name of Flavius, and adhered to Rome throughout all her wars against his country. Arminius remained unbought by honors or wealth, uncorrupted by refinement or luxury. He aspired to and obtained from Roman enmity a higher title than ever could have been given him by Roman favor. It is in the page of Rome's greatest historian that his name has come down to us with the proud addition of "Liberator haud dubiè Germaniæ."[4]

Often must the young chieftain, while meditating the exploit which has thus immortalized him, have anxiously revolved in his mind the fate of the many great men who had been crushed in the attempt which he was about to renew—the attempt to stay the chariot-wheels of triumphant Rome. Could he hope to succeed where Hannibal and Mithridates had perished? What had been the doom of Viriathus? and what warning against vain valor was written on the desolate site where Numantia once had nourished? Nor was a caution wanting in scenes nearer home and more recent times. The Gauls had fruitlessly struggled for eight years against Cæsar; and the gallant Vercingetorix, who in the last year of the war had roused all his countrymen to insurrection, who had cut off Roman detachments, and brought Cæsar himself to the extreme of peril at Alesia—he, too, had finally succumbed, had been led captive in Cæsar's triumph, and had then been butchered in cold blood in a Roman dungeon.

It was true that Rome was no longer the great military republic which for so many ages had shattered the kingdoms of the world. Her system of government was changed; and after a century of revolution and civil war, she had placed herself under the despotism of a single ruler. But the discipline of her troops was yet unimpaired, and her warlike spirit seemed unabated. The first year of the empire had been signalized by conquests as valuable as any gained by the republic in a corresponding period. It is a great fallacy, though apparently sanctioned by great authorities, to suppose that the foreign policy pursued by Augustus was pacific; he certainly recommended such a policy to his successors (*incertum metu an per invidiam, — TAC., Ann.,* i., 11), but he himself, until Arminius broke his spirit, had followed a very different course. Besides his Spanish wars, his generals, in a series of generally aggressive campaigns, had extended the Roman frontier from the Alps to the Danube, and had reduced into subjection the large and important countries that now form the territories of all Austria south of that river, and of East Switzerland, Lower Wirtemberg, Bavaria, the Valtelline, and the Tyrol. While the progress of the Roman arms thus pressed the Germans from the south, still more formidable inroads had been made by the imperial legions on the west. Roman armies, moving from the province of Gaul, established a chain of fortresses along the right as well as the left bank of the Rhine, and, in a series of victorious campaigns, advanced their eagles as far as the Elbe, which now seemed added to the list of vassal rivers, to the Nile, the Rhine, the Rhone, the Danube, the Tagus, the Seine, and many more, that acknowledged the supremacy of the Tiber. Roman fleets also, sailing from the harbors of Gaul along the German coasts and up the estuaries, co-operated with the land-forces of the empire, and seemed to display, even more decisively than her armies, her overwhelming superiority over the rude Germanic tribes. Throughout the territory thus invaded, the Romans had with their usual military skill, established fortified posts; and a powerful army of occupation was kept on foot, ready to move instantly on any spot where any popular outbreak might be attempted.

Vast, however, and admirably organized as the fabric of Roman power appeared on the frontiers and in the provinces, there was rottenness at the core. In Rome's unceasing hostilities with foreign foes, and still more in her long series of desolating civil wars, the free middle classes of Italy had almost wholly disappeared. Above the position which they had occupied, an oligarchy of wealth had reared itself; beneath that position, a degraded mass of poverty and misery was fermenting. Slaves, the chance sweepings of every conquered country, shoals of Africans, Sardinians, Asiatics, Illyrians, and others, made up the bulk of the population of the Italian peninsula. The foulest profligacy of manners was general in all ranks. In universal weariness of revolution and civil war, and in consciousness of being too debased for self-government, the nation had submitted itself to the absolute authority of Augustus. Adulation was now the chief function of the senate; and the gifts of genius and accomplishments of art were devoted to the elaboration of eloquently false panegyrics upon the prince and his favorite courtiers. With bitter indignation must the German chieftain have beheld all this and contrasted with it the rough worth of his own countrymen: their bravery, their fidelity to their word, their manly independence of spirit, their love of their national free institutions, and their loathing of every pollution and meanness. Above all, he must have thought of the domestic virtues that hallowed a German home; of the respect there shown to the female character, and of the pure affection by which that respect was repaid. His soul must have burned within him at the contemplation of such a race yielding to these debased Italians.

Still, to persuade the Germans to combine, in spite of their frequent feuds among themselves, in one sudden outbreak against Rome; to keep the scheme concealed from the Romans until the hour for action arrived; and then, without possessing a single walled town, without military stores, without training, to teach his insurgent countrymen to defeat veteran armies and storm fortifications, seemed so perilous an enterprise, that probably Arminius would have receded from it had not a stronger feeling even than patriotism urged him on. Among the Germans of high rank who had most readily submitted to the invaders, and become zealous partisans of Roman authority, was a chieftain named Segestes. His daughter, Thusnelda, was pre-eminent among the noble maidens of Germany. Arminius had sought her hand in marriage; but Segestes, who probably discerned the young chief's disaffection to Rome, forbade his suit, and strove to preclude all communication between him and his daughter. Thusnelda, however, sympathized far more with the heroic spirit of her lover than with the time-serving policy of her father. An elopement baffled the precautions of Segestes, who, disappointed in his hope of preventing the marriage, accused Arminius before the Roman governor of having carried off his daughter, and of planning treason against Rome. Thus assailed, and dreading to see his bride torn from him by the officials of the foreign oppressor, Arminius delayed no longer, but bent all his energies to organize and execute a general insurrection of the great mass of his countrymen, who hitherto had submitted in sullen hatred to the Roman dominion.

A change of governors had recently taken place, which, while it materially favored the ultimate success of the insurgents, served, by the immediate aggravation of the Roman oppressions, which it produced, to make the native population more universally eager to take arms. Tiberius, who was afterwards emperor, had recently been recalled from the command in Germany, and sent into Pannonia to put down a dangerous revolt which had broken out against the Romans in that province. The German patriots were thus delivered from the stern supervision of one of the most suspicious of mankind, and were also relieved from having to contend against the high military talents of a veteran commander, who thoroughly understood their national character, and also the nature of the country, which he himself had principally subdued. In the room of Tiberius, Augustus sent into Germany Quintilius Varus, who had lately returned from the pro-consulate of Syria. Varus was a true representative of the higher classes of the Romans, among whom a general taste for literature, a keen susceptibility to all intellectual gratifications, a minute acquaintance with the principles and practice of their own national jurisprudence, a careful training in the schools of the rhetoricians and a fondness for either partaking in or watching the intellectual strife of forensic oratory, had become generally diffused, without, however, having humanized the old Roman spirit of cruel indifference for human feelings and human sufferings, and without acting as the least checks on unprincipled avarice and ambition, or on habitual and gross profligacy. Accustomed to govern the depraved and debased natives of Syria, a country where courage in man and virtue in woman had for centuries been unknown, Varus thought that he might gratify his licentious and rapacious passions with equal impunity among the high-minded sons and pure-spirited daughters of Germany. When the general of any army sets the example of outrages of this description, he is soon faithfully imitated by his officers, and surpassed by his still more brutal soldiery. The Romans now habitually indulged in those violations of the sanctity of the domestic shrine, and those insults upon honor and modesty, by which far less gallant spirits than those of our Teutonic ancestors have often been maddened into insurrection.[5]

Arminius found among the other German chiefs many who sympathized with him in his indignation at their country's abasement, and many whom private wrongs had stung yet more deeply. There was little difficulty in collecting bold leaders for an attack on the oppressors, and little fear of the population not rising readily at those leaders' call. But to declare open war against Rome, and to encounter Varus' army in a pitched battle, would have been merely rushing upon certain destruction. Varus had three legions under him, a force which, after allowing for detachments, cannot be estimated at less than fourteen thousand Roman infantry. He had also eight or nine hundred Roman cavalry, and at least an equal number of horse and foot sent from the allied states, or raised among those provincials who had not received the Roman franchise.

It was not merely the number, but the quality of this force that made them formidable; and, however contemptible Varus might be as general, Arminius well knew how admirably the Roman armies were organized and officered and how perfectly the legionaries understood every manœuvre and every duty which the varying emergencies of a stricken field might require. Stratagem was, therefore, indispensable; and it was necessary to blind Varus to their schemes until a favorable opportunity should arrive for striking a decisive blow.

For this purpose, the German confederates frequented the head-quarters of Varus, which seem to have been near the centre of the modern country of Westphalia, where the Roman general conducted himself with all the arrogant security of the governor of a perfectly submissive province. There Varus gratified at once his vanity, his rhetorical tastes, and his avarice, by holding courts, to which he summoned the Germans for the settlement of all their disputes, while a bar of Roman advocates attended to argue the cases before the tribunal of Varus, who did not omit the opportunity of exacting court-fees and accepting bribes. Varus trusted implicitly to the respect which the Germans pretended to pay to his abilities as a judge, and to the interest which they affected to take in the forensic eloquence of their conquerors. Meanwhile, a succession of heavy rains rendered the country more difficult for the operations of regular troops, and Arminius, seeing that the infatuation of Varus was complete, secretly directed the tribes near the Weser and the Ems to take up arms in open revolt against the Romans. This was represented to Varus as an occasion which required his prompt attendance at the spot; but he was kept in studied ignorance of its being part of a concerted national rising; and he still looked on Arminius as his submissive vassal, whose aid he might rely on in facilitating the march of his troops against the rebels, and in extinguishing the local disturbance. He therefore set his army in motion, and marched eastward in a line parallel to the course of the Lippe. For some distance his route lay along a level plain; but on arriving at the tract between the curve of the upper part of that stream and the sources of the Ems, the country assumes a very different character; and here, in the territory of the modern little principality of Lippe, it was that Arminius had fixed the scene of his enterprise.

A woody and hilly region intervenes between the heads of the two rivers, and forms the water-shed of their streams. This region still retains the name (Teutobergenwald=Teutobergiensis saltus) which it bore in the days of Arminius. The nature of the ground has probably also remained unaltered. The eastern part of it, round Detmold, the modern capital of the principality of Lippe, is described by a modern German scholar, Dr. Plate, as being a "table-land intersected by numerous deep and narrow valleys, which in some places form small plains, surrounded by steep mountains and rocks, and only accessible by narrow defiles. All the valleys are traversed by rapid streams, shallow in the dry season, but subject to sudden swellings in autumn and winter. The vast forests which cover the summits and slopes of the hills consist chiefly of oak; there is little underwood, and both men and horse would move with ease in the forests if the ground were not broken by gulleys, or rendered impracticable by fallen trees." This is the district to which Varus is supposed to have marched; and Dr. Plate adds, that "the names of several localities on and near that spot seem to indicate that a great battle has once been fought there. We find the names 'das Winnefeld' (the field of victory), 'die Knochenbahn' (the bone-lane), 'die Knochenleke' (the bone-brook), 'der Mordkessel' (the kettle of slaughter), and others."[6]

Contrary to the usual strict principles of Roman discipline, Varus had suffered his army to be accompanied and impeded by an immense train of baggage-wagons and by a rabble of camp followers, as if his troops had been merely changing their quarters in a friendly country. When the long array quitted the firm, level ground, and began to wind its way among the woods, the marshes, and the ravines, the difficulties of the march, even without the intervention of an armed foe, became fearfully apparent. In many places, the soil, sodden with rain, was impracticable for cavalry, and even for infantry, until trees had been felled, and a rude causeway formed through the morass.

The duties of the engineer were familiar to all who served in the Roman armies. But the crowd and confusion of the columns embarrassed the working parties of the soldiery, and in the midst of their toil and disorder the word was suddenly passed through their ranks that the rear guard was attacked by the barbarians. Varus resolved on pressing forward: but a heavy discharge of missiles from the woods on either flank taught him how serious was the peril, and he saw his best men falling round him without the opportunity of retaliation; for his light-armed auxiliaries, who were principally of Germanic race, now rapidly deserted, and it was impossible to deploy the legionaries on such broken ground for a charge against the enemy. Choosing one of the most open and firm spots which they could force their way to, the Romans halted for the night; and, faithful to their national discipline and tactics, formed their camp amid the harassing attacks of the rapidly thronging foes, with the elaborate toil and systematic skill, the traces of which are impressed permanently on the soil of so many European countries, attesting the presence in the olden time of the imperial eagles.

On the morrow the Romans renewed their march, the veteran officers who served under Varus now probably directing the operations, and hoping to find the Germans drawn up to meet them; in which case they relied on their own superior discipline and tactics for such a victory as should reassure the supremacy of Rome. But Arminius was far too sage a commander to lead on his followers, with their unwieldly broad-swords and inefficient defensive armor, against the Roman legionaries, fully armed with helmet, cuirass, greaves, and shield, who were skilled to commence the conflict with a murderous volley of heavy javelins, hurled upon the foe when a few yards distant, and then, with their short cut-and-thrust swords, to hew their way through all opposition, preserving the utmost steadiness and coolness, and obeying each word of

command in the midst of strife and slaughter with the same precision and alertness as if upon parade.[7] Arminius suffered the
Romans to march out from their camp, to form first in line for
action, and then in column for marching, without the show of
opposition. For some distance Varus was allowed to move on, only
harassed by slight skirmishes, but struggling with difficulty
through the broken ground, the toil and distress of his men being
aggravated by heavy torrents of rain, which burst upon the
devoted legions, as if the angry gods of Germany were pouring out
the vials of their wrath upon the invaders. After some little time
their van approached a ridge of high woody ground, which is one
of the offshoots of the great Hircynian forest, and is situate
between the modern villages of Driburg and Bielefeld. Arminius
had caused barricades of hewn trees to be formed here, so as to
add to the natural difficulties of the passage. Fatigue and discouragement now began to betray themselves in the Roman ranks.
Their line became less steady; baggage-wagons were abandoned
from the impossibility of forcing them along; and, as this happened, many soldiers left their ranks and crowded round the wagons to secure the most valuable portions of their property; each
was busy about his own affairs, and purposely slow in hearing the
word of command from his officers. Arminius now gave the signal
for a general attack. The fierce shouts of the Germans pealed
through the gloom of the forests, and in thronging multitudes
they assailed the flanks of the invaders, pouring in clouds of darts
on the encumbered legionaries, as they struggled up the glens or
floundered in the morasses, and watching every opportunity of
charging through the intervals of the disjointed column, and so
cutting off the communication between its several brigades.
Arminius, with a chosen band of personal retainers round him,
cheered on his countrymen by voice and example. He and his
men aimed their weapons particularly at the horses of the Roman
cavalry. The wounded animals, slipping about in the mire and
their own blood, threw their riders and plunged among the ranks
of the legions, disordering all round them. Varus now ordered the

troops to be countermarched, in the hope of reaching the nearest Roman garrison on the Lippe.[8] But retreat now was as impracticable as advance; and the falling back of the Romans only augmented the courage of their assailants, and caused fiercer and more frequent charges on the flanks of the disheartened army. The Roman officer who commanded the cavalry, Numonius Vala, rode off with his squadrons in the vain hope of escaping by thus abandoning his comrades. Unable to keep together, or force their way across the woods and swamps, the horsemen were overpowered in detail, and slaughtered to the last man. The Roman infantry still held together and resisted, but more through the instinct of discipline and bravery than from any hope of success or escape. Varus, after being severely wounded in a charge of the Germans against his part of the column, committed suicide to avoid falling into the hands of those whom he had exasperated by his oppressions. One of the lieutenant generals of the army fell fighting; the other surrendered to the enemy. But mercy to a fallen foe had never been a Roman virtue, and those among her legions who now laid down their arms in hope of quarter, drank deep of the cup of suffering, which Rome had held to the lips of many a brave but unfortunate enemy. The infuriated Germans slaughtered their oppressors with deliberate ferocity, and those prisoners who were not hewn to pieces on the spot were only preserved to perish by a more cruel death in cold blood.

The bulk of the Roman army fought steadily and stubbornly, frequently repelling the masses of the assailants, but gradually losing the compactness of their array, and becoming weaker and weaker beneath the incessant shower of darts and the reiterated assaults of the vigorous and unencumbered Germans. At last, in a series of desperate attacks, the column was pierced through and through, two of the eagles captured, and the Roman host, which on the yester morning had marched forth in such pride and might, now broken up into confused fragments, either fell fighting beneath the overpowering numbers of the enemy, or perished in the swamps and woods in unavailing efforts at flight. Few, very few, ever saw again the left bank of the Rhine. One body of brave veterans, arraying themselves in a ring on a little mound, beat off every charge of the Germans, and prolonged their honorable resistance to the close of that dreadful day. The traces of a feeble attempt at forming a ditch and mound attested in after years the spot where the last of the Romans passed their night of suffering and despair. But on the morrow, this remnant also, worn out with hunger, wounds, and toil, was charged by the victorious Germans, and either massacred on the spot, or offered up in fearful rites at the altars of the deities of the old mythology of the North.

A gorge in the mountain ridge, through which runs the modern road between Paderborn and Pyrmont, leads from the spot where the heat of the battle raged to the Extersteinc, a cluster of bold and grotesque rocks of sandstone, near which is a small sheet of water, overshadowed by a grove of aged trees. According to local tradition, this was one of the sacred groves of the ancient Germans, and it was here that the Roman captives were slain in sacrifice by the victorious warriors of Arminius.[9]

Never was victory more decisive, never was the liberation of an oppressed people more instantaneous and complete. Throughout Germany the Roman garrisons were assailed and cut off; and within a few weeks after Varus had fallen, the German soil was freed from the foot of an invader.

At Rome the tidings of the battle were received with an agony of terror, the reports of which we should deem exaggerated, did they not come from Roman historians themselves. They not only tell emphatically how great was the awe which the Romans felt of the prowess of the Germans, if their various tribes could be brought to unite for a common purpose,[10] but also they reveal how weakened and debased the population of Italy had become. Dion Cassius says (lib. lvi., sec. 23): "Then Augustus, when he heard the calamity of Varus, rent his garment, and was in great affliction for the troops he had lost, and for terror respecting the Germans and the Gauls. And his chief alarm was that he expected them to push on against Italy and Rome; and there remained no Roman youth fit for military duty that were worth speaking of, and the allied populations, that were at all serviceable, had been wasted away. Yet he prepared for the emergency as well as his means allowed; and when none of the citizens of military age were willing to enlist, he made them cast lots, and punished by confiscation of goods and disfranchisement every fifth man among those under thirty-five, and every tenth man of those above that age. At last, when he found that not even thus could he make many come forward, he put some of them to death. So he made a conscription of discharged veterans and of emancipated slaves, and, collecting as large a force as he could, sent it, under Tiberius, with all speed into Germany."

Dion mentions, also, a number of terrific portents that were believed to have occurred at the time, and the narration of which is not immaterial, as it shows the state of the public mind, when such things were so believed in and so interpreted. The summits of the Alps were said to have fallen, and three columns of fire to have blazed up from them. In the Campus Martius, the temple of the war-god, from whom the founder of Rome had sprung, was struck by a thunderbolt. The nightly heavens glowed several times, as if on fire. Many comets blazed forth together; and fiery meteors, shaped like spears, had shot from the northern quarter of the sky down into the Roman camps. It was said, too, that a statue of Victory, which had stood at a place on the frontier, pointing the way towards Germany, had, of its own accord, turned round, and now pointed to Italy. These and other prodigies were believed by the multitude to accompany the slaughter of Varus' legions, and to manifest the anger of the gods against Rome. Augustus himself was not free from superstition; but on this occasion no supernatural terrors were needed to increase the alarm and grief that he felt, and which made him, even months after the news of the battle had arrived, often beat his head against the wall, and exclaim, "Quintilius Varus, give me back my legions." We learn this from his biographer Suetonius; and, indeed, every ancient writer who alludes to the overthrow of Varus attests the importance of the blow against the Roman power, and the bitterness with which it was felt.[11]

The Germans did not pursue their victory beyond their own territory; but that victory secured at once and forever the independence of the Teutonic race. Rome sent, indeed, her legions again into Germany, to parade a temporary superiority, but all hopes of permanent conquests were abandoned by Augustus and his successors.

The blow which Arminius had struck never was forgotten. Roman fear disguised itself under the specious title of moderation, and the Rhine became the acknowledged boundary of the two nations until the fifth century of our era, when the Germans became the assailants, and carved with their conquering swords the provinces of imperial Rome into the kingdoms of modern Europe.

ARMINIUS.

I have said above that the great Cheruscan is more truly one of our national heroes than Caractacus is. It may be added that an Englishman is entitled to claim a closer degree of relationship with Arminius than can be claimed by any German of modern Germany. The proof of this depends on the proof of four facts: first, that the Cheruscans were Old Saxons, or Saxons of the interior of Germany; secondly, that the Anglo-Saxons, or Saxons of the coast of Germany, were more closely akin than other German tribes were to the Cheruscan Saxons; thirdly, that the Old Saxons were almost exterminated by Charlemagne; fourthly, that the Anglo-Saxons are our immediate ancestors. The last of these may be assumed as an axiom in English history. The proofs of the other three are partly philological and partly historical. I have not space to go into them here, but they will be found in the early chapters of the great work of my friend, Dr. Robert Gordon Latham, on the "English Language," and in the notes to his edition of the "Germania of Tacitus." It may be, however, here remarked, that the present Saxons of Germany are of the High Germanic division of the German race, whereas both the Anglo-Saxon and Old Saxon were of the Low Germanic.

Being thus the nearest heirs of the glory of Arminius, we may fairly devote more attention to his career than, in such a work as the present, could be allowed to any individual leader; and it is interesting to trace how far his fame survived during the Middle Ages, both among the Germans of the Continent and among ourselves.

It seems probable that the jealousy with which Maroboduus, the king of the Suevi and Marcomanni, regarded Arminius, and which ultimately broke out into open hostilities between those German tribes and the Cherusci, prevented Arminius from leading the confederate Germans to attack Italy after his first victory. Perhaps he may have had the rare moderation of being content with the liberation of his country, without seeking to retaliate on her former oppressors. When Tiberius marched into Germany in the year 10, Arminius was too cautious to attack him on ground favorable to the legions, and Tiberius was too skilful to entangle his troops in the difficult parts of the country. His march and countermarch were as unresisted as they were unproductive. A few years later, when a dangerous revolt of the Roman legions near the frontier caused their generals to find them active employment by leading them into the interior of Germany, we find Arminius again active in his country's defence. The old quarrel between him and his father-in-law, Segestes, had broken out afresh. Segestes now called in the aid of the Roman general, Germanicus, to whom he surrendered himself; and by his contrivance, his daughter Thusnelda, the wife of Arminius, also came into the hands of the Romans, being far advanced in pregnancy. She showed, as Tacitus relates,[12] more of the spirit of her husband than of her father, a spirit that could not be subdued into tears or supplications. She was sent to Ravenna, and there gave birth to a son, whose life we know, from an allusion in Tacitus, to have been eventful and unhappy; but the part of the great historian's work which narrated his fate has perished, and we only know from another quarter that the son of Arminius was, at the age of four years, led captive in a triumphal pageant along the streets of Rome.

The high spirit of Arminius was goaded almost into frenzy by these bereavements. The fate of his wife, thus torn from him, and of his babe doomed to bondage even before its birth, inflamed the elequent invectives with which he roused his countrymen against the home-traitors, and against their invaders, who thus made war upon women and children. Germanicus had marched his army to the place where Varus had perished, and had there paid funeral honors to the ghastly relics of his predecessor's legions that he found heaped around him.[13] Arminius lured him to advance a little further into the country, and then assailed him, and fought a battle, which, by the Roman accounts, was a drawn one. The effect of it was to make Germanicus resolve on retreating to the Rhine. He himself, with part of his troops, embarked in some vessels on the Ems, and returned by that river, and then by sea; but part of his forces were intrusted to a Roman general named Cæcina, to lead them back by land to the Rhine. Arminius followed this division on its march, and fought several battles with it, in which he inflicted heavy loss on the Romans, captured the greater part of their baggage, and would have destroyed them completely, had not his skilful system of operations been finally thwarted by the haste of Inguiomerus, a confederate German chief, who insisted on assaulting the Romans in their camp, instead of waiting till they were entangled in the difficulties of the country, and assailing their columns on the march.

In the following year the Romans were inactive, but in the year afterwards Germanicus led a fresh invasion. He placed his army on shipboard, and sailed to the mouth of the Ems, where he disembarked, and marched to the Weser, where he encamped, probably in the neighborhood of Minden. Arminius had collected his army on the other side of the river; and a scene occurred, which is powerfully told by Tacitus, and which is the subject of a beautiful poem by Praed. It has been already mentioned that the brother of Arminius, like himself, had been trained up while young to serve in the Roman armies; but, unlike Arminius, he not only refused to quit the Roman service for that of his country, but fought against his country with the legions of Germanicus. He had assumed the Roman name of Flavius, and had gained considerable distinction in the Roman service, in which he had lost an eye from a wound in battle. When the Roman outposts approached the River Weser, Arminius called out to them from the opposite bank, and expressed a wish to see his brother. Flavius stepped forward, and Arminius ordered his own followers to retire, and requested that the archers should be removed from the Roman bank of the river. This was done; and the brothers, who apparently had not seen each other for some years, began a conversation from the opposite sides of the stream, in which Arminius questioned his brother respecting the loss of his eye, and what battle it had been lost in, and what reward he had received for his wound. Flavius told him how the eye was lost, and mentioned the increased pay that he had on account of its loss, and showed the collar and other military decorations that had been given him. Arminius mocked at these as badges of slavery; and then each began to try to win the other over. Flavius boasting the power of Rome, and her generosity to the submissive; Arminius appealing to him in the name of their country's gods, of the mother that had borne them and by the holy names of fatherland and freedom, not to prefer being the betrayer to being the champion of his country. They soon proceeded to mutual taunts and menaces, and Flavius called aloud for his horse and his arms, that he might dash across the river and attack his brother; nor would he have been checked from doing so, had not the Roman general Stertinius run up to him and forcibly detained him. Arminius stood on the other bank, threatening the renegade, and defying him to battle.

I shall not be thought to need apology for quoting here the stanzas in which Praed has described this scene — a scene among the most affecting, as well as the most striking, that history supplies. It makes us reflect on the desolate position of Arminius, with his wife and child captives in the enemy's hands, and with his brother a renegade in arms against him. The great liberator of our German race was there, with every source of human happiness denied him except the consciousness of doing his duty to his country.

"Back, back! he fears not foaming flood
Who fears not steel-clad line:
No warrior thou of German blood,
No brother thou of mine.
Go, earn Rome's chain to load thy neck,
Her gems to deck thy hilt;
And blazon honor's hapless wreck
With all the gauds of guilt.

"But wouldst thou have *me* share the prey?
By all that I have done,
The Varian bones that day by day
Lie whitening in the sun,
The legion's trampled panoply,
The eagle's shatter'd wing —
I would not be for earth or sky
So scorn'd and mean a thing.

"Ho, call me here the wizard, boy,
Of dark and subtle skill,
To agonize but not destroy,
To torture, not to kill.
When swords are out, and shriek and shout
Leave little room for prayer,
No fetter on man's arm or heart
Hangs half so heavy there.

"I curse him by the gifts the land
Hath won from him and Rome,
The riving axe, the wasting brand,
Rent forest, blazing home.

I curse him by our country's gods,
  The terrible, the dark,
. The breakers of the Roman rods,
  The smiters of the bark.

"Oh, misery that such a ban
  On such a brow should be!
Why comes he not in battle's van
  His country's chief to be?
To stand a comrade by my side,
  The sharer of my fame,
And worthy of a brother's pride
  And of a brother's name?

"But it is past! where heroes press
  And cowards bend the knee,
Arminius is not brotherless,
  His brethren are the free.
They come around: one hour, and light
  Will fade from turf and tide,
Then onward, onward to the fight,
  With darkness for our guide.

"To-night, to-night, when we shall meet
  In combat face to face,
Then only would Arminius greet
  The renegade's embrace.
The canker of Rome's guilt shall be
  Upon his dying name;
And as he lived in slavery,
  So shall he fall in shame."

On the day after the Romans had reached the Weser,
Germanicus led his army across that river, and a partial
encounter took place, in which Arminius was successful. But on
the succeeding day a general action was fought, in which

Arminius was severely wounded, and the German infantry
routed with heavy loss. The horsemen of the two armies encountered, without either party gaining the advantage. But the
Roman army remained master of the ground, and claimed a
complete victory. Germanicus erected a trophy in the field, with
a vaunting inscription, that the nations between the Rhine and
the Elbe had been thoroughly conquered by his army. But that
army speedily made a final retreat to the left bank of the Rhine;
nor was the effect of their campaign more durable than their
trophy. The sarcasm with which Tacitus speaks of certain other
triumphs of Roman generals over Germans may apply to the pageant which Germanicus celebrated on his return to Rome from
his command of the Roman army of the Rhine. The Germans
were "*triumphati potius quam victi.*"

After the Romans had abandoned their attempts on Genmany,
we find Arminius engaged in hostilities with Maroboduus, the
king of the Suevi and Marcomanni, who was endeavoring to bring
the other German tribes into a state of dependency on him.
Arminius was at the head of the Germans who took up arms
against this home invader of their liberties. After some minor
engagements, a pitched battle was fought between the two confed-
eracies, AD 19, in which the loss on each side was equal, but
Maroboduus confessed the ascendancy of his antagonist by avoiding a renewal of the engagement, and by imploring the intervention of the Romans in his defence. The younger Drusus then
commanded the Roman legions in the province of Illyricum, and
by his mediation a peace was concluded between Arminius and
Maroboduus, by the terms of which it is evident that the latter
must have renounced his ambitious schemes against the freedom
of the other German tribes.

Arminius did not long survive this second war of independence, which he successfully waged for his country. He was assassinated in the thirty-seventh year of his age by some of his own
kinsmen, who conspired against him. Tacitus says that this happened while he was engaged in a civil war, which had been caused

by his attempts to make himself king over his countrymen. It is far more probable (as one of the best biographers[14] has observed) that Tacitus misunderstood an attempt of Arminius to extend his influence as elective war-chieftain of the Cherusci, and other tribes, for an attempt to obtain the royal dignity. When we remember that his father-in-law and his brother were renegades, we can well understand that a party among his kinsmen may have been bitterly hostile to him, and have opposed his authority with the tribe by open violence, and when that seemed ineffectual, by secret assassination.

Arminius left a name which the historians of the nation against which he combated so long and so gloriously have delighted to honor. It is from the most indisputable source, from the lips of enemies, that we know his exploits.[15] His countrymen made history, but did not write it. But his memory lived among them in the days of their bards, who recorded

> "The deeds he did, the fields he won,
> The freedom he restored."

Tacitus, writing years after the death of Arminius, says of him, "Canitur adhuc barbaras apud gentes." As time passed on, the gratitude of ancient Germany to her great deliverer grew into adoration, and divine honors were paid for centuries to Arminius by every tribe of the Low Germanic division of the Teutonic races. The Irmin-sul, or the column of Herman, near Eresburgh, the modern Stadtberg, was the chosen object of worship to the descendants of the Cherusci, the Old Saxons, and in defence of which they fought most desperately against Charlemagne and his Christianized Franks. "Irmin, in the cloudy Olympus of Teutonic belief, appears as a king and a warrior; and the pillar, the 'Irmin-sul,' bearing the statue, and considered as the symbol of the deity, was the Palladium of the Saxon nation until the temple of Eresburgh was destroyed by Charlemagne, and the column itself transferred to the monastery of Corbey, where perhaps a portion of the rude rock idol yet remains, covered by the ornaments of the Gothic era."[16] Traces of the worship of Arminius are to be found among our Anglo-Saxon ancestors, after their settlement in this island. One of the four great highways was held to be under the protection of the deity, and was called the "Irmin street." The name Arminius is, of course, the mere Latinized form of "Herman," the name by which the hero and the deity were known by every man of Low German blood on either side of the German Sea. It means, etymologically, the "Warman," the "man of hosts." No other explanation of the worship of the "Irmin-sul," and of the name of the "Irmin street," is so satisfactory as that which connects them with the deified Arminius. We know for certain of the existence of other columns of an analogous character. Thus there was the Roland-seule in North Germany; there was a Thor-seule in Sweden, and (what is more important) there was an Athelstan-seule in Saxon England.[17]

There is at the present moment a song respecting the Irmin-sul current in the bishopric of Minden, one version of which might seem only to refer to Charkmagne having pulled down the Irmin-sul.

> "Herman, sla dermen,
> Sla pipen, sla trummen,
> De Kaiser will kummen,
> Met hamer un stangen,
> Will Herman uphangen."

But tnere is another version, which probably is the oldest, and which clearly refers to the great Arminius.

> "Un Herman slaug dermen,
> Slaug pipen, slaug trummen;
> De fürsten sind kammen,
> Met all eren-mannen
> Hebt *Varus* uphangen."[18]

About ten centuries and a half after the demolition of the Irmin-sul, and nearly eighteen after the death of Arminius, the modern Germans conceived the idea of rendering tardy homage to their great hero, and accordingly, some eight or ten years ago, a general subscription was organized in Germany for the purpose of erecting on the Osning—a conical mountain, which forms the highest summit of the Teutoberger Wald, and is eighteen hundred feet above the level of the sea—a colossal bronze statue of Arminius. The statue was designed by Bandel. The hero was to stand uplifting a sword in his right hand, and looking towards the Rhine. The height of the statue was to be eighty feet from the base to the point of the sword, and was to stand on a circular Gothic temple ninety feet high, and supported by oak trees as columns. The mountain, where it was to be erected, is wild and stern, and overlooks the scene of the battle. It was calculated that the statue would be clearly visible at a distance of sixty miles. The temple is nearly finished, and the statue itself has been cast at the copper works at Lemgo. But there, through want of funds to set it up, it has lain for some years, in disjointed fragments, exposed to the mutilating homage of relic-seeking travellers. The idea of honoring a hero, who belongs to *all* Germany, is not one which the present rulers of that divided country[19] have any wish to encourage; and the statue may long continue to lie there, and present too true a type of the condition of Germany herself.[20]

Surely this is an occasion in which Englishmen might well prove, by acts as well as words, that we also rank Arminius among our heroes.

I have quoted the noble stanzas of one of our modern English poets on Arminius, and I will conclude this memoir with one of the odes of the great poet of modern Germany, Klopstock, on the victory to which we owe our freedom, and Arminius mainly owes his fame. Klopstock calls it the "Battle of Winfield." The epithet of "sister of Cannæ" shows that Klopstock followed some chronologers, according to whom Varus was defeated on the anniversary of the day on which Paulus and Varro were defeated by Hannibal.

SONG OF TRIUMPH AFTER THE VICTORY OF HERRMAN, THE DELIVERER OF GERMANY FROM THE ROMANS.

FROM KLOPSTOCK'S "HERRMAN UND DIE FÚRSTEN,"

Supposed to be sung by a chorus of Bards.

A CHORUS.

Sister of Cannæ![21] Winfield's[22] fight!
We saw thee with thy streaming, bloody hair,
With fiery eye, bright with the world's despair,
Sweep by Walhalia's bards from out our sight.

Herrman outspake: "Now Victory or Death!"
The Romans . . . " Victory!"
And onward rushed their eagles with the cry.
So ended the *first* day.

"Victory or Death!" began
Then, first, the Roman chief; and Herrman spake
Not, but home-struck: the eagles fluttered—brake.
So sped the *second* day.

TWO CHORUSES.

And the third came . . . the cry was "Flight or Death!"
Flight left they not for them who'd make them slaves —
Men who stab children! flight for them! . . . no! graves!
" 'Twas their *last* day."

TWO BARDS.

Yet spared they messengers: they came to Rome —
How drooped the plume—the lance was left to trail
Down in the dust behind—their cheek was pale —
So came the messengers to Rome.

High in his hall the imperator sat —
Octavianus Cæsar Augustus sat.
They filled up wine-cups, wine-cups filled they up
For him the highest—wine-cups filled they up
For him the highest, Jove of all their state.

The flutes of Lydia hushed before their voice,
Before the messengers—the "Highest" sprung —
The god[23] against the marble pillars, wrung
By the dread words, striking his brow, and thrice
Cried he aloud in anguish, "Varus! Varus!
Give back my legions, Varus!"
And now the world-wide conquerors shrunk and feared
For fatherland and home,
The lance to raise; and 'mongst those false to Rome

The death-lot rolled,[24] and still they shrunk and feared;
"For she her face hath turned
The victor goddess," cried those cowards— (for aye
Be it!) —"from Rome and Romans, and her day
Is done"—and still be mourned,
And cried aloud in anguish, "Varus! Varus!
Give back my legions, Varus!"[25]

Synopsis of Events between Arminius' Victory Over Varus and the Battle of Chalons.

AD 43. The Romans commence the conquest of Britain, Claudius being then Emperor of Rome. The population of this island was then Celtic. In about forty years all the tribes south of the Clyde were subdued, and their land made a Roman province.

58–60. Successful campaigns of the Roman general Corbulo against the Parthians.

64. First persecution of the Christians at Rome under Nero.

68–70. Civil wars in the Roman world. The Emperors Nero, Galba, Otho, and Vitellius cut off successively by violent deaths. Vespasian becomes emperor.

70. Jerusalem destroyed by the Romans under Titus.

83. Futile attack of Domitian on the Germans.

86. Beginning of the wars between the Romans and the Dacians.

98–117. Trajan emperor of Rome. Under him the empire acquires its greatest territorial extent by his conquests in Dacia and in the East. His successor, Hadrian, abandons the provinces beyond the Euphrates which Trajan had conquered.

138–180. Era of the Antonines.

167–176. A long and desperate war between Rome and a great confederacy of the German nations. Marcus Antoninus at last succeeds in repelling them.

192–197. Civil wars throughout the Roman world. Severus becomes emperor. He relaxes the discipline of the soldiers. After his death, in 211, the series of military insurrections, civil wars, and murders of emperors recommences.

226. Artaxerxes (Ardisheer) overthrows the Parthian, and restores the Persian kingdom in Asia. He attacks the Roman possessions in the East.

250. The Goths invade the Roman provinces. The Emperor Decius is defeated and slain by them.

253–260. The Franks and Alemanni invade Gaul, Spain, and Africa. The Goths attack Asia Minor and Greece. The Persians conquer Armenia. Their king. Sapor, defeats the Roman Emperor Valerian, and takes him prisoner. General distress of the Roman empire.

268–283. The Emperors Claudius, Aurelian, Tacitus, Pro-bus, and Carus defeat the various enemies of Rome, and restore order in the Roman state.

285. Diocletian divides and reorganizes the Roman empire. After his abdication in 305 a fresh series of civil wars and confusion ensues. Constantine, the first Christian emperor, reunites the empire in 324.

330. Constantine makes Constantinople the seat of empire instead of Rome.

363. The Emperor Julian is killed in action against the Persians.

364–375. The empire is again divided, Valentinian being emperor of the West, and Valens of the East. Valentinian repulses the Alemanni, and other German invaders from Gaul. Splendor of the Gothic kingdom under Hermanric, north of the Danube.

375–395. The Huns attack the Goths, who implore the protection of the Roman emperor of the East. The Goths are allowed to pass the Danube, and to settle in the Roman provinces. A war soon breaks out between them and the Romans, and the Emperor Valens and his army are destroyed by them. They ravage the Roman territories. The Emperor Theodosius reduces them to submission. They retain settlements in Thrace and Asia Minor.

395. Final division of the Roman empire between Arcadius and Honorius, the two sons of Theodosius. The Goths revolt, and under Alaric attack various parts of both the Roman empires.

410. Alaric takes the city of Rome.

412. The Goths march into Gaul, and in 414 into Spain, which had been invaded by hosts of Vandals, Suevi, Alani, and other Germanic nations. Britain is formally abandoned by the Roman empire of the West.

428. Genseric, king of the Vandals, conquers the Roman province of North Africa.

441. The Huns attack the Eastern empire.

CHAPTER VI

THE BATTLE OF CHALONS, AD 451

"The discomfiture of the mighty attempt of Attila to found a new anti-Christian dynasty upon the wreck of the temporal power of Rome, at the end of the term of twelve hundred years, to which its duration had been limited by the forebodings of the heathen."

— Herbert.

ABROAD expanse of plains, the Campi Catalaunici of the ancients, spreads far and wide around the city of Châlons, in the northeast of France. The long rows of poplars, through which the River Marne winds its way, and a few thinly scattered villages, are almost the only objects that vary the monotonous aspect of the greater part of this region. But about five miles from Châlons, near the little hamlets of Chape and Cuperly, the ground is indented and heaped up in ranges of grassy mounds and trenches, which attest the work of man's hands in ages past, and which, to the practised eye, demonstrate that this quiet spot has once been the fortified position of a huge military host.

Local tradition gives to these ancient earth-works the name of Attila's Camp. Nor is there any reason to question the correctness of the title, or to doubt that behind these very ramparts it was that 1,400 years ago the most powerful heathen king that ever ruled in Europe mustered the remnants of his vast army, which had striven on these plains against the Christian soldiery of Toulouse and Rome. Here it was that Attila prepared to resist to the death his victors in the field; and here he heaped up the treasures of his

148

camp in one vast pile, which was to be his funeral pyre should his camp be stormed. It was here that the Gothic and Italian forces watched, but dared not assail their enemy in his despair, after that great and terrible day of battle when

> "The sound
> Of conflict was o'erpast, the shout of all
> Whom earth could send from her remotest bounds,
> Heathen or faithful; from thy hundred mouths,
> That feed the Caspian with Riphean snows.
> Huge Volga! from famed Hypanis, which once
> Cradled the Hun; from all the countless realms
> Between Imaus and that utmost strand
> Where columns of Herculean rock confront
> The blown Atlantic; Roman, Goth, and Hun,
> And Scythian strength of chivalry, that tread
> The cold Codanian shore, or what far lands
> Inhospitable drink Cimmerian floods,
> Franks, Saxons, Suevic, and Sarmatian chiefs,
> And who from green Armorica or Spain
> Flocked to the work of death."[1]

The victory which the Roman general, Aëtius, with his Gothic allies, had then gained over the Huns, was the last victory of imperial Rome. But among the long Fasti of her triumphs, few can be found that, for their importance and ultimate benefit to mankind, are comparable with this expiring effort of her arms. It did not, indeed, open to her any new career of conquest—it did not consolidate the relics of her power—it did not turn the rapid ebb of her fortunes. The mission of imperial Rome was, in truth, already accomplished. She had received and transmitted through her once ample dominion the civilization of Greece. She had broken up the barriers of narrow nationalities among the various states and tribes that dwelt around the coasts of the Mediterranean. She had fused these and many other races into one organized empire, bound together by a community of laws, of government and institutions. Under the shelter of her full power the True Faith had arisen in the earth, and during the years of her decline it had been nourished to maturity, it had overspread all the provinces that ever obeyed her sway.[2] For no beneficial purpose to mankind could the dominion of the seven-hilled city have been restored or prolonged. But it was all-important to mankind what nations should divide among them Rome's rich inheritance of empire. Whether the Germanic and Gothic warriors should form states and kingdoms out of the fragments of her dominions, and become the free members of the commonwealth of Christian Europe; or whether pagan savages, from the wilds of Central Asia, should crush the relics of classic civilization and the early institutions of the Christianized Germans in one hopeless chaos of barbaric conquest. The Christian Visigoths of King Theodoric fought and triumphed at Châlons side by side with the legions of Aëtius. Their joint victory over the Hunnish host not only rescued for a time from destruction the old age of Rome, but preserved for centuries of power and glory the Germanic element in the civilization of modern Europe.

In order to estimate the full importance to mankind of the battle of Châlons, we must keep steadily in mind who and what the Germans were, and the important distinctions between them and the numerous other races that assailed the Roman empire; and it is to be understood that the Gothic and Scandinavian nations are included in the German race. Now, "in two remarkable traits, the Germans differed from the Sarmatic as well as from the Slavic nations, and, indeed, from all those other races to whom the Greeks and Romans gave the designation of barbarians. I allude to their personal freedom and regard for the rights of men; secondly, to the respect paid by them to the female sex, and the chastity for which the latter were celebrated among the people of the North. These were the foundations of that probity of character, self-respect, and purity of manners which may be traced among the Germans and Goths even during pagan times, and which, when their sentiments were enlightened by Christianity, brought out those splendid traits of character which distinguish the age of chivalry and romance."[3] What the intermixture of the German stock with the classic, at the fall of the Western empire, has done for mankind, may be best felt by watching, with Arnold, over how large a portion of the earth the influence of the German element is now extended.

"It affects, more or less, the whole west of Europe, from the head of the Gulf of Bothnia to the most southern promontory of Sicily, from the Oder and the Adriatic to the Hebrides and to Lisbon. It is true that the language spoken over a large portion of this space is not predominantly German; but even in France, and Italy, and Spain, the influence of the Franks, Burgundians, Visigoths, Ostrogoths, and Lombards while it has colored even the language, has in blood and institutions left its mark legibly and indelibly. Germany, the Low Countries, Switzerland for the most part, Denmark, Norway, and Sweden, and our own islands are all in language, in blood, and in institutions, German most decidedly. But all South America is peopled with Spaniards and Portuguese; all North America, and all Australia with Englishmen. I say nothing of the prospects and influence of the German race in Africa and in India: it is enough to say that half of Europe, and all America and Australia, are German, more or less completely, in race, in language, or in institutions, or in all."[4]

By the middle of the fifth century, Germanic nations had settled themselves in many of the fairest regions of the Roman empire, had imposed their yoke on the provincials, and had undergone, to a considerable extent, that moral conquest which the arts of refinements of the vanquished in arms have so often achieved over the rough victor. The Visigoths held the north of Spain, and Gaul south of the Loire. Franks, Alemanni, Alans, and Burgundians had established themselves in other Gallic provinces, and the Suevi were masters of a large southern portion of the Spanish peninsula. A king of the Vandals reigned in North Africa; and the Ostrogoths had firmly planted themselves in the provinces north of Italy. Of these powers and principalities, that of the Visigoths, under their king Theodoric, son of Alaric, was by far the first in power and in civilization.

The pressure of the Huns upon Europe had first been felt in the fourth century of our era. They had long been formidable to the Chinese empire, but the ascendency in arms which another nomadic tribe of Central Asia, the Sienpi, gained over them, drove the Huns from their Chinese conquest westward; and this movement once being communicated to the whole chain of barbaric nations that dwelt northward of the Black Sea and the Roman empire, tribe after tribe of savage warriors broke in upon the barriers of civilized Europe. "Velut unda supervenit undam." The Huns crossed the Tanais into Europe in 375, and rapidly reduced to subjection the Alans, the Ostrogoths, and other tribes that were then dwelling along the course of the Danube. The armies of the Roman emperor that tried to check their progress were cut to pieces by them, and Pannonia and other provinces south of the Danube were speedily occupied by the victorious cavalry of these new invaders. Not merely the degenerate Romans but the bold and hardy warriors of Germany and Scandinavia, were appalled at the number, the ferocity, the ghastly appearance, and the lightning-like rapidity of the Huns. Strange and loathsome legends were coined and credited which attributed their origin to the union of

"Secret, black, and midnight hags,"

with the evil spirits of the wilderness.

Tribe after tribe, and city after city, fell before them. Then came a pause in their career of conquest in southwestern Europe, caused probably by dissensions among their chiefs, and also by their arms being employed in attacks upon the Scandinavian nations. But when Attila (or Atzel, as he is called in the Hungarian language) became their ruler, the torrent of their arms was directed with augmented terrors upon the west and the south, and their myriads marched beneath the guidance of one master-mind to the overthrow both of the new and the old powers of the earth.

Recent events have thrown such a strong interest over everything connected with the Hungarian name, that even the terrible renown of Attila now impresses us the more vividly through our sympathizing admiration of the exploits of those who claim to be descended from his warriors, and "ambitiously insert the name of Attila among their native kings." The authenticity of this martial genealogy is denied by some writers and questioned by more. But it is at least certain that the Magyars of Arpad, who are the immediate ancestors of the bulk of the modern Hungarians, and who conquered the country which bears the name of Hungary in AD 889, were of the same stock of mankind as were the Huns of Attila, even if they did not belong to the same subdivision of that stock. Nor is there any improbability in the tradition that after Attila's death many of his warriors remained in Hungary, and that their descendants afterwards joined the Huns of Arpad in their career of conquest. It is certain that Attila made Hungary the seat of his empire. It seems also susceptible of clear proof that the territory was then called Hungvar and Attila's soldiers Hungvari. Both the Huns of Attila and those of Arpad came from the family of nomadic nations whose primitive regions were those vast wildernesses of High Asia which are included between the Altaic and the Himalayan mountain chains. The inroads of these tribes upon the lower regions of Asia and into Europe have caused many of the most remarkable revolutions in the history of the world. There is every reason to believe that swarms of these nations made their way into distant parts of the earth, at periods long before the date of the Scythian invasion of Asia, which is the earliest inroad of the nomadic race that history records. The first, as far as we can conjecture, in respect to the time of their descent, were the Finnish and Ugrian tribes, who appear to have come down from the Altaic border of High Asia towards the northwest, in which direction they advanced to the Uralian Mountains. There they established themselves; and that mountain chain, with its valleys and pasture lands, became to them a new country, whence they sent out colonies on every side; but the Ugrian colony, which, under Arpad, occupied Hungary, and became the ancestors of the bulk of the present Hungarian nation, did not quit their settlements on the Uralian Mountains till a very late period, and not until four centuries after the time when

Attila led from the primary seats of the nomadic races in High Asia the host with which he advanced into the heart of France.[5] That host was Turkish, but closely allied in origin, language, and habits with the Finno-Ugrian settlers on the Ural.

Attila's fame has not come down to us through the partial and suspicious medium of chroniclers and poets of his own race. It is not from Hunnish authorities that we learn the extent of his might: it is from his enemies, from the literature and the legends of the nations whom he afflicted with his arms, that we draw the unquestionable evidence of his greatness. Besides the express narratives of Byzantine, Latin, and Gothic writers, we have the strongest proof of the stern reality of Attila's conquests in the extent to which he and his Huns have been the themes of the earliest German and Scandinavian lays. Wild as many of those legends are, they bear concurrent and certain testimony to the awe with which the memory of Attila was regarded by the bold warriors who composed and delighted in them. Attila's exploits, and the wonders of his unearthly steed and magic sword, repeatedly occur in the Sagas of Norway and Iceland; and the celebrated Niebelungen Lied, the most ancient of Germanic poetry, is full of them. There Etsel, or Attila, is described as the wearer of twelve mighty crowns, and as promising to his bride the lands of thirty kings, whom his irresistible sword had subdued. He is, in fact, the hero of the latter part of this remarkable poem; and it is at his capital city, Etselenburgh, which evidently corresponds to the modern Buda, that much of its action takes place.

When we turn from the legendary to the historic Attila, we see clearly that he was not one of the vulgar herd of barbaric conquerors. Consummate military skill may be traced in his campaigns; and he relied far less on the brute force of armies for the aggrandizement of his empire, than on the unbounded influence over the affections of friends and the fears of foes which his genius enabled him to acquire. Austerely sober in his private life — severely just on the judgment seat — conspicuous among a nation of warriors for hardihood, strength, and skill in every martial exercise — grave and deliberate in counsel, but rapid and remorseless in execution, he gave safety and security to all who were under his dominion, while he waged a warfare of extermination against all who opposed or sought to escape from it. He watched the national passions, the prejudices, the creeds, and the superstitions of the varied nations over which he ruled, and of those which he sought to reduce beneath his sway: all these feelings he had the skill to turn to his own account. His own warriors believed him to be the inspired favorite of their deities, and followed him with fanatic zeal; his enemies looked on him as the pre-appointed minister of heaven's wrath against themselves; and though they believed not in his creed, their own made them tremble before him.

In one of his early campaigns he appeared before his troops with an ancient iron sword in his grasp, which he told them was the god of war whom their ancestors had worshipped. It is certain that the nomadic tribes of Northern Asia, whom Herodotus described under the name of Scythians, from the earliest times worshipped as their god a bare sword. That sword-god was supposed, in Attila's time, to have disappeared from earth; but the Hunnish king now claimed to have received it by special revelation. It was said that a herdsman, who was tracking in the desert a wounded heifer by the drops of blood, found the mysterious sword standing fixed in the ground, as if it had darted down from heaven. The herdsmen bore it to Attila, who thenceforth was believed by the Huns to wield the Spirit of Death in battle, and their seers prophesied that that sword was to destroy the world. A Roman,[6] who was on an embassy to the Hunnish camp, recorded in his memoirs Attila's acquisition of this supernatural weapon, and the immense influence over the minds of the barbaric tribes which its possession gave him. In the title which he assumed we shall see the skill with which he availed himself of the legends and creeds of other nations as well as of his own. He designated himself "ATTILA, Descendant of the Great Nimrod. Nurtured in Engaddi. By the Grace of God, King of the Huns, the Goths, the Danes, and the Medes. The Dread of the World."

Herbert states that Attila is represented on an old medallion with a Teraphim, or a head, on his breast; and the same writer adds," We know, from the 'Hamartigenea' of Prudentius, that Nimrod, with a snaky-haired head, was the object of adoration of the heretical followers of Marcion; and the same head was the palladium set up by Antiochus Epiphanes over the gates of Antioch, though it has been called the visage of Charon. The memory of Nimrod was certainly regarded with mystic veneration by many; and by asserting himself to be the heir of that mighty hunter before the Lord, he vindicated to himself at least the whole Babylonian kingdom.

"The singular assertion in his style, that he was nurtured in Engaddi, where he certainly had never been, will be more easily understood on reference to the twelfth chapter of the Book of Revelation, concerning the woman clothed with the sun, who was to bring forth in the wilderness —'where she hath a place prepared of God'—a man-child, who was to contend with the dragon having seven heads and ten horns, and rule all nations with a rod of iron. This prophecy was at that time understood universally by the sincere Christians to refer to the birth of Constantine, who was to overwhelm the paganism of the city on the seven hills, and it is still so explained; but it is evident that the heathens must have looked on it in a different light, and have regarded it as a foretelling of the birth of that Great one who should master the temporal power of Rome. The assertion, therefore, that he was nurtured in Engaddi, is a claim to be looked upon as that man-child who was to be brought forth in a place prepared of God in the wilderness. Engaddi means a place of palms and vines in the desert; it was hard by Zoar, the city of refuge, which was saved in the Vale of Siddim, or Demons, when the rest were destroyed by fire and brimstone from the Lord in heaven and might, therefore, be especially called a place prepared of God in the wilderness."

It is obvious enough why he styled himself "By the Grace of God, King of the Huns and Goths"; and it seems far from difficult to see why he added the names of the Medes and the Danes. His armies had been engaged in warfare against the Persian kingdom of the Sassanidæ, and it is certain[7] that he meditated the invasion and overthrow of the Medo-Persian power. Probably some of the northern provinces of that kingdom had been compelled to pay him tribute; and this would account for his styling himself King of the Medes, they being his remotest subjects to the south. From a similar cause, he may have called himself King of the Danes, as his power may well have extended northward as far as the nearest of the Scandinavian nations, and this mention of Medes and Danes as his subjects would serve at once to indicate the vast extent of his dominion.[8]

The immense territory north of the Danube and Black Sea and eastward of Caucasus, over which Attila ruled, first in conjunction with his brother Bleda, and afterwards alone, cannot be very accurately defined, but it must have comprised within it, besides the Huns, many nations of Slavic, Gothic, Teutonic, and Finnish origin. South also of the Danube, the country, from the River Sau, as far as Novi in Thrace, was a Hunnish province. Such was the empire of the Huns in AD 445; a memorable year, in which Attila founded Buda on the Danube as his capital city, and ridded himself of his brother by a crime which seems to have been prompted not only by selfish ambition, but also by a desire of turning to his purpose the legends and forebodings which then were universally spread throughout the Roman empire, and must have been well known to the watchful and ruthless Hun.

The year 445 of our era completed the twelfth century from the foundation of Rome, according to the best chronologers. It had always been believed among the Romans that the twelve vultures, which were said to have appeared to Romulus when he founded the city, signified the time during which the Roman power should endure. The twelve vultures denoted twelve centuries. This interpretation of the vision of the birds of destiny was current among learned Romans, even when there were yet many of the twelve centuries to run, and while the imperial city was at the zenith of its power. But as the allotted time drew nearer and nearer to its conclusion, and as Rome grew weaker and weaker beneath the blows of barbaric invaders, the terrible omen was more and more talked and thought of; and in Attila's time, men watched for the momentary extinction of the Roman state with the last beat of the last vulture's wing. Moreover, among the numerous legends connected with the foundation of the city, and the fratricidal death of Remus, there was one most terrible one, which told that Romulus did not put his brother to death in accident or in hasty quarrel, but that

> "He slew his gallant twin
> With inexpiable sin,"

deliberately and in compliance with the warnings of supernatural powers. The shedding of a brother's blood was believed to have been the price at which the founder of Rome had purchased from destiny her twelve centuries of existence.[9]

We may imagine, therefore, with what terror in this, the twelve hundredth year after the foundation of Rome, the inhabitants of the Roman empire must have heard the tidings that the royal brethren, Attila and Bleda, had founded a new capital on the Danube, which was designed to rule over the ancient capital on the Tiber; and that Attila, like Romulus, had consecrated the foundations of his new city by murdering his brother; so that for the new cycle of centuries then about to commence, dominion had been bought from the gloomy spirits of destiny in favor of the Hun by a sacrifice of equal awe and value with that which had formerly obtained it for the Roman.

It is to be remembered that not only the pagans, but also the Christians of that age, knew and believed in these legends and omens, however they might differ as to the nature of the super-human agency by which such mysteries had been made known to mankind. And we may observe, with Herbert, a modern learned dignitary of our church, how remarkably this augury was ful-filled; for "if to the twelve centuries denoted by the twelve vul-tures that appeared to Romulus, we add for the six birds that appeared to Remus six lustra, or periods of five years each, by which the Romans were wont to number their time, it brings us precisely to the year 476, in which the Roman empire was finally extinguished by Odoacer."

An attempt to assassinate Attila, made, or supposed to have been made, at the instigation of Theodoric the younger, the Emperor of Constantinople, drew the Hunnish armies, in 445, upon the Eastern empire, and delayed for a time the destined blow against Rome. Probably a more important cause of delay was the revolt of some of the Hunnish tribes to the north of the Black Sea against Attila, which broke out about this period, and is cursorily mentioned by the Byzantine writers. Attila quelled this revolt, and having thus consolidated his power, and having punished the presumption of the Eastern Roman emperor by fearful ravages of his fairest provinces, Attila, in 450 AD, prepared to set vast forces in motion for the conquest of Western Europe. He sought unsuccessfully by diplomatic intrigues to detach the King of the Visigoths from his alliance with Rome, and he resolved first to crush the power of Theodoric, and then to advance with overwhelming power to trample out the last sparks of the doomed Roman empire.

A strong invitation from a Roman princess gave him a pretext for the war, and threw an air of chivalric enterprise over his invasion. Honoria, sister of Valentinian III., the Emperor of the West, had sent to Attila to offer him her hand and her supposed right to share in the imperial power. This had been discovered by the Romans, and Honoria had been forthwith closely imprisoned. Attila now pretended to take up arms in behalf of his self-promised bride, and proclaimed that he was about to march to Rome to redress Honoria's wrongs. Ambition and spite against her brother must have been the sole motives that led the lady to woo the royal Hun; for Attila's face and person had all the natural ugliness of his race, and the description given of him by a Byzantine ambassador must have been well known in the imperial courts. Herbert has well versified the portrait drawn by Priscus of the great enemy of both Byzantium and Rome:

"Terrific was his semblance, in no mould
Of beautiful proportion cast; his limbs
Nothing exalted, but with sinews braced
Of chalybæan temper, agile, lithe,
And swifter than the roe; his ample chest
Was overbrow'd by a gigantic head,
With eyes keen, deeply sunk, and small, that gleam'd
Strangely in wrath as though some spirit unclean
Within that corporal tenement install'd
Look'd from its windows, but with temper'd fire
Beam'd mildly on the unresisting. Thin
His beard and hoary; his flat nostrils crown'd
A cicatrized, swart visage; but, withal,
That questionable shape such glory wore
That mortals quail'd beneath him."

Two chiefs of the Franks, who were then settled on the Lower
Rhine, were at this period engaged in a feud with each other, and
while one of them appealed to the Romans for aid, the other
invoked the assistance and protection of the Huns. Attila thus
obtained an ally whose co-operation secured for him the passage
of the Rhine, and it was this circumstance which caused him to
take a northward route from Hungary for his attack upon Gaul.
The muster of the Hunnish hosts was swollen by warriors of every
tribe that they had subjugated; nor is there any reason to suspect
the old chroniclers of wilful exaggeration in estimating Attila's
army at seven hundred thousand strong. Having crossed the
Rhine probably a little below Coblentz, he defeated the King of
the Burgundians, who endeavored to bar his progress. He then
divided his vast forces into two armies, one of which marched
northwest upon Tongres and Arras, and the other cities of that
part of France, while the main body, under Attila himself,
advanced up the Moselle, and destroyed Besançon, and other
towns in the country of Burgundians. One of the latest and best
biographers of Attila[10] well observes, that, "having thus conquered

the eastern part of France, Attila prepared for an invasion of the West Gothic territories beyond the Loire. He marched upon Orleans, where he intended to force the passage of that river, and only a little attention is requisite to enable us to perceive that he proceeded on a systematic plan: he had his right wing on the north for the protection of his Frank allies; his left wing on the south for the purpose of preventing the Burgundians from rallying, and of menacing the passes of the Alps from Italy; and he led his centre towards the chief object of the campaign — the conquest of Orleans, and an easy passage into the West Gothic dominion. The whole plan is very like that of the allied powers in 1814, with this difference, that their left wing entered France through the denies of the Jura, in the direction of Lyons, and that the military object of the campaign was the capture of Paris."

It was not until the year 451 that the Huns commenced the siege of Orleans; and during their campaign in Eastern Gaul, the Roman general Aëtius had strenuously exerted himself in collecting and organizing such an army as might, when united to the soldiery of the Visigoths, be fit to face the Huns in the field. He enlisted every subject of the Roman empire whom patriotism, courage, or compulsion could collect beneath the standards; and round these troops, which assumed the once proud title of the legions of Rome, he arrayed the large forces of barbaric auxiliaries, whom pay, persuasion, or the general hate and dread of the Huns brought to the camp of the last of the Roman generals. King Theodoric exerted himself with equal energy. Orleans resisted her besiegers bravely as in after times. The passage of the Loire was skilfully defended against the Huns; and Aëtius and Theodoric, after much manoeuvring and difficulty, effected a junction of their armies to the south of that important river. On the advance of the allies upon Orleans, Attila instantly broke up the siege of that city, and retreated towards the Marne. He did not choose to risk a decisive battle with only the central corps of his army against the combined power of his enemies, and he therefore fell back upon his base of operations, calling in his wings from Arras and

Besançon, and concentrating the whole of the Hunnish forces on the vast plains of Châlons-sur-Marne. A glance at the map will show how scientifically this place was chosen by the Hunnish general as the point for his scattered forces to converge upon; and the nature of the ground was eminently favorable for the operations of cavalry, the arm in which Attila's strength peculiarly lay.

It was during the retreat from Orleans that a Christian hermit is reported to have approached the Hunnish king, and said to him, "Thou art the Scourge of God for the chastisement of the Christians." Attila instantly assumed this new title of terror, which thenceforth became the appellation by which he was most widely and most fearfully known.

The confederate armies of Romans and Visigoths at last met their great adversary face to face on the ample battle-ground of the Châlons plains. Aëtius commanded on the right of the allies; King Theodoric on the left; and Sangipan, king of the Alans, whose fidelity was suspected, was placed purposely in the centre, and in the very front of the battle. Attila commanded his centre in person, at the head of his own countrymen, while the Ostrogoths, the Gepidæ, and the other subject allies of the Huns were drawn up on the wings. Some manœuvring appears to have occurred before the engagement, in which Aëtius had the advantage, inasmuch as he succeeded in occupying a sloping hill, which commanded the left flank of the Huns. Attila saw the importance of the position taken by Aëtius on the high ground, and commenced the battle by a furious attack on this part of the Roman line, in which he seems to have detached some of his best troops from his centre to aid his left. The Romans, having the advantage of the ground, repulsed the Huns, and, while the allies gained this advantage on their right, their left, under King Theodoric, assailed the Ostrogoths, who formed the right of Attila's army. The gallant king was himself struck down by a javelin, as he rode onward at the head of his men; and his own cavalry, charging over him, trampled him to death in the confusion. But the Visigoths, infuriated, not dispirited, by their monarch's fall, routed the enemies opposed to them, and then wheeled upon the flank of the Hunnish centre, which had been engaged in a sanguinary and indecisive contest with the Alans.

In this peril Attila made his centre fall back upon his camp; and when the shelter of its intrenchments and wagons had once been gained, the Hunnish archers repulsed, without difficulty, the charges of the vengeful Gothic cavalry. Aëtius had not pressed the advantage which he gained on his side of the field, and, when night fell over the wild scene of havoc, Attila's left was still undefeated, but his right had been routed, and his centre forced back upon his camp.

Expecting an assault on the morrow, Attila stationed his best archers in front of the cars and wagons, which were drawn, up as a fortification along his lines, and made every preparation for a desperate resistance. But the "Scourge of God" resolved that no man should boast of the honor of having either captured or slain him, and he caused to be raised in the centre of his encampment a huge pyramid of the wooden saddles of his cavalry: round it he heaped the spoils and the wealth that he had won; on it he stationed his wives who had accompanied him in the campaign; and on the summit Attila placed himself, ready to perish in the flames, and balk the victorious foe of their choicest booty, should they succeed in storming his defences.

But when the morning broke and revealed the extent of the carnage with which the plains were heaped for miles, the successful allies saw also and respected the resolute attitude of their antagonist. Neither were any measures taken to blockade him in his camp, and so to extort by famine that submission which it was too plainly perilous to enforce with the sword. Attila was allowed to march back the remnants of his army without molestation, and even with the semblance of success.

It is probable that the crafty Aëtius was unwilling to be too victorious. He dreaded the glory which his allies the Visigoths had acquired, and feared that Rome might find a second Alaric in Prince Thorismund, who had signalized himself in the battle, and had been chosen on the field to succeed his father, Theodoric. He persuaded the young king to return at once to his capital, and thus relieved himself at the same time of the presence of a dangerous friend, as well as of a formidable though beaten foe.

Attila's attacks on the Western empire were soon renewed, but never with such peril to the civilized world as had menaced it before his defeat at Châlons; and on his death, two years after that battle, the vast empire which his genius had founded was soon dissevered by the successful revolts of the subject nations. The name of the Huns ceased for some centuries to inspire terror in Western Europe, and their ascendency passed away with the life of the great king by whom it had been so fearfully augmented.[11]

Synopsis of Events between the Battle of Chalons, AD 451, and the Battle of Tours, AD 732.

AD 476. The Roman empire of the West extinguished by Odoacer.

481. Establishment of the French monarchy in Gaul by Clovis.

455–582. The Saxons, Angles, and Frisians conquer Britain, except the northern parts and the districts along the west coast. The German conquerors found eight independent kingdoms.

533–568. The generals of Justinian, the Emperor of Constantinople, conquer Italy and North Africa; and these countries are for a short time annexed to the Roman empire of the East.

568–570. The Lombards conquer great part of Italy.

570–627. The wars between the emperors of Constantinople and the kings of Persia are actively continued.

622. The Mohammedan era of the Hegira. Mohammed is driven from Mecca, and is received as prince of Medina.

629–632. Mohammed conquers Arabia.

632–651. The Mohammedan Arabs invade and conquer Persia.

632–709. They attack the Roman empire of the East. They conquer Syria, Egypt, and Africa.

709–713. They cross the straits of Gibraltar, and invade and conquer Spain.

CHAPTER VII

THE BATTLE OF TOURS, AD 732

"The events that rescued our ancestors of Britain and our neighbors of Gaul from the civil and religious yoke of the Koran."

— *Gibbon.*

THE broad tract of champaign country which intervenes between the cities of Poitiers and Tours is principally composed of a succession of rich pasture lands, which are traversed and fertilized by the Cher, the Creuse, the Vienne, the Claine, the Indre, and other tributaries of the River Loire. Here and there the ground swells into picturesque eminences and occasionally a belt of forest land, a brown heath, or a clustering series of vineyards breaks the monontony of the widespread meadows; but the general character of the land is that of a grassy plain, and it seems naturally adapted for the evolutions of numerous armies, especially of those vast bodies of cavalry which principally decided the fate of nations during the centuries that followed the downfall of Rome, and preceded the consolidation of the modern European powers.

This region has been signalized by more than one memorable conflict; but it is principally interesting to the historian by having been the scene of the great victory won by Charles Martel over the Saracens, AD 732, which gave a decisive check to the career of Arab conquest in Western Europe, rescued Christendom from Islam, preserved the relics of ancient and the germs of modern civilization, and re-established the old superiority of the Indo-European over the Semitic family of mankind.

Sismondi and Michelet have underrated the enduring interest of this great Appeal of Battle between the champions of the Crescent and the Cross. But, if French writers have slighted the exploits of their national hero, the Saracenic trophies of Charles Martel have had full justice done to them by English and German historians. Gibbon devotes several pages of his great work[1] to the narrative of the battle of Tours, and to the consideration of the consequences which probably would have resulted if Abderrahman's enterprise had not been crushed by the Frankish chief. Schlegel[2] speaks of this "mighty victory" in terms of fervent gratitude, and tells how "the arm of Charles Martel saved and delivered the Christian nations of the West from the deadly grasp of all-destroying Islam"; and Ranke[3] points out, as "one of the most important epochs in the history of the world, the commencement of the eighth century, when on the one side Mohammedanism threatened to overspread Italy and Gaul, and on the other the ancient idolatry of Saxony and Friesland once more forced its way across the Rhine. In this peril of Christian institutions, a youthful prince of Germanic race, Karl Martell, arose as their champion, maintained them with all the energy which the necessity for self-defence calls forth, and finally extended them into new regions."

Arnold[4] ranks the victory of Charles Martel even higher than the victory of Arminius, "among those signal deliverances which have affected for centuries the happiness of mankind." In fact, the more we test its importance, the higher we shall be led to estimate it; and, though all authentic details which we possess of its circumstances and its heroes are but meagre, we can trace enough of its general character to make us watch with deep interest this encounter between the rival conquerors of the decaying Roman empire. That old classic world, the history of which occupies so large a portion of our early studies, lay, in the eighth century of our era, utterly exanimate and overthrown. On the north the German, on the south the Arab, was rending away its provinces. At last the spoilers encountered one another, each striving for the full master of the prey. Their conflict brought back upon the memory of Gibbon the old Homeric simile, where the strife of Hector and Patroclus over the dead body of Cebriones is compared to the combat of two lions, that in their hate and hunger fight together on the mountain tops over the carcass of a slaughtered stag; and the reluctant yielding of the Saracen power to the superior might of the Northern warriors might not inaptly recall those other lines of the same book of the Iliad, where the downfall of Patroclus beneath Hector is likened to the forced yielding of the panting and exhausted wild boar, that had long and furiously fought with a superior beast of prey for the possession of the scanty fountain among the rocks at which each burned to drink.[5]

Although three centuries had passed away since the Germanic conquerors of Rome had crossed the Rhine, never to repass that frontier stream, no settled system of institutions or government, no amalgamation of the various races into our people, no uniformity of language or habits had been established in the country at the time when Charles Martel was called to repel the menacing tide of Saracenic invasion from the south. Gaul was not yet France. In that, as in other provinces of the Roman empire of the West, the dominion of the Cæsars had been shattered as early as the fifth century, and barbaric kingdoms and principalities had promptly arisen on the ruins of the Roman power. But few of these had any permanency, and none of them consolidated the rest, or any considerable number of the rest, into one coherent and organized civil and political society. The great bulk of the population still consisted of the conquered provincials, that is to say, of Romanized Celts, of a Gallic race which had long been under the dominion of the Cæsars, and had acquired, together with no slight infusion of Roman blood, the language, the literature, the laws, and the civilization of Latium. Among these, and dominant over them, roved or dwelt the German victors; some retaining nearly all the rude independence of their primitive national character, others softened and disciplined by the aspect and contact of the manners and institutions of civilized life; for it is to be borne in mind that the Roman empire in the West was not crushed by any sudden avalanche of barbaric invasion. The

German conquerors came across the Rhine, not in enormous hosts, but in bands of a few thousand warriors at a time. The conquest of a province was the result of an infinite series of partial local invasions, carried on by little armies of this description. The victorious warriors either retired with their booty, or fixed themselves in the invaded district, taking care to keep sufficiently concentrated for military purposes, and ever ready for some fresh foray, either against a rival Teutonic band, or some hitherto unassailed city of the provincials. Gradually, however, the conquerors acquired a desire for permanent landed possessions. They lost somewhat of the restless thirst for novelty and adventure which had first made them throng beneath the banner of the boldest captains of their tribe, and leave their native forests for a roving military life on the left bank of the Rhine. They were converted to the Christian faith, and gave up with their old creed much of the coarse ferocity which must have been fostered in the spirits of the ancient warriors of the North by a mythology which promised, as the reward of the brave on earth, an eternal cycle of fighting and drunkenness in heaven.

But, although their conversion and other civilizing influences operated powerfully upon the Germans in Gaul, and although the Franks (who were originally a confederation of the Teutonic tribes that dwelt between the Rhine, the Maine, and the Weser) established a decisive superiority over the other conquerors of the province, as well as over the conquered provincials, the country long remained a chaos of uncombined and shifting elements. The early princes of the Merovingian dynasty were generally occupied in wars against other princes of their house, occasioned by the frequent subdivisions of the Frank monarchy; and the ablest and best of them had found all their energies tasked to the utmost to defend the barrier of the Rhine against the pagan Germans who strove to pass that river and gather their share of the spoils of the empire.

The conquests which the Saracens effected over the southern and eastern provinces of Rome were far more rapid than those achieved by the Germans in the north, and the new organizations of society which the Moslems introduced were summarily and uniformly enforced. Exactly a century passed between the death of Mohammed and the date of the battle of Tours. During that century the followers of the Prophet had torn away half the Roman empire; and, besides their conquests over Persia, the Saracens had overrun Syria, Egypt, Africa, and Spain, in an uncheckered and apparently irresistible career of victory. Nor, at the commencement of the eighth century of our era, was the Mohammedan world divided against itself, as it subsequently became. All these vast regions obeyed the caliph; throughout them all, from the Pyrenees to the Oxus, the name of Mohammed was invoked in prayer, and the Koran revered as the book of the law.

It was under one of their ablest and most renowned commanders, with a veteran army, and with every apparent advantage of time, place, and circumstance, that the Arabs made their great effort at the conquest of Europe north of the Pyrenees. The victorious Moslem soldiery in Spain,

> "A countless multitude;
> Syrian, Moor, Saracen, Greek renegade,
> Persian, and Copt, and Tartar, in one bond
> Of erring faith conjoined—strong in the youth
> And heat of zeal—a dreadful brotherhood,"

were eager for the plunder of more Christian cities and shrines, and full of fanatic confidence in the invincibility of their arms.

> "Nor were the chiefs
> Of victory less assured, by long success
> Elate, and proud of that o'erwhelming strength
> Which, surely they believed, as it had rolled
> Thus far uncheck'd, would roll victorious on,
> Till, like the Orient, the subjected West
> Should bow in reverence at Mohammed's name;
> And pilgrims from remotest Arctic shores
> Tread with religious feet the burning sands
> Of Araby and Mecca's stony soil."
>
> — Southey's *Roderick.*

It is not only by the modern Christian poet, but by the old Arabian chroniclers also, that these feelings of ambition and arrogance are attributed to the Moslems who had overthrown the Visigoth power in Spain. And their eager expectations of new wars were excited to the utmost on the reappointment by the caliph of Abderrahman Ibn Abdillah Alghafeki to the government of that country, AD 729, which restored them a general who had signalized his skill and prowess during the conquests of Africa and Spain, whose ready valor and generosity had made him the idol of the troops, who had already been engaged in several expeditions into Gaul, so as to be well acquainted with the national character and tactics of the Franks, and who was known to thirst, like a good Moslem, for revenge for the slaughter of some detachments of the True Believers, which had been cut off on the north of the Pyrenees.

In addition to his cardinal military virtues, Abderrahman is described by the Arab writers as a model of integrity and justice. The first two years of his second administration in Spain were occupied in severe reforms of the abuses which under his predecessors had crept into the system of government, and in extensive preparations for his intended conquest in Gaul. Besides the troops which he collected from his province, he obtained from Africa a large body of chosen Berber cavalry, officered by Arabs of proved skill and valor; and in the summer of 732, he crossed the Pyrenees at the head of an army which some Arab writers rate at eighty thousand strong, while some of the Christian chroniclers swell its numbers to many hundreds of thousands more. Probably the Arab account diminishes, but of the two keeps nearer to the truth. It was from this formidable host, after Eudes, the Count of Aquitaine, had vainly striven to check it, after many strong cities had fallen before it, and half the land had been overrun, that Gaul and Christendom were at last rescued by the strong arm of Prince Charles, who acquired a surname,[6] like that of the war-god of his forefathers' creed, from the might with which he broke and shattered his enemies in the battle.

The Merovingian kings had sunk into absolute insignificance, and had become mere puppets of royalty before the eighth century. Charles Martel, like his father, Pepin Heristal, was Duke of the Austrasian Franks, the bravest and most thoroughly Germanic part of the nation, and exercised, in the name of the titular king, what little paramount authority the turbulent minor rulers of districts and towns could be persuaded or compelled to acknowledge. Engaged with his national competitors in perpetual conflicts for power, and in more serious struggles for safety against the fierce tribes of the unconverted Frisians, Bavarians, Saxons, and Thuringians, who at that epoch assailed with peculiar ferocity the Christianized Germans on the left bank of the Rhine, Charles Martel added experienced skill to his natural courage, and he had also formed a militia of veterans among the Franks. Hallam has thrown out a doubt whether, in our admiration of his victory at Tours, we do not judge a little too much by the event, and whether there was not rashness in his risking the fate of France on the result of a general battle with the invaders. But when we remember that Charles had no standing army, and the independent spirit of the Frank warriors who followed his standard, it seems most probable that it was not in his power to adopt the cautious policy of watching the invaders, and wearing out their strength by delay. So dreadful and so widespread were the ravages of the Saracenic light cavalry throughout Gaul, that it must have been impossible to restrain for any length of time the indignant ardor of the Franks. And, even if Charles could have persuaded his men to look tamely on while the Arabs stormed more towns and desolated more districts, he could not have kept an army together when the usual period of a military expedition had expired. If, indeed, the Arab account of the disorganization of the Moslem forces be correct, the battle was as well timed on the part of Charles, as it was, beyond all question, well fought.

The monkish chroniclers, from whom we are obliged to glean a narrative of this memorable campaign, bear full evidence to the terror which the Saracen invasion inspired, and to the agony of that great struggle. The Saracens, say they, and their king, who was called Abdirames, came out of Spain, with all their wives, and their children, and their substance, in such great multitudes that no man could reckon or estimate them. They brought with them all their armor, and whatever they had, as if they were thenceforth always to dwell in France.[7]

"Then Abderrahman, seeing the land filled with the multitude of his army, pierces through the mountains, tramples over rough and level ground, plunders far into the country of the Franks, and smites all with the sword, insomuch that when Eudo came to battle with him at the River Garonne, and fled before him, God alone knows the number of the slain. Then Abderrahman pursued after Count Eudo, and, while he strives to spoil and burn the holy shrine at Tours, he encounters the chief of the Austrasian Franks, Charles, a man of war from his youth up, to whom Eudo had sent warning. There for nearly seven days they strive intensely, and at last they set themselves in battle array, and the nations of the North standing firm as a wall, and impenetrable as a zone of ice, utterly slay the Arabs with the edge of the sword."[8]

The European writers all concur in speaking of the fall of Abderrahman as one of the principal causes of the defeat of the Arabs; who, according to one writer, after finding that their leader was slain, dispersed in the night, to the agreeable surprise of the Christians, who expected the next morning to see them issue from their tents and renew the combat. One monkish chronicler puts the loss of the Arabs at 375,000 men, while he says that only 1,007 Christians fell; a disparity of loss which he feels bound to account for by a special interposition of Providence. I have translated above some of the most spirited passages of these writers; but it is impossible to collect from them anything like a full or authentic description of the great battle itself, or of the operations which preceded and followed it.

Though, however, we may have cause to regret the meagre-ness and doubtful character of these narratives, we have the great advantage of being able to compare the accounts given of

Abderrahman's expedition by the national writers of each side. This is a benefit which the inquirer into antiquity so seldom can obtain, that the fact of possessing it, in the case of the battle of Tours, makes us think the historical testimony respecting that great event more certain and satisfactory than is the case in many other instances, where we possess abundant details respecting military exploits, but where those details come to us from the annalist of one nation only, and where we have, consequently, no safeguard against the exaggerations, the distortions, and the fictions which national vanity has so often put forth in the garb and under the title of history. The Arabian writers who recorded the conquests and wars of their countrymen in Spain have narrated also the expedition into Gaul of their great emir, and his defeat and death near Tours, in battle with the host of the Franks under King Caldus, the name into which they metamorphose Charles Martel.[9]

They tell us how there was war between the count of the Frankish frontier and the Moslems, and how the count gathered together all his people, and fought for a time with doubtful success. "But," say the Arabian chroniclers, "Abderrahman drove them back; and the men of Abderrahman were puffed up in spirit by their repeated successes, and they were full of trust in the valor and the practice in war of their emir. So the Moslems smote their enemies, and passed the River Garonne, and laid waste the country, and took captives without number. And that army went through all places like a desolating storm. Prosperity made these warriors insatiable. At the passage of the river, Abderrahman overthrew the count, and the count retired into his stronghold, but the Moslems fought against it, and entered it by force and slew the count; for everything gave way to their cimeters, which were the robbers of lives. All the nations of the Franks trembled at that terrible army, and they betook them to their king Caldus, and told him of the havoc made by the Moslem horsemen, and how they rode at their will through all the land of Narbonne, Toulouse, and Bordeaux, and they told the king of the death of their count. Then the king bade them be of good cheer, and offered to aid them. And in the 114th year[10] he mounted his horse, and he took with him a host that could not be numbered, and went against the Moslems. And he came upon them at the great city of Tours. And Abderrahman and other prudent cavaliers saw the disorder of the Moslem troops, who were loaded with spoil; but they did not venture to displease the soldiers by ordering them to abandon everything except their arms and war-horses. And Abderrahman trusted in the valor of his soldiers, and in the good fortune which had ever attended him. But (the Arab writer remarks) such defect of discipline always is fatal to armies. So Abderrahman and his host attacked Tours to gain still more spoil, and they fought against it so fiercely that they stormed the city almost before the eyes of the army that came to save it; and the fury and the cruelty of the Moslems towards the inhabitants of the city were like the fury and cruelty of raging tigers. It was manifest," adds the Arab, "that God's chastisement was sure to follow such excesses; and Fortune thereupon turned her back upon the Moslems.

"Near the River Owar,[11] the two great hosts of the two languages and the two creeds were set in array against each other. The hearts of Abderrahman, his captains, and his men, were filled with wrath and pride, and they were the first to begin the fight. The Moslem horsemen dashed fierce and frequent forward against the battalions of the Franks, who resisted manfully, and many fell dead on either side, until the going down of the sun. Night parted the two armies; but in the gray of the morning the Moslems returned to the battle. Their cavaliers had soon hewn their way into the centre of the Christian host. But many of the Moslems were fearful for the safety of the spoil which they had stored in their tents, and a false cry arose in their ranks that some of the enemy were plundering the camp; whereupon several squadrons of the Moslem horsemen rode off to protect their tents. But it seemed as if they fled; and all the host was troubled. And, while Abderrahman strove to check their tumult, and to lead them back to battle, the warriors of the Franks came around him, and he was pierced through with many spears, so that he died. Then all the host fled before the enemy and many died in the flight. This deadly defeat of the Moslems, and the loss of the great leader and good cavalier, Abderrahman, took place in the hundred and fifteenth year."

It would be difficult to expect from an adversary a more explicit confession of having been thoroughly vanquished than the Arabs here accord to the Europeans. The points on which their narrative differs from those of the Christians—as to how many days the conflict lasted, whether the assailed city was actually rescued or not, and the like—are of little moment compared with the admitted great fact that there was a decisive trial of strength between Frank and Saracen, in which the former conquered. The enduring importance of the battle of Tours in the eyes of the Moslems is attested not only by the expressions of "the deadly battle" and "the disgraceful overthrow" which their writers constantly employ when referring to it, but also by the fact that no more serious attempts at conquest beyond the Pyrenees were made by the Saracens. Charles Martel, and his son and grandson, were left at leisure to consolidate and extend their power. The new Christian Roman empire of the West, which the genius of Charlemagne founded, and throughout which his iron will imposed peace on the old anarchy of creeds and races, did not indeed retain its integrity after its great ruler's death. Fresh troubles came over Europe; but Christendom, though disunited, was safe. The progress of civilization, and the development of the nationalities and governments of modern Europe, from that time forth went forward in not uninterrupted, but ultimately certain career.

Synopsis of Events between the Battle of Tours, AD 732, and the Battle of Hastings, AD 1066.

AD 768–814. Reign of Charlemagne. This monarch has justly been termed the principal regenerator of Western Europe, after the destruction of the Roman empire. The early death of his brother Carloman left him sole master of the dominion of the Franks, which, by a succession of victorious wars, he enlarged into the new empire of the West. He conquered the Lombards, and re-established the pope at Rome, who, in return, acknowledged Charles as suzerain of Italy. And in the year 800, Leo III., in the name of the Roman people, solemnly crowned Charlemagne at Rome as emperor of the Roman empire of the West. In Spain, Charlemagne ruled the country between the Pyrenees and the Ebro; but his most important conquests were effected on the eastern side of his original kingdom, over the Sclavonians of Bohemia, the Avars of Pannonia, and over the previously uncivilized German tribes, who had remained in their fatherland. The old Saxons were his most obstinate antagonists, and his wars with them lasted for thirty years. Under him the greater part of Germany was compulsorily civilized and converted from paganism to Christianity. His empire extended eastward as far as the Elbe, the Saale, the Bohemian Mountains, and a line drawn from thence crossing the Danube above Vienna, and prolonged to the Gulf of Istria.[12]

Throughout this vast assemblage of provinces, Charlemagne established an organized and firm government. But it is not as a mere conqueror that he demands admiration. "In a life restlessly active, we see him reforming the coinage and establishing the legal divisions of money; gathering about him the learned of every country; founding schools and collecting libraries; interfering, with the air of a king, in religious controversies; attempting, for the sake of commerce, the magnificent enterprise of uniting the Rhine and the Danube, and meditating to mould the discordant code of Roman and barbarian laws into a uniform system."[13]

814–888. Repeated partitions of the empire and civil wars between Charlemagne's descendants. Ultimately the kingdom of France is finally separated from Germany and Italy. In 962, Otho the Great of Germany revives the imperial dignity.

827. Egbert, king of Wessex, acquires the supremacy over the other Anglo-Saxon kingdoms.

832. The first Danish squadron attacks part of the English coast. The Danes, or Northmen, had begun their ravages in France a few years earlier. For two centuries Scandinavia sends out fleet after fleet of sea rovers, who desolate all the western kingdoms of Europe and in many cases effect permanent conquests.

871–900. Reign of, Alfred in England. After a long and varied struggle, he rescues England from the Danish invaders.

911. The French king cedes Neustria to Hrolf the Northman. Hrolf (or Duke Rollo, as he thenceforth was termed) and his army of Scandinavian warriors, become the ruling class of the population of the province, which is called, after them, Normandy.

1016. Four knights from Normandy, who had been on a pilgrimage to the Holy Land, while returning through Italy, head the people of Salerno in repelling an attack of a band of Saracen corsairs. In the next year many adventurers from Normandy settle in Italy, where they conquer Apulia (1040), and afterwards (1060) Sicily.

1017. Canute, king of Denmark, becomes king of England. On the death of the last of his sons, in 1041, the Saxon line is restored, and Edward the Confessor (who had been bred in the court of the Duke of Normandy) is called by the English to the throne of this island, as the representative of the house of Cedric.

1035. Duke Robert of Normandy dies on his return from a pilgrimage to the Holy Land, and his son William (afterward the conqueror of England) succeeds to the dukedom of Normandy.

CHAPTER VIII

THE BATTLE OF HASTINGS, AD 1066

"Eis vos la Bataille assemblée,
Dunc encore est grant renomée."
—*Roman de Rou, l. 3183.*

ARLETTA'S pretty feet twinkling in the brook made her the mother of William the Conqueror. Had she not thus fascinated Duke Robert the Liberal of Normandy, Harold would not have fallen at Hastings, no Anglo-Norman dynasty could have arisen, no British empire. The reflection is Sir Francis Palgrave's;[1] and it is emphatically true. If any one should write a history of "Decisive loves that have materially influenced the drama of the world in all its subsequent scenes," the daughter of the tanner of Falaise would deserve a conspicuous place in his pages. But it is her son, the victor of Hastings, who is now the object of our attention; and no one who appreciates the influence of England and her empire upon the destinies of the world will ever rank that victory as one of secondary importance.

It is true that in the last century some writers of eminence on our history and laws mentioned the Norman Conquest in terms from which it might be supposed that the battle of Hastings led to little more than the substitution of one royal family on the throne of this country, and to the garbling and changing of some of our laws through the "cunning of the Norman lawyers." But, at least since the appearance of the work of Augustin Thierry on the

Norman Conquest, these forensic fallacies have been exploded. Thierry made his readers keenly appreciate the magnitude of that political and social catastrophe. He depicted in vivid colors the atrocious cruelties of the conquerors, and the sweeping and enduring innovations that they wrought, involving the overthrow of the ancient constitution, as well as of the last of the Saxon kings. In his pages we see new tribunals and tenures superseding the old ones, new divisions of race and class introduced, whole districts devastated to gratify the vengeance or the caprice of the new tyrant, the greater part of the lands of the English confiscated and divided among aliens, the very name of Englishmen turned into a reproach, the English language rejected as servile and barbarous, and all the high places in church and state for upward of a century filled exclusively by men of foreign race.

No less true than eloquent is Thierry's summing up of the social effects of the Norman Conquest on the generation that witnessed it, and on many of their successors. He tells his reader that, "if he would form a just idea of England conquered by William of Normandy, he must figure to himself—not a mere change of political rule—not the triumph of one candidate over another candidate—of the man of one party over the man of another party, but the intrusion of one people into the bosom of another people—the violent placing of one society over another society which it came to destroy, and the scattered fragments of which it retained only as personal property, or (to use the words of an old act) as 'the clothing of the soil'; he must not picture to himself, on the one hand, William a king and a despot—on the other, subjects of William's, high and low, rich and poor, all inhabiting England, and consequently all English; he must imagine two nations, of one of which William is a member and the chief—two nations which (if the term must be used) were both *subject* to William, but as applied to which the word has quite different senses, meaning, in the one case, *subordinate*—in the other, subjugated. He must consider that there are two countries, two soils, included in the same geographical circumference—that of the Normans, rich and free;

that of the Saxons, poor and serving, vexed by *rent* and *toilage:* the former full of spacious mansions, and walled and moated castles; the latter scattered over with huts and straw, and ruined hovels; that peopled with the happy and the idle—with men of the army and of the court—with knights and nobles; this with men of pain and labor—with farmers and artisans: on the one side, luxury and insolence; on the other, misery and envy—not the envy of the poor at the sight of opulence they cannot reach, but the envy of the despoiled when in presence of the despoilers."

Perhaps the effect of Thierry's work has been to cast into the shade the ultimate good effects on England of the Norman Conquest. Yet these are as undeniable as are the miseries which that conquest inflicted on our Saxon ancestors from the time of the battle of Hastings to the time of the signing of the Great Charter at Runnymede. That last is the true epoch of English nationality; it is the epoch when Anglo-Norman and Anglo-Saxon ceased to keep aloof from each other—the one in haughty scorn, the other in sullen abhorrence; and when all the free men of the land, whether barons, knights, yeomen, or burghers, combined to lay the foundations of English freedom.

Our Norman barons were the chiefs of that primary constitutional movement; those "iron barons," whom Chatham has so nobly eulogized. This alone should make England remember her obligations to the Norman Conquest, which planted far and wide, as a dominant class in her land, a martial nobility of the bravest and most energetic race that ever existed.

It may sound paradoxical, but it is in reality no exaggeration to say, with Guizot,[2] that England's liberties are owing to her having been conquered by the Normans. It is true that the Saxon institutions were the primitive cradle of English liberty, but by their own intrinsic force they could never have founded the enduring free English Constitution. It was the Conquest that infused into them a new virtue, and the political liberties of England arose from the situation in which the Anglo-Saxon and the Anglo-Norman populations and laws found themselves placed relatively to each other in this island. The state of England under her last Anglo-Saxon kings closely resembled the state of France under the last Carlovingian and the first Capetian princes. The crown was feeble, the great nobles were strong and turbulent; and although there was more national unity in Saxon England than in France—although the English local free institutions had more reality and energy than was the case with anything analogous to them on the Continent in the eleventh century—still the probability is that the Saxon system of polity, if left to itself, would have fallen into utter confusion, out of which would have arisen, first, an aristocratic hierarchy, like that which arose in France; next, an absolute monarchy; and, finally, a series of anarchical revolutions, such as we now behold aroused, but not among us.[3]

The latest conquerors of this island were also the bravest and the best. I do not except even the Romans. And, in spite of our sympathies with Harold and Hereward, and our abhorrence of the founder of the New Forest and the desolator of Yorkshire, we must confess the superiority of the Normans to the Anglo-Saxons and Anglo-Danes, whom they met here in 1066, as well as to the degenerate Frank noblesse, and the crushed and servile Romanesque provincials, from whom, in 912, they had wrested the district in the north of Gaul, which still bears the name of Normandy.

It was not merely by extreme valor and ready subordination to military discipline that the Normans were pre-eminent among all the conquering races of the Gothic stock, but also by an instinctive faculty of appreciating and adopting the superior civilizations which they encountered. Thus Duke Rollo and his Scandinavian warriors readily embraced the creed, the language, the laws, and the arts, which France, in those troubled and evil times with which the Capetian dynasty commenced, still inherited from imperial Rome and imperial Charlemagne. "They adopted the customs, the duties, the obedience that the capitularies of emperors and kings had established; but that which they brought to the application of those laws, was the spirit of life, the spirit of liberty—the habits also of military subordination, and the aptness for a state politic which could reconcile the security of all with the independence of each."[4] So, also, in all chivalric feelings, in enthusiastic religious zeal, in almost idolatrous respect to females of gentle birth, in generous fondness for the nascent poetry of the time, in a keen intellectual relish for subtle thought and disputation, in a taste for architectural magnificence, and all courtly refinement and pageantry. The Normans were the Paladins of the world. Their brilliant qualities were sullied by many darker traits of pride, of merciless cruelty, and of brutal contempt for the industry, the rights, and the feelings of all whom they considered the lower classes of mankind.

Their gradual blending with the Saxons softened these harsh and evil points of their national character, and in return they fired the duller Saxon mass with a new spirit of animation and power. As Campbell boldly expressed it, "*They high-mettled the blood of our veins.*" Small had been the figure which England made in the world before the coming over of the Normans, and without them she never would have emerged from insignificance. The authority of Gibbon may be taken as decisive when he pronounces that "assuredly England was a gainer by the Conquest." And we may proudly adopt the comment of the Frenchman Rapin, who, writing of the battle of Hastings more than a century ago, speaks of the revolution effected by it as "the first step by which England is arrived to the height of grandeur and glory we behold it in at present."[5]

The interest of this eventful struggle, by which William of Normandy became king of England, is materially enhanced by the high personal character of the competitors for our crown. They were three in number. One was a foreign prince from the north; one was a foreign prince from the south; and one was a native hero of the land. Harald Hardrada, the strongest and the most chivalric of the kings of Norway,[6] was the first; Duke William of Normandy was the second; and the Saxon Harold, the son of Earl Godwin, was the third. Never was a nobler prize sought by nobler champions, or striven for more gallantly. The Saxon triumphed over the Norwegian, and the Norman triumphed over the Saxon;

but Norse valor was never more conspicuous than when Harald Hardrada and his host fought and fell at Stamford Bridge; nor did Saxons ever face their foes more bravely than our Harold and his men on the fatal day of Hastings.

During the reign of King Edward the Confessor over this land, the claims of the Norwegian king to our crown were little thought of; and though Hardrada's predecessor, King Magnus of Norway, had on one occasion asserted that, by virtue of a compact with our former king, Hardicanute, he was entitled to the English throne, no serious attempt had been made to enforce his pretensions. But the rivalry of the Saxon Harold and the Norman William was foreseen and bewailed by the Confessor, who was believed to have predicted on his death-bed the calamities that were impending over England. Duke William was King Edward's kinsman. Harold was the head of the most powerful noble house, next to the royal blood, in England; and, personally, he was the bravest and most popular chieftain in the land. King Edward was childless, and the nearest collateral heir was a puny unpromising boy. England had suffered too severely, during royal minorities, to make the accession of Edgar Atheling desirable; and long before King Edward's death, Earl Harold was the destined king of the nation's choice, though the favor of the Confessor was believed to lead towards the Norman duke.

A little time before the death of King Edward, Harold was in Normandy. The causes of the voyage of the Saxon earl to the Continent are doubtful; but the fact of his having been, in 1065, at the ducal court, and in the power of his rival, is indisputable. William made skilful and unscrupulous use of the opportunity. Though Harold was treated with outward courtesy and friendship, he was made fully aware that his liberty and life depended on his compliance with the duke's requests. William said to him, in apparent confidence and cordiality, "When King Edward and I once lived like brothers under the same roof, he promised that if ever he became King of England, he would make me heir to his throne. Harold, I wish that thou wouldst assist me to realize this promise." Harold replied with expressions of assent; and further agreed, at William's request, to marry William's daughter, Adela, and to send over his own sister to be married to one of William's barons. The crafty Norman was not content with this extorted promise; he determined to bind Harold by a more solemn pledge, the breach of which would be a weight on the spirit of the gallant Saxon, and a discouragement to others from adopting his cause. Before a full assembly of the Norman barons, Harold was required to do homage to Duke William, as the heir apparent of the English crown. Kneeling down, Harold placed his hands between those of the duke, and repeated the solemn form by which he acknowledged the duke as his lord, and promised to him fealty and true service. But William exacted more. He had caused all the bones and relics of saints, that were preserved in the Norman monasteries and churches, to be collected in a chest, which was placed in the council-room, covered over with a cloth of gold. On the chest of relics, which were thus concealed, was laid a missal. The duke then solemnly addressed his titular guest and real captive, and said to him, "Harold, I require thee, before this noble assembly, to confirm by oath the promises which thou hast made me, to assist me in obtaining the crown of England after King Edward's death, to marry my daughter Adela, and to send me thy sister, that I may give her in marriage to one of my barons." Harold, once more taken by surprise, and not able to deny his former words, approached the missal, and laid his hand on it, not knowing that the chest of relics was beneath. The old Norman chronicler, who describes the scene most minutely,[7] says, when Harold placed his hand on it, the hand trembled, and the flesh quivered; but he swore, and promised upon his oath to take Ele [Adela] to wife, and to deliver up England to the duke and thereunto to do all in his power, according to his might and wit, after the death of Edward, if he himself should live; so help him God. Many cried, "God grant it!" and when Harold rose from his knees, the duke made him stand close to the chest, and took off the pall that had covered it, and showed Harold upon what holy relics he had sworn; and Harold was sorely alarmed at the sight.

Harold was soon after permitted to return to England; and, after a short interval, during which he distinguished himself by the wisdom and humanity with which he pacified some formidable tumults of the Anglo-Danes in Northumbria, he found himself called on to decide whether he would keep the oath which the Norman had obtained from him, or mount the vacant throne of England in compliance with the nation's choice. King Edward the Confessor died on the 5th of January, 1066, and on the following day an assembly of the thanes and prelates present in London, and of the citizens of the metropolis, declared that Harold should be their king. It was reported that the dying Edward had nominated him as his successor. But the sense which his countrymen entertained of his preeminent merit was the true foundation of his title to the crown. Harold resolved to disregard the oath which he made in Normandy as violent and void, and on the 7th day of that January he was anointed King of England, and received from the archbishop's hands the golden crown and sceptre of England, and also an ancient national symbol, a weighty battle-axe. He had truly deep and speedy need of this significant part of the insignia of Saxon royalty.

A messenger from Normandy soon arrived to remind Harold of the oath which he had sworn to the duke "with his mouth, and his hand upon good and holy relics." "It is true," replied the Saxon king, "that I took an oath to William; but I took it under constraint: I promised what did not belong to me—what I could not in any way hold; my royalty is not my own; I could not lay it down against the will of the country, nor can I, against the will of the country, take a foreign wife. As for my sister, whom the duke claims that he may marry her to one of his chiefs, she has died within the year; would he have me send her corpse?"

William sent another message, which met with a similar answer; and then the duke published far and wide through Christendom what he termed the perjury and bad faith of his rival, and proclaimed his intention of asserting his rights by the sword before the year should expire, and of pursuing and punishing the perjurer even in those places where he thought he stood most strongly and most securely.

Before, however, he commenced hostilities, William, with deep-laid policy, submitted his claims to the decision of the pope. Harold refused to acknowledge this tribunal, or to answer before an Italian priest for his title as an English king. After a formal examination of William's complaints by the pope and the cardinals, it was solemnly adjudged at Rome that England belonged to the Norman duke; and a banner was sent to William from the Holy See, which the pope himself had consecrated and blessed for the invasion of this island. The clergy throughout the Continent were now assiduous and energetic in preaching up William's enterprise as undertaken in the cause of God. Besides these spiritual arms (the effect of which in the eleventh century must not be measured by the philosophy or the indifferentism of the nineteenth), the Norman duke applied all the energies of his mind and body, all the resources of his duchy, and all the influence he possessed among vassals or allies, to the collection of "the most remarkable and formidable armament which the Western nations had witnessed."[8] All the adventurous spirits of Christendom flocked to the holy banner, under which Duke William, the most renowned knight and sagest general of the age, promised to lead them to glory and wealth in the fair domains of England. His army was filled with the chivalry of Continental Europe, all eager to save their souls by fighting at the pope's bidding, eager to signalize their valor in so great an enterprise, and eager also for the pay and the plunder which William liberally promised. But the Normans themselves were the pith and the flower of the army, and William himself was the strongest, the sagest, and the fiercest spirit of them all.

Throughout the spring and summer of 1066, all the seaports of Normandy, Picardy, and Brittany rang with the busy sound of preparation. On the opposite side of the Channel King Harold collected the army and the fleet with which he hoped to crush the southern invaders. But the unexpected attack of King Harald Hardrada of Norway upon another part of England disconcerted the skilful measures which the Saxon had taken against the menacing armada of Duke William.

Harold's renegade brother, Earl Tostig, had excited the Norse king to this enterprise, the importance of which has naturally been eclipsed by the superior interest attached to the victorious expedition of Duke William, but which was on a scale of grandeur which the Scandinavian ports had rarely, if ever, before witnessed. Hardrada's fleet consisted of two hundred war-ships and three hundred other vessels, and all the best warriors of Norway were in his host. He sailed first to the Orkneys, where many of the islanders joined him, and then to Yorkshire. After a severe conflict near York, he completely routed Earls Edwin and Morcar, the governors of Northumbria. The city of York opened its gates, and all the country, from the Tyne to the Humber, submitted to him. The tidings of the defeat of Edwin and Morcar compelled Harold to leave his position on the southern coast, and move instantly against the Norwegians. By a remarkably rapid march he reached Yorkshire in four days, and took the Norse king and his confederates by surprise. Nevertheless, the battle which ensued, and which was fought near Stamford Bridge, was desperate, and was long doubtful. Unable to break the ranks of the Norwegian phalanx by force, Harold at length tempted them to quit their close order by a pretended flight. Then the English columns burst in among them, and a carnage ensued, the extent of which may be judged of by the exhaustion and inactivity of Norway for a quarter of a century afterwards. King Harald Hardrada, and all the flower of his nobility, perished on the 25th of September, 1066, at Stamford Bridge, a battle which was a Flodden to Norway.

Harold's victory was splendid; but he had bought it dearly by the fall of many of his best officers and men, and still more dearly by the opportunity which Duke William had gained of effecting an unopposed landing on the Sussex coast. The whole of William's shipping had assembled at the mouth of the Dive, a little river between the Seine and the Orne, as early as the middle of August. The army which he had collected amounted to fifty thousand knights and ten thousand soldiers of inferior degree. Many of the knights were mounted, but many must have served on foot, as it is hardly possible to believe that William could have found transports for the conveyance of fifty thousand war-horses across the Channel. For a long time the winds were adverse, and the duke employed the interval that passed before he could set sail in completing the organization and in improving the discipline of his army, which he seems to have brought into the same state of perfection as was seven centuries and a half afterwards the boast of another army assembled on the same coast, and which Napoleon designed (but providentially in vain) for a similar descent upon England.

It was not till the approach of the equinox that the wind veered from the northeast to the west, and gave the Normans an opportunity of quitting the weary shores of the Dive. They eagerly embarked, and set sail, but the wind soon freshened to a gale, and drove them along the French coast to St. Valery, where the greater part of them found shelter; but many of their vessels were wrecked, and the whole coast of Normandy was strewn with the bodies of the drowned. William's army began to grow discouraged and averse to the enterprise, which the very elements thus seemed to fight against; though, in reality, the northeast wind, which had cooped them so long at the mouth of the Dive, and the western gale, which had forced them into St. Valery, were the best possible friends to the invaders. They prevented the Normans from crossing the Channel until the Saxon king and his army of defence had been called away from the Sussex coast to encounter Harald Hardrada in Yorkshire; and also until a formidable English fleet, which by King Harold's orders had been cruising in the Channel to intercept the Normans, had been obliged to disperse temporarily for the purpose of refitting and taking in fresh stores of provisions.

Duke William used every expedient to reanimate the drooping spirits of his men at St. Valery; and at last he caused the body of the patron saint of the place to be exhumed and carried in solemn procession, while the whole assemblage of soldiers, mariners, and appurtenant priests implored the saint's intercession for a change of wind. That very night the wind veered; and enabled the mediæval Agamemnon to quit his Aulis.

With full sails, and a following southern breeze, the Norman Armada left the French shores and steered for England. The invaders crossed an undefended sea, and found an undefended coast. It was in Pevensey Bay, in Sussex, at Bulverhithe, between the castle of Pevensey and Hastings, that the last conquerors of this island landed on the 29th of September, 1066.

Harold was at York, rejoicing over his recent victory, which had delivered England from her ancient Scandinavian foes, and resettling the government of the counties which Harald Hardrada had overrun, when the tidings reached him that Duke William of Normandy and his host had landed on the Sussex shore. Harold instantly hurried southward to meet this long-expected enemy. The severe loss which his army had sustained in the battle with the Norwegians must have made it impossible for many of his veteran troops to accompany him in his forced march to London, and thence to Sussex. He halted at the capital only six days, and during that time gave orders for collecting forces from the southern and midland counties, and also directed his fleet to reassemble off the Sussex coast. Harold was well received in London, and his summons to arms was promptly obeyed by citizen, by thane, by sokman, and by ceorl, for he had shown himself, during his brief reign, a just and wise king, affable to all men, active for the good of his country, and (in the words of the old historian) sparing himself from no fatigue by land or by sea.[9] He might have gathered a much more numerous army than that of William; but his recent victory had made him over-confident, and he was irritated by the reports of the country being ravaged by the invaders. As soon, therefore, as he had collected a small army in London, he marched off towards the coast, pressing forward as rapidly as his men could traverse Surrey and Sussex, in the hope of taking the Normans unawares, as he had recently, by a similar forced march, succeeded in surprising the Norwegians. But he had now to deal with a foe equally brave with Harald Hardrada, and far more skilful and wary.

The old Norman chroniclers describe the preparations of William on his landing with a graphic vigor, which would be wholly lost by transfusing their racy Norman couplets and terse Latin prose into the current style of modern history. It is best to follow them closely, though at the expense of much quaintness and occasional uncouthness of expression. They tell us how Duke William's own ship was the first of the Norman fleet. It was called the Mora, and was the gift of his duchess Matilda. On the head of the ship, in the front, which mariners call the prow, there was a brazen child bearing an arrow with a bended bow. His face was turned towards England, and thither he looked, as though he was about to shoot. The breeze became soft and sweet, and the sea was smooth for their landing. The ships ran on dry land, and each ranged by the other's side. There you might see the good sailors, the sergeants, and squires sally forth and unload the ships; cast the anchors, haul the ropes, bear out shields and saddles, and land the war-horses and the palfreys. The archers came forth, and touched land the first, each with his bow strung, and with his quiver full of arrows slung at his side. All were shaven and shorn; and all clad in short garments, ready to attack, to shoot, to wheel about and skirmish. All stood well equipped, and of good courage for the fight; and they scoured the whole shore, but found not an armed man there. After the archers had thus gone forth, the knights landed all armed, with their hauberks on, their shields slung at their necks, and their helmets laced. They formed together on the shore, each armed, and mounted on his war-horse; all had their swords girded on, and rode forward into the country with their lances raised. Then the carpenters landed, who had great axes in their hands, and planes and adzes hung at their sides. They took counsel together, and sought for a good spot to place a castle on. They had brought with them in the fleet three wooden castles from Normandy in pieces, all ready for framing together, and they took the materials of one of these out of the ships, all shaped and pierced to receive the pins which they had brought cut and ready in large barrels; and before evening had set in, they had finished a good fort on the English ground, and there they placed their stores. All then ate and drank enough, and were right glad that they were ashore.

When Duke William himself landed, as he stepped on the shore, he slipped and fell forward upon his two hands. Forthwith all raised a loud cry of distress. "An evil sign," said they, "is here." But he cried out lustily, "See, my lords, by the splendor of God,[10] I have taken possession of England with both my hands. It is now mine, and what is mine is yours."

The next day they marched along the sea-shore to Hastings. Near that place the duke fortified a camp, and set up the two other wooden castles. The foragers, and those who looked out for booty, seized all the clothing and provisions they could find, lest what had been brought by the ships should fail them. And the English were to be seen fleeing before them, driving off their cattle, and quitting their houses. Many took shelter in burying-places, and even there they were in grievous alarm.

Besides the maurauders from the Norman camp, strong bodies of cavalry were detached by William into the country, and these, when Harold and his army made their rapid march from London southward, fell back in good order upon the main body of the Normans, and reported that the Saxon king was rushing on like a madman. But Harold, when he found that his hopes of surprising his adversary were vain, changed his tactics, and halted about seven miles from the Norman lines. He sent some spies, who spoke the French language, to examine the number and preparations of the enemy, who, on their return, related with astonishment that there were more priests in William's camp than there were fighting men in the English army. They had mistaken for priests all the Norman soldiers who had short hair and shaven chins, for the English laymen were then accustomed to wear long hair and mustachios. Harold, who knew the Norman usages, smiled at their words, and said, "Those whom you have seen in such numbers are not priests, but stout soldiers, as they will soon make us feel."

Harold's army was far inferior in number to that of the Normans, and some of his captains advised him to retreat upon London and lay waste the country, so as to starve down the strength of the invaders. The policy thus recommended was unquestionably the wisest, for the Saxon fleet had now reassembled, and intercepted all William's communications with Normandy; and as soon as his stores of provisions were exhausted, he must have moved forward upon London, where Harold, at the head of the full military strength of the kingdom, could have defied his assault, and probably might have witnessed his rival's destruction by famine and disease, without having to strike a single blow. But Harold's bold blood was up, and his kindly heart could not endure to inflict on the South Saxon subjects even the temporary misery of wasting the country. "He would not burn houses and villages, neither would he take away the substance of his people."

Harold's brothers, Gurth and Leofwine, were with him in the camp, and Gurth endeavored to persuade him to absent himself from the battle. The incident shows how well devised had been William's scheme of binding Harold by the oath on the holy relics. "My brother," said the young Saxon prince, "thou canst not deny that either by force or free will thou hast made Duke William an oath on the bodies of saints. Why then risk thyself in the battle with a perjury upon thee? To us, who have sworn nothing, this is a holy and a just war, for we are fighting for our country. Leave us then alone to fight this battle, and he who has the right will win." Harold replied that he would not look on while others risked their lives for him. Men would hold him a coward, and blame him for sending his best friends where he dared not go himself. He resolved, therefore, to fight, and to fight in person; but he was still too good a general to be the assailant in the action; and he posted his army with great skill along a ridge of rising ground which opened southward, and was covered on the back by an extensive wood. He strengthened his position by a palisade of stakes and osier hurdles, and there he said he would defend himself against whoever should seek him.

The ruins of Battle Abbey at this hour attest the place where Harold's army was posted; and the high altar of the abbey stood on the very spot where Harold's own standard was planted during the fight, and where the carnage was the thickest. Immediately after his victory, William vowed to build an abbey on the site; and a fair and stately pile soon rose there, where for many ages the monks prayed and said masses for the souls of those who were slain in the battle, whence the abbey took its name. Before that time the place was called Senlac. Little of the ancient edifice now remains; but it is easy to trace in the park and the neighborhood the scenes of the chief incidents in the action; and it is impossible to deny the generalship shown by Harold in stationing his men, especially when we bear in mind that he was deficient in cavalry, the arm in which his adversary's main strength consisted.

William's only chance of safety lay in bringing on a general engagement; and he joyfully advanced his army from their camp on the hill over Hastings, nearer to the Saxon position. But he neglected no means of weakening his opponent, and renewed his summonses and demands on Harold with an ostentatious air of sanctity and moderation.

"A monk, named Hugues Maigrot, came in William's name to call upon the Saxon king to do one of three things—either to resign his royalty in favor of William, or to refer it to the arbitration of the pope to decide which of the two ought to be king, or to let it be determined by the issue of a single combat. Harold abruptly replied, 'I will not resign my title, I will not refer it to the pope, nor will I accept the single combat.' He was far from being deficient in bravery; but he was no more at liberty to stake the crown, which he had received from a whole people, in the chance of a duel, than to deposit it in the hands of an Italian priest. William, not at all ruffled by the Saxon's refusal, but steadily pursuing the course of his calculated measures, sent the Norman monk again, after giving him these instructions: 'Go and tell Harold that if he will keep his former compact with me, I will leave to him all the country which is beyond the Humber, and will give his brother Gurth all the lands which Godwin held. If he still persist in refusing my offers, then thou shalt tell him, before all his people, that he is a perjurer and a liar; that he and all who shall support him are excommunicated by the mouth of the pope, and that the bull to that effect is in my hands.'

"Hugues Maigrot delivered this message in a solemn tone; and the Norman chronicle says that at the word *excommunication,* the English chiefs looked at one another as if some great danger were impending. One of them then spoke as follows: 'We must fight, whatever may be the danger to us; for what we have to consider is not whether we shall accept and receive a new lord, as if our king were dead; the case in quite otherwise. The Norman has given our lands to his captains, to his knights, to all his people, the greater part of whom have already done homage to him for them: they will all look for their gift if their duke become our king; and he himself is bound to deliver up to them our goods, our wives, and our daughters: all is promised to them beforehand. They come, not only to ruin us, but to ruin our descendants also, and to take from us the country of our ancestors. And what shall we do—whither shall we go, when we have no longer a country?' The English promised, by a unanimous oath, to make neither peace, nor truce, nor treaty with the invader, but to die, or drive away the Normans."[11]

The 13th of October was occupied in these negotiations, and at night the duke announced to his men that the next day would be the day of battle. That night is said to have been passed by the two armies in very different manners. The Saxon soldiers spent it in joviality, singing their national songs, and draining huge horns of ale and wine round their camp-fires. The Normans, when they had looked to their arms and horses, confessed themselves to the priests with whom their camp was thronged, and received the sacrament by thousands at a time.

On Saturday, the 14th of October, was fought the great battle.

It is not difficult to compose a narrative of its principal incidents from the historical information which we possess, especially if aided by an examination of the ground. But it is far better to adopt the spirit-stirring words of the old chroniclers, who wrote while the recollections of the battle were yet fresh; and while the feelings and prejudices of the combatants yet glowed in the bosoms of living men. Robert Wace, the Norman poet, who presented his "Roman de Rou" to our Henry II., is the most picturesque and animated of the old writers, and from him we can obtain a more vivid and full description of the conflict than even the most brilliant romance-writer of the present time can supply. We have also an antique memorial of the battle more to be relied on than either chronicler or poet (and which confirms Wace's narrative remarkably), in the celebrated Bayeux tapestry which represents the principal scenes of Duke William's expedition, and of the circumstances connected with it, in minute though occasionally grotesque details, and which was undoubtedly the production of the same age in which the battle took place, whether we admit or reject the legend that Queen Matilda and the ladies of her court wrought it with their own hands in honor of the royal conqueror.

Let us therefore suffer the old Norman chronicler to transport our imaginations to the fair Sussex scenery northwest of Hastings, as it appeared on the morning of the fourteenth of October, seven hundred and eighty-five years ago. The Norman host is pouring forth from its tents, and each troop and each company is forming fast under the banner of its leader. The masses have been sung, which were finished betimes in the morning; the barons have all assembled round Duke William; and the duke has ordered that the army shall be formed in three divisions, so as to make the attack upon the Saxon position in three places. The duke stood on a hill where he could best see his men; the barons surrounded him, and he spake to them proudly. He told them how he trusted them, and how all that he gained should be theirs, and how sure he felt of conquest, for in all the world there was not so brave an army, or such good men and true as were then forming around him. Then they cheered him in turn, and cried out, " 'You will not see one coward; none here will fear to die for love of you, if need be.' And he answered them, 'I thank you well. For God's sake, spare not;

strike hard at the beginning; stay not to take spoil; all the booty shall be in common, and there will be plenty for every one. There will be no safety in asking quarter or in flight; the English will never love or spare a Norman. Felons they were, and felons they are; false they were, and false they will be. Show no weakness towards them, for they will have no pity on you; neither the coward for running well, nor the bold man for smiting well, will be the better liked by the English, nor will any be the more spared on either account. You may fly to the sea, but you can fly no farther; you will find neither ships nor bridge there; there will be no sailors to receive you; and the English will overtake you there, and slay you in your shame. More of you will die in flight than in battle. Then, as flight will not secure you, fight, and you will conquer. I have no doubt of the victory; we are come for glory; the victory is in our hands, and we may make sure of obtaining it if we so please.' As the duke was speaking thus and would yet have spoken more, William Fitz Osber rode up with his horse all coated with iron: 'Sire,' said he, 'we tarry here too long; let us all arm ourselves. *Allons! allons!*'

"Then all went to their tents, and armed themselves as they best might; and the duke was very busy, giving every one his orders; and he was courteous to all the vassals, giving away many arms and horses to them. When he prepared to arm himself, he called first for his hauberk, and a man brought it on his arm, and placed it before him, but in putting his head in, to get it on, he unawares turned it the wrong way, with the back part in front. He soon changed it; but when he saw that those who stood by were sorely alarmed, he said, 'I have seen many a man who, if such a thing had happened to him, would not have borne arms, or entered the field the same day; but I never believed in omens, and I never will. I trust in God, for he does in all things his pleasure, and ordains what is to come to pass according to his will. I have never liked fortune-tellers, nor believed in diviners; but I commend myself to Our Lady. Let not this mischance give you trouble. The hauberk which was turned wrong, and then set right by me, signifies that a change will arise out of the matter which we are now stirring. You shall see the name of duke changed into king. Yea, a king shall I be, who hitherto have been but duke.' Then he crossed himself, and straightway took his hauberk, stooped his head, and put it on aright; and laced his helmet, and girt on his sword, which a varlet brought him. Then the duke called for his good horse — a better could not be found. It had been sent him by a king of Spain, out of very great friendship. Neither arms nor the press of fighting men did it fear, if its lord spurred it on. Walter Giffard brought it. The duke stretched out his hand, took the reins, put foot in stirrup, and mounted; and the good horse pawed, pranced, reared himself up, and curveted. The Viscount of Toarz saw how the duke bore himself in arms, and said to his people that were around him, 'Never have I seen a man so fairly armed, nor one who rode so gallantly, or bore his arms, or became his hauberk so well; neither any one who bore his lance so gracefully, or sat his horse and managed him so nobly. There is no such knight under heaven! a fair count he is, and fair king he will be. Let him fight, and he shall overcome; shame be to the man who shall fail him.'

"Then the duke called for the standard which the pope had sent him, and he who bore it having unfolded it, the duke took it and called to Raol de Conches. 'Bear my standard,' said he, 'for I would not but do you right; by right and by ancestry your line are standard-bearers of Normandy, and very good knights have they all been.' But Raol said that he would serve the duke that day in other guise, and would fight the English with his hand as long as life should last. Then the duke bade Galtier Giffart bear the standard. But he was old and white-headed, and bade the duke give the standard to some younger and stronger man to carry. Then the duke said fiercely, 'By the splendor of God, my lords, I think you mean to betray and fail me in this great need.' 'Sire,' said Giffart, 'not so! we have done no treason, nor do I refuse from any felony toward you; but I have to lead a great chivalry, both hired men and the men of my fief. Never had I such good means of serving you as I now have; and, if God please, I will serve you; if need be, I will die for you, and will give my own heart for yours.'

.

" 'By my faith,' quoth the duke, 'I always loved thee, and now I
love thee more; if I survive this day, thou shalt be the better for it
all thy days.' Then he called out a knight, whom he had heard
much praised, Tosteins Fitz-Rou Ie Blanc by name, whose abode
was at Bec-en-Caux. To him he delivered the standard; and
Tosteins took it right cheerfully, and bowed low to him in thanks,
and bore it gallantly, and with good heart. His kindred still have
quittance of all service for their inheritance on this account, and
their heirs are entitled so to hold their inheritance forever.

"William sat on his war-horse, and called out Rogier, whom they
call De Montgomeri. 'I rely much on you,' said he; 'lead your men
thitherward, and attack them from that side. William, the son of
Osber, the seneschal, a right good vassal, shall go with you and
help in the attack, and you shall have the men of Boilogne and
Poix, and all my soldiers. Alain Fergert and Ameri shall attack on
the other side; they shall lead the Poitevins and the Bretons, and
all the barons of Maine; and I, with my own great men, my friends
and kindred, will fight in the middle throng, where the battle shall
be the hottest.'

"The barons, and knights, and men-at-arms were all now
armed; the foot-soldiers were well equipped, each bearing bow
and sword; on their heads were caps, and to their feet were
bound buskins. Some had good hides which they had bound
round their bodies; and many were clad in frocks, and had quivers and bows hung to their girdles. The knights had hauberks
and swords, boots of steel, and shining helmets; shields at their
necks, and in their hands lances. And all had their cognizances,
so that each might know his fellow, and Norman might not strike
Norman, nor Frenchman kill his countryman by mistake. Those
on foot led the way, with serried ranks, bearing their bows. The
knights rode next, supporting the archers from behind. Thus
both horse and foot kept their course and order of march as they
began, in close ranks at a gentle pace, that the one might not
pass or separate from the other. All went firmly and compactly,
bearing themselves gallantly.

"Harold had summoned his men, earls, barons, and vavassors, from the castles and the cities, from the ports, the villages and boroughs. The peasants were also called together from the villages, bearing such arms as they found; clubs and great picks, iron forks and stakes. The English had enclosed the place where Harold was with his friends and the barons of the country whom he had summoned and called together.

"Those of London had come at once, and those of Kent, of Hertfort, and of Essesse; those of Surée and Susesse, of St. Edmund and Sufoc; of Norwis and Norfoc; of Cantorbierre and Stanfort; Bedefort and Hundestone. The men of Northanton also came; and those of Eurowic and Bokinkeham, of Bed and Notinkeham, Lindesie and Nichole. There came also from the west all who heard the summons; and very many were to be seen coming from Salebiere and Dorset, from Bat and from Sumerset. Many came, too, from about Glocestre, and many from Wirecestre, from Wincestre, Hontesire and Brichesire; and many more from other counties that we have not named, and cannot, indeed, recount. All who could bear arms, and had learned the news of the duke's arrival, came to defend the land. But none came from beyond Humbre, for they had other business upon their hands, the Danes and Tosti having much damaged and weakened them.

"Harold knew that the Normans would come and attack him hand to hand, so he had early enclosed the field in which he had placed his men. He made them arm early, and range themselves for the battle, he himself having put on arms and equipments that became such a lord. The duke, he said, ought to seek him, as he wanted to conquer England; and it became him to abide the attack who had to defend the land. He commanded the people, and counselled his barons to keep themselves all together, and defend themselves in a body; for if they once separated, they would with difficulty recover themselves. 'The Normans,' he said, are good vassals, valiant on foot and on horseback; good knights are they on horseback, and well used to battle; all is lost if they once penetrate our ranks. They have brought long lances and swords, but you have pointed lances and keen-edged bills; and I do not expect that their arms can stand against yours. Cleave whenever you can; it will be ill done if you spare aught.'

"The English had built up a fence before them with their shields, and with ash and other wood, and had well joined and wattled in the whole work, so as not to leave even a crevice; and thus they had a barricade in their front through which any Norman who would attack them must first pass. Being covered in this way by their shields and barricades, their aim was to defend themselves; and if they had remained steady for that purpose, they would not have been conquered that day; for every Norman who made his way in, lost his life in dishonor, either by hatchet or bill, by club or other weapon. They wore short and close hauberks, and helmets that hung over their garments. King Harold issued orders, and made proclamation round, that all should be ranged with their faces toward the enemy, and that no one should move from where he was, so that whoever came might find them ready; and that whatever any one, be he Norman or other, should do, each should do his best to defend his own place. Then he ordered the men of Kent to go where the Normans were likely to make the attack; for they say that the men of Kent are entitled to strike first; and that whenever the king goes to battle, the first blow belongs to them. The right of the men of London is to guard the king's body, to place themselves around him, and to guard his standard; and they were accordingly placed by the standard to watch and defend it.

"When Harold had made all ready, and given his orders, he came into the midst of the English and dismounted by the side of the standard; Leofwin and Gurth, his brothers, were with him; and around him he had barons enough, as he stood by his standard, which was, in truth, a noble one, sparkling with gold and precious stones. After the victory William sent it to the pope, to prove and commemorate his great conquest and glory. The English stood in close ranks, ready and eager for the fight; and they, moreover, made a fosse, which went across the field, guarding one side of their army.

"Meanwhile the Normans appeared advancing over the ridge of a rising ground, and the first division of their troops moved onward along the hill and across a valley. And presently another division, still larger, came in sight, close following upon the first, and they were led towards another part of the field, forming together as the first body had done. And, while Harold saw and examined them, and was pointing them out to Gurth, a fresh company came in sight, covering all the plain; and in the midst of them was raised the standard that came from Rome. Near it was the duke, and the best men and greatest strength of the army were there. The good knights, the good vassals and brave warriors were there; and there were gathered together the gentle barons, the good archers, and the men-at-arms, whose duty it was to guard the duke, and range themselves around him. The youths and common herd of the camp, whose business was not to join in the battle, but to take care of the harness and stores, moved off towards a rising ground. The priests and the clerks also ascended a hill, there to offer up prayers to God, and watch the event of the battle.

"The English stood firm on foot in close ranks, and carried themselves right boldly. Each man had his hauberk on, with his sword girt, and his shield at his neck. Great hatchets were also slung at their necks, with which they expected to strike heavy blows.

"The Normans brought on the three divisions of their army to attack at different places. They set out in three companies, and in three companies did they fight. The first and second had come up, and then advanced the third, which was the greatest; with that came the duke with his own men, and all moved boldly forward.

"As soon as the two armies were in full view of each other, great noise and tumult arose. You might hear the sound of many trumpets, of bugles, and of horns; and then you might see men ranging themselves in line, lifting their shields, raising their lances, bending their bows, handling their arrows, ready for assault and defense.

"The English stood ready to their post, the Normans still moved on; and when they drew near, the English were to be seen stirring to and fro; were going and coming; troops ranging themselves in order; some with their color rising, others turning pale; some making ready their arms, others raising their shields; the brave man rousing himself to fight, the coward trembling at the approach of danger.

"Then Taillefer, who sang right well, rode, mounted on a swift horse, before the duke, singing of Charlemagne and of Roland, of Oliver, and the peers who died in Roncesvalles. And when they drew nigh to the English, 'A boon, sire!' cried Taillefer; 'I have long served you, and you owe me for all such service. To-day, so please you, you shall repay it. I ask as my guerdon, and beseech you for it earnestly, that you will allow me to strike the first blow in the battle!' And the duke answered, 'I grant it.' Then Taillefer put his horse to a gallop, charging before all the rest, and struck an Englishman dead, driving his lance below the breast into his body, and stretching him upon the ground. Then he drew his sword, and struck another, crying out, 'Come on, come on! What do ye, sirs? Lay on, lay on!' At the second blow he struck, the English pushed forward, and surrounded, and slew him. Forthwith arose the noise and cry of war, and on either side the people put themselves in motion.

"The Normans moved on to the assault, and the English defended themselves well. Some were striking, others urging onward; all were bold, and cast aside fear. And now, behold, that battle was gathered whereof the fame is yet mighty.

"Loud and far resounded the bray of the horns; and the shocks of the lances, the mighty strokes of maces, and the quick clashing of swords. One while the Englishmen rushed on, another while they fell back; one while the men from over sea charged onward, and again at other times retreated. The Normans shouted Dex Aie, the English people Out. Then came the cunning manoeuvres, the rude shocks and strokes of the lance and blows of the swords, among the sergeants and soldiers, both English and Norman.

"When the English fall the Normans shout. Each side taunts and defies the other, yet neither knoweth what the other saith; and the Normans say the English bark, because they understand not their speech.

"Some wax strong, others weak: the brave exult, but the cowards tremble, as men who are sore dismayed. The Normans press on the assault, and the English defend their post well; they pierce the hauberks, and cleave the shields, receive and return mighty blows. Again, some press forward, others yield; and thus, in various ways, the struggle proceeds. In the plain was a fosse, which the Normans had now behind them, having passed it in the fight without regarding it. But the English charged and drove the Normans before them till they made them fall back upon this fosse, overthrowing into it horses and men. Many were to be seen falling therein, rolling one over the other, with their faces to the earth, and unable to rise. Many of the English, also, whom the Normans drew down along with them, died there. At no time during the day's battle did so many Normans die as perished in that fosse. So those said who saw the dead.

"The varlets who were set to guard the harness began to abandon it as they saw the loss of the Frenchmen, when thrown back upon the fosse without power to recover themselves. Being greatly alarmed at seeing the difficulty in restoring order, they began to quit the harness, and sought around, not knowing where to find shelter. Then Duke William's brother, Odo, the good priest, the Bishop of Bayeux, galloped up, and said to them, 'Stand fast! Stand fast! Be quiet and move not! fear nothing; for, if God please, we shall conquer yet.' So they took courage, and rested where they were; and Odo returned galloping back to where the battle was most fierce, and was of great service on that-day. He had put a hauberk on over a white aube, wide in the body, with the sleeve tight, and sat on a white horse, so that all might recognize him. In his hand he held a mace, and wherever he saw most need he held up and stationed the knights, and often urged them on to assault and strike the enemy.

"From nine o'clock in the morning, when the combat began, till three o'clock came, the battle was up and down, this way and that, and no one knew who would conquer and win the land. Both sides stood so firm and fought so well, that no one could guess which would prevail. The Norman archers with their bows shot thickly upon the English; but they covered themselves with their shields, so that the arrows could not reach their bodies, nor do any mischief, how true soever was their aim, or however well they shot. Then the Normans determined to shoot their arrows upward into the air, so that they might fall on their enemies' heads, and strike their faces. The archers adopted this scheme, and shot up into the air towards the English; and the arrows, in falling, struck their heads and faces, and put out the eyes of many; and all feared to open their eyes, or leave their faces unguarded.

"The arrows now flew thicker than rain before the wind; fast sped the shafts that the English called 'wibetes.' Then it was that an arrow, that had been thus shot upward, struck Harold above his right eye, and put it out. In his agony he drew the arrow and threw it away, breaking it with his hands; and the pain to his head was so great that he leaned upon his shield. So the English were wont to say, and still say to the French, that the arrow was well shot which was so sent up against their king, and that the archer won them great glory who thus put out Harold's eye.

"The Normans saw that the English defended themselves well, and were so strong in their position that they could do little against them. So they consulted together privily, and arranged to draw off, and pretend to flee, till the English should pursue and scatter themselves over the field; for they saw that, if they could once get their enemies to break their ranks, they might be attacked and discomfited much more easily. As they had said, so they did. The Normans by little and little fled, the English following them. As the one fell back, the other pressed after; and, when the Frenchmen retreated, the English thought and cried out that the men of France fled, and would never return.

"Thus they were deceived by the pretended flight, and great mischief thereby befell them; for, if they had not moved from their position, it is not likely that they would have been conquered at all; but, like fools, they broke their lines and pursued.

"The Normans were to be seen following up their stratagem, retreating slowly so as to draw the English farther on. As they still flee, the English pursue; they push out their lances and stretch forth their hatchets; following the Normans as they go, rejoicing in the success of their scheme, and scattering themselves over the plain. And the English meantime jeered and insulted their foes with words. 'Cowards,' they cried, 'you came hither in an evil hour, wanting our lands, and seeking to seize our property, fools that ye were to come! Normandy is too far off, and you will not easily reach it. It is of little use to run back; unless you can cross the sea at a leap, or can drink it dry, your sons and daughters are lost to you.'

"The Normans bore it all; but, in fact, they knew not what the English said: their language seemed like the baying of dogs, which they could not understand. At length, they stopped and turned round, determined to recover their ranks; and the barons might be heard crying Dex Aie! fora halt. Then the Normans resumed their former position, turning their faces towards the enemy; and their men were to be seen facing round and rushing onward to a fresh *mêlée*, the one party assaulting the other; this man striking, another pressing onward. One hits, another misses; one flies, another pursues; one is aiming a stroke, while another discharges his blow. Norman strives with Englishman again, and aims his blows afresh. One flies, another pursues swiftly: the combatants are many, the plain wide, the battle and the *mêlée* fierce. On every hand they fight hard, the blows are heavy, and the struggle becomes fierce.

"The Normans were playing their part well, when an English knight came rushing up, having in his company a hundred men, furnished with various arms. He wielded a northern hatchet, with the blade a full foot long, and was well armed after his manner, being tall, bold, and of noble carriage. In the front of the battle, where the Normans thronged most, he came bounding on swifter than the stag, many Normans falling before him and his company. He rushed straight upon a Norman who was armed and riding on a war-horse, and tried with his hatchet of steel to cleave his helmet; but the blow miscarried, and the sharp blade glanced down before the saddle-bow, driving through the horse's neck down to the ground, so that both horse and master fell together to the earth. I know not whether the Englishman struck another blow; but the Normans who saw the stroke were astonished, and about to abandon the assault, when Roger de Montgomeri came galloping up, with his lance set, and heeding not the long-handled ax which the Englishman wielded aloft, struck him down, and left him stretched on the ground. Then Roger cried out, 'Frenchmen, strike! The day is ours!' And again a fierce *mêlée* was to be seen, with many a blow of lance and sword; the English still defending themselves, killing the horses and cleaving the shields.

"There was a French soldier of noble mien, who sat his horse gallantly. He spied two Englishmen who were also carrying themselves boldly. They were both men of great worth, and had become companions in arms and fought together, the one protecting the other. They bore two long and broad bills, and did great mischief to the Normans, killing both horses and men. The French soldier looked at them and their bills, and was sore alarmed, for he was afraid of losing his good horse, the best that he had, and would willingly have turned to some other quarter, if it would not have looked like cowardice. He soon, however, recovered his courage, and, spurring his horse, gave him the bridle, he raised his shield, and struck one of the Englishmen with his lance on the breast, so that the iron passed out at his back. At the moment that he fell, the lance broke, and the Frenchman seized the mace that hung at his right side, and struck the other Englishman a blow that completely fractured his skull.

"On the other side was an Englishman who much annoyed the French, continually assaulting them with a keen-edged hatchet. He had a helmet made of wood, which he had fastened down to his coat, and laced round his neck, so that no blows could reach his head. The ravage he was making was seen by a gallant Norman knight, who rode a horse that neither fire nor water could stop in its career, when its master urged it on. The knight spurred, and his horse carried him on well till he charged the Englishman, striking him over the helmet, so that it fell down over his eyes; and, as he stretched out his hand to raise it and uncover his face, the Norman cut off his right hand, so that his hatchet fell to the ground. Another Norman sprang forward and eagerly seized the prize with both his hands, but he kept it little space, and paid dearly for it, for, as he stooped to pick up the hatchet, an Englishman with his long-handled ax struck him over the back, breaking all his bones, so that his entrails and lungs gushed forth. The knight of the good horse meantime returned without injury; but on his way he met another Englishman and bore him down under his horse, wounding him grievously and trampling him altogether under foot.

"And now might be heard the loud clang and cry of battle, and the clashing of lances. The English stood firm in their barricades, and shivered the lances, beating them into pieces with their bills and maces. The Normans drew their swords and hewed down the barricades, and the English, in great trouble, fell back upon their standard, where were collected the maimed and wounded.

"There were many knights of Chauz who jousted and made attacks. The English knew not how to joust, or bear arms on horse-back, but fought with hatchets and bills. A man, when he wanted to strike with one of their hatchets, was obliged to hold it with both his hands, and could not at the same time, as it seems to me, both cover himself and strike with any freedom.

"The English fell back towards the standard, which was upon a rising ground, and the Normans followed them across the valley, attacking them on foot and horseback. Then Hue de Mortemer, with the Sires D'Auviler, D'Onebac, and Saint Cler, rode up and charged, overthrowing many.

"Robert Fitz Erneis fixed his lance, took his shield, and gallop-ing towards the standard, with his keen-edged sword struck an Englishman who was in front, killed him, and then, drawing back his sword, attacked many others, and pushed straight for the standard, trying to beat it down; but the English surrounded it and killed him with their bills. He was found on the spot, when they afterwards sought for him, dead and lying at the standard's foot.

"Duke William pressed upon the English with his lance striving hard to reach the standard with the great troop he led and seeking earnestly for Harold, on whose account the whole war was. The Normans follow their lord, and press around him, they ply their blows upon the English; and these defend themselves stoutly, striving hard with their enemies, returning blow for blow.

"One of them was a man of great strength, a wrestler, who did great mischief to the Normans with his hatchet; all feared him, for he struck down a great many Normans. The Duke spurred on his horse, and aimed a blow at him, but he stooped, and so escaped the stroke; then, jumping on one side, he lifted his hatchet aloft, and, as the duke bent to avoid the blow, the Englishman boldly struck him on the head, and beat in his helmet, though without doing much injury. He was very near falling, however; but, bearing on his stirrups, he recovered himself immediately; and, when he thought to have revenged himself upon the churl by killing him, he had escaped, dreading the duke's blow. He ran back in among the English, but he was not safe even there; for the Normans seeing him, pursued and caught him, and, having pierced him through and through with their lances, left him dead on the ground.

"Where the throng of the battle was greatest, the men of Kent and Essex fought wondrously well, and made the Normans again retreat, but without doing them much injury. And when the duke saw his men fall back and the English triumphing over them, his spirit rose high, and he seized his shield and his lance, which a vassal handed to him, and took his post by his standard.

"Then those who kept close guard by him, and rode where he rode, being about a thousand armed men, came and rushed with closed ranks upon the English; and with the weight of their good horses, and the blows the knights gave, broke the press of the enemy, and scattered the crowd before them, the good duke leading them on in front. Many pursued and many fled; many were the

Englishmen who fell around, and were trampled under the horses, crawling upon the earth, and not able to rise. Many of the richest and noblest men fell in the rout, but still the English rallied in places, smote down those whom they reached, and maintained the combat the best they could, beating down the men and killing the horses. One Englishman watched the duke, and plotted to kill him; he would have struck him with his lance, but he could not, for the duke struck him first, and felled him to the earth.

"Loud was now the clamor, and great the slaughter; many a soul then quitted the body it inhabited. The living marched over the heaps of dead, and each side was weary of striking. He charged on who could, and he who could no longer strike still pushed forward. The strong struggled with the strong; some failed, others triumphed; the cowards fell back, the brave pressed on; and sad was his fate who fell in the midst, for he had little chance of rising again; and many in truth fell who never rose at all, being crushed under the throng.

"And now the Normans had pressed on so far, that at last they had readied the standard. There Harold had remained, defending himself to the utmost; but he was sorely wounded in his eye by the arrow, and suffered grievous pain from the blow. An armed man came in the throng of the battle, and struck him on the ventaille of his helmet, and beat him to the ground; and as he sought to recover himself a knight beat him down again, striking him on the thick of his thigh, down to the bone.

"Gurth saw the English falling around, and that there was no remedy. He saw his race hastening to ruin, and despaired of any aid; he would have fled, but could not, for the throng continually increased. And the duke pushed on till he reached him, and struck him with great force. Whether he died of that blow I know not, but it was said that he fell under it, and rose no more.

"The standard was beaten down, the golden standard was taken, and Harold and the best of his friends were slain; but there was so much eagerness, and throng of so many around, seeking to kill him, that I know not who it was that slew him.

"The English were in great trouble at having lost their king, and at the duke's having conquered and beat down the standard; but they still fought on, and defended themselves long, and, in fact, till the day drew to a close. Then it clearly appeared to all that the standard was lost, and the news had spread throughout the army that Harold, for certain, was dead; and all saw that there was no longer any hope, so they left the field, and those fled who could.

"William fought well; many an assault did he lead, many a blow did he give, and many receive, and many fell dead under his hand. Two horses were killed under him, and he took a third when necessary, so that he fell not to the ground, and lost not a drop of blood. But, whatever any one did, and whoever lived or died, this is certain, that William conquered, and that many of the English fled from the field, and many died on the spot. Then he returned thanks to God, and in his pride ordered his standard to be brought and set up on high, where the English standard had stood; and that was the signal of his having conquered, and beaten down the standard. And he ordered his tent to be raised on the spot among the dead, and had his meat brought thither, and his supper prepared there.

"Then he took off his armor; and the barons and knights, pages and squires came, when he had unstrung his shield; and they took the helmet from his head, and the hauberk from his back, and saw the heavy blows upon his shield, and how his helmet was dinted in. And all greatly wondered, and said: 'Such a baron (ber) never bestrode war-horse, nor dealt such blows, nor did such feats of arms; neither has there been on earth such a knight since Rollant and Oliver.'

"Thus they lauded and extolled him greatly, and rejoiced in what they saw, but grieving also for their friends who were slain in the battle. And the duke stood meanwhile among them, of noble stature and mien, and rendered thanks to the King of glory, through whom he had the victory; and thanked the knights around him, mourning also frequently for the dead. And he ate and drank among the dead, and made his bed that night upon the field.

"The morrow was Sunday; and those who had slept upon the field of battle, keeping watch around, and suffering great fatigue, bestirred themselves at break of day, and sought out and buried such of the bodies of their dead friends as they might find. The noble ladies of the land also came, some to seek their husbands, and others their fathers, sons, or brothers. They bore the bodies to their villages, and interred them at the churches; and the clerks and priests of the country were ready, and, at the request of their friends, took the bodies that were found, and prepared graves and lay them therein.

"King Harold was carried and buried at Varham; but I know not who it was that bore him thither, neither do I know who buried him. Many remained on the field, and many had fled in the night."

Such is a Norman account of the battle of Hastings,[12] which does full justice to the valor of the Saxons, as well as to the skill and bravery of the victors. It is, indeed, evident that the loss of the battle by the English was owing to the wound which Harold received in the afternoon, and which must have incapacitated him from effective command. When we remember that he had himself just won the battle of Stamford Bridge over Harald Hardrada by the manoeuvre of a feigned flight, it is impossible to suppose that he could be deceived by the same stratagem on the part of the Normans at Hastings. But his men, when deprived of his control, would very naturally be led by their inconsiderate ardor into the pursuit that proved so fatal to them. All the narratives of the battle, however much they vary as to the precise time and manner of Harold's fall, eulogize the generalship and the personal prowess which he displayed, until the fatal arrow struck him. The skill with which he had posted his army was proved both by the slaughter which it cost the Normans to force the position, and also by the desperate rally which some of the Saxons made after the battle in the forest in the rear, in which they cut off a large number of the pursuing Normans. This circumstance is particularly mentioned by William of Poitiers, the Conqueror's own chaplain. Indeed, if Harold, or either of his brothers, had survived, the remains of the English army might have formed again in the wood, and could at least have effected an orderly retreat, and prolonged the war. But both Gurth and Leofwine, and all the bravest Thanes of Southern England lay dead on Senlac, around their fallen king and the fallen standard of their country. The exact number that perished on the Saxon's side is unknown; but we read that on the side of the victors, out of sixty thousand men who had been engaged, no less than a fourth perished. So well had the English billmen "plyed the ghastly blow," and so sternly had the Saxon battle-axe cloven Norman's casque and mail.[13] The old historian Daniel justly, as well as forcibly, remarks:[14] "Thus was tried, by the great assize of God's judgment in battle, the right of power between the English and Norman nations; a battle the most memorable of all others; and, however miserably lost, yet most nobly fought on the part of England."

Many a pathetic legend was told in after years respecting the discovery and the burial of the corpse of our last Saxon king. The main circumstances, though they seem to vary, are perhaps reconcilable.[15] Two of the monks of Waltham Abbey, which Harold had founded a little time before his election to the throne, had accompanied him to the battle. On the morning after the slaughter, they begged and gained permission of the Conqueror to search for the body of their benefactor. The Norman soldiery and camp-followers had stripped and gashed the slain, and the two monks vainly strove to recognize from among the mutilated and gory heaps around them the features of their former king. They sent for Harold's mistress, Edith, surnamed "the Fair," and "the swan-necked," to aid them. The eye of love proved keener than the eye of gratitude, and the Saxon lady even in that Aceldama knew her Harold.

The king's mother now sought the victorious Norman, and begged the dead body of her son. But William at first answered, in his wrath and the hardness of his heart, that a man who had been false to his word and his religion should have no other sepulchre than the sand of the shore. He added, with a sneer, "Harold mounted guard on the coast while he was alive, he may continue his guard now he is dead." The taunt was an unintentional eulogy; and a grave washed by the spray of the Sussex waves would have been the noblest burial-place for the martyr of Saxon freedom. But Harold's mother was urgent in her lamentations and her prayers; the Conqueror relented: like Achilles, he gave up the dead body of his fallen foe to a parent's supplications, and the remains of King Harold were deposited with regal honors in Waltham Abbey.

On Christmas day in the same year William the Conqueror was crowned at London King of England.

SYNOPSIS OF EVENTS BETWEEN THE BATTLE OF HASTINGS, AD 1066, AND JOAN OF ARC'S VICTORY AT ORLEANS, A.D. 1429.

AD 1066–1087. Reign of William the Conqueror. Frequent risings of the English against him, which are quelled with merciless rigor.

1096. The first Crusade.

1112. Commencement of the disputes about investitures between the emperors and the popes.

1140. Foundation of the city of Lubec, whence originated the Hanseatic League. Commencement of the feuds in Italy between the Guelfs and the Ghibellines.

1146. The second Crusade.

1154. Henry II. becomes King of England. Under him Thomas à Becket is made Archbishop of Canterbury: the first instance of any man of the Saxon race being raised to high office in Church or State since the Conquest.

1170. Strongbow, earl of Pembroke, lands with an English army in Ireland.

1189. Richard Cœur de Lion becomes King of England. He and King Philip Augustus of France join in the third Crusade.

1199–1204. On the death of King Richard, his brother John claims and makes himself master of England and Normandy, and the other large continental possessions of the early Plantagenet princes. Philip Augustus asserts the cause of Prince Arthur, John's nephew, against him. Arthur is murdered, but the French king continues the war against John, and conquers from him Normandy, Brittany, Anjou, Maine, Touraine, and Poitiers.

1215. The barons, the freeholders, the citizens, and the yeomen of England rise against the tyranny of John and his foreign favorites. They compel him to sign Magna Charta. This is the commencement of our nationality; for our history from this time forth is the history of a national life, then complete and still in being. All English history before this period is a mere history of elements, of their collisions, and of the processes of their fusion. For upwards of a century after the Conquest, Anglo-Norman and Anglo-Saxon had kept aloof from each other: the one in haughty scorn, the other in sullen abhorrence. They were two peoples, though living in the same land. It is not until the thirteenth century, the period of the reigns of John and his son and grandson, that we can perceive the existence of any feeling of common nationality among them. But in studying the history of these reigns, we read of the old dissensions no longer. The Saxon no more appears in civil war against the Norman, the Norman no longer scorns the language of the Saxon, or refuses to bear together with him the name of Englishman. No part of the community think themselves foreigners to another part. They feel that they are all one people, and they have learned to unite their efforts for the common purpose of protecting the rights and promoting the welfare of all. The fortunate loss of the Duchy of Normandy in John's reign greatly promoted these new feelings. Thenceforth our barons' only homes were in England. One language had, in the reign of Henry III., become the language of the land, and that, also, had then assumed the form in which we still possess it. One law, in the eye of which all freemen are equal without distinction of race, was modelled, and steadily enforced, and still continues to form the ground-work of our judicial system.[16]

1273. Rudolph of Hapsburg chosen Emperor of Germany.

1283. Edward I. conquers Wales.

1346. Edward III. invades France, and gains the battle of Crecy.

1356. Battle of Poitiers.

1360. Treaty of Bretigny between England and France. By it Edward III. renounces his pretensions to the French crown. The treaty is ill kept, and indecisive hostilities continue between the forces of the two countries.

1414. Henry V. of England claims the crown of France, and resolves to invade and conquer that kingdom. At this time France was in the most deplorable state of weakness and suffering, from the factions that raged among her nobility, and from the cruel oppressions which the rival nobles practised on the mass of the community. "The people were exhausted by taxes, civil wars, and military executions; and they had fallen into that worst of all states of mind, when the independence of one's country is thought no longer a paramount and sacred object. 'What can the English do to us worse than the thing we suffer at the hands of our own princes?' was a common exclamation among the poor people of France."[17]

1415. Henry invades France, takes Harfleur, and wins the great battle of Agincourt.

1417–1419. Henry conquers Normandy. The French dauphin assassinates the Duke of Burgundy, the most powerful of the French nobles, at Montereau. The successor of the murdered duke becomes the active ally of the English.

1420. The treaty of Troyes is concluded between Henry V. of England and Charles VI. of France, and Philip, duke of Burgundy. By this treaty it was stipulated that Henry should marry the Princess Catharine of France; that King Charles, during his life-time, should keep the title and dignity of King of France, but that Henry should succeed him, and should at once be intrusted with the administration of the government, and that the French crown should descend to Henry's heirs; that France and England should forever be united under one king, but should still retain their several usages, customs, and privileges; that all the princes, peers, vassals, and communities of France should swear allegiance to Henry as their future king, and should pay him present obedience as regent. That Henry should unite his arms to those of King Charles and the Duke of Burgundy, in order to subdue the adherents of

Charles, the pretended dauphin; and that these three princes should make no peace or truce with the dauphin but by the common consent of all three.

1421. Henry V. gains several victories over the French, who refuse to acknowledge the treaty of Troyes. His son, afterwards Henry VI., is born.

1422. Henry V. and Charles VI. of France die. Henry VI. is proclaimed at Paris King of England and France. The followers of the French dauphin proclaim him Charles VII., king of France. The Duke of Bedford, the English regent in France, defeats the army of the dauphin at Crevant.

1424. The Duke of Bedford gains the great victory of Verneuil over the French partisans of the dauphin and their Scotch auxiliaries.

1428. The English begin the siege of Orleans.

CHAPTER IX

JOAN OF ARC'S VICTORY OVER THE ENGLISH AT ORLEANS, AD 1429

"The eyes of all Europe were turned towards this scene, where it was reasonably supposed the French were to make their last stand for maintaining the independence of their monarchy and the rights of their sovereign."

— *Hume.*

WHEN, after their victory at Salamis, the generals of the various Greek states voted the prizes for distinguished individual merit, each assigned the first place of excellence to himself, but they all concurred in giving their second votes to Themistocles.[1] This was looked on as a decisive proof that Themistocles ought to be ranked first of all. If we were to endeavor, by a similar test, to ascertain which European nation had contributed the most to the progress of European civilization, we should find Italy, Germany, England, and Spain each claiming the first degree, but each also naming France as clearly next in merit. It is impossible to deny her paramount importance in history. Besides the formidable part that she has for nearly three centuries played, as the Bellona of the European commonwealth of states, her influence during all this period over the arts, the literature, the manners, and the feelings of mankind, has been such as to make the crisis of her earlier fortunes a point of world-wide interest; and it may be asserted, without exaggeration, that the future career of every nation was involved in the result of the struggle by which the unconscious heroine of France, in the beginning of the fifteenth century, rescued her country from becoming a second Ireland under the yoke of the triumphant English.

Seldom has the extinction of a nation's independence appeared more inevitable than was the case in France when the English invaders completed their lines round Orleans, four hundred and twenty-two years ago. A series of dreadful defeats had thinned the chivalry of France, and daunted the spirits of her soldiers. A foreign king had been proclaimed in her capital; and foreign armies of the bravest veterans, and led by the ablest captains then known in the world, occupied the fairest portions of her territory. Worse to her, even, than the fierceness and the strength of her foes, were the factions, the vices, and the crimes of her own children. Her native prince was a dissolute trifler, stained with the assassination of the most powerful noble of the land, whose son, in revenge, had leagued himself with the enemy. Many more of her nobility, many of her prelates, her magistrates, and rulers, had sworn fealty to the English king. The condition of the peasantry amid the general prevalence of anarchy and brigandage, which were added to the customary devastations of contending armies, was wretched beyond the power of language to describe. The sense of terror and wretchedness seemed to have extended itself even to the brute creation.

"In sooth, the estate of France was then most miserable. There appeared nothing but a horrible face, confusion, poverty, desolation, solitarinesse, and feare. The lean and bare laborers in the country did terrifie even theeves themselves, who had nothing left them to spoile but the carkasses of these poore miserable creatures, wandering up and down like ghostes drawne out of their graves. The least farmes and hamlets were fortified by these robbers, English, Bourguegnons, and French, every one striving to do his worst: all men-of-war were well agreed to spoile the countryman and merchant. *Even the cattell, accustomed to the larume bell, the signe of the enemy's approach, would run home of themselves without any guide by this accustomed misery.*"[2]

In the autumn of 1428, the English, who were already masters of all France north of the Loire, prepared their forces for the conquest of the southern provinces, which yet adhered to the cause of the dauphin. The city of Orleans, on the banks of that river, was looked upon as the last stronghold of the French national party. If the English could once obtain possession of it, their victorious progress through the residue of the kingdom seemed free from any serious obstacle. Accordingly, the Earl of Salisbury, one of the bravest and most experienced of the English generals, who had been trained under Henry V., marched to the attack of the all-important city; and, after reducing several places of inferior consequence in the neighborhood, appeared with his army before its walls on the 12th of October, 1428.

The city of Orleans itself was on the north side of the Loire, but its suburbs extended far on the southern side, and a strong bridge connected them with the town. A fortification, which in modern military phrase would be termed a tete-du-pont, defended the bridge head on the southern side, and two towers, called the Tourelles, were built on the bridge itself, at a little distance from the tete-du-pont. Indeed, the solid masonry of the bridge terminated at the Tourelles; and the communication thence with the tete-du-pont and the southern shore was by means of a draw-bridge. The Tourelles and the tete-du-pont formed together a strong-fortified post, capable of containing a garrison of considerable strength; and so long as this was in possession of the Orleannais, they could communicate freely with the southern provinces, the inhabitants of which, like the Orleannais themselves, supported the cause of their dauphin against the foreigners. Lord Salisbury rightly judged the capture of the Tourelles to be the most material step towards the reduction of the city itself. Accordingly, he directed his principal operations against this post, and after some severe repulses he carried the Tourelles by storm on the 23d of October. The French, however, broke down the arches of the bridge that were nearest to the north bank, and thus rendered a direct assault from the Tourelles upon the city impossible.

But the possession of this post enabled the English to distress the town greatly by a battery of cannon which they planted there, and which commanded some of the principal streets.

It has been observed by Hume that this is the first siege in which any important use appears to have been made of artillery. And even at Orleans both besiegers and besieged seem to have employed their cannons merely as instruments of destruction against their enemy's men, and not to have trusted to them as engines of demolition against their enemy's walls and works. The efficacy of cannon in breaching solid masonry was taught Europe by the Turks a few years afterwards, at the memorable siege of Constantinople.[3] In our French wars, as in the wars of the classic nations, famine was looked on as the surest weapon to compel the submission of a well-walled town; and the great object of the besiegers was to effect a complete circumvallation. The great ambit of the walls of Orleans, and the facilities which the river gave for obtaining succors and supplies, rendered the capture of the town by this process a matter of great difficulty. Nevertheless, Lord Salisbury, and Lord Suffolk, who succeeded him in command of the English after his death by a cannon ball, carried on the necessary works with great skill and resolution. Six strongly-fortified posts, called bastilles, were formed at certain intervals round the town, and the purpose of the English engineers was to draw strong lines between them. During the winter, little progress was made with the intrenchments, but, when the spring of 1429 came, the English resumed their work, with activity; the communications between the city and the country became more difficult, and the approach of want began already to be felt in Orleans.

The besieging force also fared hardly for stores and provisions, until relieved by the effects of a brilliant victory which Sir John Fastolfe, one of the best English generals, gained at Rouvrai, near Orleans, a few days after Ash Wednesday, 1429. With only sixteen hundred fighting men, Sir John completely defeated an army of French and Scots, four thousand strong, which had been collected for the purpose of aiding the Orleannais and harassing the besiegers. After this encounter, which seemed decisively to con-firm the superiority of the English in battle over their adversaries, Fastolfe escorted large supplies of stores and food to Suffolk's camp, and the spirits of the English rose to the highest pitch at the prospect of the speedy capture of the city before them, and the consequent subjection of all France beneath their arms.

The Orleannais now, in their distress, offered to surrender the city into the hands of the Duke of Burgundy, who, though the ally of the English, was yet one of their native princes. The Regent Bedford refused these terms, and the speedy submission of the city to the English seemed inevitable. The Dauphin Charles, who was now at Chinon with his remnant of a court, despaired of con-tinuing any longer the struggle for his crown, and was only pre-vented from abandoning the country by the more masculine spirits of his mistress and his queen. Yet neither they, nor the bold-est of Charles' captains, could have shown him where to find resources for prolonging war; and least of all could any human skill have predicted the quarter whence rescue was to come to Orleans and to France.

In the village of Domremy, on the borders of Lorraine, there was a poor peasant of the name of Jacques d'Arc, respected in his station of life, and who had reared a family in virtuous habits and in the practice of the strictest devotion. His eldest daughter was named by her parents Jannette, but she was called Jeanne by the French, which was Latinized into Johanna, and Anglicized into Joan.[4]

At the time when Joan first attracted attention, she was about eighteen years of age. She was naturally of a susceptible disposition, which diligent attention to the legends of saints and tales of fairies, aided by the dreamy loneliness of her life while tending her father's flocks,[5] had made peculiarly prone to enthusiastic fervor. At the same time, she was eminent for piety and purity of soul, and for her compassionate gentleness to the sick and the distressed.

The district where she dwelt had escaped comparatively free from the ravages of war, but the approach of roving bands of Burgundian or English troops frequently spread terror through

Domremy. Once the village had been plundered by some of these marauders, and Joan and her family had been driven from their home, and forced to seek refuge for a time at Neufchâteau. The peasantry in Domremy were principally attached to the house of Orleans and the dauphin, and all the miseries which France endured were there imputed to the Burgundian faction and their allies, the English, who were seeking to enslave unhappy France.

Thus, from infancy to girlhood, Joan had heard continually of the woes of the war, and had herself witnessed some of the wretchedness that it caused. A feeling of intense patriotism grew in her with her growth. The deliverance of France from the English was the subject of her reveries by day and her dreams by night. Blended with these aspirations were recollections of the miraculous interpositions of Heaven in favor of the oppressed, which she had learned from the legends of her Church. Her faith was undoubting; her prayers were fervent. "She feared no danger, for she felt no sin," and at length she believed herself to have received the supernatural inspiration which she sought. According to her own narrative, delivered by her to her merciless inquisitors in the time of her captivity and approaching death, she was about thirteen years old when her revelations commenced. Her own words describe them best.[6] "At the age of thirteen, a voice from God came to her to help her in ruling herself, and that voice came to her about the hour of noon, in summer time, while she was in her father's garden. And she had fasted the day before. And she heard the voice on her right, in the direction of the church; and when she heard the voice, she saw also a bright light." Afterwards St. Michael, and St. Margaret, and St. Catharine appeared to her. They were always in a halo of glory; she could see that their heads were crowned with jewels; and she heard their voices, which were sweet and mild. She did not distinguish their arms or limbs. She heard them more frequently than she saw them; and the usual time when she heard them was when the church bells were sounding for prayer. And if she was in the woods when she heard them, she could plainly distinguish their voices drawing near to her. When she thought that she discerned the Heavenly Voices, she knelt down, and bowed herself to the ground. Their presence gladdened her even to tears; and, after they departed, she wept because they had not taken her with them back to Paradise. They always spoke soothingly to her. They told her that France would be saved, and that she was to save it. Such were the visions and the voices that moved the spirit of the girl of thirteen; and, as she grew older, they became more frequent and more clear. At last the tidings of the siege of Orleans reached Domremy. Joan heard her parents and neighbors talk of the sufferings of its population, of the ruin which its capture would bring on their lawful sovereign, and of the distress of the dauphin and his court. Joan's heart was sorely troubled at the thought of the fate of Orleans; and her voices now ordered her to leave her home; and warned her that she was the instrument chosen by Heaven for driving away the English from that city, and for taking the dauphin to be anointed king at Rheims. At length she informed her parents of her divine mission, and told them that she must go to the Sire de Baudricourt, who commanded at Vaucouleurs, and who was the appointed person to bring her into the presence of the king, whom she was to save. Neither the anger nor the grief of her parents, who said that they would rather see her drowned than exposed to the contamination of the camp, could move her from her purpose. One of her uncles consented to take her to Vaucouleurs, where De Baudricourt at first thought her mad, and derided her; but by degrees was led to believe, if not in her inspiration, at least in her enthusiasm, and in its possible utility to the dauphin's cause.

The inhabitants of Vaucouleurs were completely won over to her side by the piety and devoutness which she displayed, and by her firm assurance in the truth of her mission. She told them that it was God's will that she should go to the king, and that no one but her could save the kingdom of France. She said that she herself would rather remain with her poor mother, and spin; but the Lord had ordered her forth. The fame of "The Maid," as she was termed, the renown of her holiness, and of her mission, spread far and wide. Baudricourt sent her with an escort to Chinon, where the Dauphin Charles was dallying away his time. Her Voices had bidden her assume the arms and the apparel of a knight; and the wealthiest inhabitants of Vaucouleurs had vied with each other in equipping her with war-horse, armor, and sword. On reaching Chinon, she was, after some delay, admitted into the presence of the dauphin. Charles designedly dressed himself far less richly than many of his courtiers were apparelled, and mingled with them, when Joan was introduced, in order to see if the Holy Maid would address her exhortations to the wrong person. But she instantly singled him out, and, kneeling before him, said: "Most noble dauphin, the King of Heaven announces to you by me that you shall be anointed and crowned king in the city of Rheims, and that you shall be his viceregent in France." His features may probably have been seen by her previously in portraits, or have been described to her by others; but she herself believed that her Voices inspired her when she addressed the king;[7] and the report soon spread abroad that the Holy Maid had found the king by a miracle; and this, with many other similar rumors, augmented the renown and influence that she now rapidly acquired.

The state of public feeling in France was now favorable to an enthusiastic belief in a divine interposition in favor of the party that had hitherto been unsuccessful and oppressed. The humiliations which had befallen the French royal family and nobility were looked on as the just judgments of God upon them for their vice and impiety. The misfortunes that had come upon France as a nation were believed to have been drawn down by national sins. The English, who had been the instruments of Heaven's wrath against France, seemed now, by their pride and cruelty, to be fitting objects of it themselves. France in that age was a profoundly religious country. There was ignorance, there was superstition, there was bigotry; but there was Faith — a faith that itself worked true miracles, even while it believed in unreal ones. At this time, also, one of those devotional movements began among the clergy in France, which from time to time occur in national churches, without it being possible for the historian to assign any adequate human cause for their immediate date or extension. Numberless friars and priests traversed the rural districts and towns of France, preaching to the people that they must seek from Heaven a deliverance from the pillages of the soldiery and the insolence of the foreign oppressors.[8] The idea of a Providence that works only by general laws was wholly alien to the feelings of the age. Every political event, as well as every natural phenomenon, was believed to be the immediate result of a special mandate of God. This led to the belief that his holy angels and saints were constantly employed in executing his commands and mingling in the affairs of men. The Church encouraged these feelings, and at the same time sanctioned the concurrent popular belief that hosts of evil spirits were also ever actively interposing in the current of earthly events, with whom sorcerers and wizards could league themselves, and thereby obtain the exercise of supernatural power.

Thus, all things favored the influence which Joan obtained both over friends and foes. The French nation, as well as the English and Burgundians, readily admitted that superhuman beings inspired her; the only question was whether these beings were good or evil angels; whether she brought with her "airs from heaven or blasts from hell." This question seemed to her countrymen to be decisively settled in her favor by the austere sanctity of her life, by the holiness of her conversation, but still more by her exemplary attention to all the services and rites of the Church. The dauphin at first feared the injury that might be done to his cause if he laid himself open to the charge of having leagued himself with a sorceress. Every imaginable test, therefore, was resorted to in order to set Joan's orthodoxy and purity beyond suspicion. At last Charles and his advisers felt safe in accepting her services as those of a true and virtuous Christian daughter of the Holy Church.

It is, indeed, probable that Charles himself and some of his counselors may have suspected Joan of being a mere enthusiast, and it is certain that Dunois, and others of the best generals, took considerable latitude in obeying or deviating from the military orders that she gave. But over the mass of the people and the soldiery her influence was unbounded. While Charles and his doctors of theology, and court ladies, had been deliberating as to recognizing or dismissing the Maid, a considerable period had passed away, during which a small army, the last gleanings, at is seemed, of the English sword, had been assembled at Blois, under Dunois, La Hire, Xaintrailles, and other chiefs, who to their natural valor were now beginning to unite the wisdom that is taught by misfortune. It was resolved to send Joan with this force and a convoy of provisions to Orleans. The distress of that city had now become urgent. But the communication with the open country was not entirely cut off: the Orleannais had heard of the Holy Maid whom Providence had raised up for their deliverance, and their messengers earnestly implored the dauphin to send her to them without delay.

Joan appeared at the camp at Blois, clad in a new suit of brilliant white armor, mounted on a stately black war-horse, and with a lance in her right hand, which she had learned to wield with skill and grace.[9] Her head was unhelmeted, so that all could behold her fair and expressive features, her deep-set and earnest eyes, and her long black hair, which was parted across her forehead, and bound by a ribbon behind her back. She wore at her side a small battle-axe, and the consecrated sword, marked on the blade with five crosses, which had at her bidding been taken for her from the shrine of St. Catharine at Fierbois. A page carried her banner, which she had caused to be made and embroidered as her Voices enjoined. It was white satin,[10] strewn with fleurs-de-lis; and on it were the words "Jhesus Maria," and the representation of the Saviour in his glory. Joan afterwards generally bore her banner herself in battle; she said that, though she loved her sword much, she loved her banner forty times as much; and she loved to carry it, because it could not kill any one.

Thus accoutred, she came to lead the troops of France, who looked with soldierly admiration on her well-proportioned and upright figure, the skill with which she managed her war-horse, and the easy grace with which she handled her weapons. Her military education had been short, but she had availed herself of it well. She had also the good sense to interfere little with the manoeuvres of the troops, leaving these things to Dunois, and others whom she had the discernment to recognize as the best officers in the camp. Her tactics in action were simple enough. As she herself described it, "I used to say to them,' Go boldly in among the English,' and then I used to go boldly in myself."[11] Such, as she told her inquisitors, was the only spell she used, and it was one of power. But, while interfering little with the military discipline of the troops, in all matters of moral discipline she was inflexibly strict. All the abandoned followers of the camp were driven away. She compelled both generals and soldiers to attend regularly at confessional. Her chaplain and other priests marched with the army under her orders; and at every halt, an altar was set up and the sacrament administered. No oath or foul language passed without punishment or censure. Even the roughest and most hardened veterans obeyed her. They put off for a time the bestial coarseness which had grown on them during a life of bloodshed and rapine; they felt that they must go forth in a new spirit to a new career, and acknowledged the beauty of the holiness in which the heaven-sent Maid was leading them to certain victory.

Joan marched from Blois on the 25th of April with a convoy of provisions for Orleans, accompanied by Dunois, La Hire, and the other chief captains of the French, and on the evening of the 28th they approached the town. In the words of the old chronicler Hall:[12] "The Englishmen, perceiving that thei within could not long continue for faute of vitaile and pouder, kepte not their watche so diligently as thei were accustomed, nor scoured now the countrey environed as thei before had ordained. Whiche negligence the citizens shut in perceiving, sent worde thereof to the French captaines, which, with Pucelle, in the dedde tyme of the nighte, and in a greate rayne and thundere, with all their vitaile and artillery, entered into the citie."

When it was day, the Maid rode in solemn procession through the city, clad in complete armor, and mounted on a white horse. Dunois was by her side, and all the bravest knights of her army and of the garrison followed in her train. The whole population thronged around her; and men, women, and children strove to touch her garments, or her banner, or her charger. They poured forth blessings on her, whom they already considered their deliverer. In the words used by two of them afterwards before the tribunal which reversed the sentence, but could not restore the life of the Virgin-martyr of France, "the people of Orleans, when they first saw her in their city, thought that it was an angel from Heaven that had come down to save them." Joan spoke gently in reply to their acclamations and addresses. She told them to fear God, and trust in Him for safety from the fury of their enemies. She first went to the principal church, where *Te Deum* was chanted; and then she took up her abode at the house of Jacques Bourgier, one of the principal citizens, and whose wife was a matron of good repute. She refused to attend a splendid banquet which had been provided for her, and passed nearly all her time in prayer.

When it was known by the English that the Maid was in Orleans, their minds were not less occupied about her than were the minds of those in the city; but it was in a very different spirit. The English believed in her supernatural mission as firmly as the French did, but they thought her a sorceress who had come to overthrow them by her enchantments. An old prophecy, which told that a damsel from Lorraine was to save France, had long been current, and it was known and applied to Joan by foreigners, as well as by the natives. For months the English had heard of the coming Maid, and the tales of miracles which she was said to have wrought had been listened to by the rough yeomen of the English camp with anxious curiosity and secret awe. She had sent a herald to the English generals before she marched for Orleans, and he had summoned the English generals in the name of the Most High to give up to the Maid, who was sent by Heaven, the keys of the French cities which they had wrongfully taken; and he also solemnly adjured the English troops, whether archers, or men of the companies of war, or gentlemen, or others, who were before the city of Orleans, to depart thence to their homes, under peril of being visited by the judgment of God. On her arrival in Orleans, Joan sent another similar message; but the English scoffed at her from their towers, and threatened to burn her heralds. She determined, before she shed the blood of the besiegers, to repeat the warning with her own voice; and, accordingly, she mounted one of the boulevards of the town, which was within hearing of the Tourelles, and thence she spoke to the English, and bade them depart, otherwise they would meet with shame and woe. Sir William Gladsdale (whom the French call *Glacidas*) commanded the English post at the Tourelles, and he and another English officer replied by bidding her go home and keep her cows, and by ribald jests, that brought tears of shame and indignation into her eyes. But, though the English leaders vaunted aloud, the effect produced on their army by Joan's presence in Orleans was proved four days after her arrival, when, on the approach of re-enforcements and stores to the town, Joan and La Hire marched out to meet them, and escorted the long train of provision wagons safely into Orleans, between the bastilles of the English, who cowered behind their walls, instead of charging fiercely and fearlessly, as had been their wont, on any French band that dared to show itself within reach.

Thus far she had prevailed without striking a blow; but the time was now come to test her courage amid the horrors of actual slaughter. On the afternoon of the day on which she had escorted the re-enforcements into the city, while she was resting fatigued at home, Dunois had seized an advantageous opportunity of attacking the English bastille of St. Loup, and a fierce assault of the Orleannais had been made on it, which the English garrison of the fort stubbornly resisted. Joan was roused by a sound which she believed to be that of her Heavenly Voices; she called for her arms and horse, and, quickly equipping herself, she mounted to ride off to where the fight was raging. In her haste she had forgotten her banner; she rode back, and, without dismounting, had it given to her from the window, and then she galloped to the gate whence the sally had been made. On her way she met some of the wounded French who had been carried back from the fight. "Ha!" she exclaimed, "I never can see French blood flow without my hair standing on end." She rode out of the gate, and met the tide of her countrymen, who had been repulsed from the English fort, and were flying back to Orleans in confusion. At the sight of the Holy Maid and her banner they rallied, and renewed the assault. Joan rode forward at their head, waving her banner and cheering them on. The English quailed at what they believed to be the charge of hell; Saint Loup was stormed, and its defenders put to the sword, except some few, whom Joan succeeded in saving. All her woman's gentleness returned when the combat was over. It was the first time she had ever seen a battle-field. She wept at the sight of so many bleeding corpses; and her tears flowed doubly when she reflected that they were the bodies of Christian men who had died without confession.

The next day was Ascension day, and it was passed by Joan in prayer. But on the following morrow it was resolved by the chiefs of the garrison to attack the English forts on the south of the river. For this purpose they crossed the river in boats, and, after some severe fighting, in which the Maid was wounded in the heel, both the English bastilles of the Augustins and St. Jean de Blanc were captured. The Tourelles were now the only post which the besiegers held on the south of the river. But that post was formidably strong, and, by its command of the bridge, it was the key to the deliverance of Orleans. It was known that a fresh English army was approaching under Fastolfe to re-enforce the besiegers, and, should that army arrive while the Tourelles were yet in the possession of their comrades, there was great peril of all the advantages which the French had gained being nullified, and of the siege being again actively carried on.

It was resolved, therefore, by the French to assail the Tourelles at once, while the enthusiasm which the presence and the heroic valor of the Maid had created was at its height. But the enterprise was difficult. The rampart of the tête-du-pont, or landward bulwark, of the Tourelles was steep and high, and Sir John Gladsdale occupied this all-important fort with five hundred archers and men-at-arms, who were the very flower of the English army.

Early in the morning of the 7th of May, some thousands of the best French troops in Orleans heard mass and attended the confessional by Joan's orders, and then, crossing the river in boats, as on the preceding day, they assailed the bulwark of the Tourelles "with light hearts and heavy hands." But Gladsdale's men, encouraged by their bold and skilful leader, made a resolute and able defence. The Maid planted her banner on the edge of the fosse, and then, springing down into the ditch, she placed the first ladder against the wall, and began to mount. An English archer sent an arrow at her, which pierced her corselet, and wounded her severely between the neck and shoulder. She fell bleeding from the ladder; and the English were leaping down from the wall to capture her, but her followers bore her off. She was carried to the rear, and laid upon the grass; her armor was taken off, and the anguish of her wound and the sight of her blood made her at first tremble and weep. But her confidence in her celestial mission soon returned: her patron saints seemed to stand before her, and reassure her. She sat up and drew the arrow out with her own hands. Some of the soldiers who stood by wished to stanch the blood by saying a charm over the wound; but she forbade them, saying that she did not wish to be cured by unhallowed means. She had the wound dressed with a little oil, and then, bidding her confessor come to her, she betook herself to prayer.

In the mean while, the English in the bulwark of the Tourelles had repulsed the oft-renewed efforts of the French to scale the wall. Dunois, who commanded the assailants, was at last discouraged, and gave orders for a retreat to be sounded.

Joan sent for him and the other generals, and implored them not to despair. "By my God," she said to them, "you shall soon enter in there. Do not doubt it. When you see my banner wave again up to the wall, to your arms again! The fort is yours. For the present, rest a little, and take some food and drink." "They did so," says the old chronicler of the siege,[13] "for they obeyed her marvellously." The faintness caused by her wound had now passed off, and she headed the French in another rush against the bulwark. The English, who had thought her slain, were alarmed at her reappearance, while the French pressed furiously and fanatically forward. A Biscayan soldier was carrying Joan's banner. She had told the troops that directly the banner touched the wall, they should enter. The Biscayan waved the banner forward from the edge of the fosse, and touched the wall with it; and then all the French host swarmed madly up the ladders that now were raised in all directions against the English fort. At this crisis, the efforts of the English garrison were distracted by an attack from another quarter. The French troops who had been left in Orleans had placed some planks over the broken arch of the bridge, and advanced across them to the assault of the Tourelles on the northern side. Gladsdale resolved to withdraw his men from the landward bulwark, and concentrate his whole force in the Tourelles themselves. He was passing for this purpose across the drawbridge that connected the Tourelles and the tête-du-pont, when Joan, who by this time had scaled the wall of the bulwark, called out to him, "Surrender! Surrender to the King of Heaven! Ah, Glacidas, you have foully wronged me with your words, but I have great pity on your soul and the souls of your men." The Englishman, disdainful of her summons, was striding on across the drawbridge, when a cannon shot from the town carried it away, and Gladsdale perished in the water that ran beneath. After his fall, the remnant of the English abandoned all further resistance. Three hundred of them had been killed in the battle, and two hundred were made prisoners.

The broken arch was speedily repaired by the exulting Orleannais, and Joan made her triumphant re-entry into the city by the bridge that had so long been closed. Every church in Orleans rang out its gratulating peal; and throughout the night, the sounds of rejoicing echoed, and the bonfires blazed up from the city. But in the lines and forts which the besiegers yet retained on the northern shore, there was anxious watching of the generals, and there was desponding gloom among the soldiery. Even Talbot now counselled retreat. On the following morning, the Orleannais, from their walls, saw the great forts called "London" and "St. Lawrence" in flames, and witnessed their invaders busy in destroying the stores and munitions which had been relied on for the destruction of Orleans. Slowly and sullenly the English army retired; and not before it had drawn up in battle array opposite to the city, as if to challenge the garrison to an encounter. The French troops were eager to go out and attack, but Joan forbade it. The day was Sunday. "In the name of God," she said, "let them depart, and let us return thanks to God." She led the soldiers and citizens forth from Orleans, but not for the shedding of blood. They passed in solemn procession round the city walls, and then, while their retiring enemies were yet in sight, they knelt in thanksgiving to God for the deliverance which he had vouchsafed them.

Within three months from the time of her first interview with the dauphin, Joan had fulfilled the first part of her promise, the raising of the siege of Orleans. Within three months more she had fulfilled the second part also, and had stood with her banner in her hand by the high altar at Rheims, while he was anointed and crowned as King Charles VII. of France. In the interval she had taken Jargeau, Troyes, and other strong places, and she had defeated an English army in a fair field at Patay. The enthusiasm of her countrymen knew no bounds; but the importance of her services, and especially of her primary achievement at Orleans, may perhaps be best proved by the testimony of her enemies. There is extant a fragment of a letter from the Regent Bedford to his royal nephew, Henry VI., in which he bewails the turn that the war has taken, and especially attributes it to the raising of the siege of Orleans by Joan. Bedford's own words, which are preserved in Rymer,[14] are as follows:

"And alle thing there prospered for you til the tyme of the Siege of Orleans taken in hand God knoweth by what advis.

"At the whiche tyme, after the adventure fallen to the persone of my cousin of Salisbury, whom God assoille, there felle, by the hand of God as it seemeth, a great strook upon your peuple that was assembled there in grete nombre, caused in grete partie, as y trowe, of lakke of sadde beleve, and of unlevefulle doubte, that thei hadde of a disciple and lyme of the Feende, called the Pucelle, that used fals enchantments and sorcerie.

"The whiche strooke and discomfiture nott oonly lessed in grete partie the nombre of your peuple there, but as well withdrewe the courage of the remenant in merveillous wyse, and couraiged your adverse partie and ennemys to assemble them forthwith in grete nombre."

When Charles had been anointed King of France, Joan believed that her mission was accomplished. And in truth, the deliverance of France from the English, though not completed for many years afterwards, was then insured. The ceremony of a royal coronation and anointment was not in those days regarded as a mere costly formality. It was believed to confer the sanction and the grace of Heaven upon the prince, who had previously ruled with mere human authority. Thenceforth he was the Lord's Anointed. Moreover, one of the difficulties that had previously lain in the way of many Frenchmen when called on to support Charles VII. was now removed. He had been publicly stigmatized, even by his own parents, as no true son of the royal race of France. The queen-mother, the English, and the partisans of Burgundy called him the "Pretender to the title of Dauphin"; but those who had been led to doubt his legitimacy were cured of their scepticism by the victories of the Holy Maid, and by the fulfilment of her pledges. They thought that Heaven had now declared itself in favor of Charles as the true heir of the crown of St. Louis, and the tales about his being spurious were thenceforth regarded as mere English calumnies. With this strong tide of national feeling in his favor, with victorious generals and soldiers round him, and a dispirited and divided enemy before him, he could not fail to conquer, though his own imprudence and misconduct, and the stubborn valor which the English still from time to time displayed, prolonged the war in France until the civil war of the Roses broke out in England, and left France to peace and repose.

Joan knelt before the French king in the cathedral of Rheims and shed tears of joy. She said that she had then fulfilled the work which the Lord had commanded her. The young girl now asked for her dismissal. She wished to return to her peasant home, to tend her parents' flocks again, and live at her own will in her native village.[15] She had always believed that her career would be a short one. But Charles and his captains were loath to lose the presence of one who had such an influence upon the soldiery and the people. They persuaded her to stay with the army. She still showed the same bravery and zeal for the cause of France. She still was as fervent as before in her prayers, and as exemplary in all religious duties. She still heard her Heavenly Voices, but she now no longer thought herself the appointed minister of Heaven to lead her countrymen to certain victory. Our admiration for her courage and patriotism ought to be increased a hundred fold by her conduct throughout the latter part of her career, amid dangers, against which she no longer believed herself to be divinely secured. Indeed, she believed herself doomed to perish in a little more than a year;[16] but she still fought on as resolutely, if not as exultingly as ever.

As in the case of Arminius, the interest attached to individual heroism and virtue makes us trace the fate of Joan of Arc after she had saved her country. She served well with Charles' army in the capture of Laon, Soissons, Compiègne, Beauvais, and other strong places; but in a premature attack on Paris, in September, 1429, the French were repulsed, and Joan was severely wounded. In the winter she was again in the field with some of the French troops, and in the following spring she threw herself into the fortress of Compiegne, which she had herself won for the French king in the preceding autumn, and which was now besieged by a strong Burgundian force.

She was taken prisoner in a sally from Compiegne, on the 24th of May, and was imprisoned by the Burgundians first at Arras, and then at a place called Crotoy, on the Flemish coast, until November, when, for payment of a large sum of money, she was given up to the English, and taken to Rouen, which then was their main stronghold in France.

> "Sorrow it were, and shame to tell,
> The butchery that there befell."

And the revolting details of the cruelties practised upon this young girl may be left to those whose duty, as avowed biographers, it is to describe them.[17] She was tried before an ecclesiastical tribunal on the charge of witchcraft, and on the 30th of May, 1431, she was burned alive in the market-place at Rouen.

I will add but one remark on the character of the truest heroine that the world has ever seen.

If any person can be found in the present age who would join in the scoffs of Voltaire against the Maid of Orleans and the Heavenly Voices by which she believed herself inspired, let him read the life of the wisest and best man that the heathen nations produced. Let him read of the Heavenly Voices by which Socrates believed himself to be constantly attended; which cautioned him on his way from the field of battle at Delium, and which, from his boyhood to the time of his death, visited him with unearthly warnings.[18] Let the modern reader reflect upon this; and then, unless he is prepared to term Socrates either fool or impostor, let him not dare to deride or villify Joan of Arc.

Synopsis of Events between Joan of Arc's Victory at Orleans, AD 1429, and the Defeat of the Spanish Armada, AD 1588.

AD 1452. Final expulsion of the English from France.

1453. Constantinople taken, and the Roman empire of the East destroyed by the Turkish Sultan Mohammed II.

1455. Commencement of the civil wars in England between the houses of York and Lancaster.

1479. Union of the Christian kingdoms of Spain under Ferdinand and Isabella.

1492. Capture of Grenada by Ferdinand and Isabella, and end of the Moorish dominion in Spain.

1492. Columbus discovers the New World.

1494. Charles VIII. of France invades Italy.

1497. Expedition of Vasco da Gama to the East Indies round the Cape of Good Hope.

1503. Naples conquered from the French by the great Spanish general, Gonsalvo of Cordova.

1508. League of Cambray by the Pope, the Emperor, and the King of France, against Venice.

1509. Albuquerque establishes the empire of the Portuguese in the East Indies.

1516. Death of Ferdinand of Spain; he is succeeded by his grandson Charles, afterwards the Emperor Charles V.

1517. Dispute between Luther and Tetzel respecting the sale of indulgences, which leads to the Reformation.

1519. Charles V. is elected Emperor of Germany.

1520. Cortez conquers Mexico.

1525. Francis First of Spain defeated and taken prisoner by the imperial army at Pavia.

1529. League of Smalcald formed by the Protestant princes of Germany.

1533. Henry VIII. renounces the papal supremacy.

1533. Pizarro conquers Peru.

1556. Abdication of the Emperor Charles V., Philip II. becomes King of Spain, and Ferdinand I. Emperor of Germany.

1557. Elizabeth becomes Queen of England.

1557. The Spaniards defeat the French at the battle of St Quentin.

1571. Don John of Austria, at the head of the Spanish fleet, aided by the Venetian and the papal squadrons, defeats the Turks at Lepanto.

1572. Massacre of the Protestants in France on St. Bartholomew's day.

1579. The Netherlands revolt against Spain.

1580. Philip II. conquers Portugal.

CHAPTER X

THE DEFEAT OF THE SPANISH
ARMADA, AD 1588

"In that memorable year, when the dark cloud gathered round our coasts, when Europe stood by in fearful suspense to behold what should be the result of that great cast in the game of human politics, what the craft of Rome, the power of Philip, the genius of Farnese could achieve against the island-queen, with her Drakes and Cecils— in that agony of the Protestant faith and English name."
—Hallam, Const. Hist., vol. i., p. 220.

ON the afternoon of the 19th of July, AD 1588, a group of English captains was collected at the Bowling Green on the Hoe at Plymouth, whose equals have never before or since been brought together, even at that favorite mustering place of the heroes of the British navy. There was Sir Francis Drake, the first English circumnavigator of the globe, the terror of every Spanish coast in the Old World and the New; there was Sir John Hawkins, the rough veteran of many a daring voyage on the African and American seas, and of many a desperate battle; there was Sir Martin Frobisher, one of the earliest explorers of the Arctic seas, in search of that Northwest Passage which is still the darling object of England's boldest mariners. There was the high admiral of England, Lord Howard of Effingham, prodigal of all things in his country's cause, and who had recently had the noble daring to refuse to dismantle part of the fleet, though the queen had sent him orders to do so, in consequence of an exaggerated report that the enemy had been driven back and shattered by a storm. Lord Howard (whom contemporary writers describe as being of a wise and noble courage, skilful in sea matters, wary and provident, and of great esteem among the sailors) resolved to risk his sovereign's anger, and to keep the ships afloat at his own charge, rather than that England should run the peril of losing their protection.

Another of our Elizabethan sea-kings, Sir Walter Raleigh, was at that time commissioned to raise and equip the land-forces of Cornwall; but we may well believe that he must have availed himself of the opportunity of consulting with the lord admiral and the other high officers, which was offered by the English fleet putting into Plymouth; and we may look on Raleigh as one of the group that was assembled at the Bowling Green on the Hoe. Many other brave men and skilful mariners, besides the chiefs whose names have been mentioned, were there, enjoying, with true sailor-like merriment, their temporary relaxation from duty. In the harbor lay the English fleet with which they had just returned from a cruise to Corunna in search of information respecting the real condition and movements of the hostile Armada. Lord Howard had ascertained that our enemies, though tempest-tossed, were still formidably strong; and fearing that part of their fleet might make for England in his absence, he had hurried back to the Devonshire coast. He resumed his station at Plymouth, and waited there for certain tidings of the Spaniard's approach.

A match at bowls was being played, in which Drake and other high officers of the fleet were engaged, when a small armed vessel was seen running before the wind into Plymouth harbor with all sails set. Her commander landed in haste, and eagerly sought the place where the English lord admiral and his captains were standing. His name was Fleming; he was the master of a Scotch privateer; and he told the English officers that he had that morning seen the Spanish Armada off the Cornish coast. At this exciting information the captains began to hurry down to the water, and there was a shouting for the ships' boats; but Drake coolly checked

THE DECISIVE ACTION WITH THE ARMADA
OFF GRAVELINES, JULY 30, 1588.

Photogravure from the original painting by Oswald W. Brierly.

his comrades, and insisted that the match should be played out. He said that there was plenty of time both to win the game and beat the Spaniards. The best and bravest match that ever was scored was resumed accordingly. Drake and his friends aimed their last bowls with the same steady, calculating coolness with which they were about to point their guns. The winning cast was made; and then they went on board and prepared for action with their hearts as light and their nerves as firm as they had been on the Hoe Bowling Green.

Meanwhile the messengers and signals had been despatched fast and far through England, to warn each town and village that the enemy had come at last. In every sea-port there was instant making ready by land and by sea; in every shire and every city there was instant mustering of horse and man.[1] But England's best defence then, as ever, was in her fleet; and after warping laboriously out of Plymouth harbor against the wind, the lord admiral stood westward under easy sail, keeping an anxious look-out for the Armada, the approach of which was soon announced by Cornish fisher-boats and signals from the Cornish cliffs.

The England of our own days is so strong, and the Spain of our own days is so feeble, that it is not easy, without some reflection and care, to comprehend the full extent of the peril which England then ran from the power and the ambition of Spain, or to appreciate the importance of that crisis in the history of the world. We had then no Indian or colonial empire, save the feeble germs of our North American settlements, which Raleigh and Gilbert had recently planted. Scotland was a separate kingdom; and Ireland was then even a greater source of weakness and a worse nest of rebellion than she has been in after times Queen Elizabeth had found at her accession an encumbered revenue, a divided people, and an unsuccessful foreign war, in which the last remnant of our possessions in France had been lost; she had also a formidable pretender to her crown, whose interests were favored by all the Roman Catholic powers; and even some of her subjects were warped by religious bigotry to deny her title, and to look on her as a heretical usurper. It is true that during the years of her reign which had passed away before the attempted invasion of 1588, she had revived the commercial prosperity, the national spirit, and the national loyalty of England. But her resources to cope with the colossal power of Philip II. still seemed most scanty; and she had not a single foreign ally, except the Dutch, who were themselves struggling hard, and, as it seemed, hopelessly, to maintain their revolt against Spain.

On the other hand, Philip II. was absolute master of an empire so superior to the other states of the world in extent, in resources, and especially in military and naval forces, as to make the project of enlarging that empire into a universal monarchy seem a perfectly feasible scheme; and Philip had both the ambition to form that project, and the resolution to devote all his energies and all his means to its realization. Since the downfall of the Roman empire no such preponderating power had existed in the world. During the mediæval centuries the chief European kingdoms were slowly moulding themselves out of the feudal chaos; and though the wars with each other were numerous and desperate, and several of their respective kings figured for a time as mighty conquerors, none of them in those times acquired the consistency and perfect organization which are requisite for a long-sustained career of aggrandizement After the consolidation of the great kingdoms, they for some time kept each other in mutual check. During the first half of the sixteenth century, the balancing system was successfully practised by European statesmen. But Philip II. reigned, France had become so miserably weak through her civil wars, that he had nothing to dread from the rival state which had so long curbed his father, the Emperor Charles V. In Germany, Italy, and Poland he had either zealous friends and dependents, or weak and divided enemies. Against the Turks he had gained great and glorious successes; and he might look round the continent of Europe without discerning a single antagonist of whom he could stand in awe. Spain, when he acceded to the throne, was at the zenith of her power. The hardihood and spirit which the Aragonese, the Castilians, and the other nations of the peninsula had acquired during centuries of free institutions and successful war against the Moors, had not yet become obliterated. Charles V. had, indeed, destroyed the liberties of Spain; but that had been done too recently for its full evil to be felt in Philip's time. A people cannot be debased in a single generation; and the Spaniards under Charles V. and Philip II. proved the truth of the remark, that no nation is ever so formidable to its neighbors for a time, as a nation which, after being trained up in self-government, passes suddenly under a despotic ruler. The energy of democratic institutions survives for a few generations, and to it are superadded the decision and certainty which are the attributes of government when all its powers are directed by a single mind. It is true that this preternatural vigor is short-lived: national corruption and debasement gradually follow the loss of the national liberties; but there is an interval before their workings are felt, and in that interval the most ambitious schemes of foreign conquest are often successfully undertaken.

Philip had also the advantage of finding himself at the head of a large standing army in a perfect state of discipline and equipment, in an age when, except some few insignificant corps, standing armies were unknown in Christendom. The renown of the Spanish troops was justly high, and the infantry in particular was considered the best in the world. His fleet, also, was far more numerous, and better appointed than that of any other European power; and both his soldiers and his sailors had the confidence in themselves and their commanders which a long career of successful warfare alone can create

Besides the Spanish crown, Philip succeeded to the kingdom of Naples and Sicily, the duchy of Milan, Franche-Comté, and the Netherlands. In Africa he possessed Tunis, Oran, the Cape Verde, and the Canary Islands; and in Asia, the Philippine and Sunda Islands, and a part of the Moluccas. Beyond the Atlantic he was lord of the most splendid portions of the New World, which Columbus found "for Castile and Leon" The empires of Peru and Mexico, New Spain, and Chili, with their abundant mines of the precious metals, Hispaniola and Cuba, and many other of the American islands, were provinces of the sovereign of Spain

Philip had, indeed, experienced the mortification of seeing the inhabitants of the Netherlands revolt against his authority, nor could he succeed in bringing back beneath the Spanish sceptre all the possessions which his father had bequeathed to him. But he had reconquered a large number of the towns and districts that originally took up arms against him. Belgium was brought more thoroughly into implicit obedience to Spain than she had been before her insurrection, and it was only Holland and the six other northern states that still held out against his arms The contest had also formed a compact and veteran army on Philip's side, which, under his great general, the Prince of Parma, had been trained to act together under all difficulties and all vicissitudes of warfare, and on whose steadiness and loyalty perfect reliance might be placed throughout any enterprise, however difficult and tedious, Alexander Farnese, prince of Parma, captain general of the Spanish armies, and governor of the Spanish possessions in the Netherlands, was beyond all comparison the greatest military genius of his age. He was also highly distinguished for political wisdom and sagacity, and for his great administrative talents. He was idolized by his troops, whose affections he knew how to win without relaxing their discipline or diminishing his own authority. Pre-eminently cool and circumspect in his plans, but swift and energetic when the moment arrived for striking a decisive blow, neglecting no risk that caution could provide against, conciliating even the populations of the districts which he attacked by his scrupulous good faith, his moderation, and his address, Farnese was one of the most formidable generals that ever could be placed at the head of an army designed not only to win battles, but to effect conquests. Happy it is for England and the world that this island was saved from becoming an arena for the exhibition of his powers.

Whatever diminution the Spanish empire might have sustained in the Netherlands seemed to be more than compensated by the acquisition of Portugal, which Philip had completely conquered in 1580. Not only that ancient kingdom itself, but all the fruits of the maritime enterprises of the Portuguese, had fallen into Philip's hands. All the Portuguese colonies in America, Africa, and the East Indies acknowledged the sovereignty of the King of Spain, who thus not only united the whole Iberian peninsula under his single sceptre, but had acquired a transmarine empire little inferior in wealth and extent to that which he had inherited at his accession. The splendid victory which his fleet, in conjunction with the papal and Venetian galleys, had gained at Lepanto over the Turks, had deservedly exalted the fame of the Spanish marine throughout Christendom; and when Philip had reigned thirty-five years, the vigor of his empire seemed unbroken, and the glory of the Spanish arms had increased, and was increasing throughout the world.

One nation only had been his active, his persevering, and his successful foe. England had encouraged his revolted subjects in Flanders against him, and given them the aid in men and money, without which they must soon have been humbled in the dust. English ships had plundered his colonies; had defied his supremacy in the New World as well as the Old; they had inflicted ignominious defeats on his squadrons; they had captured his cities, and burned his arsenals on the very coasts of Spain. The English had made Philip himself the object of personal insult. He was held up to ridicule in their stage-plays and masks, and these scoffs at the man had (as is not unusual in such cases) excited the anger of the absolute king even more vehemently than the injuries inflicted on his power.[2] Personal as well as political revenge urged him to attack England. Were she once subdued, the Dutch must submit; France could not cope with him, the empire would not oppose him; and universal dominion seemed sure to be the result of the conquest of that malignant island.

There was yet another and a stronger feeling which armed King Philip against England. He was one of the sincerest and one of the sternest bigots of his age. He looked on himself, and was looked on by others, as the appointed champion to extirpate heresy and re-establish the papal power throughout Europe. A powerful reaction against Protestantism had taken place since the commencement of the second half of the sixteenth century, and he looked on himself as destined to complete it. The Reformed doctrines had been thoroughly rooted out from Italy and Spain. Belgium, which had previously been half Protestant, had been reconquered both in allegiance and creed by Philip, and had become one of the most Catholic countries in the world. Half Germany had been won back to the old faith. In Savoy, in Switzerland, and in many other countries, the progress of the counter-Reformation had been rapid and decisive. The Catholic league seemed victorious in France. The papal court itself had shaken off the supineness of recent centuries, and at the head of the Jesuits and the other new ecclesiastical orders, was displaying a vigor and a boldness worthy of the days of Hildebrand, or Innocent III.

Throughout Continental Europe, the Protestants, discomfited and dismayed, looked to England as their protector and refuge. England was the acknowledged central point of Protestant power and policy; and to conquer England was to stab Protestantism to the very heart. Sixtus V., the then reigning pope, earnestly exhorted Philip to this enterprise. And when the tidings reached Italy and Spain that the Protestant Queen of England had put to death her Catholic prisoner, Mary Queen of Scots, the fury of the Vatican and Escurial knew no bounds. Elizabeth was denounced as the murderous heretic whose destruction was an instant duty. A formal treaty was concluded (in June, 1587), by which the pope bound himself to contribute a million of scudi to the expenses of the war; the money to be paid as soon as the king had actual possession of an English port. Philip, on his part, strained the resources of his vast empire to the utmost. The French Catholic chiefs eagerly co-operated with him. In the sea-ports of the Mediterranean, and along almost the whole coast from Gibraltar to Jutland, the preparations for the great armament were urged forward with all the earnestness of religious zeal as well as of angry ambition. "Thus," says the German historian of the popes,[3] "thus did the united powers of Italy and Spain, from which such mighty influences had gone forth over the whole world, now rouse themselves for an attack upon England! The king had already compiled, from the archives of Simancas, a statement of the claims which he had to the throne of that country on the extinction of the Stuart line; the most brilliant prospects, especially that of a universal dominion of the seas, were associated in his mind with this enterprise. Everything seemed to conspire to such an end; the predominancy of Catholicism in Germany, the renewed attack upon the Huguenots in France, the attempt upon Geneva, and the enterprise against England. At the same moment, a thoroughly Catholic prince, Sigismund III., ascended the throne of Poland, with the prospect also of future succession to the throne of Sweden. But whenever any principle or power, be it what it may, aims at unlimited supremacy in Europe, some vigorous resistance to it, having its origin in the deepest springs of human nature, invariably arises. Philip II. had to encounter newly-awakened powers, braced by the vigor of youth, and elevated by a sense of their future destiny. The intrepid corsairs, who had rendered every sea insecure, now clustered round the coasts of their native island. The Protestants in a body—even the Puritans, although they had been subjected to as severe oppressions as the Catholics—rallied round their queen, who now gave admirable proof of her masculine courage, and her princely talent of winning the affections, and leading the minds, and preserving the allegiance of men."

Ranke should have added that the English Catholics at this crisis proved themselves as loyal to their queen and true to their country as were the most vehement anti-Catholic zealots in the island. Some few traitors there were; but as a body, the Englishmen who held the ancient faith stood the trial of their patriotism nobly. The lord admiral himself was a Catholic, and (to adopt the words of Hallam) "then it was that the Catholics in every county repaired to the standard of the lord lieutenant, imploring that they might not be suspected of bartering the national independence for their religion itself." The Spaniard found no partisans in the country which he assailed, nor did England, self-wounded,

> "Lie at the proud foot of her enemy."

Each party at this time thought it politic to try to amuse its adversary by pretending to treat for peace, and negotiations were opened at Ostend in the beginning of 1588, which were prolonged during the first six months of that year. Nothing real was effected, and probably nothing real had been intended to be effected, by them.

Meanwhile in England, from the sovereign on the throne to the peasant in the cottage, all hearts and hands made ready to meet the imminent deadly peril. Circular letters from the queen were sent round to the lords lieutenant of the several counties, requiring them to "call together the best sort of gentlemen under their lieutenancy, and to declare unto them these great preparations and arrogant threatenings, now burst forth in action upon the seas, wherein every man's particular state, in the highest degree, could be touched in respect of country, liberty, wives, children, lands, lives, and (which was specially to be regarded) the profession of the true and sincere religion of Christ. And to lay before them the infinite and unspeakable miseries that would fall out upon any such change, which miseries were evidently seen by the fruits of that hard and cruel government holden in countries not far distant. We do look," said the queen, "that the most part of them should have, upon this instant extraordinary occasion, a larger proportion of furniture, both for horsemen and footmen, but especially horsemen, than hath been certified thereby to be in their best strength against any attempt, or to be employed about our own person, or otherwise. Hereunto as we doubt not but by your good endeavors they will be the rather conformable, so also we assure ourselves that Almighty God will so bless these their loyal hearts borne towards us, their loving sovereign, and their natural country, that all the attempts of any enemy whatsoever shall be made void and frustrate, to their confusion, your comfort, and to God's high glory."[4]

Letters of a similar kind were also sent by the council to each of the nobility, and to the great cities. The primate called on the clergy for their contributions; and by every class of the community the appeal was responded to with liberal zeal, that offered more even than the queen required. The boasting threats of the Spaniards had roused the spirit of the nation, and the whole people "were thoroughly irritated to stir up their whole forces for their defence against such prognosticated conquests; so that, in a very short time, all her whole realm, and every corner, were furnished with armed men, on horseback and on foot; and those continually trained, exercised, and put into bands in warlike manner, as in no age ever was before in this realm. There was no sparing of money to provide horse, armor, weapons, powder, and all necessaries; no, nor want of provision of pioneers, carriages, and victuals, in every county of the realm, without exception, to attend upon the armies. And to this general furniture every man voluntarily offered, very many their services personally without wages, others money for armor and weapons, and to wage soldiers; a matter strange, and never the like heard of in this realm or elsewhere. And this general reason moved all men to large contributions, that when a conquest was to be withstood wherein all should be lost, it was no time to spare a portion."[5]

Our lion-hearted queen showed herself worthy of such a people. A camp was formed at Tilbury; and there Elizabeth rode through the ranks, encouraging her captains and her soldiers by her presence and her words. One of the speeches which she addressed to them during this crisis has been preserved; and, though often quoted, it must not be omitted here.

"My loving people," she said, "we have been persuaded by some that are careful of our safety to take heed how we commit ourselves to armed multitudes, for fear of treachery; but I assure you I do not desire to live to distrust my faithful and loving people. Let tyrants fear! I have always so behaved myself, that, under God, I have placed my chiefest strength, and safeguard in the loyal hearts and good-will of my subjects; and, therefore, I am come among you, as you see, at this time, not for my recreation and disport, but being resolved, in the midst and heat of the battle, to live or die among you all, to lay down for my God, for my kingdom, and for my people, my honor and my blood even in the dust. I know I have the body but of a weak and feeble woman, but I have the heart and stomach of a king, and of a King of England, too, and think it foul scorn that Parma, or Spain, or any prince of Europe should dare to invade the borders of my realm, to which rather than any dishonor shall grow by me, I myself will take up arms, I myself will be your general, judge, and rewarder of every one of your virtues in the field. I know already, for your forwardness, you have deserved rewards and crowns; and we do assure you, on the word of a prince, they shall be duly paid you. In the mean time, my lieutenant general shall be in my stead, than whom never prince commanded a more noble or worthy subject, not doubting but by your obedience to my general, by your concord in the camp, and your valor in the field, we shall shortly have a famous victory over those enemies of my God, of my kingdom, and of my people."

Some of Elizabeth's advisers recommended that the whole care and resources of the government should be devoted to the equipment of the armies, and that the enemy, when he attempted to land, should be welcomed with a battle on the shore. But the wiser counsels of Raleigh and others prevailed, who urged the importance of fitting out a fleet that should encounter the Spaniards at sea, and, if possible, prevent them from approaching the land at all. In Raleigh's great work on the "History of the World," he takes occasion, when discussing some of the events of the first Punic war, to give his reasonings on the proper policy of England when menaced with invasion. Without doubt, we have there the substance of the advice which he gave to Elizabeth's council; and the remarks of such a man on such a subject have a general and enduring interest, beyond the immediate crisis which called them forth. Raleigh says:[6] "Surely I hold that the best way is to keep our enemies from treading upon our ground; wherein if we fail, then must we seek to make him wish that he had stayed at his own home. In such a case, if it should happen, our judgments are to weigh many particular circumstances, that belongs not unto this discourse. But making the question general, the positive, *Whether* England, *without the help of her fleet, be able to debar an enemy from landing,* I hold that it is unable so to do, and therefore I think it most dangerous to make the adventure; for the encouragement of a first victory to an enemy, and the discouragement of being beaten to the invaded, may draw after it a most perilous consequence.

"Great difference I know there is, and a diverse consideration to be had, between such a country as France is, strengthened with many fortified places, and this of ours, where our ramparts are but the bodies of men. But I say that an army to be transported over sea, and to be landed again in an enemy's country, and the place left to the choice of the invader, cannot be resisted on the coast of England without a fleet to impeach it; no, nor on the coast of France, or any other country, except every creek, port, or sandy bay had a powerful army in each of them to make opposition. For let the supposition be granted that Kent is able to furnish twelve thousand foot, and that those twelve thousand be layed in the three best landing-places within that country, to wit, three thousand at Margat, three thousand at the Nesse, and six thousand at Foulkstone, that is, somewhat equally distant from them both, as also that two of these troops (unless some other order be thought more fit) be directed to strengthen the third, when they shall see the enemy's fleet to head towards it: I say, that notwithstanding this provision, if the enemy, setting sail from the Isle of Wight, in the first watch of the night, and towing their long boats at their sterns, shall arrive by dawn of day at the Nesse, and thrust their army on shore there, it will be hard for those three thousand that are at Margat (twenty-and-four long miles from thence) to come time enough to re-enforce their fellows at the Nesse. Nay, how shall they at Foulkstone be able to do it, who are nearer by more than half the way? seeing that the enemy, at his first arrival, will either make his entrance by force, with three or four shot of great artillery, and quickly put the first three thousand that are intrenched at the Nesse to run, or else give them so much to do that they shall be glad to send for help to Foulkstone, and perhaps to Margat, whereby those places will be left bare. Now, let us suppose that all the twelve thousand Kentish soldiers arrive at the Nesse ere the enemy can be ready to disembarque his army, so that he will find it unsafe to land in the face of so many prepared to withstand him, yet must we believe that he will play the best of his own game (having liberty to go which way he list), and under covert of the night, set sail towards the east, where what shall hinder him to take ground either at Margat, the Downes, or elsewhere, before they at the Nesse can be well aware of his departure? Certainly there is nothing more easy than to do it. Yea, the like may be said of Weymouth, Purbeck, Poole, and of all landing-places on the southwest; for there is no man ignorant that ships, without putting themselves out of breath, will easily outrun the soldiers that coast them. '*Les armées ne volent point en poste,*' 'Armies neither fly, nor run post,' saith a marshal of France. And I know it to be true, that a fleet of ships may be seen at sunset, and after it at the Lizard, yet by the next morning they may recover Portland, whereas an army of foot shall not be able to march it in six dayes. Again, when those troops lodged on the sea-shores shall be forced to run from place to place in vain, after a fleet of ships, they will at length sit down in the midway, and leave all at adventure. But say it were otherwise, that the invading enemy will offer to land in some such place where there shall be an army of ours ready to receive him; yet it cannot be doubted but that when the choice of all our trained bands, and the choice of our commanders and captains, shall be drawn together (as they were at Tilbury in the year 1588) to attend the person of the prince, and for the defence of the city of London, they that remain to guard the

THE DEFEAT OF THE SPANISH ARMADA

THE DEFEAT OF THE SPANISH ARMADA

coast can be of no such force as to encounter an army like unto that wherewith it was intended that the Prince of Parma should have landed in England.

"For end of this digression, I hope that this question shall never come to trial: his majesty's many movable forts will forbid the experience. And although the English will no less disdain, than any nation under heaven can do, to be beaten upon their own ground, or elsewhere, by a foreign enemy, yet to entertain those that shall assail us, with their own beef in their bellies, and before they eat of our Kentish capons, I take it to be the wisest way; to do which his majesty, after God, will employ his good ships on the sea, and not trust in any intrenchment upon the shore."

The introduction of steam as a propelling power at sea has added ten-fold weight to these arguments of Raleigh. On the other hand, a well-constructed system of railways, especially of coast lines, aided by the operation of the electric telegraph, would give facilities for concentrating a defensive army to oppose an enemy on landing, and for moving troops from place to place in observation of the movements of the hostile fleet, such as would have astonished Sir Walter, even more than the sight of vessels passing rapidly to and fro without the aid of wind or tide. The observation of the French marshal, whom he quotes, is now no longer correct. Armies can be made to pass from place to place almost with the speed of wings, and far more rapidly than any post-travelling that was known in the Elizabethan or any other age. Still, the presence of a sufficient armed force at the right spot, at the right time, can never be made a matter of certainty, and even after the changes that have taken place, no one can doubt but that the policy of Raleigh is that which England should ever seek to follow in defensive war. At the time of the Armada, that policy certainly saved the country, if not from conquest, at least from deplorable calamities. If indeed the enemy had landed, we may be sure that he would have been heroically opposed. But history shows us so many examples of the superiority of veteran troops over new levies, however numerous and brave, that, without disparaging our countrymen's soldierly merits, we may well be thankful that no trial of them was then made on English land. Especially must we feel this when we contrast the high military genius of the Prince of Parma, who would have headed the Spaniards, with the imbecility of the Earl of Leicester, to whom the deplorable spirit of favoritism, which formed the great blemish on Elizabeth's character, had then committed the chief command of the English armies.

The ships of the royal navy at this time amounted to no more than thirty-six; but the most serviceable merchant vessels were collected from all the ports of the country; and the citizens of London, Bristol, and the other great seats of commerce showed as liberal a zeal in equipping and manning vessels as the nobility and gentry displayed in mustering forces by land. The seafaring population of the coast, of every rank and station, was animated by the same ready spirit; and the whole number of seamen who came forward to man the English fleet was 17,472. The number of the ships that were collected was 191, and the total amount of their tonnage 31,985. There was one ship in the fleet (the Triumph) of 1,100 tons, one of 1,000, one of 900, two of 800 each, three of 600, five of 500, five of 400, six of 300, six of 250, twenty of 200, and the residue of inferior burden. Application was made to the Dutch for assistance; and, as Stowe expresses it, "The Hollanders came roundly in, with threescore sail, brave ships of war, fierce and full of spleen, not so much for England's aid, as in just occasion for their own defence: these men foreseeing the greatness of the danger that might ensue if the Spaniards should chance to win the day and get the mastery over them; in due regard whereof, their manly courage was inferior to none."

We have more minute information of the number and equipment of the hostile forces than we have of our own. In the first volume of Hakluyt's "Voyages," dedicated to Lord Effingham, who commanded against the Armada, there is given (from the contemporary foreign writer, Meteran) a more complete and detailed catalogue than has perhaps ever appeared of a similar armament.

"A very large and particular description of this navie was put in print and published by the Spaniards, wherein were set downe the number, names, and burthens of the shippes, the number of mariners and soldiers throughout the whole fleete; likewise the quantitie of their ordinance, of their armor, of bullets, of match, of gun-poulder, of victuals, and of all their navall furniture was in the saide description particularized. Unto all these were added the names of the governours, captaines, noblemen, and gentlemen voluntaries, of whom there was so great a multitude, that scarce was there any family of accompt, or any one principall man throughout all Spaine, that had not a brother, sonne, or kinsman in that fleete; who all of them were in good hope to purchase unto themselves in that navie (as they termed it) invincible, endless glory and renown, and to possess themselves of great seigniories and riches in England and in the Low Countreys. But because the said description was translated and published out of Spanish into divers other languages, we will here only make an abridgement or brief rehearsal thereof.

"Portugall furnished and set foorth under the conduct of the Duke of Medina Sidonia, generall of the fleete, 10 galeons, 2 zabraes, 1300 mariners, 3300 souldiers, 300 great pieces, with all requisite furniture.

"Biscay, under the conduct of John Martines de Ricalde, admiral of the whole fleete, set forth 10 galeons, 4 pataches, 700 mariners, 2000 souldiers, 250 great pieces, &c.

"Guipusco, under the conduct of Michael de Oquendo, 10 galeons, 4 pataches, 700 mariners, 2000 souldiers, 310 great pieces.

"Italy, with the Levant islands, under Martine de Vertendona, 10 galeons, 800 mariners, 2000 souldiers, 310 great pieces, &c.

"Castile, under Diego Flores de Valdez, 14 galeons, 2 pataches, 1700 mariners, 2400 souldiers, and 380 great pieces, &c.

"Andaluzia, under the conduct of Petro de Valdez, 10 galeons, 1 patache, 800 mariners, 2400 souldiers, 280 great pieces, &c.

"Item, under the conduct of John Lopez de Medina, 23 great Flemish hulkes, with 700 mariners, 3200 souldiers, and 400 great pieces.

"Item, under Hugo de Moncada, 4 galliasses, containing 1200 gally-slaves, 460 mariners, 870 souldiers, 200 great pieces, &c.

"Item, under Diego de Mandrana, 4 gallies of Portugall, with 888 gally-slaves, 360 mariners, 20 great pieces, and other requisite furniture.

"Item, under Anthonie de Mendoza, 22 pataches and zabraes, with 574 mariners, 488 souldiers, and 193 great pieces.

"Besides the ships aforementioned, there were 20 caravels rowed with oares, being appointed to performe necessary services under the greater ships, insomuch that all the ships appertayning to this navie amounted unto the summe of 150, eche one being sufficiently provided of furniture and victuals.

"The number of mariners in the saide fleete were above 8000, of slaves 2088, of souldiers 20,000 (besides noblemen and gentlemen voluntaries), of great cast pieces 2600. The foresaid ships were of an huge and incredible capacitie and receipt, for the whole fleete was large enough to containe the burthen of 60,000 tunnes.

"The galeons were 64 in number, being of an huge bignesse, and very flately built, being of marvellous force also, and so high that they resembled great castles, most fit to defend themselves and to withstand any assault, but in giving any other ships the encounter farr inferiour unto the English and Dutch ships, which can with great dexteritie weild and turne themselves at all assayes. The upper worke of the said galeons was of thicknesse and strength sufficient to beare off musket-shot. The lower worke and the timbers thereof were out of measure strong, being framed of plankes and ribs foure or five foote in thicknesse, insomuch that no bullets could pierce them but such as were discharged hard at hand, which afterward prooved true, for a great number of bullets were founde to sticke fast within the massie substance of those thicke plankes. Great and well-pitched cables were twined about the masts of their shippes, to strengthen them against the battery of shot.

"The galliasses were of such bignesse that they contained within them chambers, chapels, turrets, pulpits, and other commodities of great houses. The galliasses were rowed with great oares, there being in eche one of them 300 slaves for the same purpose, and were able to do great service with the force of their ordinance. All these, together with the residue aforenamed, were furnished and beautified with trumpets, streamers, banners, warlike ensignes, and other such like ornaments.

"Their pieces of brazen ordinance were 1600, and of yron a 1000.

"The bullets thereto belonging were 120,000.

"Item of gun-poulder, 5600 quintals. Of matche, 1200 quintals. Of muskets and kaleivers, 7000. Of haleberts and partisans, 10,000.

"Moreover, they had great stores of canons, double-canons, culverings and field-pieces for land services.

"Likewise they were provided of all instruments necessary on land to conveigh and transport their furniture from place to place, as namely of carts, wheeles, wagons, &c. Also they had spades, mattocks, and baskets to set pioners on worke. They had in like sort great store of mules and horses, and whatsoever else was requisite for a land armie. They were so well stored of biscuit, that for the space of halfe a yeere they might allow eche person in the whole fleete halfe a quintall every moneth, whereof the whole summe amounteth unto an hundreth thousand quintals.

"Likewise of wine they had 147,000 pipes, sufficient also for halfe a yeere's expedition. Of bacon, 6500 quintals. Of cheese, 3000 quintals. Besides fish, rise, beanes, pease, oile, vinegar, &c.

"Moreover, they had 12,000 pipes of fresh water, and all other necessary provision, as namely candles, lanternes, lampes, sailes, hempe, oxe-hides, and lead, to stop holes that should be made with the battery of gunshot. To be short, they brought all things expedient, either for a fleete by sea, or for an armie by land.

"This navie (as Diego Pimentelli afterward confessed) was esteemed by the king himseife to containe 32,000 persons, and to cost him every day 30,000 ducates.

"There were in the said navie five terzaes of Spaniards (which terzaes the Frenchmen call regiments), under the command of five governours, termed by the Spaniards masters of the field, and among the rest there were many olde and expert souldiers chosen out of the garisons of Sicilie, Naples, and Terçera. Their captaines or colonels were Diego Pimentelli, Don Francisco de Toledo, Don Alonço de Luçon, Don Nicolas de Isia, Don Augustin de Mexia, who had eche of them thirty-two companies under their conduct. Besides the which companies, there were many bands also of Castilians and Portugals, every one of which had their peculiar governours, captains, officers, colors, and weapons."

While this huge armament was making ready in the southern ports of the Spanish dominions, the Duke of Parma, with almost incredible toil and skill, collected a squadron of war-ships at Dunkirk, and a large flotilla of other ships and of flat-bottomed boats for the transport to England of the picked troops, which were designed to be the main instruments in subduing England. Thousands of workmen were employed, night and day, in the construction of these vessels in the ports of Flanders and Brabant. One hundred of the kind called hendes, built at Antwerp, Bruges, and Ghent, and laden with provision and ammunition, together with sixty flat-bottomed boats, each capable of carrying thirty horses, were brought, by means of canals and fosses dug expressly for the purpose, to Nieuport and Dunkirk. One hundred smaller vessels were equipped at the former place, and thirty-two at Dunkirk, provided with twenty thousand empty barrels and with materials for making pontoons, for stopping up the harbors and raising forts and entrenchments. The army which these vessels were designed to convey to England amounted to thirty thousand strong, besides a body of four thousand cavalry, stationed at Courtroi, composed chiefly of the ablest veterans of Europe; invigorated by rest (the siege of Sluys having been the only enterprise in which they were employed during the last campaign) and excited by the hopes of plunder and the expectation of certain conquest.

Philip had been advised by the deserter, Sir William Stanley, not to attack England in the first instance, but first to effect a landing and secure a strong position in Ireland; his admiral, Santa Cruz, had recommended him to make sure, in the first instance, of some large harbor on the coast of Holland or Zealand, where the Armada, having entered the Channel, might find shelter in case of storm, and whence it could sail without difficulty for England; but Philip rejected both these counsels, and directed that England itself should be made the immediate object of attack; and on the 20th of May the Armada left the Tagus, in the pomp and pride of supposed invincibility, and amid the shouts of thousands who believed that England was already conquered. But, steering to the northward, and before it was clear of the coast of Spain, the Armada was assailed by a violent storm, and driven back with considerable damage to the ports of Biscay and Galicia. It had, however, sustained its heaviest loss before it left the Tagus, in the death of the veteran admiral Santa Cruz, who had been destined to guide it against England.

This experienced sailor, notwithstanding his diligence and success, had been unable to keep pace with the impatient ardor of his master. Philip II. had approached him with his dilatoriness, and had said, with ungrateful harshness, "You make an ill return for all my kindness to you." These words cut the veteran's heart, and proved fatal to Santa Cruz. Overwhelmed with fatigue and grief, he sickened and died. Philip II. had replaced him by Alonzo Perez de Gusman, Duke of Medina-Sidonia, one of the most powerful of the Spanish grandees, but wholly unqualified to command such an expedition. He had, however, as his lieutenants two seamen of proved skill and bravery, Juan de Martinez Recalde, of Biscay, and Miguel Oquendo, of Guipuzcoa.

The report of the storm which had taken back the Armada reached England with much exaggeration, and it was supposed by some of the queen's counsellors that the invasion would now be deferred to another year. But Lord Howard of Effingham, the lord high admiral of the English fleet, judged more wisely that the danger was not yet passed, and, as already mentioned, had the moral courage to refuse to dismantle his principal ships, though he received orders to that effect. But it was not Howard's design to keep the English fleet in costly inaction and to wait patiently in our own harbors till the Spaniards had recruited their strength and sailed forth again to attack us. The English seamen of that age (like their successors) loved to strike better than to parry, though, when emergency required, they could be patient and cautious in their bravery. It was resolved to proceed to Spain to learn the enemy's real condition, and to deal him any blow for which there might be opportunity. In this bold policy we may well believe him to have been eagerly seconded by those who commanded under him. Howard and Drake sailed accordingly to Corunna, hoping to surprise and attack some part of the Armada in that harbor; but when near the coast of Spain, the north wind, which had blown up to that time, veered suddenly to the south; and, fearing that the Spaniards might put to sea and pass him unobserved, Howard returned to the entrance of the Channel, where he cruised for some time on the lookout for the enemy. In part of a letter written by him at this period, he speaks of the difficulty of guarding so large a breadth of sea—a difficulty that ought not to be forgotten when modern schemes of defence against hostile fleets from the south are discussed. "I myself," he wrote, "do lie in the midst of the Channel, with the greatest force; Sir Francis Drake hath twenty ships and four or five pinnaces, which lie towards Ushant; and Mr. Hawkins, with as many more, lieth towards Scilly. Thus we are fain to do, or else with this wind they might pass us by, and we never the wiser. The Sleeve is another manner of thing than it was taken for: we find it by experience and daily observation to be 100 miles over—a large room tor me to look unto!" But, after some time, further reports that the Spaniards were inactive in their harbor, where they were suffering severely from sickness, caused Howard also to relax in his vigilance; and he returned to Plymouth with the greater part of his fleet.

On the 12th of July, the Armada, having completely refitted, sailed again for the Channel, and reached it without obstruction or observation by the English.

The design of the Spaniards was that the Armada should give them, at least for a time, the command of the sea, and that it should join the squadron that Parma had collected off Calais.

Then, escorted by an overpowering naval force, Parma and his army were to embark in their flotilla, and cross the sea to England, where they were to be landed, together with the troops which the Armada brought from the ports of Spain. The scheme was not dissimilar to one formed against England a little more than two centuries afterwards.

As Napoleon, in 1805, waited with his army and flotilla at Boulogne, looking for Villeneuve to drive away the English cruisers, and secure him a passage across the Channel, so Parma, in 1588, waited for Medina-Sidonia to drive away the Dutch and English squadrons that watched his flotilla, and to enable his veterans to cross the sea to the land that they were to conquer. Thanks to Providence, in each case England's enemy waited in vain!

Although the numbers of sail which the queen's government and the patriotic zeal of volunteers had collected for the defence of England exceeded the number of sail in the Spanish fleet, the English ships were, collectively, far inferior in size to their adversaries, their aggregate tonnage being less by half than that of the enemy. In the number of guns and weight of metal, the disproportion was still greater. The English admiral was also obliged to subdivide his force; and Lord Henry Seymour, with forty of the best Dutch and English ships, was employed in blockading the hostile ports in Flanders, and in preventing the Duke of Parma from coming out of Dunkirk.

The orders of King Philip to the Duke de Medina-Sidonia were, that he should, on entering the Channel, keep near the French coast, and, if attacked by the English ships, avoid an action and steer on to Calais Roads, where the Prince of Parma's squadron was to join him. The hope of surprising and destroying the English fleet in Plymouth led the Spanish admiral to deviate from these orders and to stand across to the English shore; but, on finding that Lord Howard was coming out to meet him, he resumed the original plan, and determined to bend his way steadily toward Calais and Dunkirk, and to keep merely on the defensive against such squadrons of the English as might come up with him.

It was on Saturday, the 20th of July, that Lord Effingham came in sight of his formidable adversaries. The Armada was drawn up in form of a crescent, which from horn to horn measured some seven miles. There was a southwest wind, and before it the vast vessels sailed slowly on. The English let them pass by, and then, following in the rear, commenced an attack on them. A running fight now took place, in which some of the best ships of the Spaniards were captured; many more received heavy damage, while the English vessels, which took care not to close with their huge antagonists, but availed themselves of their superior celerity in tacking and manoeuvring, suffered little comparative loss. Each day added not only to the spirit, but to the number of Effingham's force. Raleigh, Oxford, Cumberland, and Sheffield joined him; and "the gentlemen of England hired ships from all parts at their own charge, and with one accord came flocking thither as to a set field, where glory was to be attained, and faithful service performed unto their prince and their country."

Raleigh justly praises the English admiral for his skilful tactics. Raleigh says,[7] "Certainly, he that will happily perform a fight at sea must be skilful in making choice of vessels to fight in: he must believe that there is more belonging to a good man of war, upon the waters, than great daring; and must know, that there is a great deal of difference between fighting loose or at large and grappling. The guns of a slow ship pierce as well and make as great holes, as those in a swift. To clap ships together, without consideration, belongs rather to a madman than to a man of war; for by such an ignorant bravery was Peter Strossie lost at the Azores, when he fought against the Marquis of Santa Cruza. In like sort had the Lord Charles Howard, admiral of England, been lost in the year 1588, if he had not been better advised than a great many malignant fools were that found fault with his demeanor. The Spaniards had an army aboard them, and he had none; they had more ships than he had, and of higher building and charging; so that, had he entangled himself with those great and powerful vessels, he had greatly endangered this kingdom of England; for twenty men upon the defences are equal to a hundred that board and enter; whereas then, contrariwise, the Spaniards had a hundred, for twenty of ours, to defend themselves withal. But our admiral knew his advantage, and held it; which had he not done, he had not been worthy to have held his head up."

The Spanish admiral also showed great judgment and firmness in following the line of conduct that had been traced out for him; and on the 27th of July, he brought his fleet unbroken, though sorely distressed, to anchor in Calais Roads. But the King of Spain had calculated ill the number and the activity of the English and Dutch fleets; as the old historian expresses it, "It seemeth that the Duke of Parma and the Spaniards grounded upon a vain and presumptuous expectation, that all the ships of England and of the Low Countreys would at the first sight of the Spanish and Dunkirk navie have betaken themselves to flight, yeelding them sea-room, and endeavoring only to defend themselues, their havens, and sea-coasts from invasion. Wherefore their intent and purpose was, that the Duke of Parma, in his small and flat-bottomed ships, should, as it were under the shadow and wings of the Spanish fleet, convey over all his troupes, armor, and war-like provisions, and with their forces so united, should invade England; or while the English fleet were busied in fight against the Spanish, should enter upon any part of the coast, which he thought to be most convenient. Which invasion (as the captives afterward confessed) the Duke of Parma thought first to have attempted by the River of Thames; upon the bankes whereof having at the first arrivall landed twenty or thirty thousand of his principall souldiers, he supposed that he might easily have wonne the citie of London; both because his small shippes should have followed and assisted his land forces, and also for that the citie it-selfe was but meanely fortified and easie to ouercome, by reason of the citizens' delicacie and discontinuance from the warres, who, with continuall and constant labor, might be vanquished, if they yielded not at the first assault."[8]

But the English and Dutch found ships and mariners enough to keep the Armada itself in check, and at the same time to block up Parma's flotilla. The greater part of Seymour's squadron left its cruising-ground off Dunkirk to join the English admiral off Calais; but the Dutch manned about five-and-thirty sail of good ships, with a strong force of soldiers on board, all well seasoned to the sea-service, and with these they blockaded the Flemish ports that were in Parma's power. Still it was resolved by the Spanish admiral and the prince to endeavor to effect a junction, which the English seamen were equally resolute to prevent; and bolder measures on our side now became necessary.

The Armada lay off Calais, with its largest ships ranged outside, "like strong castles fearing no assault, the lesser placed in the middleward." The English admiral could not attack them in their position without great disadvantage, but on the night of the 29th he sent eight fire-ships among them, with almost equal effect to that of the fire-ships which the Greeks so often employed against the Turkish fleets in their late war of independence. The Spaniards cut their cables and put to sea in confusion. One of the largest galeasses ran foul of another vessel and was stranded. The rest of the fleet was scattered about on the Flemish coast, and when the morning broke, it was with difficulty and delay that they obeyed their admiral's signal to range themselves round him near Gravelines. Now was the golden opportunity for the English to assail them, and prevent them from ever letting loose Parma's flotilla against England, and nobly was that opportunity used. Drake and Fenner were the first English captains who attacked the unwieldly leviathans; then came Fenton, Southwell, Burton, Cross, Raynor, and then the lord admiral, with Lord Thomas Howard and Lord Sheffield. The Spaniards only thought of forming and keeping close together, and were driven by the English past Dunkirk, and far away from the Prince of Parma, who, in watching their defeat from the coast, must, as Drake expressed it, have chafed like a bear robbed of her whelps. This was indeed the last and the decisive battle between the two fleets. It is, perhaps, best described in the very words of the contemporary writer, as we may read them in Hakluyt.[9]

"Upon the 29 of July in the morning, the Spanish fleet after the forsayd tumult, having arranged themselues againe into order, were, within sight of Greveling, most bravely and furiously encountered by the English, where they once again got the wind of the Spaniards, who suffered themselues to be deprived of the commodity of the place in Caleis Road, and of the advantage of the wind neer unto Dunkerk, rather than they would change their array or separate their forces now conjoyned and united together, standing only upon their defence.

"And albeit there were many excellent and warlike ships in the English fleet, yet scarce were there 22 or 23 among them all, which matched 90 of the Spanish ships in the bigness, or could conveniently assault them. Wherefore the English shippes using their prerogative of nimble steerage, whereby they could turn and wield themselues with the wind which way they listed, came often times very near upon the Spaniards, and charged them so sore, that now and then they were but a pike's length asunder; and so continually giving them one broadside after another, they discharged all their shot, both great and small, upon them, spending one whole day, from morning till night, in that violent kind of conflict, untill such time as powder and bullets failed them. In regard of which want they thought it convenient not to pursue the Spaniards any longer, because they had many great vantages of the English, namely, for the extraordinary bigness of their shippes, and also for that they were so neerely conjoyned, and kept together in so good array, that they could by no meanes be fought withall one to one. The English thought, therefore, that they had right well acquitted themselues in chasing the Spaniards first from Caleis, and then from Dunkerk, and by that means to have hindered them from joyning with the Duke of Parma his forces, and getting the wind of them, to have driven them from their own coasts.

"The Spaniards that day sustained great loss and damage, having many of their shippes shot thorow and thorow, and they discharged likewise great store of ordinance against the English, who, indeed, sustained some hinderance, but not comparable to the Spaniard's loss; for they lost not any one ship or person of account; for very diligent inquisition being made, the Englishmen all that time wherein the Spanish navy sayled upon their seas, are not found to haue wanted aboue one hundred of their people; albeit Sir Francis Drake's ship was pierced with shot aboue forty times, and his very cabben was twice shot thorow, and about the conclusion of the fight, the bed of a certaine gentleman lying weary thereupon, was taken quite from under him with the force of a bullet. Likewise, as the Earle of Northumberland and Sir Charles Blunt were at dinner upon a time, the bullet of a demy-culvering brake thorow the middest of their cabben, touched their feet, and strooke downe two of the standers-by, with many such accidents befalling the English shippes, which it were tedious to rehearse."

It reflects little credit on the English government that the English fleet was so deficiently supplied with ammunition as to be unable to complete the destruction of the invaders. But enough was done to insure it. Many of the largest Spanish ships were sunk or captured in the action of this day. And at length the Spanish admiral, despairing of success, fled northward with a southerly wind, in the hope of rounding Scotland, and so returning to Spain without a farther encounter with the English fleet. Lord Effingham left a squadron to continue the blockade of the Prince of Parma's armament; but that wise general soon withdrew his troops to more promising fields of action. Meanwhile the lord admiral himself, and Drake, chased the vincible Armada, as it was now termed, for some distance northward; and then, when they seemed to bend away from the Scotch coast towards Norway, it was thought best, in the words of Drake, "to leave them to those boisterous and uncouth Northern seas."

The sufferings and losses which the unhappy Spaniards sustained in their flight round Scotland and Ireland are well known. Of their whole Armada only fifty-three shattered vessels brought back their beaten and wasted crews to the Spanish coast, which they had quitted in such pageantry and pride. Some passages from the writings of those who took part in the struggle have been already quoted, and the most spirited description of the defeat of the Armada which ever was penned may perhaps be taken from the letter which our brave Vice-Admiral Drake wrote in answer to some mendacious stories by which the Spaniards strove to hide their shame. Thus does he describe the scenes in which he played so important a part:[10]

"They were not ashamed to publish, in sundry languages in print, great victories in words, which they pretended to have obtained against this realm, and spread the same in a most false sort over all parts of France, Italy, and elsewhere; when, shortly afterward, it was happily manifested in very deed to all nations, how their navy, which they termed invincible, consisting of one hundred and forty sail of ships, not only of their own kingdom, but strengthened with the greatest argosies, Portugal carracks, Florentines, and large hulks of other countries, were by thirty of her majesty's own ships of war, and a few of our own merchants, by the wise, valiant, and advantageous conduct of the Lord Charles Howard, high admiral of England, beaten and shuffled together even from the Lizard in Cornwall, first to Portland, when they shamefully left Don Pedro de Valdez with his mighty ship; from Portland to Calais, where they lost Hugh de Moncado, with the galleys of which he was captain; and from Calais, driven with squibs from their anchors, were chased out of the sight of England, round about Scotland and Ireland; where, for the sympathy of their religion, hoping to find succor and assistance, a great part of them were crushed against the rocks, and those others that landed, being very many in number, were, notwithstanding, broken, slain, and taken, and so sent from village to village, coupled in halters to be shipped into England, where her majesty, of her princely and invincible disposition, disdaining to put them to death, and scorning either to retain or to entertain them, they were all sent back again to their countries, to witness and recount the worthy achievement of their invincible and dreadful navy. Of which the number of soldiers, the fearful burden of their ships, the commanders' names of every squadron, with all others, their magazines of provision, were put in print, as an army and navy irresistible and disdaining prevention; with all which their great and terrible ostentation, they did not in all their sailing round about England so much as sink or take one ship, barque, pinnace, or cock-boat of ours, or even burn so much as one sheep-cote on this land."

Synopsis of Events between the Defeat of the Spanish Armada, AD 1588, and the Battle of Blenheim, AD 1704.

AD 1594. Henry IV. of France conforms to the Roman Catholic Church, and ends the civil wars that had long desolated France.

1598. Philip II. of Spain dies, leaving a ruined navy and an exhausted kingdom.

1603. Death of Queen Elizabeth. The Scotch dynasty of the Stuarts succeeds to the throne of England.

1619. Commencement of the Thirty Years' War in Germany.

1624–1642. Cardinal Richelieu is minister of France. He breaks the power of the nobility, reduces the Huguenots to complete subjection, and by aiding the Protestant German princes in the latter part of the Thirty Years' War, he humiliates France's ancient rival, Austria.

1630. Gustavus Adolphus, King of Sweden, marches into Germany to the assistance of the Protestants, who were nearly crushed by the Austrian armies. He gains several great victories, and, after his death, Sweden, under his statesmen and generals, continues to take a leading part in the war.

1640. Portugal throws off the Spanish yoke; and the house of Braganza begins to reign.

1642. Commencement of the civil war in England between Charles I. and his Parliament.

1648. The Thirty Years' War in Germany ended by the treaty of Westphalia.

1653. Oliver Cromwell Lord Protector of England.

1660. Restoration of the Stuarts to the English throne.

1661. Louis XIV. takes the administration of affairs in France into his own hands.

1667–1668. Louis XIV. makes war on Spain, and conquers a large part of the Spanish Netherlands.

1672. Louis makes war upon Holland, and almost overpowers it. Charles II., of England, is his pensioner, and England helps the French in their attacks upon Holland until 1674. Heroic resistance of the Dutch under the Prince of Orange.

1674. Louis conquers Franche-Comté.

1679. Peace of Nimeguen.

1681. Louis invades and occupies Alsace.

1682. Accession of Peter the Great to the throne of Russia.

1685. Louis commences a merciless persecution of his Protestant subjects.

1688. The glorious Revolution in England. Expulsion of James II. William of Orange is made King of England. James takes refuge at the French court, and Louis undertakes to restore him. General war in the west of Europe.

1697. Treaty of Ryswick. Charles XII. becomes King of Sweden.

1700. Charles II., of Spain, dies, having bequeathed his dominions to Philip of Anjou, Louis XIV.'s grandson. Defeat of the Russians at Narva by Charles XII.

1701. William III. forms a "Grand Alliance" of Austria, the Empire, the United Provinces, England, and other powers, against France.

1702. King William dies; but his successor, Queen Anne, adheres to the Grand Alliance, and war is proclaimed against France.

CHAPTER XI

THE BATTLE OF BLENHEIM, AD 1704

"The decisive blow struck at Blenheim resounded through every part of Europe: it at once destroyed the vast fabric of power which it had taken Louis XIV., aided by the talents of Turenne and the genius of Vauban, so long to construct."

—*Alison.*

THOUGH more slowly moulded and less imposingly vast than the empire of Napoleon, the power which Louis XIV. had acquired and was acquiring at the commencement of the eighteenth century was almost equally menacing to the general liberties of Europe. If tested by the amount of *permanent* aggrandizement which each procured for France, the ambition of the royal Bourbon was more successful than were the enterprises of the imperial Corsican. All the provinces that Bonaparte conquered were rent again from France within twenty years from the date when the very earliest of them was acquired. France is not stronger by a single city or a single acre for all the devastating wars of the Consulate and the Empire. But she still possesses Franche-Comté, Alsace, and part of Flanders. She has still the extended boundaries which Louis XIV. gave her; and the royal Spanish marriages a few years ago proved clearly how enduring has been the political influence which the arts and arms of France's "Grand Monarque" obtained for her southward of the Pyrenees.

When Louis XIV. took the reins of government into his own hands, after the death of Cardinal Mazarin, there was a union of ability with opportunity such as France had not seen since the days of Charlemagne. Moreover, Louis' career was no brief one. For upwards of forty years, for a period nearly equal to the duration of Charlemagne's reign, Louis steadily followed an aggressive and a generally successful policy. He passed a long youth and manhood of triumph before the military genius of Marlborough made him acquainted with humiliation and defeat. The great Bourbon lived too long. He should not have outstayed our two English kings, one his dependent, James II., the other his antagonist, William III. Had he died when they died, his reign would be cited as unequalled in the French annals for its prosperity. But he lived on to see his armies beaten, his cities captured and his kingdom wasted year after year by disastrous war. It is as if Charlemagne had survived to be defeated by the Northmen, and to witness the misery and shame that actually fell to the lot of his descendants.

Still, Louis XIV. had forty years of success; and from the permanence of their fruits, we may judge what the results would have been if the last fifteen years of his reign had been equally fortunate. Had it not been for Blenheim, all Europe might at this day suffer under the effect of French conquests resembling those of Alexander in extent and those of the Romans in durability.

When Louis XIV. began to govern, he found all the materials for a strong government ready to his hand. Richelieu had completely tamed the turbulent spirit of the French nobility, and had subverted the "imperium in imperio" of the Huguenots. The faction of the Frondeurs in Mazarin's time had had the effect of making the Parisian Parliament utterly hateful and contemptible in the eyes of the nation. The Assemblies of the States-General were obsolete. The royal authority alone remained. The king was the state. Louis knew his position. He fearlessly avowed it, and he fearlessly acted up to it.[1]

Not only was his government a strong one, but the country which he governed was strong—strong in its geographical situation, in the compactness of its territory, in the number and martial spirit of its inhabitants, and in their complete and undivided nationality. Louis had neither a Hungary nor an Ireland in his dominions. The civil war in the Cévennes was caused solely by his own persecuting intolerance; and that did not occur till late in his reign, when old age had made his bigotry more gloomy, and had given fanaticism the mastery over prudence.

Like Napoleon in after times, Louis XIV, saw clearly that the great wants of France were "ships, colonies, and commerce." But Louis did more than see these wants: by the aid of his great minister, Colbert, he supplied them. One of the surest proofs of the genius of Louis was his skill in finding out genius in others and his promptness in calling it into action. Under him, Louvois organized, Turenne, Condé, Villars, and Berwick led the armies of France, and Vauban fortified her frontiers. Throughout his reign, French diplomacy was marked by skilfulness and activity, and also by comprehensive farsightedness, such as the representatives of no other nation possessed. Guizot's testimony to the vigor that was displayed through every branch of Louis XIV.'s government, and to the extent to which France at present is indebted to him, is remarkable. He says that, "taking the public services of every kind, the finances, the departments of roads and public works, the military administration, and all the establishments which belong to every branch of administration, there is not one that will not be found to have had its origin, its development, or its greatest perfection under the reign of Louis XIV."[2] And he points out to us that "the government of Louis XIV. was the first that presented itself to the eyes of Europe as a power acting upon sure grounds, which had not to dispute its existence with inward enemies, but was at ease as to its territory and its people, and solely occupied with the task of administering government, properly so called. All the European governments had been previously thrown into incessant wars, which deprived them of all security as well as of all leisure, or so pestered by internal parties or antagonists that their time was passed in fighting for existence. The government of Louis XIV. was the first to appear as a busy, thriving administration of affairs, as a power at once definitive and progressive, which was not afraid to innovate, because it could reckon securely on the future. There have been, in fact, very few governments equally innovating. Compare it with a government of the same nature, the unmixed monarchy of Philip II. in Spain; it was more absolute than that of Louis XIV., and yet it was far less regular and tranquil. How did Philip II. succeed in establishing absolute power in Spain? By stifling all activity in the country, opposing himself to every species of amelioration, and rendering the state of Spain completely stagnant. The government of Louis XIV., on the contrary, exhibited alacrity for all sorts of innovations, and showed itself favorable to the progress of letters, arts, wealth—in short, of civilization. This was the veritable cause of its preponderance in Europe, which arose to such a pitch, that it became the type of a government, not only to sovereigns, but also to nations, during the seventeenth century."

While France was thus strong and united in herself, and ruled by a martial, an ambitious, and (with all his faults) an enlightened and high-spirited sovereign, what European power was there fit to cope with her or keep her in check?

"As to Germany, the ambitious projects of the German branch of Austria had been entirely defeated, the peace of the empire had been restored, and almost a new constitution formed, or an old revived, by the treaties of Westphalia; *nay, the imperial eagle was not only fallen, but her wings were clipped.*"[3]

As to Spain, the Spanish branch of the Austrian house had sunk equally low. Philip II. left his successors a ruined monarchy. He left them something worse; he left them his example and his principles of government, founded in ambition, in pride, in ignorance, in bigotry, and all the pedantry of state.[4]

It is not, therefore, to be wondered at, that France, in the first war of Louis XIV., despised the opposition of both branches of the once predominant house of Austria. Indeed, in Germany, the French king acquired allies among the princes of the empire against the emperor himself. He had a still stronger support in

Austria's misgovernment of her own subjects. The words of Bolingbroke on this are remarkable, and some of them sound as if written within the last three years. Bolingbroke says, "It was not merely the want of cordial cooperation among the princes of the empire that disabled the emperor from acting with vigor in the cause of his family then, nor that has rendered the house of Austria a dead weight upon all her allies ever since. Bigotry, and its inseparable companion, cruelty, as well as the tyranny and avarice of the court of Vienna, created in those days, and has maintained in ours, almost a perpetual diversion of the imperial arms from all effectual opposition to France. *I mean to speak of the troubles in Hungary. Whatever they became in their progress, they were caused originally by the usurpations and persecutions of the emperor; and when the Hungarians were called rebels first, they were called so for no other reason than this, that they would not be slaves.* The dominion of the emperor being less sup-portable than that of the Turks, this unhappy people opened a door to the latter to infest the empire, instead of making their country, what it had been before, a barrier against the Ottoman power. France became a sure though secret ally of the Turks as well as the Hungarians, and has found her account in it by keeping the emperor in perpetual alarms on that side, while she has ravaged the empire and the Low Countries on the other."[5]

If, after having seen the imbecility of Germany and Spain against the France of Louis XIV., we turn to the two only remaining European powers of any importance at that time, to England and to Holland, we find the position of our own country as to European politics, from 1660 to 1688, most painful to contemplate; nor is our external history during the last twelve years of the eighteenth century by any means satisfactory to national pride, though it is infinitely less shameful than that of the preceding twenty-eight years. From 1660 to 1668, "England, by the return of the Stuarts, was reduced to a nullity." The words are Michelet's,[6] and, though severe, they are just. They are, in fact, not severe enough; for when England, under her restored dynasty of the Stuarts, did take any part in European politics, her conduct, or, rather, her king's conduct, was almost invariably wicked and dishonorable.

Bolingbroke rightly says that, previous to the revolution of 1688, during the whole progress that Louis XIV. made towards acquiring such exorbitant power as gave him well-grounded hopes of acquiring at last to his family the Spanish monarchy, England had been either an idle spectator of what passed on the Continent, or a faint and uncertain ally against France, or a warm and sure ally on her side, or a partial mediator between her and the powers confederated together in their common defence. But though the court of England submitted to abet the usurpations of France, and the King of England stooped to be her pensioner, the crime was not national. On the contrary, the nation cried out loudly against it, even while it was committing.[7]

Holland alone, of all the European powers, opposed from the very beginning a steady and uniform resistance to the ambition and power of the French king. It was against Holland that the fiercest attacks of France were made, and, though often apparently on the eve of complete success, they were always ultimately baffled by the stubborn bravery of the Dutch, and the heroism of their great leader, William of Orange. When he became King of England, the power of this country was thrown decidedly into the scale against France; but though the contest was thus rendered less unequal, though William acted throughout "with invincible firmness, like a patriot and a hero,"[8] France had the general superiority in every war and in every treaty; and the commencement of the eighteenth century found the last league against her dissolved, all the forces of the confederates against her dispersed and many disbanded; while France continued armed, with her veteran forces by sea and land increased, and held in readiness to act on all sides, whenever the opportunity should arise for seizing on the great prizes which, from the very beginning of his reign, had never been lost sight of by her king.

This is not the place for any narrative of the first essay which Louis XIV. made of his power in the war of 1667; of his rapid conquest of Flanders and Franche-Comté; of the treaty of Aix-la-Chapelle, which "was nothing more than a composition between the bully and the bullied";[9] of his attack on Holland in 1672; of the districts and barrier towns of the Spanish Netherlands, which were secured to him by the treaty of Nimeguen in 1678; of how, after this treaty, he "continued to vex both Spain and the empire, and to extend his conquests in the Low Countries and on the Rhine, both by the pen and the sword; how he took Luxembourg by force, stole Strasburg, and bought Casal"; of how the league of Augsburg was formed against him in 1686, and the election of William of Orange to the English throne in 1688 gave a new spirit to the opposition which France encountered; of the long and checkered war that followed, in which the French armies were generally victorious on the Continent, though his fleet was beaten at La Hogue, and his dependent, James II., was defeated at the Boyne; or of the treaty of Ryswick, which left France in possession of Roussillon, Artois, and Strasburg, which gave Europe no security against her claims on the Spanish succession, and which Louis regarded as a mere truce, to gain breathing-time before a more decisive struggle. It must be borne in mind that the ambition of Louis in these wars was two-fold. It had its immediate and its ulterior objects. Its immediate object was to conquer and annex to France the neighboring provinces and towns that were most convenient for the increase of her strength; but the ulterior object of Louis, from the time of his marriage to the Spanish Infanta in 1659, was to acquire for the house of Bourbon the whole empire of Spain. A formal renunciation of all right to the Spanish succession had been made at the time of the marriage; but such renunciations were never of any practical effect, and many casuists and jurists of the age even held them to be intrinsically void. As the time passed on, and the prospect of Charles II. of Spain dying without lineal heirs became more and more certain, so did the claims of the house of Bourbon to the Spanish crown after his death become matters of urgent interest to French ambition on the one hand, and to the other powers of Europe on the other. At length the unhappy King of Spain died. By his will he appointed Philip, Duke of Anjou, one of Louis XIV.'s grandsons, to succeed him on the throne of Spain, and strictly forbade any partition of his dominions. Louis well knew that a general European war would follow if he accepted for his house the crown thus bequeathed. But he had been preparing for this crisis throughout his reign. He sent his grandson into Spain as King Philip V. of that country, addressing to him, on his departure, the memorable words, "There are no longer any Pyrenees."

The empire, which now received the grandson of Louis as its king, comprised, besides Spain itself, the strongest part of the Netherlands, Sardinia, Sicily, Naples, the principality of Milan, and other possessions in Italy, the Philippines and Manilla Islands in Asia, and, in the New World, besides California and Florida, the greatest part of Central and of Southern America. Philip was well received in Madrid, where he was crowned as King Philip V. in the beginning of 1701. The distant portions of his empire sent in their adhesion; and the house of Bourbon, either by its French or Spanish troops, now had occupation both of the kingdom of Francis I. and of the fairest and amplest portions of the empire of the great rival of Francis, Charles V.

Loud was the wrath of Austria, whose princes were the rival claimants of the Bourbons for the empire of Spain. The indignation of our William III., though not equally loud, was far more deep and energetic. By his exertions, a league against the house of Bourbon was formed between England, Holland, and the Austrian emperor, which was subsequently joined by the Kings of Portugal and Prussia, by the Duke of Savoy, and by Denmark. Indeed, the alarm throughout Europe was now general and urgent. It was evident that Louis aimed at consolidating France and the Spanish dominions into one preponderating empire. At the moment when Philip was departing to take possession of Spain, Louis had issued letters-patent in his favor to the effect of preserving his rights to the throne of France. And Louis had himself obtained possession of the important frontier of the Spanish Netherlands with its numerous fortified cities, which were given up to his troops under pretence of securing them for the young King of Spain. Whether the formal union of the two crowns was likely to take place speedily or not, it was evident that the resources of the whole Spanish monarchy were now virtually at the French king's disposal.

The peril that seemed to menace the empire, England, Holland, and the other independent powers, is well summed up by Alison —"Spain had threatened the liberties of Europe in the end of the sixteenth century, France had all but overthrown them in the close of the seventeenth. What hope was there of their being able to make head against them both, united under such a monarch as Louis XIV.?"[10]

Our knowledge of the decayed state into which the Spanish power had fallen ought not to make us regard their alarms as chimerical. Spain possessed enormous resources, and her strength was capable of being regenerated by a vigorous ruler. We should remember what Alberoni effected even after the close of the War of Succession. By what that minister did in a few years, we may judge what Louis XIV. would have done in restoring the maritime and military power of that great country, which nature had so largely gifted, and which man's misgovernment had SO debased.

The death of King William, on the 8th of March, 1702, at first seemed likely to paralyze the league against France; "for notwithstanding the ill success with which he made war generally, he was looked upon as the sole centre of union that could keep together the great confederacy then forming; and how much the French feared from his life had appeared a few years before, in the extravagant and indecent joy they expressed on a false report of his death. A short time showed how vain the fears of some and the hopes of others were."[11] Queen Anne, within three days after her accession, went down to the House of Lords, and there declared her resolution to support the measures planned by her predecessor, who had been "the great support, not only of these kingdoms, but of all Europe." Anne was married to Prince George of Denmark, and by her accession to the English throne the confederacy against Louis obtained the aid of the troops of Denmark; but Anne's strong attachment to one of her female friends led to far more important advantages to the anti-Gallican confederacy than the acquisition of many armies, for it gave them Marl-borough as their captain-general.

There are few successful commanders on whom Fame has shone so unwillingly as upon John Churchill, Duke of Marl-borough, prince of the Holy Roman Empire, victor of Blenheim, Ramillies, Oudenarde, and Malplaquet, captor of Liege, Bonn, Limburg, Landau, Ghent, Bruges, Antwerp, Oudenarde, Ostend, Menin, Dendermonde, Ath, Lille, Tournay, Mons, Douay, Aire, Bethune, and Bouchain; who never fought a battle that he did not win, and never besieged a place that he did not take. Marlborough's own character is the cause of this. Military glory may, and too often does, dazzle both contemporaries and posterity, until the crimes as well as the vices of heroes are forgotten. But even a few stains of personal meanness will dim a soldiers reputation irreparably; and Marlborough's faults were of a peculiarly base and mean order. Our feelings towards historical personages are in this respect like our feelings towards private acquaintances. There are actions of that shabby nature, that however much they may be outweighed by a man's good deeds on a general estimate of his character, we never can feel any cordial liking for the person who has once been guilty of them. Thus, with respect to the Duke of Marlborough, it goes against our feelings to admire the man who owed his first advancement in life to the court favor which he and his family acquired through his sister becoming one of the mistresses of the Duke of York. It is repulsive to know that Marlborough laid the foundation of his wealth by being the paid lover of one of the fair and frail favorites of Charles II.[12] His treachery, and his ingratitude to his patron and benefactor, James II., stand out in dark relief even in that age of thankless perfidy. He was almost equally disloyal to his new master, King William; and a more un-English act cannot be recorded than Godolphin's and Marlborough's betrayal to the French court in 1694 of the expedition then designed against Brest, a piece of treachery which caused some hundreds of English soldiers and sailors to be helplessly slaughtered on the beach in Cameret Bay.

It is, however, only in his military career that we have now to consider him; and there are very few generals, of either ancient or modern times, whose campaigns will bear a comparison with those of Marlborough, either for the masterly skill with which they were planned, or for the bold yet prudent energy with which each plan was carried into execution. Marlborough had served while young under Turenne, and had obtained the marked praise of that great tactician. It would be difficult, indeed, to name a single quality which a general ought to have, and with which Marlborough was not eminently gifted. What principally attracted the notice of contemporaries was the imperturbable evenness of his spirit. Voltaire[13] says of him:

"He had, to a degree above all other generals of his time, that calm courage in the midst of tumult, that serenity of soul in danger, which the English call *a cool head* [que les Anglais appellent *cold head, tête froide*], and it was, perhaps, this quality, the greatest gift of nature for command, which formerly gave the English so many advantages over the French in the plains of Cressy, Poictiers, and Agincourt."

King William's knowledge of Marlborough's high abilities, though he knew his faithlessness equally well, is said to have caused that sovereign in his last illness to recommend Marl-borough to his successor as the fittest person to command her armies; but Marlborough's favor with the new queen, by means of his wife, was so high, that he was certain of obtaining the highest employment; and the war against Louis opened to him a glorious theatre for the display of those military talents, which he had previously only had an opportunity of exercising in a subordinate character, and on far less conspicuous scenes.

He was not only made captain-general of the English forces at home and abroad, but such was the authority of England in the council of the Grand Alliance, and Marlborough was so skilled in winning golden opinions from all whom he met with, that, on his reaching the Hague, he was received with transports of joy by the Dutch, and it was agreed by the heads of that republic, and the minister of the emperor, that Marl-borough should have the chief command of all the allied armies.

It must, indeed, in Justice to Marlborough, be borne in mind that mere military skill was by no means all that was required of him in this arduous and invidious station. Had it not been for his unrivalled patience and sweetness of temper, and his marvellous ability in discerning the character of those whom he had to act with, his intuitive perception of those who were to be thoroughly trusted, and of those who were to be amused with the mere semblance of respect and confidence; had not Marlborough possessed and employed, while at the head of the allied armies, all the qualifications of a polished courtier and a great statesman, he never would have led the allied armies to the Danube. The confederacy would not have held together for a single year. His great political adversary, Bolingbroke, does him ample justice here. Bolingbroke, after referring to the loss which King William's death seemed to inflict on the cause of the allies, observes that, "By his death the Duke of Marlborough was raised to the head of the army, and, indeed, of the confederacy; where he, a new, a private man, a subject, acquired by merit and by management a more deciding influence than high birth, confirmed authority, and even the crown of Great Britain had given to King William. Not only all the parts of that vast machine, the Grand Alliance, were kept more compact and entire, but a more rapid and vigorous motion was given to the whole; and, instead of languishing and disastrous campaigns, we saw every scene of the war full of action. All those wherein he appeared, and many of those wherein he was not then an actor, but abettor, however, of their action, were crowned with the most triumphant success.

"I take with pleasure this opportunity of doing justice to that great man, whose faults I knew, whose virtues I admired; and whose memory, as the greatest general and the greatest minister that our country, or perhaps any other, has produced, I honor."[14]

War was formally declared by the allies against France on the 4th of May, 1702. The principal scenes of its operation were, at first, Flanders, the Upper Rhine, and North Italy. Marlborough headed the allied troops in Flanders during the first two years of the war, and took some towns from the enemy, but nothing decisive occurred. Nor did any actions of importance take place during this period between the rival armies in Italy. But in the centre of that line from north to south, from the mouth of the Scheldt to the mouth of the Po, along which the war was carried on, the generals of Louis XIV. acquired advantages in 1703 which threatened one chief member of the Grand Alliance with utter destruction. France had obtained the important assistance of Bavaria as her confederate in the war. The elector of this powerful German state made himself master of the strong fortress of Ulm, and opened a communication with the French armies on the Upper Rhine. By this junction, the troops of Louis were enabled to assail the emperor in the very heart of Germany. In the autumn of the year 1703, the comoined armies of the elector and French king completely defeated the Imperialists in Bavaria; and in the following winter they made themselves masters of the important cities of Augsburg and Passau. Meanwhile the French army of the Upper Rhine and Moselle had beaten the allied armies opposed to them, and taken Trêves and Landau. At the same time, the discontents in Hungary with Austria again broke out into open insurrection, so as to distract the attention and complete the terror of the emperor and his council at Vienna.

Louis XIV. ordered the next campaign to be commenced by his troops on a scale of grandeur and with a boldness of enterprise such as even Napoleon's military schemes have seldom equalled. On the extreme left of the line of the war, in the Netherlands, the French armies were to act only on the defensive.

The fortresses in the hands of the French there were so many and so strong that no serious impression seemed likely to be made by the allies on the French frontier in that quarter during one campaign, and that one campaign was to give France such triumphs elsewhere as would (it was hoped) determine the war. Large detachments were therefore to be made from the French force in Flanders, and they were to be led by Marshal Villeroy to the Moselle and Upper Rhine. The French army already in the neighborhood of those rivers was to march under Marshal Tallard through the Black Forest, and join the Elector of Bavaria, and the French troops that were already with the elector under Marshal Marsin. Meanwhile the French army of Italy was to advance through the Tyrol into Austria, and the whole forces were to combine between the Danube and the Inn. A strong body of troops was to be despatched into Hungary, to assist and organize the insurgents in that kingdom; and the French grand army of the Danube was then in collected and irresistible might to march upon Vienna, and dictate terms of peace to the emperor. High military genius was shown in the formation of this plan, but it was met and baffled by a genius higher still.

Marlborough had watched, with the deepest anxiety, the progress of the French arms on the Rhine and in Bavaria, and he saw the futility of carrying on a war of posts and sieges in Flanders, while death-blows to the empire were being dealt on the Danube. He resolved, therefore, to let the war in Flanders languish for a year, while he moved with all the disposable forces that he could collect to the central scenes of decisive operations. Such a march was in itself difficult; but Marlborough had, in the first instance, to overcome the still greater difficulty of obtaining the consent and cheerful cooperation of the allies, especially of the Dutch, whose frontier it was proposed thus to deprive of the larger part of the force which had hitherto been its protection. Fortunately, among the many slothful, the many foolish, the many timid, and the not few treacherous rulers, statesmen, and generals of different nations with whom he had to deal, there were two men, eminent both in ability and integrity, who entered fully into Marlborough's projects, and who, from the stations which they occupied, were enabled materially to forward them. One of these was the Dutch statesman Heinsius, who had been the cordial supporter of King William, and who now, with equal zeal and good faith, supported Marlborough in the councils of the allies; the other was the celebrated general, Prince Eugene, whom the Austrian cabinet had recalled from the Italian frontier to take the command of one of the emperor's armies in Germany. To these two great men, and a few more, Marlborough communicated his plan freely and unreservedly; but to the general councils of his allies he only disclosed part of his daring scheme. He proposed to the Dutch that he should march from Flanders to the Upper Rhine and Moselle with the British troops and part of the foreign auxiliaries, and commence vigorous operations against the French armies in that quarter, while General Auverquerque, with the Dutch and the remainder of the auxiliaries, maintained a defensive war in the Netherlands. Having with difficulty obtained the consent of the Dutch to this portion of his project, he exercised the same diplomatic zeal, with the same success, in urging the King of Prussia, and other princes of the empire, to increase the number of the troops which they supplied, and to post them in places convenient for his own intended movements.

Marlborough commenced his celebrated march on the 19th of May. The army which he was to lead had been assembled by his brother, General Churchill, at Bedburg, not far from Maestricht, on the Meuse: it included sixteen thousand English troops, and consisted of fifty-one battalions of foot and ninety-two squadrons of horse. Marlborough was to collect and join with him on his march the troops of Prussia, Luneburg, and Hesse, quartered on the Rhine, and eleven Dutch battalions that were stationed at Rothweil.[15] He had only marched a single day, when the series of interruptions, complaints, and requisitions from the other leaders of the allies began, to which he seemed subjected throughout his enterprise, and which would have caused its failure in the hands of any one not gifted with the firmness and the exquisite temper of Marlborough. One specimen of these annoyances and of Marlborough's mode of dealing with them, may suffice. On his encamping at Kupen on the 20th, he received an express from Auverquerque pressing him to halt, because Villeroy, who commanded the French army in Flanders, had quitted the lines which he had been occupying, and crossed the Meuse at Namur with thirty-six battalions and forty-five squadrons, and was threatening the town of Huys. At the same time Marlborough received letters from the Margrave of Baden and Count Wratislaw, who commanded the Imperialist forces at Stollhoffen, near the left bank of the Rhine, stating that Tallard had made a movement, as if intending to cross the Rhine, and urging him to hasten his march towards the lines of Stollhoffen. Marlborough was not diverted by these applications from the prosecution of his grand design. Conscious that the army of Villeroy would be too much reduced to undertake offensive operations, by the detachments which had already been made towards the Rhine, and those which must follow his own march, he halted only a day to quiet the alarms of Auverquerque. To satisfy also the margrave, he ordered the troops of Hompesch and Bulow to draw towards Philipsburg, though with private injunctions not to proceed beyond a certain distance. He even exacted a promise to the same effect from Count Wratislaw, who at the juncture arrived at the camp to attend him during the whole campaign.[16]

Marlborough reached the Rhine at Coblentz, where he crossed that river, and then marched along its left bank to Broubach and Mentz. His march, though rapid, was admirably conducted, so as to save the troops from all necessary fatigue; ample supplies of provisions were ready, and the most perfect discipline was maintained. By degrees Marlborough obtained more re-enforcements from the Dutch and the other confederates, and he also was left more at liberty by them to follow his own course. Indeed, before even a blow was struck, his enterprise had paralyzed the enemy, and had materially relieved Austria from the pressure of the war.

Villeroy, with his detachments from the French Flemish army, was completely bewildered by Marlborough's movements; and, unable to divine where it was that the English general meant to strike his blow, wasted away the early part of the summer between Flanders and the Moselle without effecting anything.[17]

Marshal Tallard, who commanded forty-five thousand French at Strasburg, and who had been destined by Louis to march early in the year into Bavaria, thought that Marl-borough's march along the Rhine was preliminary to an attack upon Alsace; and the marshal therefore kept his forty-five thousand men back in order to protect France in that quarter. Marlborough skilfully encouraged his apprehensions, by causing a bridge to be constructed across the Rhine at Philipsburg, and by making the Landgrave of Hesse advance his artillery at Manheim, as if for a siege of Landau. Meanwhile the Elector of Bavaria and Marshal Marsin, suspecting that Marlborough's design might be what it really proved to be, forbore to press upon the Austrians opposed to them, or to send troops into Hungary; and they kept back so as to secure their communications with France. Thus, when Marlborough, at the beginning of June, left the Rhine and marched for the Danube, the numerous hostile armies were uncombined and unable to check him.

"With such skill and science had this enterprise been concerted that at the very moment when it assumed a specific direction the enemy was no longer enabled to render it abortive. As the march was now to be bent towards the Danube, notice was given for the Prussians, Palatines, and Hessians, who were stationed on the Rhine, to order their march so as to join the main body in its progress. At the same time directions were sent to accelerate the advance of the Danish auxiliaries, who were marching from the Netherlands."[18]

Crossing the River Neckar, Marlborough marched in a southeastern direction to Mundelshene, where he had his first personal interview with Prince Eugene, who was destined to be his colleague on so many glorious fields. Thence, through a difficult and dangerous country, Marlborough continued his march against the Bavarians, whom he encountered on the 2d of July on the heights of the Schullenberg, near Donauwert. Marlborough stormed their intrenched camp, crossed the Danube, took several strong places in Bavaria, and made himself completely master of the elector's dominions, except the fortified cities of Munich and Augsburg. But the elector's army, though defeated at Donauwert, was still numerous and strong; and at last Marshal Tallard, when thoroughly apprised of the real nature of Marlborough's movements, crossed the Rhine; and being suffered, through the supineness of the German general at Stollhoffen, to march without loss through the Black Forest, he united his powerful army at Biberbach, near Augsburg, with that of the elector and the French troops under Marshal Marsin, who had previously co-operating with the Bavarians.

On the other hand, Marlborough recrossed the Danube, and on the 11th of August united his army with the Imperialist forces under Prince Eugene. The combined armies occupied a position near Hochstadt, a little higher up the left bank of the Danube than Donauwert, the scene of Marlborough's recent victory, and almost exactly on the ground where Marshal Villars and the elector had defeated an Austrian army in the preceding year. The French marshals and the elector were now in position a little farther to the east, between Blenheim and Lutzingen, and with the little stream of the Nebel between them and the troops of Marlborough and Eugene. The Gallo-Bavarian army consisted of about sixty thousand men, and they had sixty-one pieces of artillery. The army of the allies was about fifty-six thousand strong, with fifty-two guns.

Although the French army of Italy had been unable to penetrate into Austria, and although the masterly strategy of Marlborough had hitherto warded off the destruction with which the cause of the allies seemed menaced at the beginning of the campaign, the peril was still more serious. It was absolutely necessary for Marlborough to attack the enemy before Villeroy should be roused into action. There was nothing to stop that general and his army from marching into Franconia, whence the allies drew their principal supplies; and besides thus distressing them, he might, by marching on and joining his army to those of Tallard and the elector, form a mass which would overwhelm the force under Marlborough and Eugene. On the other hand, the chances of a battle seemed perilous, and the fatal consequences of a defeat were certain. The disadvantage of the allies in point of number was not very great, but still it was not to be disregarded; and the advantage which the enemy seemed to have in the composition of their troops was striking. Tallard and Marsin had forty-five thousand Frenchmen under them, all veterans and all trained to act together; the elector's own troops also were good soldiers. Marlborough, like Wellington at Waterloo, headed an army, of which the larger proportion consisted not of English, but of men of many different nations and many different languages. He was also obliged to be the assailant in the action, and thus to expose his troops to comparatively heavy loss at the commencement of the battle, while the enemy would fight under the protection of the villages and lines which they were actively engaged in strengthening. The consequences of a defeat of the confederated army must have broken up the Grand Alliance, and realized the proudest hopes of the French king. Mr. Alison, in his admirable military history of the Duke of Marlborough, has truly stated the effects which would have taken place if France had been successful in the war; and when the position of the confederates at the time when Blenheim was fought is remembered—when we recollect the exhaustion of Austria, the menacing insurrection of Hungary, the feuds and jealousies of the German princes, the strength and activity of the Jacobite party in England, and the imbecility of nearly all the Dutch statesmen of the time, and the weakness of Holland if deprived of her allies, we may adopt his words in speculating on what would have ensued if France had been victorious in the battle, and "if a power, animated by the ambition, guided by the fanaticism, and directed by the ability of that of Louis XIV., had gained the ascendancy in Europe. Beyond all question, a universal despotic dominion would have been established over the bodies, a cruel spiritual thraldom over the minds, of men. France and Spain united under Bourbon princes and in a close family alliance—the empire of Charlemagne with that of Charles V.—the power which revoked the Edict of Nantes and perpetrated the massacre of St. Bartholomew, with that which banished the Moriscoes and established the Inquisition, would have proved irresistible, and beyond example destructive to the best interests of mankind.

"The Protestants might have been driven, like the pagan heathens of old by the son of Pepin, beyond the Elbe; the Stuart race, and with them Romish ascendancy, might have been re-established in England; the fire lighted by Latimer and Ridley might have been extinguished in blood; and the energy breathed by religious freedom into the Anglo-Saxon race might have expired. The destinies of the world would have been changed. Europe, instead of a variety of independent states, whose mutual hostility kept alive courage, while their national rivalry stimulated talent, would have sunk into the slumber attendant on universal dominion. The colonial empire of England would have withered away and perished, as that of Spain has done in the grasp of the Inquisition. The Anglo-Saxon race would have been arrested in its mission to overspread the earth and subdue it. The centralized despotism of the Roman empire would have been renewed on Continental Europe; the chains of Romish tyranny, and with them the general infidelity of France before the Revolution, would have extinguished or perverted thought in the British Islands."[19]

Marlborough's words at the council of war, when a battle was resolved on, are remarkable, and they deserve recording. We know them on the authority of his chaplain, Mr. (afterward Bishop) Hare, who accompanied him throughout the campaign, and in whose journal the biographers of Marlborough have found many of their best materials. Marlborough's words to the officers who remonstrated with him on the seeming temerity of attacking the enemy in their position were, "I know the danger, yet a battle is absolutely necessary, and I rely on the bravery and discipline of the troops, which will make amends for our disadvantages." In the evening orders were issued for a general engagement, and received by the army with an alacrity which justified his confidence.

The French and Bavarians were posted behind a little stream called the Nebel, which runs almost from north to south into the Danube immediately in front of the village of Blenheim. The Nebel flows along a little valley, and the French occupied the rising ground to the west of it. The village of Blenheim was the extreme right of their position, and the village of Lutzingen, about three miles north of Blenheim, formed their left. Beyond Lutzingen are the rugged high grounds of the Godd Berg and Eich Berg, on the skirts of which some detachments were posted, so as to secure the Gallo-Bavarian position from being turned on the left flank. The Danube secured their right flank; and it was only in front that they could be attacked. The villages of Blenheim and Lutzingen had been strongly palisaded and intrenched; Marshal Tallard, who held the chief command, took his station at Blenheim; the elector and Marshal Marsin commanded on the left. Tallard garrisoned Blenheim with twenty-six battalions of French infantry and twelve squadrons of French cavalry. Marsin and the elector had twenty-two battalions of infantry and thirty-six squadrons of cavalry in front of the village of Lutzingen. The centre was occupied by fourteen battalions of infantry, including the celebrated Irish brigade. These were posted in the little hamlet of Oberglau, which lies somewhat nearer to Lutzingen than to Blenheim. Eighty squadrons of cavalry and seven battalions of foot were ranged between Oberglau and Blenheim. Thus the French position was very strong at each extremity, but was comparatively weak in the centre. Tallard seems to have relied on the swampy state of the part of the valley that reaches from below Oberglau to Blenheim for preventing any serious attack on this part of his line.

The army of the allies was formed into two great divisions, the largest being commanded by the duke in person, and being destined to act against Tallard, while Prince Eugene led the other division, which consisted chiefly of cavalry, and was intended to oppose the enemy under Marsin and the elector. As they approached the enemy, Marlborough's troops formed the left and the centre, while Eugene's formed the right of the entire army. Early in the morning of the 13th of August the allies left their own camp and marched towards the enemy. A thick haze covered the ground, and it was not until the allied right and centre had advanced nearly within cannon shot of the enemy that Tallard was aware of their approach. He made his preparations with what haste he could, and about eight o'clock a heavy fire of artillery was opened from the French right on the advancing left wing of the British. Marl-borough ordered up some of his batteries to reply to it, and while the columns that were to form the allied left and centre deployed, and took up their proper stations in the line, a warm cannonade was kept up by the guns on both sides.

The ground which Eugene's columns had to traverse was peculiarly difficult, especially for the passage of the artillery, and it was nearly mid-day before he could get his troops into line opposite to Lutzingen. During this interval, Marlborough ordered divine service to be performed by the chaplains at the head of each regiment, and then rode alone the lines, and found both officers and men in the highest spirits, and waiting impatiently for the signal for the attack. At length an aide-de-camp galloped up from the right with the welcome news that Eugene was ready. Marlborough instantly sent Lord Cutts, with a strong brigade of infantry, to assault the village of Blenheim, while he himself led the main body down the eastward slope of the valley of the Nebel, and prepared to effect the passage of the stream.

The assault on Blenheim, though bravely made, was repulsed with severe loss, and Marlborough, finding how strongly that village was garrisoned, desisted from any further attempts to carry it, and bent all his energies to breaking the enemy's line between

Blenheim and Oberglau. Some temporary bridges had been prepared, and planks and fascines had been collected; and by the aid of these, and a little stone bridge which crossed the Nebel, near a hamlet called Unterglau, that lay in the centre of the valley, Marlborough succeeded in getting several squadrons across the Nebel, though it was divided into several branches, and the ground between them was soft, and, in places, little better than a mere marsh. But the French artillery was not idle. The cannon balls plunged incessantly among the advancing squadrons of the allies, and bodies of French cavalry rode frequently down from the western ridge, to charge them before they had time to form on the firm ground. It was only by supporting his men by fresh troops, and by bringing up infantry, who checked the advance of the enemy's horse by their steady fire, that Marlborough was able to save his army in this quarter from a repulse, which, succeeding the failure of the attack upon Blenheim, would probably have been fatal to the allies. By degrees, his cavalry struggled over the bloodstained streams; the infantry were also now brought across, so as to keep in check the French troops who held Blenheim, and who, when no longer assailed in front, had begun to attack the allies on their left with considerable effect.

Marlborough had thus at last succeeded in drawing up the whole left wing of his army beyond the Nebel, and was about to press forward with it, when he was called away to another part of the field by a disaster that had befallen his centre. The Prince of Holstein-Beck had, with eleven Hanoverian battalions, passed the Nebel opposite to Oberglau, when he was charged and utterly routed by the Irish brigade which held that village. The Irish drove the Hanoverians back with heavy slaughter, broke completely through the line of the allies, and nearly achieved a success as brilliant as that which the same brigade afterwards gained at Fontenoy. But at Blenheim their ardor in pursuit led them too far. Marlborough came up in person, and dashed in upon the exposed flank of the brigade with some squadrons of British cavalry. The Irish reeled back, and as they strove to regain the height of Oberglau, their column was raked through and through by the fire of three battalions of the allies, which Marlborough had summoned up from the reserve. Marlborough having re-established the order and communications of the allies in this quarter, now, as he returned to his own left wing, sent to learn how his colleague fared against Marsin and the elector, and to inform Eugene of his own success.

Eugene had hitherto not been equally fortunate. He had made three attacks on the enemy opposed to him, and had been thrice driven back. It was only by his own desperate personal exertions, and the remarkable steadiness of the regiments of Prussian infantry, which were under him, that he was able to save his wing from being totally defeated. But it was on the southern part of the battlefield, on the ground which Marlborough had won beyond the Nebel with such difficulty, that the crisis of the battle was to be decided.

Like Hannibal, Marlborough relied principally on his cavalry for achieving his decisive successes, and it was by his cavalry that Blenheim, the greatest of his victories, was won. The battle had lasted till five in the afternoon. Marlborough had now eight thousand horsemen drawn up in two lines, and in the most perfect order for a general attack on the enemy's line along the space between Blenheim and Oberglau. The infantry was drawn up in battalions in their rear, so as to support them if repulsed, and to keep in check the large masses of the French that still occupied the village of Blenheim. Tallard now interlaced his squadrons of cavalry with battalions of infantry, and Marlborough, by a corresponding movement, brought several regiments of infantry and some pieces of artillery to his front line at intervals between the bodies of horse. A little after five, Marlborough commenced the decisive movement, and the allied cavalry, strengthened and supported by foot and guns, advanced slowly from the lower ground near the Nebel up the slope to where the French cavalry, ten thousand strong, awaited them. On riding over the summit of the acclivity, the allies were received with so hot a fire from the French artillery and small arms that at first the cavalry recoiled, but without abandoning the high ground. The guns and the infantry which they had brought with them maintained the contest with spirit and effect. The French fire seemed to slacken. Marlborough instantly ordered a charge along the line. The allied cavalry galloped forward at the enemy's squadrons, and the hearts of the French horsemen failed them. Discharging their carbines at an idle distance, they wheeled round and spurred from the field, leaving the nine infantry battalions of their comrades to be ridden down by the torrent of the allied cavalry. The battle was now won. Tallard and Marsin, severed from each other, thought only of retreat. Tallard drew up the squadrons of horse that he had left, in a line extended towards Blenheim, and sent orders to the infantry in that village to leave it and join him without delay. But, long ere his orders could be obeyed, the conquering squadrons of Marlborough had wheeled to the left and thundered down on the feeble array of the French marshal. Part of the force which Tallard had drawn up for this last effort was driven into the Danube; part fled with their general to the village of Senderheim, where they were soon surrounded by the victorious allies, and compelled to surrender. Meanwhile, Eugene had renewed his attack upon the Gallo-Bavarian left, and Marsin, finding his colleague utterly routed, and his own right flank uncovered prepared to retreat. He and the elector succeeded in withdrawing a considerable part of their troops in tolerable order to Dillingen; but the large body of French who garrisoned Blenheim were left exposed to certain destruction. Marlborough speedily occupied all the outlets from the village with his victorious troops, and then, collecting his artillery round it, he commenced a cannonade that speedily would have destroyed Blenheim itself and all who were in it. After several gallant but unsuccessful attempts to cut their way through the allies, the French in Blenheim were at length compelled to surrender at discretion; and twenty-four battalions and twelve squadrons, with all their officers, laid down their arms, and became the captives of Marlborough.

"Such," says Voltaire, "was the celebrated battle which the French called the battle of Hochstet, the Germans Plentheim, and the English Blenheim. The conquerors had about five thousand killed and eight thousand wounded, the greater part being on the side of Prince Eugene. The French army was almost entirely destroyed: of sixty thousand men, so long victorious, there never reassembled more than twenty thousand effective. About twelve thousand killed, fourteen thousand prisoners, all the cannon, a prodigious number of colors and standards, all the tents and equipages, the general of the army, and one thousand two hundred officers of mark in the power of the conqueror, signalized that day!"

Ulm, Landau, Trêves, and Traerbach surrendered to the allies before the close of the year. Bavaria submitted to the emperor, and the Hungarians laid down their arms. Germany was completely delivered from France, and the military ascendancy of the arms of the allies was completely established. Throughout the rest of the war Louis fought only in defence. Blenheim had dissipated forever his once proud visions of almost universal conquest.

Synopsis of Events between the Battle of Blenheim, AD 1704, and the Battle of Pultowa, AD 1709.

AD 1705. The Archduke Charles lands in Spain with a small English army under Lord Peterborough, who takes Barcelona.

1706. Marlborough's victory at Ramillies.

1707. The English army in Spain is defeated at the battle of Almanza.

1708. Marlborough's victory at Oudenarde.

CHAPTER XII

THE BATTLE OF PULTOWA, AD 1709

"Dread Pultowa's day,
When fortune left the royal Swede,
Around a slaughtered army lay,
No more to combat and to bleed.
The power and fortune of the war
Had passed to the triumphant Czar."

—*Byron.*

NAPOLEON prophesied, at St. Helena, that all Europe would soon be either Cossack or republican. Three years ago the fulfilment of the last of these alternatives appeared most probable. But the democratic movements of 1848 were sternly repressed in 1849. The absolute authority of a single ruler and the austere stillness of martial law are now paramount in the capitals of the Continent, which lately owned no sovereignty save the will of the multitude, and where that which the Democrat calls his sacred right of insurrection was so loudly asserted and so often fiercely enforced. Many causes have contributed to bring about this reaction, but the most effective and the most permanent have been Russian influence and Russian arms. Russia is now the avowed and acknowledged champion of monarchy against democracy; of constituted authority, however acquired, against revolution and change, for whatever purpose desired; of the imperial supremacy of strong states over their weaker neighbors against all claims for political independence and all strivings for separate nationality. She had crushed the heroic Hungarians; and Austria, for whom nominally she crushed them, is now one of her dependents. Whether the rumors of her being about to engage in fresh enterprises be well or ill founded, it is certain that recent events must have fearfully augmented the power of the Muscovite empire, which, even previously, had been the object of well-founded anxiety to all Western Europe.

It was truly stated, eleven years ago, that "the acquisitions which Russia has made within the [then] last sixty-four years are equal in extent and importance to the whole empire she had in Europe before that time; that the acquisitions she has made from Sweden are greater than what remains of that ancient kingdom; that her acquisitions from Poland are as large as the whole Austrian empire; that the territory she has wrested from Turkey in Europe is equal to the dominions of Prussia, exclusive of her Rhenish provinces; and that her acquisitions from Turkey in Asia are equal in extent to all the smaller states of Germany, the Rhenish provinces of Prussia, Belgium, and Holland taken together; that the country she has conquered from Persia is about the size of England; that her acquisitions in Tartary have an area equal to Turkey in Europe, Greece, Italy, and Spain. In sixty-four years she has advanced her frontier eight hundred and fifty miles towards Vienna, Berlin, Dresden, Munich, and Paris; she has approached four hundred and fifty miles nearer to Constantinople; she has possessed herself of the capital of Poland, and has advanced to within a few miles of the capital of Sweden, from which, when Peter the First mounted the throne, her frontier was distant three hundred miles. Since that time she has stretched herself forward about one thousand miles towards India, and the same distance towards the capital of Persia."[1]

Such, at that period, had been the recent aggrandizement of Russia; and the events of the last few years, by weakening and disuniting all her European neighbors, have immeasurably augmented the relative superiority of the Muscovite empire over all the other Continental powers.

With a population exceeding sixty millions, all implicitly obeying the impulse of a single ruling mind; with a territorial area of six millions and a half of square miles; with a standing army eight hundred thousand strong; with powerful fleets on the Baltic and Black seas; with a skilful host of diplomatic agents planted in every court and among every tribe; with the confidence which unexpected success creates, and the sagacity which long experience fosters, Russia now grasps, with an armed right hand, the tangled thread of European politics, and issues her mandates as the arbitress of the movements of the age. Yet a century and a half have hardly elapsed since she was first recognized as a member of the drama of modern European history—previous to the battle of Pultowa, Russia played no part. Charles V. and his great rival, our Elizabeth and her adversary Philip of Spain, the Guises, Sully, Richelieu, Cromwell, De Witt, William of Orange, and the other leading spirits of the sixteenth and seventeenth centuries, thought no more about the Muscovite Czar than we now think about the King of Timbuctoo. Even as late as 1735, Lord Bolingbroke, in his admirable "Letters on History," speaks of the history of the Muscovites as having no relation to the knowledge which a practical English statesman ought to acquire.[2] It may be doubted whether a cabinet council often takes place now in our Foreign Office without Russia being uppermost in every English statesman's thoughts.

But, though Russia remained thus long unheeded among her snows, there *was* a Northern power, the influence of which was acknowledged in the principal European quarrels, and whose good-will was sedulously courted by many of the boldest chiefs and ablest counsellors of the leading states. This was Sweden; Sweden, on whose ruins Russia has risen, but whose ascendancy over her semi-barbarous neighbor was complete, until the fatal battle that now forms our subject.

As early as 1542 France had sought the alliance of Sweden to aid her in her struggle against Charles V. And the name of Gustavus Adolphus is of itself sufficient to remind us that in the great contest for religious liberty, of which Germany was for thirty years the arena, it was Sweden that rescued the falling cause of Protestantism, and it was Sweden that principally dictated the remodelling of the European state-system at the peace of Westphalia.

From the proud pre-eminence in which the valor of the "Lion of the North," and of Torstenston, Bannier, Wrangel, and the other generals of Gustavus, guided by the wisdom of Oxenstiern, had placed Sweden, the defeat of Charles XII. at Pultowa hurled her down at once and forever. Her efforts during the wars of the French Revolution to assume a leading part in European politics met with instant discomfiture, and almost provoked derision. But the Sweden whose sceptre was bequeathed to Christina, and whose alliance Cromwell valued so highly, was a different power to the Sweden of the present day. Finland, Ingria, Livonia, Esthonia, Carelia, and other districts east of the Baltic then were Swedish provinces; and the possession of Pomerania, Rugen, and Bremen made her an important member of the Germanic empire. These territories are now all reft from her, and the most valuable of them form the staple of her victorious rival's strength. Could she resume them — could the Sweden of 1648 be reconstructed, we should have a first-class Scandinavian state in the North, well qualified to maintain the balance of power, and check the progress of Russia; whose power, indeed, never could have become formidable to Europe save by Sweden becoming weak.

The decisive triumph of Russia over Sweden at Pultowa was therefore all-important to the world, on account of what it overthrew as well as for what it established; and it is the more deeply interesting, because it was not merely the crisis of a struggle between two states, but it was a trial of strength between two great races of mankind. We must bear in mind, that while the Swedes, like the English, the Dutch, and others, belong to the Germanic race, the Russians are a Sclavonic people. Nations of Sclavonian origin have long occupied the greater part of Europe eastward of the Vistula; and the populations also of Bohemia, Croatia, Servia, Dalmatia, and other important regions westward of that river are

Sclavonic. In the long and varied conflicts between them and the Germanic nations that adjoin them, the Germanic race had, before Pultowa, almost always maintained a superiority. With the single but important exception of Poland, no Sclavonic state had made any considerable figure in history before the time when Peter the Great won his great victory over the Swedish king.[3] What Russia has done since that time we know and we feel. And some of the wisest and best men of our own age and nations, who have watched with deepest care the annals and the destinies of humanity, have believed that the Sclavonic element in the population of Europe has as yet only partially developed its powers; that, while other races of mankind (our own, the Germanic, included) have exhausted their creative energies and completed their allotted achievements, the Sclavonic race has yet a great career to run; and that the narrative of Slavonic ascendency is the remaining page that will conclude the history of the world.[4]

Let it not be supposed that in thus regarding the primary triumph of Russia over Sweden as a victory of the Sclavonic over the Germanic race, we are dealing with matters of mere ethnological pedantry, or with themes of mere speculative curiosity. The fact that Russia is a Sclavonic empire is a fact of immense practical influence at the present moment. Half the inhabitants of the Austrian empire are Sclavonians. The population of the larger part of Turkey in Europe is of the same race. Silesia, Posen, and other parts of the Prussian dominions are principally Sclavonic. And during late years, an enthusiastic zeal for blending all Sclavonians into one great united Sclavonic empire has been growing up in these countries, which, however we may deride its principle, is not the less real and active, and of which Russia, as the head and the champion of the Sclavonic race, knows well how to take her advantage.[5]

It is a singular fact that Russia owes her very name to a band of Swedish invaders who conquered her a thousand years ago. They were soon absorbed in the Sclavonic population, and every trace of the Swedish character had disappeared in Russia for many centuries before her invasion by Charles XII. She was long the victim and the slave of the Tartars; and for many considerable periods of years the Poles held her in subjugation. Indeed, if we except the expeditions of some of the early Russian chiefs against Byzantium, and the reign of Ivan Vasilovitch, the history of Russia before the time of Peter the Great is one long tale of suffering and degradation.

But, whatever may have been the amount of national injuries that she sustained from Swede, from Tartar, or from Pole in the ages of her weakness, she has certainly retaliated ten-fold during the century and a half of her strength. Her rapid transition at the commencement of that period from being the prey of every conqueror to being the conqueror of all with whom she comes into contact, to being the oppressor instead of the oppressed, is almost without a parallel in the history of nations. It was the work of a single ruler; who, himself without education, promoted science and literature among barbaric millions; who gave them fleets, commerce, arts, and arms; who, at Pultowa, taught them to face and beat the previously invincible Swedes; and who made stubborn valor and implicit subordination from that time forth the distinguishing characteristics of the Russian soldiery, which had before his time been a mere disorderly and irresolute rabble.

The career of Philip of Macedon resembles most nearly that of the great Muscovite Czar: but there is this important difference, that Philip had, while young, received in Southern Greece the best education in all matters of peace and war that the ablest philosophers and generals of the age could bestow. Peter was brought up among barbarians and in barbaric ignorance. He strove to remedy this, when a grown man, by leaving all the temptations to idleness and sensuality which his court offered, and by seeking instruction abroad. He labored with his own hands as a common artisan in Holland and England, that he might return and teach his subjects how ships, commerce, and civilization could be acquired. There is a degree of heroism here superior to anything that we know of in the Macedonian king. But Philip's consolidation of the long-disunited Macedonian empire; his raising a people, which he found the scorn of their civilized Southern neighbors, to be their dread; his organization of a brave and well-disciplined army instead of a disorderly militia; his creation of a maritime force, and his systematic skill in acquiring and improving seaports and arsenals; his patient tenacity of purpose under reverses; his personal bravery, and even his proneness to coarse amusements and pleasures,—all mark him out as the prototype of the imperial founder of the Russian power. In justice, however, to the ancient hero, it ought to be added that we find in the history of Philip no examples of that savage cruelty which deforms so grievously the character of Peter the Great.

In considering the effects of the overthrow which the Swedish arms sustained at Pultowa, and in speculating on the probable consequences that would have followed if the invaders had been successful, we must not only bear in mind the wretched state in which Peter found Russia at his accession, compared with her present grandeur, but we must also keep in view the fact that, at the time when Pultowa was fought, his reforms were yet incomplete, and his new institutions immature. He had broken up the Old Russia; and the New Russia, which he ultimately created, was still in embryo. Had he been crushed at Pultowa, his immense labors would have been buried with him, and (to use the words of Voltaire) "the most extensive empire in the world would have relapsed into the chaos from which it had been so lately taken." It is this fact that makes the repulse of Charles XII. the critical point in the fortunes of Russia. The danger which she incurred a century afterwards from her invasion by Napoleon was in reality far less than her peril when Charles attacked her, though the French emperor, as a military genius, was infinitely superior to the Swedish king, and led a host against her, compared with which the armies of Charles seem almost insignificant. But, as Fouche well warned his imperial master, when he vainly endeavored to dissuade him from his disastrous expedition against the empire of the Czars, the difference between the Russia of 1812 and the Russia of 1709 was greater than the disparity between the power of

Charles and the might of Napoleon. "If that heroic king," said Fouche, "had not, like your imperial majesty, half Europe in arms to back him, neither had his opponent, the Czar Peter, 400,000 soldiers and 50,000 Cossacks." The historians who describe the state of the Muscovite empire when revolutionary and imperial France encountered it, narrate with truth and justice how, "at the epoch of the French Revolution, this immense empire, comprehending nearly half of Europe and Asia within its dominions, inhabited by a patient and indomitable race, ever ready to exchange the luxury and adventure of the South for the hardships and monotony of the North, was daily becoming more formidable to the liberties of Europe.... The Russian infantry had then long been celebrated for its immovable firmness. Her immense population, amounting then in Europe alone to nearly thirty-five millions, afforded an inexhaustible supply of men. Her soldiers, inured to heat and cold from their infancy, and actuated by a blind devotion to their Czar, united the steady valor of the English to the impetuous energy of the French troops."[6] So, also, we read how the haughty aggressions of Bonaparte "went to excite a national feeling from the banks of the Borysthenes to the wall of China, and to unite against him the wild and uncivilized inhabitants of an extended empire, possessed by a love of their religion, their government, and their country, and having a character of stern devotion, which he was incapable of estimating."[7] But the Russia of 1709 had no such forces to oppose to an assailant. Her whole population then was below sixteen millions; and, what is far more important, this population had neither acquired military spirit nor strong nationality, nor was it united in loyal attachment to its ruler.

Peter had wisely abolished the old regular troops of the empire, the Strelitzes; but the forces which he had raised in their stead on a new and foreign plan, and principally officered with foreigners, had, before the Swedish invasion, given no proof that they could be relied on. In numerous encounters with the Swedes, Peter's soldiery had run like sheep before inferior numbers. Great discontent, also, had been excited among all classes of the community by the arbitrary changes which their great emperor introduced, many of which clashed with the most cherished national prejudices of his subjects. A career of victory and prosperity had not yet raised Peter above the reach of that disaffection, nor had superstitious obedience to the Czar yet become the characteristic of the Muscovite mind. The victorious occupation of Moscow by Charles XII. would have quelled the Russian nation as effectually, as had been the case when Batou Khan and other ancient invaders captured the capital of primitive Muscovy. How little such a triumph could effect towards subduing modern Russia, the fate of Napoleon demonstrated at once and forever.

The character of Charles XII. has been a favorite theme with historians, moralists, philosophers, and poets. But it is his military conduct during the campaign in Russia that alone requires comment here. Napoleon, in the Memoirs dictated by him at St. Helena, has given us a systematic criticism on that, among other celebrated campaigns, his own Russian campaign included. He labors hard to prove that he himself observed all the true principles of offensive war; and probably his censures on Charles' generalship were rather highly colored, for the sake of making his own military skill stand out in more favorable relief. Yet, after making all allowances, we must admit the force of Napoleon's strictures on Charles' tactics, and own that his judgment, though severe, is correct, when he pronounces that the Swedish king, unlike his great predecessor Gustavus, knew nothing of the art of war, and was nothing more than a brave and intrepid soldier. Such, however, was not the light in which Charles was regarded by his contemporaries at the commencement of his Russian expedition. His numerous victories, his daring and resolute spirit, combined with the ancient renown of the Swedish arms, then filled all Europe with admiration and anxiety. As Johnson expresses it, his name was then one at which the world grew pale. Even Louis le Grand earnestly solicited his assistance; and our own Marlborough, then in the full career of his victories, was specially sent by the English court to the camp of Charles, to propitiate the hero of the North in favor of the cause of the allies, and to prevent the Swedish sword from being flung into the scale in the French king's favor. But Charles at that time was solely bent on dethroning the sovereign of Russia, as he had already dethroned the sovereign of Poland, and all Europe fully believed that he would entirely crush the Czar, and dictate conditions of peace in the Kremlin.[8] Charles himself looked on success as a matter of certainty, and the romantic extravagance of his views was continually increasing. "One year, he thought, would suffice for the conquest of Russia. The court of Rome was next to feel his vengeance, as the pope had dared to oppose the concession of religious liberty to the Silesian Protestants. No enterprise at that time appeared impossible to him. He had even despatched several officers privately into Asia and Egypt, to take plans of the towns and examine into the strength and resources of those countries."[9]

Napoleon thus epitomizes the earlier operations of Charles' invasion of Russia:

"That prince set out from his camp at Aldstadt, near Leipsic, in September, 1707, at the head of 45,000 men, and traversed Poland; 20,000 men, under Count Lewenhaupt, disembarked at Riga; and 15,000 were in Finland. He was therefore in a condition to have brought together 80,000 of the best troops in the world. He left 10,000 men at Warsaw to guard King Stanislaus, and in January, 1708, arrived at Grodno, where he wintered. In June he crossed the forest of Minsk and presented himself before Borisov; forced the Russian army, which occupied the left bank of the Beresina; defeated 20,000 Russians who were strongly intrenched behind marshes; passed the Borysthenes at Mohilov, and vanquished a corps of 16,000 Muscovites near Smolensko on the 22d of September. He was now advanced to the confines of Lithuania, and was about to enter Russia Proper; the Czar, alarmed at his approach, made him proposals of peace. Up to this time all his movements were conformable to rule, and his communications were well secured. He was master of Poland and

Riga, and only ten days' march distant from Moscow; and it is probable that he would have reached that capital, had he not quitted the high road thither, and directed his steps towards the Ukraine, in order to form a junction with Mazeppa, who brought him only 6,000 men. By this movement, his line of operations, beginning at Sweden, exposed his flank to Russia for a distance of four hundred leagues, and he was unable to protect it, or to receive either re-enforcements or assistance."

Napoleon severely censures this neglect of one of the great rules of war. He points out that Charles had not organized his war, like Hannibal, on the principle of relinquishing all communications with home, keeping all his forces concentrated, and creating a base of operations in the conquered country. Such had been the bold system of the Carthaginian general; but Charles acted on no such principle, inasmuch as he caused Lewenhaupt, one of his generals who commanded a considerable detachment, and escorted a most important convoy, to follow him at a distance of twelve days' march. By this dislocation of his forces he exposed Lewenhaupt to be overwhelmed separately by the full force of the enemy, and deprived the troops under his own command of the aid which that general's men and stores might have afforded at the very crisis of the campaign.

The Czar had collected an army of about 100,000 effective men; and though the Swedes, in the beginning of the invasion, were successful in every encounter, the Russian troops were gradually acquiring discipline; and Peter and his officers were learning generalship from their victors, as the Thebans of old learned it from the Spartans. When Lewenhaupt, in the October of 1708, was striving to join Charles in the Ukraine, the Czar suddenly attacked him near the Borysthenes with an overwhelming force of 50,000 Russians. Lewenhaupt fought bravely for three days, and succeeded in cutting his way through the enemy with about 4,000 of his men to where Charles awaited him near the River Desna; but upwards of 8,000 Swedes fell in these battles; Lewenhaupt's cannon and ammunition were abandoned; and the whole of his important convoy of provisions, on which Charles and his half-starved troops were relying, fell into the enemy's hands. Charles was compelled to remain in the Ukraine during the winter; but in the spring of 1709 he moved forward towards Moscow, and invested the fortified town of Pultowa, on the River Vorskla, a place where the Czar had stored up large supplies of provisions and military stores, and which commanded the passes leading towards Moscow. The possession of this place would have given Charles the means of supplying all the wants of his suffering army, and would also have furnished him with a secure base of operations for his advance against the Muscovite capital. The siege was therefore hotly pressed by the Swedes; the garrison resisted obstinately; and the Czar, feeling the importance of saving the town, advanced in June to its relief, at the head of an army from fifty to sixty thousand strong.

Both sovereigns now prepared for the general action, which each saw to be inevitable, and which each felt would be decisive of his own and of his country's destiny. The Czar, by some masterly manoeuvres, crossed the Vorskla, and posted his army on the same side of that river with the besiegers, but a little higher up. The Vorskla falls into the Borysthenes about fifteen leagues below Pultowa, and the Czar arranged his forces in two lines, stretching from one river towards the other, so that if the Swedes attacked him and were repulsed, they would be driven backward into the acute angle formed by the two streams at their junction. He fortified these lines with several redoubts, lined with heavy artillery; and his troops, both horse and foot, were in the best possible condition, and amply provided with stores and ammunition. Charles' forces were about 24,000 strong. But not more than half of these were Swedes: so much had battle, famine, fatigue, and the deadly frosts of Russia thinned the gallant bands which the Swedish king and Lewenhaupt had led to the Ukraine. The other 12,000 men, under Charles, were Cossacks and Wallachians, who had joined him in the country. On hearing that the Czar was about to attack him, he deemed that his dignity required that he himself should be the assailant; and, leading his army out of their intrenched lines before the town, he advanced with them against the Russian redoubts.

He had been severely wounded in the foot in a skirmish a few days before, and was borne in a litter along the ranks into the thick of the fight. Notwithstanding the fearful disparity of numbers and disadvantage of position, the Swedes never showed their ancient valor more nobly than on that dreadful day. Nor do their Cossack and Wallachian allies seem to have been unworthy of fighting side by side with Charles' veterans. Two of the Russian redoubts were actually entered, and the Swedish infantry began to raise the cry of victory. But, on the other side, neither general nor soldiers flinched in their duty. The Russian cannonade and musketry were kept up; fresh masses of defenders were poured into the fortifications, and at length the exhausted remnants of the Swedish columns recoiled from the blood-stained redoubts. Then the Czar led the infantry and cavalry of his first line outside the works, drew them up steadily and skilfully, and the action was renewed along the whole fronts of the two armies on the open ground. Each sovereign exposed his life freely in the world-winning battle, and on each side the troops fought obstinately and eagerly under their ruler's eyes. It was not till two hours from the commencement of the action that, overpowered by numbers, the hitherto invincible Swedes gave way. All was then hopeless disorder and irreparable rout. Driven downward to where the rivers join, the fugitive Swedes surrendered to their victorious pursuers or perished in the waters of the Borysthenes. Only a few hundreds swam that river with their king and the Cossack Mazeppa, and escaped into the Turkish territory. Nearly 10,000 lay killed and wounded in the redoubts and on the field of battle.

In the joy of his heart the Czar exclaimed, when the strife was over, "That the son of the morning had fallen from heaven, and that the foundation of St. Petersburg at length stood firm." Even on that battle-field, near the Ukraine, the Russian emperor's first thoughts were of conquests and aggrandizement on the Baltic.

The peace of Nystadt, which transferred the fairest provinces of Sweden to Russia, ratified the judgment of battle which was pronounced at Pultowa. Attacks on Turkey and Persia by Russia commenced almost directly after that victory. And though the Czar failed in his first attempts against the sultan, the successors of Peter have, one and all, carried on a uniformly aggressive and uniformly successive system of policy against Turkey, and against every other state, Asiatic as well as European, which has had the misfortune of having Russia for a neighbor.

Orators and authors, who have discussed the progress of Russia, have often alluded to the similitude between the modern extension of the Muscovite empire and the extension of the Roman dominions in ancient times. But attention has scarcely been drawn to the closeness of the parallel between conquering Russia and conquering Rome, not only in the extent of conquests, but in the means of effecting conquest. The history of Rome during the century and a half which followed the close of the second Punic war, and during which her largest acquisitions of territory were made, should be minutely compared with the history of Russia for the last one hundred and fifty years. The main points of similitude can only be indicated in these pages; but they deserve the fullest consideration. Above all, the sixth chapter of Montesquieu's great treatise on Rome, "*De la conduite que les Remains tinrent pour soumettre les peuples*," should be carefully studied by every one who watches the career and policy of Russia. The classic scholar will remember the statecraft of the Roman senate, which took care in every foreign war to appear in the character of a *Protector*. Thus Rome *protected* the Ætolians and the Greek cities against Macedon; she *protected* Bithynia and other small Asiatic states against the Syrian kings; she protected Numidia against Carthage; and in numerous other instances assumed the same specious character. But "woe to the people whose liberty depends on the continued forbearance of an overmighty protector."[10] Every state which Rome protected was ultimately subjugated and absorbed by her. And Russia has been the protector of Poland — the protector of the Crimea — the protector of Courland—the protector of Georgia, Immeritia, Mingrelia, the Tcherkessian and Caucasian tribes, etc. She has first protected, and then appropriated, them all. She protects Moldavia and Wallachia. A few years ago she became the protector of Turkey from Mehemet Ali; and since the summer of 1849 she has made herself the protector of Austria.

When the partisans of Russia speak of the disinterestedness with which she withdrew her protecting troops from Constantinople and from Hungary, let us here also mark the ominous exactness of the parallel between her and Rome. While the ancient world yet contained a number of independent states, which might have made a formidable league against Rome if she had alarmed them by openly avowing her ambitious schemes, Rome's favorite policy was seeming disinterestedness and moderation. After her first war against Philip, after that against Antiochus, and many others, victorious Rome promptly withdrew her troops from the territories which they occupied. She affected to employ her arms only for the good of others. But, when the favorable moment came, she always found a pretext for marching her legions back into each coveted district, and making it a Roman province. Fear, not moderation, is the only effective check on the ambition of such powers as ancient Rome and modern Russia. The amount of that fear depends on the amount of timely vigilance and energy which other states choose to employ against the common enemy of their freedom and national independence.

Synopsis of Events between the Battle of Pultowa, AD 1709, and the Defeat of Burgoyne at Saratoga, AD 1777.

AD 1713. Treaty of Utrecht. Philip is left by it in possession of the throne of Spain. But Naples, Milan, the Spanish territories on the Tuscan coast, the Spanish Netherlands, and some parts of the French Netherlands are given to Austria. France cedes to England Hudson's Bay and Straits, the island of St. Christopher, Nova

Scotia, and Newfoundland in America. Spain cedes to England, Gibraltar and Minorca, which the English had taken during the war. The King of Prussia and the Duke of Savoy both obtain considerable additions of territory to their dominions.

1715. Death of Queen Anne. The house of Hanover begins to reign in England. A rebellion in favor of the Stuarts is put down. Death of Louis XIV.

1718. Charles XII. killed at the siege of Frederickshall.

1725. Death of Peter the Great of Russia.

1740. Frederick II. King of Prussia. He attacks the Austrian dominions, and conquers Silesia.

1742. War between France and England.

1743. Victory of the English at Dettingen.

1745. Victory of the French at Fontenoy. Rebellion in Scotland in favor of the house of Stuart; finally quelled by the battle of Culloden in the next year.

1748. Peace of Aix-la-Chapelle.

1756–1763. The Seven Years' War, during which Prussia makes a heroic resistance against the armies of Austria, Russia, and France. England, under the administration of the elder Pitt (afterward Lord Chatham), takes a glorious part in the war in opposition to France and Spain. Wolfe wins the battle of Quebec, and the English conquer Canada, Cape Breton, and St. John. Clive begins his career of conquest in India. Cuba is taken by the English from Spain.

1763. Treaty of Paris; which leaves the power of Prussia increased, and its military reputation greatly exalted.

"France, by the treaty of Paris, ceded to England Canada and the island of Cape Breton, with the islands and coasts of the gulf and river of St. Lawrence. The boundaries between the two nations in North America were fixed by a line drawn along the middle of the Mississippi, from its source to its mouth. All on the left or eastern bank of that river was given up to England, except the city of New Orleans, which was reserved to France; as was also the liberty of the fisheries on a part of the coasts of Newfoundland and the Gulf of St. Lawrence. The islands of St. Peter and Miquelon were given them as a shelter for their fishermen, but without permission to raise fortifications. The islands of Martinico, Guadaloupe, Mariegalante, Desirada, and St. Lucia were surrendered to France; while Grenada, the Grenadines, St. Vincent, Dominica, and Tobago were ceded to England. This latter power retained her conquests on the Senegal, and restored to France the island of Gorea, on the coast of Africa. France was put in possession of the forts and factories which belonged to her in the East Indies, on the coasts of Coromandel, Orissa, Malabar, and Bengal, under the restriction of keeping up no military force in Bengal.

"In Europe, France restored all the conquests she had made in Germany, as also the island of Minorca. England gave up to her Belleisle, on the coast of Brittany; while Dunkirk was kept in the same condition as had been determined by the peace of Aix-la-Chapelle. The island of Cuba, with the Havana, were restored to the King of Spain, who, on his part, ceded to England Florida, with Port Augustine and the Bay of Pensacola. The King of Portugal was restored to the same state in which he had been before the war. The colony of St. Sacrament in America, which the Spaniards had conquered, was given back to him.

"The peace of Paris, of which we have just now spoken, was the era of England's greatest prosperity. Her commerce and navigation extended over all parts of the globe, and were supported by a naval force, so much the more imposing, as it was no longer counterbalanced by the maritime power of France, which had been almost annihilated in the preceding war. The immense territories which that peace had secured her, both in Africa and America, opened up new channels for her industry; and what deserves specially to be remarked is, that she acquired at the same time vast and important possessions in the East Indies."[11]

CHAPTER XIII

VICTORY OF THE AMERICANS OVER BURGOYNE AT SARATOGA, AD 1777

"Westward the course of empire takes its way;
The first four acts already past,
A fifth shall close the drama with the day:
Time's noblest offspring is its last."

— *Bishop Berkeley.*

"Even of those great conflicts in which hundreds of thousands have been engaged and tens of thousands have fallen, none has been more fruitful of results than this surrender of thirty-five hundred fighting men at Saratoga. It not merely changed the relations of England and the feelings of Europe towards these insurgent colonies, but it has modified, for all time to come, the connection between every colony and every parent state."

— *Lord Mahon.*

Of the four great powers that now principally rule the political destinies of the world, France and England are the only two whose influence can be dated back beyond the last century and a half. The third great power, Russia, was a feeble mass of barbarism before the epoch of Peter the Great; and the very existence of the fourth great power as an independent nation commenced within the memory of living men. By the fourth great power of the world I mean the mighty commonwealth of the Western Continent which now commands the admiration of mankind. That homage is sometimes reluctantly given, and is sometimes accompanied with suspicion and ill-will. But none can refuse it. All the physical essentials for national strength are undeniably to be found in the geographical position and amplitude of territory which the United States possess; in their almost inexhaustible tracts of fertile but hitherto untouched soil, in their stately forests, in their mountain-chains and their rivers, their beds of coal and stores of metallic wealth, in their extensive sea-board along the waters of two oceans, and in their already numerous and rapidly increasing population. And when we examine the character of this population, no one can look on the fearless energy, the sturdy determination, the aptitude for local self-government, the versatile alacrity, and the unresting spirit of enterprise which characterize the Anglo-Americans, without feeling that here he beholds the true elements of progressive might.

Three-quarters of a century have not yet passed since the United States ceased to be mere dependencies of England. And even if we date their origin from the period when the first permanent European settlements out of which they grew were made on the western coast of the North Atlantic, the increase of their strength is unparalleled either in rapidity or extent.

The ancient Roman boasted, with reason, of the growth of Rome from humble beginnings to the greatest magnitude which the world had then ever witnessed. But the citizen of the United States is still more justly entitled to claim this praise. In two centuries and a half his country has acquired ampler dominion than the Roman gained in ten. And even if we credit the legend of the band of shepherds and outlaws with which Romulus is said to have colonized the Seven Hills, we find not there so small a germ of future greatness as we find in the group of a hundred and five ill-chosen and disunited emigrants who founded Jamestown in 1607, or in the scanty band of Pilgrim Fathers who, a few years later, moored their bark on the wild and rock-bound coast of the wilderness that was to become New England. The power of the United States is emphatically the "Imperium quo neque ab exordio ullum fere minus, neque incrementis toto orbe amplius humana potest memoria recordari."[1]

Nothing is more calculated to impress the mind with a sense of the rapidity with which the resources of the American republic advance, than the difficulty which the historical inquirer finds in ascertaining their precise amount. If he consults the most recent works, and those written by the ablest investigators of the subject, he finds in them admiring comments on the change which the last few years, before those books were written, had made; but when he turns to apply the estimates in those books to the present moment, he finds them wholly inadequate. Before a book on the subject of the United States has lost its novelty, those states have outgrown the descriptions which it contains. The celebrated work of the French statesman, De Tocqueville, appeared about fifteen years ago. In the passage which I am about to quote, it will be seen that he predicts the constant increase of the Anglo-American power, but he looks on the Rocky Mountains as their extreme western limit for many years to come. He had evidently no expectation of himself seeing that power dominant along the Pacific as well as along the Atlantic coast. He says:[2]

"The distance from Lake Superior to the Gulf of Mexico extends from the 47th to the 30th degree of latitude, a distance of more than 1,200 miles as the bird flies. The frontier of the United States winds along the whole of this immense line, sometimes falling within its limits, but more frequently extending far beyond it into the waste. It has been calculated that the whites advance every year a mean distance of seventeen miles along this vast boundary. Obstacles, such as an unproductive district, a lake, or an Indian nation unexpectedly encountered, are sometimes met with. The advancing column then halts for a while; its two extremities tall back upon themselves, and as soon as they are reunited they proceed onward. This gradual and continuous progress of the European race towards the Rocky Mountains has the solemnity of a providential event; it is like a deluge of men rising unabatedly, and daily driven onward by the hand of God.

"Within this first line of conquering settlers towns are built and vast states founded. In 1790 there were only a few thousand pioneers sprinkled along the valleys of the Mississippi; and at the present day these valleys contain as many inhabitants as were to be found in the whole Union in 1790. Their population amounts to nearly four millions. The City of Washington was founded in 1800, in the very centre of the Union; but such are the changes which has taken place that it now stands at one of the extremities; and the delegates of the most remote Western States are already obliged to perform a journey as long as that from Vienna to Paris.

"It must not, then, be imagined that the impulse of the British race in the New World can be arrested. The dismemberment of the Union, and the hostilities which might ensue, the abolition of republican institutions, and the tyrannical government which might succeed it, may retard this impulse, but they cannot prevent it from ultimately fulfilling the destinies to which that race is reserved. No power upon earth can close upon the emigrants that fertile wilderness, which offers resources to all industry and a refuge from all want. Future events, of whatever nature they may be, will not deprive the Americans of their climate or of their inland seas, of their great rivers or of their exuberant soil. Nor will bad news, revolutions, and anarchy be able to obliterate that love of prosperity and that spirit of enterprise which seem to be the distinctive characteristics of their race, or to extinguish that knowledge which guides them on their way.

"Thus, in the midst of the uncertain future, one event at least is sure — at a period which may be said to be near (for we are speaking of the life of a nation), the Anglo-Americans will alone cover the immense space contained between the polar regions and the tropics, extending from the coast of the Atlantic to the shores of the Pacific Ocean; the territory which will probably be occupied by the Anglo-Americans at some future time may be computed to equal three-quarters of Europe in extent. The climate of the Union is upon the whole preferable to that of Europe, and its natural advantages are not less great; it is therefore evident that its population will at some future time be proportionate to our own. Europe, divided as it is between so many different nations, and torn as it has been by incessant wars and the barbarous manners of the Middle Ages, has, notwithstanding, attained a population of 410 inhabitants to the square league. What cause can prevent the United States from having as numerous a population in time?

"The time will therefore come when one hundred and fifty millions of men will be living in North America, equal in condition, the progeny of one race, owing their origin to the same cause, and preserving the same civilization, the same language, the same religion, the same habits, the same manners, and imbued with the same opinions, propagated under the same forms. The rest is uncertain, but this is certain; and it is a fact new to the world, a fact fraught with such portentous consequences as to baffle the efforts even of the imagination."

Let us turn from the French statesman writing in 1835, to an English statesman who is justly regarded as the highest authority in all statistical subjects, and who described the United States only five years ago. Macgregor[3] tells us:

"The states which, on the ratification of independence, formed the American Republican Union, were thirteen, viz.:

"Massachusetts, New Hampshire, Connecticut, Rhode Island, New York, New Jersey, Delaware, Maryland, Pennsylvania, Virginia, North Carolina, South Carolina, and Georgia.

"The foregoing thirteen states (*the whole inhabited territory of which, with the exception of a few small settlements, was confined to the region extending between the Alleghany Mountains and the Atlantic*) were those which existed at the period when they became an acknowledged separate and independent federal sovereign power. The thirteen stripes of the standard or flag of the United States continue to represent the original number. The stars have multiplied to twenty-six,[4] according as the number of states have increased.

"The territory of the thirteen original states of the Union, including Maine and Vermont, comprehended a superficies of 371,124 English square miles; that of the whole United Kingdom of Great Britain and Ireland, 120,354; that of France, including Corsica, 214,910; that of the Austrian empire, including Hungary and all the Imperial states, 257,540 English square miles.

"The present superficies of the twenty-six constitutional states of the Anglo-American Union, and the District of Columbia, and territories of Florida, include 1,029,025 square miles; to which, if we add the Northwest or Wisconsin Territory, east of the Mississippi, and bound by Lake Superior on the north and Michigan on the east, and occupying at least 100,000 square miles, and then add the great western region, not yet well-defined territories, but at the most limited calculation comprehending 700,000 square miles, the whole unbroken in its vast length and breadth by foreign nations, comprehends a portion of the earth's surface equal to 1,729,025 English, or 1,296,770 geographical, square miles."

We may add that the population of the states when they declared their independence was about two millions and a half; it is now twenty-three millions.

I have quoted Macgregor, not only on account of the clear and full view which he gives of the progress of America to the date when he wrote, but because his description may be contrasted with what the United States have become even since his book appeared. Only three years after the time when Macgregor thus wrote, the American president truly stated:

"Within less than four years the annexation of Texas to the Union has been consummated; all conflicting title to the Oregon Territory, south of the forty-ninth degree of north latitude, adjusted; and New Mexico and Upper California have been acquired by treaty. The area of these several territories contains 1,193,061 square miles, or 763,559,040 acres; while the area of the remaining twenty-nine states, and the territory not yet organized into states east of the Rocky Mountains, contains 2,059,513 square miles, or 1,318,126,058 acres. These estimates show that the territories recently acquired and over which our exclusive jurisdiction and dominion have been extended, constitute a country more than half as large as all that which was held by the United States before their acquisition. If Oregon be excluded from the estimate, there will still remain within the limits of Texas, New Mexico, and California 851,598 square miles, or 545,012,720 acres, being an addition equal to more than one-third of all the territory owned by the United States before their acquisition, and, including Oregon, nearly as great an extent of territory as the whole of Europe, Russia only excepted. *The Mississippi, so lately the frontier of our country, is now only its centre.* With the addition of the late acquisitions, the United States are now estimated to be nearly as large as the whole of Europe. The extent of the sea-coast of Texas on the Gulf of Mexico is upwards of 400 miles; of the coast of Upper California, on the Pacific, of 970 miles, and of Oregon, including the Straits of Fuca, of 650 miles; *making the whole extent of sea-coast on the Pacific 1,620 miles,* and the whole extent on both the Pacific and the Gulf of Mexico 2,020 miles. The length of the coast on the Atlantic, from the northern limits of the United States, round the Capes of Florida to the Sabine on the eastern boundary of Texas, is estimated to be 3,100 miles, so that the addition of sea-coast, including Oregon, is very nearly two-thirds as great as all we possessed before; and, excluding Oregon, is an addition of 1,370 miles, being nearly equal to one-half of the extent of coast which we possessed before these acquisitions. We have now three great maritime fronts—on the Atlantic, the Gulf of Mexico, and the Pacific—making, in the whole, an extent of sea-coast exceeding 5,000 miles. This is the extent of the sea-coast of the United States, not including bays, sounds, and small irregularities of the main shore and of the sea islands. If these be included, the length of the shore-line of coast, as estimated by the superintendent of the Coast Survey in his report, would be 33,063 miles."

The importance of the power of the United States being then firmly planted along the Pacific applies not only to the New World, but to the Old. Opposite to San Francisco, on the coast of that ocean, lie the wealthy but decrepit empires of China and Japan. Numerous groups of islets stud the larger part of the intervening sea, and form convenient step-ping-stones for the progress of commerce or ambition. The intercourse of traffic between these ancient Asiatic monarchies and the young Anglo-American republic must be rapid and extensive. Any attempt of the Chinese or

Japanese rulers to check it will only accelerate an armed collision. The American will either buy or force his way. Between such populations as that of China and Japan on the one side, and that of the United States on the other—the former haughty, formal, and insolent; the latter bold, intrusive, and unscrupulous—causes of quarrel must sooner or later arise. The results of such a quarrel cannot be doubted. America will scarcely imitate the forbearance shown by England at the end of our late war with the Celestial Empire; and the conquests of China and Japan by the fleets and armies of the United States are events which many now living are likely to witness. Compared with the magnitude of such changes in the dominion of the Old World, the certain ascendency of the Anglo-Americans over Central and Southern America seems a matter of secondary importance. Well may we repeat De Tocqueville's words, that the growing power of this commonwealth is "un fait entièrement nouveau dans Ie monde, et dont l'imagination elle-même ne saurait saisir la portée."

An Englishman may look, and ought to look, on the growing grandeur of the Americans with no small degree of generous sympathy and satisfaction. They, like ourselves, are members of the great Anglo-Saxon nation, "whose race and language are now overrunning the world from one end of it to the other."[5] And whatever differences of form of government may exist between us and them—whatever reminiscences of the days when, though brethren, we strove together, may rankle in the minds of us, the defeated party, we should cherish the bonds of common nationality that still exist between us. We should remember, as the Athenians remembered of the Spartans at a season of jealousy and temptation, that our race is one, being of the same blood, speaking the same language, having an essential resemblance in our institutions and usages, and worshipping in the temples of the same God.[6] All this may and should be borne in mind. And yet an Englishman can hardly watch the progress of America without the regretful thought that America once was English, and that, but for the folly of our rulers, she might be English still. It is true that the commerce between the two countries has largely and beneficially increased, but this is no proof that the increase would not have been still greater had the states remained integral portions of the same great empire. By giving a fair and just participation in political rights, these, "the fairest possessions" of the British crown, might have been preserved to it. "This ancient and most noble monarchy"[7] would not have been dismembered; nor should we see that which ought to be the right arm of our strength, now menacing us in every political crisis as the most formidable rival of our commercial and maritime ascendency.

The war which rent away the North American colonies from England is, of all subjects in history, the most painful for an Englishman to dwell on. It was commenced and carried on by the British ministry in iniquity and folly, and it was concluded in disaster and shame. But the contemplation of it cannot be evaded by the historian, however much it may be abhorred. Nor can any military event be said to have exercised more important influence on the future fortunes of mankind than the complete defeat of Burgoyne's expedition in 1777; a defeat which rescued the revolted colonists from certain subjection, and which, by inducing the courts of France and Spain to attack England in their behalf, insured the independence of the United States and the formation of that trans-Atlantic power which not only America, but both Europe and Asia, now see and feel.

Still, in proceeding to describe this "decisive battle of the world," a very brief recapitulation of the earlier events of the war may be sufficient; nor shall I linger unnecessarily on a painful theme.

The five northern colonies of Massachusetts, Connecticut, Rhode Island, New Hampshire, and Vermont, usually classed together as the New England colonies, were the strongholds of the insurrection against the mother country. The feeling of resistance was less vehement and general in the central settlement of New York, and still less so in Pennsylvania, Maryland, and the other colonies of the South, although everywhere it was formidably strong. But it was among the descendants of the stern Puritans that the spirit of Cromwell and Vane breathed in all its fervor; it was from the New Englanders that the first armed opposition to the British crown had been offered; and it was by them that the most stubborn determination to fight to the last, rather than waive a single right or privilege, had been displayed. In 1775 they had succeeded in forcing the British troops to evacuate Boston; and the events of 1776 had made New York (which the Royalists captured in that year) the principal basis of operations for the armies of the mother country.

A glance at the map will show that the Hudson River, which falls into the Atlantic at New York, runs down from the north at the back of the New England States, forming an angle of about forty-five degrees with the line of the coast of the Atlantic, along which the New England States are situate. Northward of the Hudson we see a small chain of lakes communicating with the Canadian frontier. It is necessary to attend closely to these geographical points in order to understand the plan of the operations which the English attempted in 1777, and which the battle of Saratoga defeated.

The English had a considerable force in Canada, and in 1776 had completely repulsed an attack which the Americans had made upon that province. The British ministry resolved to avail themselves, in the next year, of the advantage which the occupation of Canada gave them, not merely for the purpose of defence, but for the purpose of striking a vigorous and crushing blow against the revolted colonies. With this view the army in Canada was largely re-enforced. Seven thousand veteran troops were sent out from England, with a corps of artillery abundantly supplied and led by select and experienced officers. Large quantities of military stores were also furnished for the equipment of the Canadian volunteers, who were expected to join the expedition. It was intended that the force thus collected should march southward by the line of the lakes, and thence along the banks of the Hudson River. The British army from New York (or a large detachment of it) was to make a simultaneous movement northward, up the line of the Hudson, and the two expeditions were to unite at Albany, a town on that river. By these operations all communication between the northern colonies and those of the centre and south would be cut off. An irresistible force would be concentrated, so as to crush all further opposition in New England; and when this was done, it was believed that the other colonies would speedily submit. The Americans had no troops in the field that seemed able to baffle these movements. Their principal army, under Washington, was occupied in watching over Pennsylvania and the South. At any rate, it was believed that, in order to oppose the plan intended for the new campaign, the insurgents must risk a pitched battle, in which the superiority of the Royalists, in numbers, in discipline, and in equipment, seemed to promise to the latter a crowning victory. Without question, the plan was ably formed; and had the success of the execution been equal to the ingenuity of the design, the reconquest or submission of the thirteen United States must in all human probability have followed, and the independence which they proclaimed in 1776 would have been extinguished before it existed a second year. No European power had as yet come forward to aid America. It is true that England was generally regarded with Jealousy and ill-will, and was thought to have acquired, at the treaty of Paris, a preponderance of dominion which was perilous to the balance of power; but, though many were willing to wound, none had yet ventured to strike; and America, if defeated in 1777, would have been suffered to fall unaided.

Burgoyne had gained celebrity by some bold and dashing exploits in Portugal during the last war; he was personally as brave an officer as ever headed British troops; he had considerable skill as a tactician; and his general intellectual abilities and acquirements were of a high order. He had several very able and experienced officers under him, among whom were Major-General Phillips and Brigadier-General Fraser. His regular troops amounted, exclusively of the corps of artillery, to about 7,200 men, rank and file. Nearly half of these were Germans. He had also an auxiliary force of from two to three thousand Canadians.

He summoned the warriors of several tribes of the red Indians near the Western lakes to join his army. Much eloquence was poured forth both in America and in England in denouncing the use of these savage auxiliaries. Yet Burgoyne seems to have done no more than Montcalm, Wolfe, and other French, American, and English generals had done before him. But, in truth, the lawless ferocity of the Indians, their unskilfulness in regular action, and the utter impossibility of bringing them under any discipline made their services of little or no value in times of difficulty; while the indignation which their outrages inspired went far to rouse the whole population of the invaded districts into active hostilities against Burgoyne's force.

Burgoyne assembled his troops and confederates near the River Bouquet, on the west side of Lake Champlain. He-then, on the 21st of June, 1777, gave his red allies a war feast, and harangued them on the necessity of abstaining from their usual cruel practices against unarmed people and prisoners. At the same time he published a pompous manifesto to the Americans, in which he threatened the refractory with all the horrors of war, Indian as well as European. The army proceeded by water to Crown Point, a fortification which the Americans held at the northern extremity of the inlet by which the water from Lake George is conveyed to Lake Champlain. He landed here without opposition; but the reduction of Ticonderoga, a fortification about twelve miles to the south of Crown Point, was a more serious matter, and was supposed to be the critical part of the expedition. Ticonderoga commanded the passage along the lakes, and was considered to be the key to the route which Burgoyne wished to follow. The English had been repulsed in an attack on it in the war with the French in 1758, with severe loss. But Burgoyne now invested it with great skill; and the American general, St. Clair, who had only an ill-equipped army of about 3,000 men, evacuated it on the 5th of July. It seems evident that a different course would have caused the destruction or capture of his whole army, which, weak as it was, was the chief force then in the field for the protection of the New England States, When censured by some of his countrymen for abandoning Ticonderoga, St. Clair truly replied "that he had lost a post, but saved a province." Burgoyne's troops pursued the retiring Americans, gained several advantages over them, and took a large part of their artillery and military stores.

The loss of the British in these engagements was trifling. The army moved southward along Lake George to Skenesborough, and thence, slowly and with great difficulty, across a broken country, full of creeks and marshes, and clogged by the enemy with felled trees and other obstacles, to Fort Edward, on the Hudson River, the American troops continuing to retire before them.

Burgoyne reached the left bank of the Hudson River on the 30th of July. Hitherto he had overcome every difficulty which the enemy and the nature of the country had placed in his way. His army was in excellent order and in the highest spirits, and the peril of the expedition seemed over when they were once on the bank of the river which was to be the channel of communication between them and the British army in the South. But their feelings, and those of the English nation in general, when their successes were announced, may best be learned from a contemporary writer. Burke, in the "Annual Register" for 1777, describes them thus:

"Such was the rapid torrent of success, which swept every thing away before the Northern army in its onset. It is not to be wondered at if both officers and private men were highly elated with their good fortune, and deemed that and their prowess to be irresistible; if they regarded their enemy with the greatest contempt; considered their own toils to be nearly at an end; Albany to be already in their hands; and the reduction of the northern provinces to be rather a matter of some time than an arduous task full of difficulty and danger.

"At home the joy and exultation was extreme; not only at court, but with all those who hoped or wished the unqualified subjugation and unconditional submission of the colonies. The loss in reputation was greater to the Americans, and capable of more fatal consequences, than even that of ground, of posts, of artillery, or of men. All the contemptuous and most degrading charges which had been made by their enemies, of their wanting the resolution and abilities of men, even in their defence of whatever was dear to them, were now repeated and believed. Those who still regarded them as men, and who had not yet lost all affection to them as brethren; who also retained hopes that a happy reconciliation upon constitutional principles, without sacrificing the dignity of the just authority of government on the one side, or a dereliction of the rights of freemen on the other, was not even now impossible, notwithstanding their favorable dispositions in general, could not help feeling upon this occasion that the Americans sunk not a little in their estimation. It was not difficult to diffuse an opinion that the war, in effect, was over, and that any further resistance could serve only to render the terms of their submission the worse. Such were some of the immediate effects of the loss of those grand keys of North America—Ticonderoga and the lakes."

The astonishment and alarm which these events produced among the Americans were naturally great; but in the midst of their disasters none of the colonists showed any disposition to submit. The local governments of the New England States, as well as the Congress, acted with vigor and firmness in their efforts to repel the enemy. General Gates was sent to take the command of the army at Saratoga; and Arnold, a favorite leader of the Americans, was despatched by Washington to act under him, with re-enforcements of troops and guns from the main American army. Burgoyne's employment of the Indians now produced the worst possible effects. Though he labored hard to check the atrocities which they were accustomed to commit, he could not prevent the occurrence of many barbarous outrages, repugnant both to the feelings of humanity and to the laws of civilized warfare. The American commanders took care that the reports of these excesses should be circulated far and wide, well knowing that they would make the stern New Englanders not droop, but rage. Such was their effect; and though, when each man looked upon his wife, his children, his sisters, or his aged parents, the thought of the merciless Indian "thirsting for the blood of man, woman, and child," of "the cannibal savage torturing, murdering, roasting, and eating the mangled victims of his barbarous battles,"[8] might raise terror in the bravest breasts; this very terror produced a directly contrary effect to causing submission to the royal army. It was seen that the few friends of the royal cause, as well as its enemies, were liable to be the victims of the indiscriminate rage of the savages;[9] and thus "the inhabitants of the open and frontier countries had no choice of acting: they had no means of security left but by abandoning their habitations and taking up arms. Every man saw the necessity of becoming a temporary soldier, not only for his own security, but for the protection and defence of those connections which are dearer than life itself. Thus an army was poured forth by the woods, mountains, and marshes, which in this part were thickly sown with plantations and villages. The Americans recalled their courage, and, when their regular army seemed to be entirely wasted, the spirit of the country produced a much greater and more formidable force."[10]

While resolute recruits, accustomed to the use of firearms, and all partially trained by service in the provincial militias, were thus flocking to the standard of Gates and Arnold at Saratoga, and while Burgoyne was engaged at Fort Edward in providing the means for the further advance of his army through the intricate and hostile country that still lay before him, two events occurred, in each of which the British sustained loss and the Americans obtained advantage, the moral effects of which were even more important than the immediate result of the encounters. When Burgoyne left Canada, General St. Leger was detached from that province with a mixed force of about 1,000 men and some light field-pieces across Lake Ontario against Fort Stanwix, which the Americans held. After capturing this, he was to march along the Mohawk River to its confluence with the Hudson, between Saratoga and Albany, where his force and that of Burgoyne's were to unite. But, after some successes, St. Leger was obliged to retreat, and to abandon his tents and large quantities of stores to the garrison. At the very time that General Burgoyne heard of this disaster, he experienced one still more severe in the defeat of Colonel Baum, with a large detachment of German troops, at Bennington, whither Burgoyne had sent them for the purpose of capturing some magazines of provisions, of which the British army stood greatly in need. The Americans, augmented by continual accessions of strength, succeeded, after many attacks, in breaking this corps, which fled into the woods, and left its commander mortally wounded on the field: they then marched against a force of five hundred grenadiers and light infantry, which was advancing to Colonel Baum's assistance under Lieutenant-Colonel Breyman, who, after a gallant resistance, was obliged to retreat on the main army. The British loss in these two actions exceeded six hundred men; and a party of American loyalists, on their way to join the army, having attached themselves to Colonel Baum's corps, were destroyed with it.

Notwithstanding these reverses, which added greatly to the spirit and numbers of the American forces, Burgoyne determined to advance. It was impossible any longer to keep up his communications with Canada by way of the lakes, so as to supply his army on his southward march; but having, by unremitting exertions, collected provisions for thirty days, he crossed the Hudson by means of a bridge of rafts, and, marching a short distance along its western bank, he encamped on the 14th of September on the heights of Saratoga, about sixteen miles from Albany. The Americans had fallen back from Saratoga, and were now strongly posted near Stillwater, about half way between Saratoga and Albany, and showed a determination to recede no further.

Meanwhile Lord Howe, with the bulk of the British army that had lain at New York, had sailed away to the Delaware, and there commenced a campaign against Washington, in which the English general took Philadelphia, and gained other showy but unprofitable successes. But Sir Henry Clinton, a brave and skilful officer, was left with a considerable force at New York, and he undertook the task of moving up the Hudson to co-operate with

Burgoyne. Clinton was obliged for this purpose to wait for re-enforcements which had been promised from England, and these did not arrive till September. As soon as he received them, Clinton embarked about 3,000 of his men on a flotilla, convoyed by some ships-of-war under Commander Hotham, and proceeded to force his way up the river.

The country between Burgoyne's position at Saratoga and that of the Americans at Stillwater was rugged, and seamed with creeks and water-courses; but, after great labor in making bridges and temporary causeways, the British army moved forward. About four miles from Saratoga, on the afternoon of the 19th of September, a sharp encounter took place between part of the English right wing, under Burgoyne himself, and a strong body of the enemy, under Gates and Arnold. The conflict lasted till sunset. The British remained masters of the field; but the loss on each side was nearly equal (from five to six hundred men); and the spirits of the Americans were greatly raised by having withstood the best regular troops of the English army. Burgoyne now halted again, and strengthened his position by field-works and redoubts; and the Americans also improved their defences. The two armies remained nearly within cannon-shot of each other for a considerable time, during which Burgoyne was anxiously looking for intelligence of the promised expedition from New York, which, according to the original plan, ought by this time to have been approaching Albany from the south. At last a messenger from Clinton made his way, with great difficulty, to Burgoyne's camp, and brought the information that Clinton was on his way up the Hudson to attack the American torts which barred the passage up that river to Albany. Burgoyne, in reply, on the 30th of September, urged Clinton to attack the forts as speedily as possible, stating that the effect of such an attack, or even the semblance of it, would be to move the American army from its position before his own troops. By another messenger, who reached Clinton on the 5th of October, Burgoyne informed his brother general that he had lost his communications with Canada, but had provisions which would last him till the 20th. Burgoyne described himself as strongly posted, and stated that, though the Americans in front of him were strongly posted also, he made no doubt of being able to force them and making his way to Albany; but that he doubted whether he could subsist there, as the country was drained of provisions. He wished Clinton to meet him there and to keep open a communication with New York.

Burgoyne had overestimated his resources, and in the very beginning of October found difficulty and distress pressing him hard.

The Indians and Canadians now began to desert him, while, on the other hand, Gates' army was continually re-enforced by fresh bodies of the militia. An expeditionary force was detached by the Americans, which made a bold though unsuccessful attempt to retake Ticonderoga. And finding the number and spirit of the enemy to increase daily, and his own stores of provisions to diminish, Burgoyne determined on attacking the Americans in front of him, and, by dislodging them from their position, to gain the means of moving upon Albany, or, at least, of relieving his troops from the straitened position in which they were cooped up.

Burgoyne's force was now reduced to less than 6,000 men. The right of his camp was on high ground a little to the west of the river; thence his intrenchments extended along the lower ground to the bank of the Hudson, their line being nearly at a right angle with the course of the stream. The lines were fortified with redoubts and field-works. On the extreme right a strong redoubt and entrenchments were thrown up. The numerical force of the Americans was now greater than the British, even in regular troops, and the numbers of the militia and volunteers which had joined Gates and Arnold were greater still.

General Lincoln, with 2,000 New England troops, had reached the American camp on the 29th of September. Gates gave him the command of the right wing, and took in person the command of the left wing, which was composed of two brigades under Generals Poor and Learned, of Colonel Morgan's rifle corps, and part of the fresh New England militia. The whole of the American lines had been ably fortified under the direction of the celebrated Polish general, Kosciusko, who was now serving as a volunteer in Gates's army. The right of the American position—that is to say, the part of it nearest to the river—was too strong to be assailed with any prospect of success, and Burgoyne therefore determined to endeavor to force their left. For this purpose he formed a column of 1,500 regular troops, with two twelve-pounders, two howitzers, and six six-pounders. He headed this in person, having Generals Phillips, Riedesel, and Fraser under him. The enemy's force immediately in front of his lines was so strong that he dared not weaken the troops who guarded them by detaching any more to strengthen his column of attack.

It was on the 7th of October that Burgoyne led his column on to the attack; and on the preceding day, the 6th, Clinton had successfully executed a brilliant enterprise against the two American forts which barred his progress up the Hudson. He had captured them both, with severe loss to the American forces opposed to him; he had destroyed the fleet which the Americans had been forming on the Hudson, under the protection of their forts; and the upward river was laid open to his squadron. He was now only a hundred and fifty-six miles distant from Burgoyne, and a detachment of 1,700 men actually advanced within forty miles of Albany. Unfortunately, Burgoyne and Clinton were each ignorant of the other's movements; but if Burgoyne had won his battle on the 7th, he must, on advancing, have soon learned the tidings of Clinton's success, and Clinton would have heard of his. A junction would soon have been made of the two victorious armies, and the great objects of the campaign might yet have been accomplished. All depended on the fortune of the column with which Burgoyne, on the eventful 7th of October, 1777, advanced against the American position. There were brave men, both English and German, in its ranks; and, in particular, it comprised one of the best bodies of Grenadiers in the British service.

Burgoyne pushed forward some bodies of irregular troops to distract the enemy's attention, and led his column to within three-quarters of a mile from the left of Gates's camp, and then deployed his men into line. The grenadiers under Major Ackland, and the artillery under Major Williams, were drawn up on the left; a corps of Germans under General Riedesel, and some British troops under General Phillips were in the centre, and the English light infantry and the 24th Regiment under Lord Balcarres and General Fraser were on the right. But Gates did not wait to be attacked; and directly the British line was formed and began to advance, the American general, with admirable skill, caused General Poor's brigade of New York and New Hampshire troops, and part of General Learned's brigade, to make a sudden and vehement rush against its left, and at the same time sent Colonel Morgan, with his rifle corps and other troops, amounting to 1,500, to turn the right of the English. The grenadiers under Ackland sustained the charge of superior numbers nobly. But Gates sent more Americans forward, and in a few minutes the action became general along the centre, so as to prevent the Germans from detaching any help to the grenadiers. Morgan, with his riflemen, was now pressing Lord Balcarres and General Fraser hard, and fresh masses of the enemy were observed advancing from their extreme left, with the evident intention of forcing the British right and cutting off its retreat. The English light infantry and the 24th now fell back and formed an oblique second line, which enabled them to baffle this manoeuvre and also to succor their comrades in the left wing, the gallant grenadiers, who were overpowered by superior numbers and, but for this aid, must have been cut to pieces.

The contest now was fiercely maintained on both sides. The English cannon were repeatedly taken and retaken; but when the grenadiers near them were forced back by the weight of superior numbers, one of the guns was permanently captured by the Americans, and turned upon the English. Major Williams and Major Ackland were both made prisoners, and in this part of the field the advantage of the Americans was decided. The British centre still held its ground; but now it was that the American general Arnold appeared upon the scene and did more for his countrymen than whole battalions could have effected. Arnold, when the decisive engagement of the 7th of October commenced, had been deprived of his command by Gates, in consequence of a quarrel between them about the action of the 19th of September. He had listened for a short time in the American camp to the thunder of the battle, in which he had no military right to take part, either as commander or as combatant. But his excited spirit could not long endure such a state of inaction. He called for his horse, a powerful brown charger, and, springing on it, galloped furiously to where the fight seemed to be the thickest. Gates saw him, and sent an aide-de-camp to recall him; but Arnold spurred far in advance, and placed himself at the head of three regiments which had formerly been under him, and which welcomed their old commander with joyous cheers. He led them instantly upon the British centre; and then, galloping along the American line, he issued orders for a renewed and a closer attack, which were obeyed with alacrity Arnold himself setting the example of the most daring personal bravery and charging more than once, sword in hand, into the English ranks. On the British side the officers did their duty nobly; but General Fraser was the most eminent of them all, restoring order wherever the line began to waver, and infusing fresh courage into his men by voice and example. Mounted on an iron-gray charger, and dressed in the full uniform of a general officer, he was conspicuous to foes as well as to friends. The American Colonel Morgan thought that the fate of the battle rested on this gallant man's life, and, calling several of his best marksmen round him, pointed Fraser out, and said: "That officer is General Fraser; I admire him, but he must die. Our victory depends on it. Take your stations in that clump of bushes, and do your duty." Within five minutes Fraser fell, mortally wounded, and was carried to the British camp by two grenadiers. Just previously to his being struck by the fatal bullet, one rifle-ball had cut the crupper of his saddle and another had passed through his horse's mane close behind the ears. His aide-de-camp had noticed this, and said: "It is evident that you are marked out for particular aim; would it not be prudent for you to retire from this place?" Fraser replied: "My duty forbids me to fly from danger"; and the next moment he fell.

Burgoyne's whole force was soon compelled to retreat towards their camp; the left and centre were in complete disorder; but the Light Infantry and the 24th checked the fury of the assailants, and the remains of the column with great difficulty effected their return to their camp, leaving six of their cannons in the possession of the enemy, and great numbers of killed and wounded on the field, and especially a large proportion of the artillerymen, who had stood to their guns until shot down or bayoneted beside them by the advancing Americans.

Burgoyne's column had been defeated, but the action was not yet over. The English had scarcely entered the camp, when the Americans, pursuing their success, assaulted it in several places with remarkable impetuosity, rushing in upon the intrenchments through a severe fire of grape-shot and musketry. Arnold especially, who on this day appeared maddened with the thirst of combat and carnage, urged on the attack against a part of the intrenchments which was occupied by the Light Infantry under Lord Balcarres![11] But the English received him with vigor and spirit. The struggle here was obstinate and sanguinary. At length, as it grew towards evening, Arnold having forced all obstacles, entered the works with some of the most fearless of his followers. But in this critical moment of glory and danger, he received a painful wound in the same leg which had already been injured at the assault on Quebec. To his bitter regret, he was obliged to be carried back. His party still continued the attack; but the English also continued their obstinate resistance, and at last night fell, and the assailants withdrew from this quarter of the British intrenchments. But in another part the attack had been more successful. A body of the Americans, under Colonel Brooke, forced their way in through a part of the intrenchments on the extreme right, which was defended by the Hessian reserve under Colonel Breyman. The Germans resisted well, and Breyman died in defence of his post, but the Americans made good the ground which they had won, and captured baggage, tents, artillery, and a store of ammunition, which they were greatly in need of. They had, by establishing themselves on this point, acquired the means of completely turning the right flank of the British, and gaining their rear. To prevent this calamity, Burgoyne effected during the night an entire change of position. With great skill, he removed his whole army to some heights near the river, a little northward of the former camp, and he there drew up his men, expecting to be attacked on the following day. But Gates was resolved not to risk the certain triumph which his success had already secured for him. He harassed the English with skirmishes, but attempted no regular attack. Meanwhile he detached bodies of troops on both sides of the Hudson to prevent the British from recrossing that river and to bar their retreat. When night fell, it became absolutely necessary for Burgoyne to retire again, and, accordingly, the troops were marched through a stormy and rainy night towards Saratoga, abandoning their sick and wounded, and the greater part of their baggage to the enemy.

Before the rear-guard quitted the camp, the last sad honors were paid to the brave General Fraser, who expired on the day after the action.

He had, almost with his last breath, expressed a wish to be buried in the redoubt which had formed the part of the British lines where he had been stationed, but which had now been abandoned by the English, and was within full range of the cannon which the advancing Americans were rapidly placing in position to bear upon Burgoyne's force. Burgoyne resolved, nevertheless, to comply with the dying wish of his comrade; and the interment took place under circumstances the most affecting that have ever marked a soldier's funeral. Still more interesting is the narrative of Lady Ackland's passage from the British to the American camp, after the battle, to share the captivity and alleviate the sufferings of her husband, who had been severely wounded and left in the enemy's power. The American historian Lossing has described both these touching episodes of the campaign in a spirit that does honor to the writer as well as to his subject. After narrating the death of General Fraser on the 8th of October, he says that "it was just at sunset, on that calm October evening, that the corpse of General Fraser was carried up the hill to the place of burial within the 'great redoubt.' It was attended only by the members of his military family and Mr. Brudenell, the chaplain; yet the eyes of hundreds of both armies followed the solemn procession, while the Americans, ignorant of its true character, kept up a constant cannonade upon the redoubt. The chaplain, unawed by the danger to which he was exposed, as the cannon-balls which struck the hill threw the loose soil over him, pronounced the impressive funeral service of the Church of England with an unfaltering voice. The growing darkness added solemnity to the scene. Suddenly the irregular firing ceased, and the solemn voice of a single cannon, at measured intervals, boomed along the valley, and awakened the responses of the hills. It was a minute-gun fired by the Americans in honor of the gallant dead. The moment information was given that the gathering at the redoubt was a funeral company, fulfilling, amid imminent perils, the last-breathed wishes of the noble Fraser, orders were issued to withhold the cannonade with balls and to render military homage to the fallen brave.

"The case of Major Ackland and his heroic wife presents kindred features. He belonged to the corps of grenadiers, and was an accomplished soldier. His wife accompanied him to Canada in 1776, and during the whole campaign of that year, and until his return to England after the surrender of Burgoyne, in the autumn of 1777, endured all the hardships, dangers, and privations of an active campaign in an enemy's country. At Chambly, on the Sorel, she attended him in illness, in a miserable hut; and when he was wounded in the battle of Hubbardton, Vermont, she hastened to him at Skenesborough from Montreal, where she had been persuaded to remain, and resolved to follow the army thereafter. Just before crossing the Hudson, she and her husband came near losing their lives in consequence of their tent accidentally taking fire.

"During the terrible engagement of the 7th of October, she heard all the tumult and dreadful thunder of the battle in which her husband was engaged; and when, on the morning of the 8th, the British fell back in confusion to Wilbur's Basin, she, with the other women, was obliged to take refuge among the dead and dying, for the tents were all struck, and hardly a shed was left standing. Her husband was wounded and a prisoner in the American camp. That gallant officer was shot through both legs. When Poor and Learned's troops assaulted the grenadiers and artillery on the British left, on the afternoon of the 7th, Wilkinson, Gates's adjutant-general, while pursuing the flying enemy when they abandoned their battery, heard a feeble voice exclaim, 'Protect me, sir, against that boy.' He turned and saw a lad with a musket taking deliberate aim at a wounded British officer, lying in a corner of a worm fence. Wilkinson ordered the boy to desist, and discovered the wounded man to be Major Ackland. He had him conveyed to the quarters of General Poor (now the residence of Mr. Neilson) on the heights, where every attention was paid to his wants.

"When the intelligence that he was wounded and a prisoner reached his wife, she was greatly distressed, and, by the advice of her friend, Baron Riedesel, resolved to visit the American camp and implore the favor of a personal attendance upon her husband. On the 9th she sent a message to Burgoyne by Lord Petersham, his aide, asking permission to depart. 'Though I was ready to believe,' says Burgoyne, 'that patience and fortitude, in a supreme degree, were to be found, as well as every other virtue, under the most tender forms, I was astonished at this proposal. After so long an agitation of spirits, exhausted not only for want of rest but absolute want of food, drenched in rain for twelve hours together, that a woman should be capable of such an undertaking as delivering herself to an enemy, probably in the night, and uncertain of what hands she might fall into, appeared an effort above human nature. The assistance I was enabled to give was small indeed. I had not even a cup of wine to offer her.

All I could furnish to her was an open boat, and a few lines, written upon dirty wet paper, to General Gates, recommending her to his protection.'

"The following is a copy of the note from Burgoyne to General Gates: 'Sir—Lady Harriet Ackland, a lady of the first distinction of family, rank, and personal virtues, is under such concern on account of Major Ackland, her husband, wounded and a prisoner in your hands, that I cannot refuse her request to commit her to your protection. Whatever general impropriety there may be in persons in my situation and yours to solicit favors, I cannot see the uncommon perseverance in every female grace and the exaltation of character of this lady, and her very hard fortune, without testifying that your attentions to her will lay me under obligations. I am, sir, your obedient servant, J. Burgoyne.'

"She set out in an open boat upon the Hudson, accompanied by Mr. Brudenell, the chaplain, Sarah Pollard her waiting-maid, and her husband's valet, who had been severely wounded while searching for his master upon the battle-field. It was about sunset when they started, and a violent storm of rain and wind, which had been increasing since morning, rendered the voyage tedious and perilous in the extreme. It was long after dark when they reached the American outposts; the sentinel heard their oars and hailed them. Lady Harriet returned the answer herself. The clear, silvery tones of a woman's voice amid the darkness filled the soldier on duty with superstitious fear, and he called a comrade to accompany him to the river bank. The errand of the voyagers was made known, but the faithful guard, apprehensive of treachery, would not allow them to land until they sent for Major Dearborn. They were invited by that officer to his quarters, where every attention was paid to them, and Lady Harriet was comforted by the joyful tidings that her husband was safe. In the morning she experienced parental tenderness from General Gates, who sent her to her husband, at Poor's quarters, under a suitable escort. There she remained until he was removed to Albany."

Burgoyne now took up his last position on the heights near Saratoga; and, hemmed in by the enemy, who refused any encounter, and baffled in all his attempts at finding a path of escape, he there lingered until famine compelled him to capitulate. The fortitude of the British army during this melancholy period has been justly eulogized by many native historians, but I prefer quoting the testimony of a foreign writer, as free from all possibility of partiality. Botta says:

"It exceeds the power of words to describe the pitiable condition to which the British army was now reduced. The troops were worn down by a series of toil, privation, sickness, and desperate fighting. They were abandoned by the Indians and Canadians; and the effective force of the whole army was now diminished by repeated and heavy losses, which had principally fallen on the best soldiers and the most distinguished officers, from ten thousand combatants to less than one-half that number. Of this remnant little more than three thousand were English.

"In these circumstances, and thus weakened, they were invested by an army of four times their own number, whose position extended three parts of a circle round them; who refused to fight them, as knowing their weakness, and who, from the nature of the ground, could not be attacked in any part. In this helpless condition, obliged to be constantly under arms while the enemy's cannon played on every part of their camp and even the American rifle-balls whistled in many parts of the lines, the troops of Burgoyne retained their customary firmness; and, while sinking under a hard necessity, they showed themselves worthy of a better fate. They could not be reproached with an action or a word which betrayed a want of temper or of fortitude."

At length the 13th of October arrived, and as no prospect of assistance appeared, and the provisions were nearly exhausted, Burgoyne, by the unanimous advice of a council of war, sent a messenger to the American camp to treat of a convention.

General Gates in the first instance demanded that the royal army should surrender prisoners of war. He also proposed that the British should ground their arms. Burgoyne replied, "This article is inadmissible in every extremity; sooner than this army will consent to ground their arms in their encampment, they will rush on the enemy, determined to take no quarter." After various messages, a convention for the surrender of the army was settled which provided that "the troops under General Burgoyne were to march out of their camp with the honors of war, and the artillery of the intrenchments, to the verge of the river, where the arms and artillery were to be left. The arms to be piled by word of command from their own officers. A free passage was to be granted to the army under Lieutenant-General Burgoyne to Great Britain, upon condition of not serving again in North America during the present contest."

The Articles of Capitulation were settled on the 15th of October; and on that very evening a messenger arrived from Clinton with an account of his successes, and with the tidings that part of his force had penetrated as far as Esopus, within fifty miles of Burgoyne's camp. But it was too late. The public faith was pledged; and the army was indeed too debilitated by fatigue and hunger to resist an attack, if made; and Gates certainly would have made it, if the convention had been broken off. Accordingly, on the 17th, the Convention of Saratoga was carried into effect. By this convention 5,790 men surrendered themselves as prisoners. The sick and wounded left in the camp when the British retreated to Saratoga, together with the numbers of the British, German, and Canadian troops who were killed, wounded, or taken, and who had deserted in the preceding part of the expedition, were reckoned to be 4,689.

The British sick and wounded who had fallen into the hands of the Americans after the battle of the 7th were treated with exemplary humanity; and when the Convention was executed, General Gates showed a noble delicacy of feeling, which deserves the highest degree of honor. Every circumstance was avoided which could give the appearance of triumph. The American troops remained within their lines until the British had piled their arms; and when this was done, the vanquished officers and soldiers were received with friendly kindness by their victors, and their immediate wants were promptly and liberally supplied. Discussions and disputes afterwards arose as to some of the terms of the Convention, and the American Congress refused for a long time to carry into effect the article which provided for the return of Burgoyne's men to Europe; but no blame was imputable to General Gates or his army, who showed themselves to be generous as they had proved themselves to be brave.

Gates, after the victory, immediately despatched Colonel Wilkinson to carry the happy tidings to Congress. On being introduced into the hall, he said: "The whole British army has laid down its arms at Saratoga; our own, full of vigor and courage, expect your orders. It is for your wisdom to decide where the country may still have need for their service." Honors and rewards were liberally voted by the Congress to their conquering general and his men; and it would be difficult (says the Italian historian) to describe the transports of joy which the news of this event excited among the Americans. They began to flatter themselves with a still more happy future. No one any longer felt any doubt about their achieving their independence. All hoped, and with good reason, that a success of this importance would at length determine France, and the other European powers that waited for her example, to declare themselves in favor of America. "*There could no longer be any question respecting the future, since there was no longer the risk of espousing the cause of a people too feeble to defend themselves.*"[12]

The truth of this was soon displayed in the conduct of France. When the news arrived at Paris of the capture of Ticonderoga, and of the victorious march of Burgoyne towards Albany, events which seemed decisive in favor of the English, instructions had been immediately despatched to Nantes, and the other ports of the kingdom, that no American privateers should be suffered to enter them, except from indispensable necessity; as to repair their vessels, to obtain provisions, or to escape the perils of the sea. The American commissioners at Paris, in their disgust and despair, had almost broken off all negotiations with the French government; and they even endeavored to open communications with the British ministry. But the British government, elated with the first successes of Burgoyne, refused to listen to any overtures for accommodation. But when the news of Saratoga reached Paris the whole scene was changed. Franklin and his brother commissioners found all their difficulties with the French government vanish. The time seemed to have arrived for the house of Bourbon to take a full revenge for all its humiliations and losses in previous wars. In December a treaty was arranged, and formally signed in the February following, by which France acknowledged *the Independent United States of America*. This was, of course, tantamount to a declaration of war with England. Spain soon followed France; and, before long, Holland took the same course. Largely aided by French fleets and troops, the Americans vigorously maintained the war against the armies which England, in spite of her European foes, continued to send across the Atlantic. But the struggle was too unequal to be maintained by this country for many years; and when the treaties of 1783 restored peace to the world, the independence of the United States was reluctantly recognized by their ancient parent and recent enemy, England.

Synopsis of European Events between the Defeat of Burgoyne at Saratoga, 1777, and the Battle of Valmy, 1792.

1782. Rodney's victory over the Spanish fleet. Unsuccessful siege of Gibraltar by the Spaniards and French.

1788. The States-General are convened in France; beginning of the French Revolution.

Synopsis of Events in American History between the Declaration of Independence, AD 1776, and the Battle of Gettysburg, AD 1863.

Declaration of Independence of the American Colonies, July 4, 1776.

Independence of the United States recognized by Great Britain by treaty signed at Paris, September 3, 1783.

The same treaty ratified by Congress, January 4, 1784.

Second war between the United States and Great Britain ends with the Treaty of Ghent, which is ratified by Congress, February 17, 1815.

Henry Clay's "Missouri Compromise," to effect a *modus vivendi* between the slaveholding states and those opposed to slavery, February, 1820.

Treaty of peace closing the war between the United States and Mexico, ratified, May 19, 1848.

John Brown's raid on Harper's Ferry, Virginia, October 16, 1859.

Abraham Lincoln, Republican candidate, elected President of the United States in succession to James Buchanan, November 6, 1860.

CHAPTER XIV

THE BATTLE OF VALMY, AD 1792

"Purpurei metuunt tyranni
Injurioso ne pede proruas
Stantem columnam: neu populus frequens
Ad arma cessantes ad arma
Concitet, imperiumque frangat."

—*Horat., Od.* i., 35.

"A little fire is quickly trodden out,
Which, being suffered, rivers cannot quench."

—*Shakespeare.*

A few miles distant from the little town of St. Menehould, in the northeast of France, are the village and hill of Valmy, and near the crest of that hill a simple monument points out the burial-place of the heart of a general of the French republic and a marshal of the French empire.

The elder Kellermann (father of the distinguished officer of that name, whose cavalry charge decided the battle of Marengo) held high commands in the French armies throughout the wars of the Convention, the Directory, the Consulate, and the Empire. He survived those wars, and the empire itself, dying in extreme old age in 1820. The last wish of the veteran on his death-bed was that his heart should be deposited in the battlefield of Valmy, there to repose among the remains of his old companions in arms who had fallen at his side on that spot twenty-eight years before, on the memorable day when they won the primal victory of Revolutionary France, and prevented the armies of Brunswick and the emigrant bands of Condé from marching on defenceless Paris and destroying the immature democracy in its cradle.

The Duke of Valmy (for Kellermann, when made one of Napoleon's military peers in 1802, took his title from this same battle-field) had participated, during his long and active career, in the gaining of many a victory far more immediately dazzling than the one the remembrance of which he thus cherished. He had been present at many a scene of carnage, where blood flowed in deluges, compared with which the libations of slaughter poured out at Valmy would have seemed scant and insignificant. But he rightly estimated the paramount importance of the battle with which he thus wished his appellation while living, and his memory after his death, to be identified. The successful resistance which the raw Carmagnole levies and the disorganized relics of the old monarchy's army then opposed to the combined hosts and chosen leaders of Prussia, Austria, and the French refugee *noblesse*, determined at once and forever the belligerent character of the revolution. The raw artisans and tradesmen, the clumsy burghers, the base mechanics, and low peasant-churls, as it had been the fashion to term the middle and lower classes in France, found that they could face cannon-balls, pull triggers, and cross bayonets without having been drilled into military machines, and without being officered by scions of noble houses. They awoke to the consciousness of their own instinctive soldiership. They at once acquired confidence in themselves and in each other; and that confidence soon grew into a spirit of unbounded audacity and ambition. "From the cannonade of Valmy may be dated the commencement of that career of victory which carried their armies to Vienna and the Kremlin."[1]

One of the gravest reflections that arises from the contemplation of the civil restlessness and military enthusiasm which the close of the last century saw nationalized in France, is the consideration that these disturbing influences have become perpetual.

No settled system of government, that shall endure from generation to generation, that shall be proof against corruption and
popular violence, seems capable of taking root among the French.
And every revolutionary movement in Paris thrills throughout the
rest of the world. Even the successes which the powers allied
against France gained in 1814 and 1815, important as they were,
could not annul the effects of the preceding twenty-three years of
general convulsion and war.

In 1830, the dynasty which foreign bayonets had imposed on
France was shaken off, and men trembled at the expected outbreak of French anarchy and the dreaded inroads of French ambition. They "looked forward with harassing anxiety to a period of
destruction similar to that which the Roman world experienced
about the middle of the third century of our era."[2] Louis Philippe
cajoled Revolution, and then strove with seeming success to stifle
it. But, in spite of Fieschi laws, in spite of the dazzle of Algerian
razzias and Pyrenee-effacing marriages, in spite of hundreds of
armed forts, and hundreds of thousands of coercing troops,
Revolution lived, and struggled to get free. The old Titan spirit
heaved restlessly beneath "the monarchy based on republican
institutions." At last, three years ago, the whole fabric of kingcraft
was at once rent and scattered to the winds by the uprising of the
Parisian democracy; and insurrections, barricades, and dethrone-
ments, the downfalls of coronets and crowns, the armed collisions
of parties, systems, and populations, became the commonplaces
of recent European history.

France now calls herself a republic. She first assumed that title
on the 20th of September, 1792, on the very day on which the battle of Valmy was fought and won. To that battle the democratic
spirit which in 1848, as well as in 1792, proclaimed the Republic in
Paris, owed its preservation, and it is thence that the imperishable
activity of its principles may be dated.

Far different seemed the prospects of democracy in Europe
on the eve of that battle, and far different would have been
the present position and influence of the French nation, if

Brunswick's columns had charged with more boldness, or the lines of Dumouriez resisted with less firmness. When France, in 1792, declared war with the great powers of Europe, she was far from possessing that splendid military organization which the experience of a few revolutionary campaigns taught her to assume, and which she has never abandoned. The army of the old monarchy had, during the latter part of the reign of Louis XV., sunk into gradual decay, both in numerical force and in efficiency of equipment and spirit. The laurels gained by the auxiliary regiments which Louis XVI. sent to the American war, did but little to restore the general tone of the army. The insubordination and license which the revolt of the French guards, and the participation of other troops in many of the first excesses of the Revolution, introduced among the soldiery, were soon rapidly disseminated through all the ranks. Under the Legislative Assembly every complaint of the soldier against his officer, however frivolous or ill-founded, was listened to with eagerness, and investigated with partiality, on the principles of liberty and equality. Discipline accordingly became more and more relaxed; and the dissolution of several of the old corps, under the pretext of their being tainted with an aristocratic feeling, aggravated the confusion and inefficiency of the war department. Many of the most effective regiments during the last period of the monarchy had consisted of foreigners. These had either been slaughtered in defence of the throne against insurrections, like the Swiss, or had been disbanded, and had crossed the frontier to recruit the forces which were assembled for the invasion of France. Above all, the emigration of the *noblesse* had stripped the French army of nearly all its officers of high rank, and of the greatest portion of its subalterns. Above twelve thousand of the high-born youth of France, who had been trained to regard military command as their exclusive patrimony, and to whom the nation had been accustomed to look up as its natural guides and champions in the storm of war, were now marshalled beneath the banner of Condé and the other emigrant princes for the overthrow of the French armies and the reduction of the French capital. Their successors in the French regiments and brigades had as yet acquired neither skill nor experience; they possessed neither self-reliance, nor the respect of the men who were under them.

Such was the state of the wrecks of the old army; but the bulk of the forces with which France began the war consisted of raw insurrectionary levies, which were even less to be depended on. The Carmagnoles, as the revolutionary volunteers were called, flocked, indeed, readily to the frontier from every department when the war was proclaimed, and the fierce leaders of the Jacobins shouted that the country was in danger. They were full of zeal and courage, "heated and excited by the scenes of the Revolution, and inflamed by the florid eloquence, the songs, dances, and signal-words with which it had been celebrated."[3] But they were utterly undisciplined, and turbulently impatient of superior authority or systematic control. Many ruffians, also, who were sullied with participation in the most sanguinary horrors of Paris, joined the camps, and were pre-eminent alike for misconduct before the enemy and for savage insubordination against their own officers. On one occasion during the campaign of Valmy, eight battalions of federates, intoxicated with massacre and sedition, joined the forces under Dumouriez, and soon threatened to uproot all discipline, saying openly that the ancient officers were traitors, and that it was necessary to purge the army, as they had Paris, of its aristocrats. Dumouriez posted these battalions apart from the others, placed a strong force of cavalry behind them, and two pieces of cannon on their flank. Then, affecting to review them, he halted at the head of the line, surrounded by all his staff, and an escort of a hundred hussars. "Fellows," said he, "for I will not call you either citizens or soldiers, you see before you this artillery, behind you this cavalry; you are stained with crimes, and I do not tolerate here assassins or executioners. I know that there are scoundrels among you charged to excite you to crime. Drive them from among you, or denounce them to me, for I shall hold you responsible for their conduct."[4]

One of our recent historians of the Revolution, who narrates this incident,[5] thus apostrophizes the French general:

"Patience, o Dumouriez! this uncertain heap of shriekers, mutineers, were they once drilled and inured, will become a phalanxed mass of fighters; and wheel and whirl to order swiftly, like the wind or the whirlwind; tanned mustachio-figures, often barefoot, even bare-backed, with sinews of iron, who require only bread and gunpowder; very sons of fire, the adroitest, hastiest, hottest ever seen, perhaps, since Attila's time."

Such phalanxed masses of fighters did the Carmagnoles ultimately become; but France ran a fearful risk in being obliged to rely on them when the process of their transmutation had barely commenced.

The first events, indeed, of the war were disastrous and disgraceful to France, even beyond what might have been expected from the chaotic state in which it found her armies as well as her government. In the hopes of profiting by the unprepared state of Austria, then the mistress of the Netherlands, the French opened the campaign of 1792 by an invasion of Flanders, with forces whose muster-rolls showed a numerical overwhelming superiority to the enemy, and seemed to promise a speedy conquest of that old battle-field of Europe. But the first flash of an Austrian sabre, or the first sound,of an Austrian gun, was enough to discomfit the French. Their first corps, four thousand strong, that advanced from Lille across the frontier, came suddenly upon a far inferior detachment of the Austrian garrison of Tournay. Not a shot was fired, nor a bayonet levelled. With one simultaneous cry of panic, the French broke and ran headlong back to Lille, where they completed the specimen of insubordination which they had given in the field by murdering their general and several of their chief officers. On the same day, another division under Biron, mustering ten thousand sabres and bayonets, saw a few Austrian skirmishers reconnoitring their position. The French advanced posts had scarcely given and received a volley, and only a few balls from the enemy's field-pieces had fallen among the lines, when two regiments of French dragoons raised the cry "We are betrayed," galloped off, and were followed in disgraceful rout by the rest of the whole army. Similar panics, or repulses almost equally discreditable, occurred whenever Rochambeau, or Lückner, or Lafayette, the earliest French generals in the war, brought their troops into the presence of the enemy.

Meanwhile the allied sovereigns had gradually collected on the Rhine a veteran and finely-disciplined army for the invasion of France, which for numbers, equipment, and martial renown, both of generals and men, was equal to any that Germany had ever sent forth to conquer. Their design was to strike boldly and decisively at the heart of France, and, penetrating the country through the Ardennes, to proceed by Châlons upon Paris. The obstacles that lay in their way seemed insignificant. The disorder and imbecility of the French armies had been even augmented by the forced flight of Lafayette and a sudden change of generals. The only troops posted on or near the track by which the allies were about to advance were the 23,000 men at Sedan, whom Lafayette had commanded, and a corps of 20,000 near Metz, the command of which had just been transferred from Liickner to Kellermann. There were only three fortresses which it was necessary for the allies to capture or mask—Sedan, Longwy, and Verdun. The defences and stores of all these three were known to be wretchedly dismantled and insufficient; and when once these feeble barriers were overcome and Châlons reached, a fertile and unprotected country seemed to invite the invaders to that "military promenade to Paris" which they gayly talked of accomplishing.

At the end of July, the allied army, having fully completed all preparations for the campaign, broke up from its cantonments, and, marching from Luxembourg upon Longwy, crossed the French frontier. Sixty thousand Prussians, trained in the schools, and many of them under the eye of the Great Frederick, heirs of the glories of the Seven Years' War, and universally esteemed the best troops in Europe, marched in one column against the central point of attack. Forty-five thousand Austrians, the greater part of whom were picked troops, and had served in the recent Turkish war, supplied two formidable corps that supported the flanks of the Prussians. There was also a powerful body of Hessians; and leagued with the Germans against the Parisian democracy came 15,000 of the noblest and the bravest among the sons of France. In these corps of emigrants, many of the highest born of the French nobility, scions of houses whose chivalric trophies had for centuries filled Europe with renown, served as rank and file. They looked on the road to Paris as the path which they were to carve out by their swords to victory, to honor, to the rescue of their king, to reunion with their families, to the recovery of their patrimony, and to the restoration of their order.[6]

Over this imposing army the allied sovereigns placed as generalissimo the Duke of Brunswick, one of the minor reigning princes of Germany, a statesman of no mean capacity, and who had acquired in the Seven Years' War a military reputation second only to that of the Great Frederick himself. He had been deputed a few years before to quell the popular movements which then took place in Holland, and he had put down the attempted revolution in that country with a promptitude which appeared to augur equal success to the army that now marched under his orders on a similar mission into France.

Moving majestically forward, with leisurely deliberation, that seemed to show the consciousness of superior strength, and a steady purpose of doing their work thoroughly, the allies appeared before Longwy on the 20th of August, and the dispirited and despondent garrison opened the gates of that fortress to them after the first shower of bombs. On the 2d of September, the still more important stronghold of Verdun capitulated after scarcely the shadow of resistance.

Brunswick's superior force was now interposed between Kellermann's troops on the left and the other French army near Sedan, which Lafayette's flight had, for the time, left destitute of a commander. It was in the power of the German general, by striking with an overwhelming mass to the right and left, to crush in succession each of these weak armies, and the allies might then have marched irresistible and unresisted upon Paris. But at this crisis Dumouriez, the new commander-in-chief of the French, arrived at the camp near Sedan, and commenced a series of movements by which he reunited the dispersed and disorganized forces of his country, checked the Prussian columns at the very moment when the last obstacles to their triumph seemed to have given way, and finally rolled back the tide of invasion far across the enemy's frontier.

The French fortresses had fallen; but nature herself still offered to brave and vigorous defenders of the land the means of opposing a barrier to the progress of the allies. A ridge of broken ground, called the Argonne, extends from the vicinity of Sedan towards the southwest for about fifteen or sixteen leagues. The country of L'Argonne has now been cleared and drained; but in 1792 it was thickly wooded, and the lower portions of its unequal surface were filled with rivulets and marshes. It thus presented a natural barrier of from four to five leagues broad which was absolutely impenetrable to an army, except by a few defiles, such as an inferior force might easily fortify and defend. Dumouriez succeeded in marching his army down from Sedan behind the Argonne, and in occupying its passes, while the Prussians still lingered on the northeastern side of the forest line. Ordering Kellermann to wheel round from Metz to St. Menehould and the re-enforcements from the interior and the extreme north also to concentrate at that spot, Dumouriez trusted to assemble a powerful force in the rear of the southwest extremity of the Argonne, while with the twenty-five thousand men under his immediate command he held the enemy at bay before the passes, or forced him to a long circumvolution round one extremity of the forest ridge, during which, favorable opportunities of assailing his flank were almost certain to occur. Dumouriez fortified the principal defiles, and boasted of the Thermopylæ which he had found for the invaders; but the simile was nearly rendered fatally complete for the defending force. A pass, which was thought of inferior importance, had been but slightly manned, and an Austrian corps, under Clairfayt, forced it after some sharp fighting. Dumouriez with great difficulty saved himself from being enveloped and destroyed by the hostile columns that now pushed through the forest. But instead of despairing at the failure of his plans, and falling back into the interior, to be completely severed from Kellermann's army, to be hunted as a fugitive under the walls of Paris by the victorious Germans, and to lose all chance of ever rallying his dispirited troops, he resolved to cling to the difficult country in which the armies still were grouped, to force a junction with Kellermann, and so to place himself at the head of a force which the invaders would not dare to disregard, and by which he might drag them back from the advance on Paris, which he had not been able to bar. Accordingly, by a rapid movement to the south, during which, in his own words, "France was within a hair's breadth of destruction," and after with difficulty checking several panics of his troops, in which they ran by thousands at the sight of a few Prussian hussars, Dumouriez succeeded in establishing his head-quarters in a strong position at St. Menehould, protected by the marshes and shallows of the rivers Aisne and Aube, beyond which, to the northwest, rose a firm and elevated plateau, called Dampierre's camp, admirably situated for commanding the road by Châlons to Paris, and where he intended to post Kellermann's army so soon as it came up.[7]

The news of the retreat of Dumouriez from the Argonne passes, and of the panic flight of some divisions of his troops, spread rapidly throughout the country, and Kellermann, who believed that his comrade's army had been annihilated, and feared to fall among the victorious masses of the Prussians, had halted on his march from Metz when almost close to St. Menehould. He had actually commenced a retrograde movement, when couriers from his commander-in-chief checked him from that fatal course; and then continuing to wheel round the rear and left flank of the troops at St. Menehould, Kellerman, with twenty thousand of the army of Metz, and some thousands of volunteers, who had joined him in the march, made his appearance to the west of Dumouriez on the very evening when Westerman and Thouvenot, two of the staff-officers of Dumouriez, galloped in with the tidings that Brunswick's army had come through the upper passes of the Argonne in full force, and was deploying on the heights of La Lune, a chain of eminences that stretch obliquely from southwest to northeast, opposite the high ground which Dumouriez held, and also opposite but at a shorter distance from the position which Kellermann was designed to occupy.

The allies were now, in fact, nearer to Paris than were the French troops themselves; but, as Dumouriez had foreseen, Brunswick deemed it unsafe to march upon the capital with so large a hostile force left in his rear between his advancing columns and his base of operations. The young King of Prussia, who was in the allied camp, and the emigrant princes, eagerly advocated an instant attack upon the nearest French general. Kellermann had laid himself unnecessarily open, by advancing beyond Dampierre's camp, which Dumouriez had designed for him, and moving forward across the Aube to the plateau of Valmy, a post inferior in strength and space to that which he had left, and which brought him close upon the Prussian lines, leaving him separated by a dangerous interval from the troops under Dumouriez himself. It seemed easy for the Prussian army to overwhelm him while thus isolated, and then they might surround and crush Dumouriez at their leisure.

Accordingly, the right wing of the allied army moved forward in the gray of the morning of the 20th of September to gain Kellermann's left flank and rear, and cut him off from retreat upon Châlons, while the rest of the army, moving from the heights of La Lune, which here converge semi-circularly round the plateau of Valmy, were to assail his position in front, and interpose between him and Dumouriez. An unexpected collision between some of the advanced cavalry on each side in the low ground warned Kellermann of the enemy's approach. Dumouriez had not been unobservant of the danger of his comrade, thus isolated and involved, and he had ordered up troops to support Kellermann on either flank in the event of his being attacked. These troops, however, moved forward slowly; and Kellermann's army ranged on the plateau of Valmy "projected like a cape into the midst of the lines of the Prussian bayonets."[8] A thick autumnal mist floated in waves of vapor over the plains and ravines that lay between the two armies, leaving only the crests and peaks of the hills glittering in the early light. About ten o'clock the fog began to clear off, and then the French from their promontory saw emerging from the white wreaths of mist, and glittering in the sunshine, the countless Prussian cavalry, which were to envelop them as in a net if once driven from their position, the solid columns of the infantry, that moved forward as if animated by a single will, the bristling batteries of the artillery, and the glancing clouds of the Austrian light troops, fresh from their contests with the Spahis of the east.

The best and bravest of the French must have beheld this spectacle with secret apprehension and awe. However bold and resolute a man may be in the discharge of duty, it is an anxious and fearful thing to be called on to encounter danger among comrades of whose steadiness you can fell no certainty. Each soldier of Kellermann's army must have remembered the series of panic routs which had hitherto invariably taken place on the French side during the war, and must have cast restless glances to the right and left, to see is any symptoms of wavering began to show themselves, and to calculate how long it was likely to be before a general rush of his comrades to the rear would either hurry him off with involuntary disgrace, or leave him alone and helpless to be cut down by assailing multitudes.

On that very morning, and at the self-same hour in which the allied forces and the emigrants began to descend from La Lune at the attack of Valmy, and while the cannonade was opening between the Prussian and Revolutionary batteries, the debate in the National Convention at Paris commenced on the proposal to proclaim France a republic.

The old monarchy had little chance of support in the hall of the Convention; but if its more effective advocates at Valmy had triumphed, there were yet the elements existing in France for an effective revival of the better part of the ancient institutions, and for substituting Reform for Revolution. Only a few weeks before, numerously signed addresses from the middle classes in Paris, Rouen, and other large cities had been presented to the king expressive of their horror of the anarchists, and their readiness to uphold the rights of the crown, together with the liberties of the subject. And an armed resistance to the authority of the Convention, and in favor of the king, was in reality at this time being actively organized in La Vendée and Brittany, the importance of which may be estimated from the formidable opposition which the Royalists of these provinces made to the Republican party at a later period, and under much more disadvantageous circumstances. It is a fact peculiarly illustrative of the importance of the battle of Valmy, that "during the summer of 1792 the gentlemen of Brittany entered into an extensive association for the purpose of rescuing the country from the oppressive yoke which had been imposed by the Parisian demagogues. At the head of the whole was the Marquis de la Rouarie, one of those remarkable men who rise into eminence during the stormy days of a revolution, from conscious ability to direct its current. Ardent, impetuous, and enthusiastic, he was first distinguished in the American war, when the intrepidity of his conduct attracted the admiration of the republican troops, and the same qualities rendered him at first an ardent supporter of the Revolution in France; but when the atrocities of the people began, he espoused with equal warmth the opposite side, and used the utmost efforts to rouse the *noblesse* of Brittany against the plebeian yoke which had been imposed upon them by the National Assembly. He submitted his plan to the Count d'Artois, and had organized one so extensive as would have proved extremely formidable to the Convention, if the retreat of the Duke of Brunswick, in September, 1792, had not damped the ardor of the whole of the west of France, then ready to break out into insurrection."[9]

And it was not only among the zealots of the old monarchy that the cause of the king would then have found friends. The ineffable atrocities of the September massacres had just occurred, and the reaction produced by them among thousands who had previously been active on the ultra-democratic side was fresh and powerful. The nobility had not yet been made utter aliens in the eyes of the nation by long expatriation and civil war. There was not yet a generation of youth educated in revolutionary principles, and knowing no worship save that of military glory. Louis XVI. was just and humane, and deeply sensible of the necessity of a gradual extension of political rights among all classes of his subjects. The Bourbon throne, if rescued in 1792, would have had the chances of stability such as did not exist for it in 1814, and seem never likely to be found again in France.

Serving under Kellermann on that day was one who experienced, perhaps the most deeply of all men, the changes for good and for evil which the French Revolution has produced. He who, in his second exile, bore the name of the Count de Neuilly in this country, and who lately was Louis Philippe, king of the French, figured in the French lines at Valmy as a young and gallant officer, cool and sagacious beyond his years, and trusted accordingly by Kellermann and Dumouriez with an important station in the national army. The Duc de Chartres (the title he then bore) commanded the French right, General Valence was on the left, and Kellerman himself took his post in the centre, which was the strength and key of his position.

Besides these celebrated men who were in the French army, and besides the King of Prussia, the Duke of Brunswick, and other men of rank and power who were in the lines of the allies, there was an individual present at the battle of Valmy, of little political note, but who has exercised, and exercises, a greater influence over the human mind, and whose fame is more widely spread than that of either duke, or general, or king. This was the German poet Goethe, then in early youth, and who had, out of curiosity, accompanied the allied army on its march into France as a mere spectator.

He has given us a curious record of the sensations which he experienced during the cannonade. It must be remembered that many thousands in the French ranks then, like Goethe, felt the "cannon fever" for the first time. The German poet says:[10]

"I had heard so much of the cannon fever, that I wanted to know what kind of thing it was. *Ennui,* and a spirit which every kind of danger excites to daring, nay, even to rashness, induced me to ride up quite coolly to the outwork of La Lune. This was again occupied by our people; but it presented the wildest aspect. The roofs were shot to pieces, the corn-shocks scattered about, the bodies of men mortally wounded stretched upon them here and there, and occasionally a spent cannon-ball fell and rattled among the ruins of the tile roofs.

"Quite alone, and left to myself, I rode away on the heights to the left, and could plainly survey the favorable position of the French; they were standing in the form of a semicircle, in the greatest quiet and security, Kellermann, then on the left wing, being the easiest to reach.

"I fell in with good company on the way, officers of my acquaintance, belonging to the general staff and the regiment, greatly surprised to find me here. They wanted to take me back again with them; but I spoke to them of particular objects I had in view, and they left me, without further dissuasion, to my well-known singular caprice.

"I had now arrived quite in the region where the balls were playing across me: the sound of them is curious enough, as if it were composed of the humming of tops, the gurgling of water, and the whistling of birds. They were less dangerous by reason of the wetness of the ground; wherever one fell, it stuck fast. And thus my foolish experimental ride was secured against the danger at least of the balls rebounding.

"In the midst of these circumstances, I was soon able to remark that something unusual was taking place within me. I paid close attention to it, and still the sensation can be described only by similitude. It appeared as if you were in some extremely hot place, and, at the same time, quite penetrated by the heat of it, so that you feel yourself, as it were, quite one with the element in which you are. The eyes lose nothing of their strength or clearness; but it is as if the world had a kind of brown-red tint, which makes the situation, as well as the surrounding objects, more impressive. I was unable to perceive any agitation of the blood; but everything seemed rather to be swallowed up in the glow of which I speak. From this, then, it is clear in what sense this condition can be called a fever. It is remarkable, however, that the horrible uneasy feeling arising from it is produced in us solely through the ears. For the cannon thunder, the howling and crashing of the balls through the air, is the real cause of these sensations.

"After I had ridden back and was in perfect security, I remarked, with surprise, that the glow was completely extinguished, and not the slightest feverish agitation was left behind. On the whole, this condition is one of the least desirable; as, indeed, among my dear and noble comrades, I found scarcely one who expressed a really passionate desire to try it."

Contrary to the expectations of both friends and foes, the French infantry held their ground steadily under the fire of the Prussian guns, which thundered on them from La Lune, and their own artillery replied with equal spirit and greater effect on the denser masses of the allied army. Thinking that the Prussians were slackening in their fire, Kellermann formed a column in charging order, and dashed down into the valley in the hopes of capturing some of the nearest guns of the enemy. A masked battery opened its fire on the French column, and drove it back in disorder, Kellermann having his horse shot under him, and being with difficulty carried off by his men. The Prussian columns now advanced in turn. The French artillery-men began to waver and desert their posts, but were rallied by the efforts and example of their officers, and Kellermann, reorganizing the line of his infantry, took his station in the ranks on foot, and called out to his men to let the enemy come close up, and then to charge them with the bayonet. The troops caught the enthusiasm of their general, and a cheerful shout of *Vive la nation,* taken up by one battalion from another, pealed across the valley to the assailants. The Prussians hesitated from a charge up hill against a force that seemed so resolute and formidable; they halted for a while in the hollow, and then slowly retreated up their own side of the valley.

Indignant at being thus repulsed by such a foe, the King of Prussia formed the flower of his men in person, and, riding along the column, bitterly reproached them with letting their standard be thus humiliated. Then he led them on again to the attack, marching in the front line, and seeing his staff mowed down around him by the deadly fire which the French artillery reopened. But the troops sent by Dumouriez were now cooperating effectually with Kellerman, and that general's own men, flushed by success, presented a firmer front than ever. Again the Prussians retreated, leaving eight hundred dead behind, and at nightfall the French remained victors on the heights of Valmy.

All hopes of crushing the Revolutionary armies, and of the promenade to Paris, had now vanished, though Brunswick lingered long in the Argonne, till distress and sickness wasted away his once splendid force, and finally but a mere wreck of it recrossed the frontier. France, meanwhile, felt that she possessed a giant's strength, and like a giant did she use it. Before the close of that year all Belgium obeyed the National Convention at Paris, and the kings of Europe, after the lapse of eighteen centuries, trembled once more before a conquering military republic.

Goethe's description of the cannonade has been quoted. His observation to his comrades, and the camp of the allies at the end of the battle, deserves quotation also. It shows that the poet felt (and probably he alone, of the thousands there assembled, felt) the full importance of that day. He describes the consternation and the change of demeanor which he observed among his Prussian friends that evening. He tells us that "most of them were silent, and, in fact, the power of reflection and judgment was wanting to all. At last I was called upon to say what I thought of the engagement, for I had been in the habit of enlivening and amusing the troop with short sayings. This time I said, '*From this place and from this day forth commences a new era in the world's history, and you can all say that you were present at its birth.*'"

Synopsis of Events between the Battle of Valmy, AD 1792, and the Battle of Waterloo, AD 1815.

AD 1793. Trial and execution of Louis XVI. at Paris. England and Spain declare war against France. Royalist war in La Vendée. Second invasion of France by the allies.

1794. Lord Howe's victory over the French fleet. Final partition of Poland by Russia, Prussia, and Austria.

1795. The French armies, under Pichegru, conquer Holland. Cessation of the war in La Vendée

1796. Bonaparte commands the French army of Italy, and gains repeated victories over the Austrians.

1797. Victory of Jervis off Cape St. Vincent. Peace of Campo Formio between France and Austria. Defeat of the Dutch off Camperdown by Admiral Duncan.

1798. Rebellion in Ireland. Expedition of the French under Bonaparte to Egypt. Lord Nelson destroys the French fleet at the battle of the Nile.

1799. Renewal of the war between Austria and France. The Russian emperor sends an army in aid of Austria under Suwarrow. The French are repeatedly defeated in Italy. Bonaparte returns from Egypt and makes himself First Consul of France. Massena wins the battle of Zurich. The Russian emperor makes peace with France.

1800. Bonaparte passes the Alps, and defeats the Austrians at Marengo. Moreau wins the battle of Hohenlinden.

1801. Treaty of Luneville between France and Austria. The battle of Copenhagen.

1802. Peace of Amiens.

1803. War between England and France renewed.

1804. Napoleon Bonaparte is made Emperor of France.

1805. Great preparations of Napoleon to invade England. Austria, supported by Russia, renews war with France. Napoleon marches into Germany, takes Vienna, and gains the battle of Austerlitz. Lord Nelson destroys the combined French and Spanish fleets, and is killed at the battle of Trafalgar.

1806. War between Prussia and France. Napoleon conquers Prussia at the battle of Jena.

1807. Obstinate warfare between the French and Prussian armies in East Prussia and Poland. Peace of Tilsit.

1808. Napoleon endeavors to make his brother king of Spain. Rising of the Spanish nation against him. England sends troops to aid the Spaniards. Battle of Vimiera and Corunna.

1809. War renewed between France and Austria. Battles of Asperne and Wagram. Peace granted to Austria. Lord Wellington's victory of Talavera, in Spain.

1810. Marriage of Napoleon and the Archduchess Maria Louisa. Holland annexed to France.

1812. War between England and the United States. Napoleon invades Russia. Battle of Borodino. The French occupy Moscow, which is burned. Disastrous retreat and almost total destruction of the great army of France.

1813. Prussia and Austria take up arms again against France. Battles of Lützen, Bautzen, Dresden, Culm, and Leipsic. The French are driven out of Germany. Lord Wellington gains the great battle of Vittoria, which completes the rescue of Spain from France.

1814. The allies invade France on the eastern, and Lord Wellington invades it on the southern, frontier. Battles of Laon, Montmirail, Arcis-sur-Aube, and others in the northeast of France; and of Toulouse in the south. Paris surrenders to the allies, and Napoleon abdicates. First restoration of the Bourbons. Napoleon goes to the Isle of Elba, which is assigned to him by the allies. Treaty of Ghent between the United States and England.

CHAPTER XV

BATTLE OF WATERLOO, AD 1815

"Thou first and last of fields, king-making victory!"

— *Byron.*

ENGLAND has now been blessed with thirty-six years of peace. At no other period of her history can a similarly long cessation from a state of warfare be found. It is true that our troops have had battles to fight during this interval for the protection and extension of our Indian possessions and our colonies, but these have been with distant and unimportant enemies. The danger has never been brought near our own shores, and no matter of vital importance to our empire has ever been at stake. We have not had hostilities with either France, America, or Russia; and when not at war with any of our peers, we feel ourselves to be substantially at peace. There has, indeed, throughout this long period, been no great war, like those with which the previous history of modern Europe abounds. There have been formidable collisions between particular states, and there have been still more formidable collisions between the armed champions of the conflicting principles of absolutism and democracy; but there has been no general war, like those of the French Revolution, like the American, or the Seven Years' War, or like the war of the Spanish Succession. It would be far too much to augur from this that no similar wars will again convulse the world; but the value of the period of peace which Europe has gained is incalculable, even if we look on it as only a truce, and expect again to see the nations of the earth recur to what some philosophers have termed man's natural state of warfare.

No equal number of years can be found during which science, commerce, and civilization have advanced so rapidly and so extensively as has been the case since 1815. When we trace their progress, especially in this country, it is impossible not to feel that their wondrous development has been mainly due to the land having been at peace.[1] Their good effects cannot be obliterated even if a series of wars were to recommence. When we reflect on this and contrast these thirty-six years with the period that preceded them—a period of violence, of tumult, of unrestingly destructive energy—a period throughout which the wealth of nations was scattered like sand, and the blood of nations lavished like water, it is impossible not to look with deep interest on the final crisis of that dark and dreadful epoch—the crisis out of which our own happier cycle of years has been evolved. The great battle which ended the twenty-three years' war of the first French Revolution, and which quelled the man whose genius and ambition had so long disturbed and desolated the world, deserves to be regarded by us not only with peculiar pride as one of our greatest national victories, but with peculiar gratitude for the repose which it secured for us and for the greater part of the human race.

One good test for determining the importance of Waterloo is to ascertain what was felt by wise and prudent statesmen before that battle respecting the return of Napoleon from Elba to the imperial throne of France, and the probable effects of his success. For this purpose, I will quote the words, not of any of our vehement anti-Gallican politicians of the school of Pitt, but of a leader of our Liberal party, of a man whose reputation as a jurist, an historian, and a far-sighted and candid statesman was, and is, deservedly high, not only in this country, but throughout Europe. Sir James Mackintosh, on the 20th of April, 1815, spoke thus of the return from Elba:

"Was it in the power of language to describe the evil? Wars which had raged for more than twenty years throughout Europe; which had spread blood and desolation from Cadiz to Moscow, and from Naples to Copenhagen; which had wasted the means of human enjoyment, and destroyed the instruments of social improvement; which threatened to diffuse among the European nations the dissolute and ferocious habits of a predatory soldiery—at length, by one of those vicissitudes which bid defiance to the foresight of man, had been brought to a close, upon the whole, happy, beyond all reasonable expectation, with no violent shock to national independence, with some tolerable compromise between the opinions of the age and the reverence due to ancient institutions; with no too signal or mortifying triumph over the legitimate interests or avowable feelings of any numerous body of men, and, above all, without those retaliations against nations or parties which beget new convulsions, often as horrible as those which they close, and perpetuate revenge, and hatred, and blood shed from age to age. Europe seemed to breathe after her sufferings. In the midst of this fair prospect and of these consolatory hopes. Napoleon Bonaparte escaped from Elba; three small vessels reached the coast of Provence; our hopes are instantly dispelled; the work of our toil and fortitude is undone; the blood of Europe is spilled in vain —

" 'Ibi omnis effusus labor!' "

The congress of emperors, kings, princes, generals, and statesmen who had assembled at Vienna to remodel the world after the overthrow of the mighty conqueror, and who thought that Napoleon had passed away forever from the great drama of European politics, had not yet completed their triumphant festivities and their diplomatic toils, when Talleyrand, on the 11th of March, 1815, rose up among them and announced that the ex-emperor had escaped from Elba, and was emperor of France once more. It is recorded by Sir Walter Scott, as a curious physiological fact, that the first effect of the news of an event which threatened to neutralize all their labors was to excite a loud burst of laughter from nearly every member of the congress. But the jest was a bitter one; and they were soon deeply busied in anxious deliberations respecting the mode in which they should encounter their arch-enemy, who had thus started from torpor and obscurity into renovated splendor and strength:

> "Qualis ubi in lucem coluber mala gramina pastus,
> Frigida sub terrâ tumidum quern bruma tegebat,
> Nunc positis novus exuviis nitidusque juventâ,
> Lubrica convolvit sublato pectore terga
> Arduus ad solem, et linguis micata ore trisulcis."
>
> —VERGIL, *Æneid.*

Napoleon sought to disunite the formidable confederacy which he knew would be arrayed against him, by endeavoring to negotiate separately with each of the allied sovereigns. It is said that Austria and Russia were at first not unwilling to treat with him. Disputes and jealousies had been rife among several of the Allies on the subject of the division of the conquered countries; and the cordial unanimity with which they had acted during 1813 and the first months of 1814 had grown chill during some weeks of discussions. But the active exertions of Talleyrand, who represented Louis XVIII at the congress, and who both hated and feared Napoleon with all the intensity of which his powerful spirit was capable, prevented the secession of any member of the congress from the new great league against their ancient enemy. Still, it is highly probable that if Napoleon had triumphed in Belgium over the Prussians and the English, he would have succeeded in opening negotiations with the Austrians and Russians; and he might have thus gained advantages similar to those which he had obtained on his return from Egypt, when he induced the Czar Paul to withdraw the Russian armies from co-operating with the other enemies of France in the extremity of peril to which she seemed reduced in 1799. But fortune now had deserted him, both in diplomacy and in war.

On the 13th of March, 1815, the ministers of the seven powers, Austria, Spain, England, Portugal, Prussia, Russia, and Sweden, signed a manifesto by which they declared Napoleon an outlaw; and this denunciation was instantly followed up by a treaty between England, Austria, Prussia, and Russia (to which other powers soon acceded), by which the rulers of those countries bound themselves to enforce that decree, and to prosecute the war until Napoleon should be driven from the throne of France and rendered incapable of disturbing the peace of Europe. The Duke of Wellington was the representative of England at the Congress of Vienna, and he was immediately applied to for his advice on the plan of military operations against France. It was obvious that Belgium would be the first battle-field; and by the general wish of the Allies, the English duke proceeded thither to assemble an army from the contingents of Dutch, Belgian, and Hanoverian troops that were most speedily available, and from the English regiments which his own government was hastening to send over from this country. A strong Prussian corps was near Aix-la-Chapelle, having remained there since the campaign of the preceding year. This was largely reinforced by other troops of the same nation; and Marshal Blücher, the favorite hero of the Prussian soldiery and the deadliest foe of France, assumed the command of this army, which was termed the "Army of the Lower Rhine," and which, in conjunction with Wellington's forces, was to make the van of the armaments of the allied powers. Meanwhile Prince Schwartzenberg was to collect 130,000 Austrians and 124,000 troops of other Germanic states, as the "Army of the Upper Rhine"; and 168,000 Russians, under the command of Barclay de Tolly, were to form the "Army of the Middle Rhine," and to repeat the march from Muscovy to that river's banks.

The exertions which the allied powers made at this crisis to grapple promptly with the French emperor have truly been termed gigantic, and never were Napoleon's genius and activity more signally displayed than in the celerity and skill by which he brought forward all the military resources of France, which the reverses of the three preceding years, and the pacific policy of the Bourbons during the months of their first restoration, had greatly diminished and disorganized. He re-entered Paris on the 20th of March, and by the end of May, besides sending a force into La Vendée to put down the armed risings of the Royalists in that province, and besides providing troops under Massena and Suchet for the defence of the southern frontiers of France, Napoleon had an army assembled in the northeast for active operations under his own command, which amounted to between 120,000 and 130,000 men,[2] with a superb park of artillery, and in the highest possible state of equipment, discipline, and efficiency.

The approach of the multitudinous Russian, Austrian, Bavarian, and other foes of the French Emperor to the Rhine was necessarily slow; but the two most active of the allied powers had occupied Belgium with their troops, while Napoleon was organizing his forces. Marshal Blücher was there with one hundred and sixteen thousand Prussians; and, before the end of May the Duke of Wellington was there also with about one hundred and six thousand troops, either British or in British pay.[3] Napoleon determined to attack these enemies in Belgium. The disparity of numbers was indeed great, but delay was sure to increase the proportionate numerical superiority of his enemies over his own ranks. The French Emperor considered also that "the enemy's troops were now cantoned under the command of two generals, and composed of nations differing both in interest and in feelings."[4] His own army was under his own sole command. It was composed exclusively of French soldiers, mostly of veterans, well acquainted with their officers and with each other, and full of enthusiastic confidence in their commander. If he could separate the Prussians from the British, so as to attack each singly, he felt sanguine of success, not only against these the most resolute of his many adversaries, but also against the other masses that were slowly laboring up against his eastern dominions.

The triple chain of strong fortresses which the French possessed on the Belgian frontier formed a curtain, behind which
Napoleon was able to concentrate his army, and to conceal till the
very last moment the precise line of attack which he intended to
take. On the other hand, Blücher and Wellington were obliged
to canton their troops along a line of open country of considerable length, so as to watch for the outbreak of Napoleon from
whichever point of his chain of strongholds he should please to
make it. Blücher, with his army, occupied the banks of the Sambre
and the Meuse, from Liege on his left to Charleroi on his right;
and the Duke of Wellington covered Brussels, his cantonments
being partly in front of that city, and between it and the French
frontier, and partly on its west; their extreme right reaching to
Courtray and Tournay, while their left approached Charleroi and
communicated with the Prussian right. It was upon Charleroi that
Napoleon resolved to level his attack, in hopes of severing the
two allied armies from each other, and then pursuing his favorite
tactics of assailing each separately with a superior force on the
battle-field, though the aggregate of their numbers considerably
exceeded his own.

The first French corps d'armée, commanded by Count
d'Erlon, was stationed, in the beginning of June, in and around
the city of Lille, near to the northeastern frontier of France. The
second corps, under Count Reille, was at Valenciennes, to the
right of the first one. The third corps, under Count Vandamme,
was at Mezières. The fourth, under Count Gérard, had its head-
quarters at Metz; and the sixth,[5] under Count Lobau, was at Laon.
Four corps of reserve cavalry, under Marshal Grouchy, were also
near the frontier, between the rivers Aisne and Sambre. The
Imperial Guard remained in Paris until the 8th of June, when it
marched towards Belgium, and reached Avesnes on the 13th; and
in the course of the same and the following day, the five corps
d'armée, with the cavalry reserves which have been mentioned,
were, in pursuance of skilfully combined orders, rapidly drawn
together and concentrated in and around the same place, on the

right bank of the river Sambre. On the 14th Napoleon arrived among his troops, who were exulting at the display of their commander's skill in the celerity and precision with which they had been drawn together and in the consciousness of their collective strength. Although Napoleon too often permitted himself to use language unworthy of his own character respecting his great English adversary, his real feelings in commencing this campaign may be judged from the last words which he spoke, as he threw himself into his travelling-carriage to leave Paris for the army. "I go," he said, "to measure myself with Wellington."

The enthusiasm of the French soldiers at seeing their emperor among them was still more excited by the "Order of the Day," in which he thus appealed to them:

"Napoleon, by the Grace of God, and the Constitution of the Empire, Emperor of the French, etc., to the Grand Army.

"At The Imperial Headquarters,
"*Avesnes, June 14th,* 1815.

"Soldiers! this day is the anniversary of Marengo and of Friedland, which twice decided the destiny of Europe. Then, as after Austerlitz, as after Wagram, we were too generous! We believed in the protestations and in the oaths of princes, whom we left on their thrones. Now, however, leagued together, they aim at the independence and the most sacred rights of France. They have commenced the most unjust of aggressions. Let us, then, march to meet them. Are they and we no longer the same men?

"Soldiers! at Jena, against these same Prussians, now so arrogant, you were one to three, and at Montmirail one to six!

"Let those among you who have been captives to the English describe the nature of their prison ships, and the frightful miseries they endured.

"The Saxons, the Belgians, the Hanoverians, the soldiers of the Confederation of the Rhine, lament that they are compelled to use their arms in the cause of princes, the enemies of justice and of the rights of all nations. They know that this coalition is insatiable! After having devoured twelve millions of Poles, twelve millions of Italians, one million of Saxons, and six millions of Belgians, it now wishes to devour the states of the second rank in Germany.

"Madmen! one moment of prosperity has bewildered them. The oppression and the humiliation of the French people are beyond their power. If they enter France, they will there find their grave.

"Soldiers! we have forced marches to make, battles to fight, dangers to encounter; but, with firmness, victory will be ours. The rights, the honor, and the happiness of the country will be recovered!

"To every Frenchman who has a heart, the moment is now arrived to conquer or to die.

"NAPOLEON.

"THE MARSHAL DUKE OF DALMATIA,

Major-general."

The 15th of June had scarcely dawned before the French army was in motion for the decisive campaign and crossed the frontier in three columns, which were pointed upon Charleroi and its vicinity. The French line of advance upon Brussels, which city Napoleon resolved to occupy, thus lay right through the centre of the cantonments of the Allies.

Much criticism has been expended on the supposed surprise of Wellington's army in its cantonments by Napoleon's rapid advance. These comments would hardly have been made if sufficient attention had been paid to the geography of the Waterloo campaign, and if it had been remembered that the protection of Brussels was justly considered by the allied generals a matter of primary importance. If Napoleon could, either by manœuvring or fighting, have succeeded in occupying that city, the greater part of Belgium would unquestionably have declared in his favor; and the results of such a success, gained by the emperor at the commencement of the campaign, might have decisively influenced the whole after current of events. A glance at the map will show the numerous roads that lead from the different fortresses on the French northeastern frontier and converge upon Brussels, any one of which Napoleon might have chosen for the advance of a strong force upon that city. The duke's army was judiciously arranged so as to enable him to concentrate troops on any one of these roads sufficiently in advance of Brussels to check an assailing enemy. The army was kept thus available for movement in any necessary direction, till certain intelligence arrived on the 15th of June that the French had crossed the frontier in large force near Thuin, that they had driven back the Prussian advanced troops under General Ziethen, and were also moving across the Sambre upon Charleroi.

Marshal Blücher now rapidly concentrated his forces, calling them in from the left upon Ligny, which is to the northeast of Charleroi. Wellington also drew his troops together, calling them in from the right. But even now, though it was certain that the French were in large force at Charleroi, it was unsafe for the English general to place his army directly between that place and Brussels, until it was certain that no corps of the enemy was marching upon Brussels by the western road through Mons and Hal. The duke, therefore, collected his troops in Brussels and its immediate vicinity, ready to move due southward on Quatre Bras and co-operate with Blücher, who was taking his station at Ligny, but also ready to meet and defeat any manœuvre that the enemy might make to turn the right of the Allies and occupy Brussels by a flanking movement. The testimony of the Prussian general, Baron Muffling, who was attached to the duke's staff during the campaign, and who expressly states the reasons on which the English general acted, ought forever to have silenced the "weak inventions of the enemy "about the Duke of Wellington having been deceived and surprised by his assailant, which some writers of our own nation, as well as foreigners, have incautiously repeated.

It was about three o'clock in the afternoon of the 15th that a Prussian officer reached Brussels, whom General Ziethen had sent to Müffling to inform him of the advance of the main French army upon Charleroi. Müffling immediately communicated this to the Duke of Wellington, and asked him whether he would now concentrate his army, and what would be his point of concentration, observing that Marshal Blücher in consequence of this intelligence would certainly concentrate the Prussians at Ligny. The duke replied: "If all is as General Ziethen supposes, I will concentrate on my left wing, and so be in readiness to fight in conjunction with the Prussian army. Should, however, a portion of the enemy's force come by Mons, I must concentrate more towards my centre. This is the reason why I must wait for positive news from Mons before I fix the rendezvous. Since, however, it is certain that the troops must march, though it is uncertain upon what precise spot they must march, I will order all to be in readiness and will direct a brigade to move at once towards Quatre Bras."

Later in the same day a message from Blücher himself was delivered to Müffling, in which the Prussian field-marshal informed the baron that he was concentrating his men at Sombref and Ligny, and charged Müffling to give him speedy intelligence respecting the concentration of Wellington. Müffling immediately communicated this to the duke, who expressed his satisfaction with Blücher's arrangements, but added that he could not even then resolve upon his own point of concentration before he obtained the desired intelligence from Mons. About midnight this information arrived. The duke went to the quarters of General Müffling and told him that he now had received his reports from Mons and was sure that no French troops were advancing by that route, but that the mass of the enemy's force was decidedly directed on Charleroi. He informed the Prussian general that he had ordered the British troops to move forward upon Quatre Bras; but with characteristic coolness and sagacity resolved not to give the appearance of alarm by hurrying on with them himself. A ball was to be given by the Duchess of Richmond at Brussels that night, and the duke proposed to General Müffling that they should go to the ball for a few hours, and ride forward in the morning to overtake the troops at Quatre Bras.

To hundreds who were assembled at that memorable ball the news that the enemy was advancing, and that the time for battle had come, must have been a fearfully exciting surprise, and the magnificent stanzas of Byron ("Childe Harold," Canto III) are as true as they are beautiful; but the duke and his principal officers knew well the stern termination to that festive scene which was approaching. One by one, and in such a way as to attract as little observation as possible, the leaders of the various corps left the ballroom and took their stations at the head of their men, who were pressing forward through the last hours of the short summer night to the arena of anticipated slaughter.

Napoleon's operations on the 15th had been conducted with signal skill and vigor, and their results had been very advantageous for his plan of the campaign. With his army formed in three vast columns, he had struck at the centre of the line of cantonments of his allied foes; and he had so far made good his blow that he had effected the passage of the Sambre, he had beaten with his left wing the Prussian corps of General Ziethen at Thuin, and with his centre he had in person advanced right through Charleroi upon Fleurus, inflicting considerable loss upon the Prussians that fell back before him. His right column had with little opposition moved forward as far as the bridge of Chatelet.

Napoleon had thus a powerful force immediately in front of the point which Blücher had fixed for the concentration of the Prussian army, and that concentration was still incomplete. The French emperor designed to attack the Prussians on the morrow in person with the troops of his centre and right columns, and to employ his left wing in beating back such English troops as might advance to the help of their allies, and also in aiding his own attack upon Blücher. He gave the command of his left wing to Marshal Ney. Napoleon seems not to have originally intended to employ this celebrated general in the campaign. It was only on the night of the 11h of June that Marshal Ney received at Paris an order to join the army. Hurrying forward to the Belgian frontier, he meet the emperor near Charleroi. Napoleon immediately directed him to take the command of the left wing and to press forward with it upon Quatre Bras by the line of the road which leads from Charleroi to Brussels, through Gosselies, Frasne, Quatre Bras, Genappe, and Waterloo. Ney immediately proceeded to the post assigned him; and before ten on the night of the 15th he had occupied Gosselies and Frasne, driving out without much difficulty some weak Belgian detachments which had been stationed in those villages. The lateness of the hour and the exhausted state of the French troops, who had been marching and fighting since ten in the morning, made him pause from advancing farther to attack the much more important position of Quatre Bras. In truth, the advantages which the French gained by their almost superhuman energy and activity throughout the long day of the 15th of June were necessarily bought at the price of more delay and inertness during the following night and morrow than would have been observable if they had not been thus overtasked. Ney has been blamed for want of promptness in his attack upon Quatre Bras, and Napoleon has been criticised for not having fought at Ligny before the afternoon of the 16th; but their censors should remember that soldiers are but men and that there must be necessarily some interval of time before troops that have been worn and weakened by twenty hours of incessant fatigue and strife can be fed, rested, reorganized, and brought again into action with any hope of success.

Having on the night of the 15th placed the most advanced of the French under his command in position in front of Frasne, Ney rode back to Charleroi, where Napoleon also arrived about midnight, having returned from directing the operations of the centre and right column of the French. The emperor and the marshal supped together, and remained in earnest conversation till two in the morning. An hour or two afterwards Ney rode back to Frasne, where he endeavored to collect tidings of the numbers and movements of the enemy in front of him; and also busied himself in the necessary duty of learning the amount and composition of the troops which he himself was commanding. He had been so suddenly appointed to his high station that he did not know the strength of, the several regiments under him, or even the names of their commanding officers. He now caused his aide-de-camps to prepare the requisite returns, and drew together the troops, whom he was thus learning before he used them.

Wellington remained at the Duchess of Richmond's ball at Brussels till about three o'clock in the morning of the 16th, "showing himself very cheerful," as Baron Müffling, who accompanied him, observes. At five o'clock the duke and the baron were on horseback and reached the position at Quatre Bras about eleven. As the French, who were in front of Frasne, were perfectly quiet, and the duke was informed that a very large force under Napoleon in person was menacing Blücher, it was thought possible that only a slight detachment of the French was posted at Frasne in order to mask the English army. In that event Wellington, as he told Baron Müffling, would be able to employ his whole strength in supporting the Prussians; and he proposed to ride across from Quatre Bras to Blücher's position in order to concert with him personally the measures which should be taken in order to bring on a decisive battle with the French. Wellington and Müffling rode accordingly towards Ligny, and found Marshal Blücher and his staff at the windmill of Bry, near that village. The Prussian army, 80,000 strong, was drawn up chiefly along a chain of heights, with the villages of Sombref, St. Amand, and Ligny in their front. These villages were strongly occupied by Prussian detachments, and formed the keys of Blücher's position. The heads of the columns which Napoleon was forming for the attack were visible in the distance. The duke asked Blücher and General Gneisenau (who was Blücher's adviser in matters of strategy) what they wished him to do. Müffling had already explained to them in a few words the duke's earnest desire to support the field-marshal, and that he would do all that they wished, provided they did not ask him to divide his army, which was contrary to his principles. The duke wished to advance with his army (as soon as it was concentrated) upon Frasne and Gosselies, and thence to move upon Napoleon's flank and rear. The Prussian leaders preferred that he should march his men from Quatre Bras by the Namur road, so as to form a reserve in the rear of Blücher's army. The duke replied, "Well, I will come if I am not attacked myself," and galloped back with Müffling to Quatre Bras, where the French attack was now actually raging.

Marshal Ney began the battle about two o'clock in the afternoon. He had at this time in hand about 16,000 infantry, nearly 2,000 cavalry, and 38 guns. The force which Napoleon nominally placed at his command exceeded 40,000 men. But more than one-half of these consisted of the first French corps d'armée, under Count d'Erlon; and Ney was deprived of the use of this corps at the time that he most required it, in consequence of its receiving orders to march to the aid of the emperor at Ligny. A magnificent body of heavy cavalry under Kellermann, nearly 5,000 strong, and several more battalions of artillery were added to Ney's army during the battle of Quatre Bras; but his effective infantry force never exceeded 16,000.

When the battle began, the greater part of the duke's army was yet on its march towards Quatre Bras from Brussels and the other parts of its cantonments. The force of the Allies, actually in position there, consisted only of a Dutch and Belgian division of infantry, not quite 7,000 strong, with one battalion of foot and one of horse-artillery. The Prince of Orange commanded them. A wood, called the Bois de Bossu, stretched along the right (or western) flank of the position of Quatre Bras; a farmhouse and building, called Gemiancourt, stood on some elevated ground in its front; and to the left (or east) were the enclosures of the village of Pierremont. The Prince of Orange endeavored to secure these posts; but Ney carried Gemiancourt in the centre, and Pierremont on the east, and gained occupation of the southern part of the wood of Bossu. He ranged the chief part of his artillery on the high ground of Gemiancourt, whence it played throughout the action with most destructive effect upon the Allies. He was pressing forward to further advantages, when the fifth infantry division, under Sir Thomas Picton, and the Duke of Brunswick's corps, appeared upon the scene. Wellington (who had returned to Quatre Bras from his interview with Blücher shortly before the arrival of these forces) restored the fight with them; and as fresh troops of the Allies arrived, they were brought forward to stem the fierce attacks which Ney's columns and squadrons continued to make with unabated gallantry and zeal. The only cavalry of the Anglo-allied army that reached Quatre Bras during the action consisted of Dutch and Belgians, and a small force of Brunswickers under their duke, who was killed on the field. These proved wholly unable to encounter Kellermann's cuirassiers and Piré's lancers. The Dutch and Belgian infantry also gave way early in the engagement; so that the whole brunt of the battle fell on the British and Germany infantry. They sustained it nobly. Though repeatedly charged by the French cavalry, though exposed to the murderous fire of the French batteries, which from the heights of Gemiancourt sent shot and shell into the devoted squares whenever the French horsemen withdrew, they not only repelled their assailants, but Kempt's and Pack's brigades, led on by Picton, actually advanced against and through their charging foes, and with stern determination made good to the end of the day the ground which they had thus boldly won. Some, however, of the British regiments were during the confusion assailed by the French cavalry before they could form squares, and suffered severely. One regiment, the 92d, was almost wholly destroyed by the cuirassiers. A French private soldier named Lami, of the 8th Regiment of cuirassiers, captured one of the English colors and presented it to Ney. It was a solitary trophy. The arrival of the English Guards about half-past six o'clock enabled the duke to recover the wood of Bossu, which the French had almost entirely won and the possession of which by them would have enabled Ney to operate destructively upon the allied flank and rear. Not only was the wood of Bossu recovered on the British right, but the enclosures of Pierremont were also carried on the left. When night set in the French had been driven back on all points towards Frasne; but they still held the farm of Gemiancourt in front of the duke's centre. Wellington and Müffling were unacquainted with the result of the collateral battle between Blücher and Napoleon, the cannonading of which had been distinctly audible at Quatre Bras throughout the afternoon and evening. The duke observed to Müffling that of course the two allied armies would assume the offensive against the enemy on the morrow, and, consequently, it would be better to capture the farm at once, instead of waiting till next morning. Müffling agreed in the duke's views, and Gemiancourt was forthwith attacked by the English and captured with little loss to the assailants.

Meanwhile the French and the Prussians had been fighting in and round the villages of Ligny, Sombref, and St. Amand, from three in the afternoon to nine in the evening, with a savage inveteracy almost unparalleled in modern warfare. Blücher had in the field, when he began the battle, 83,417 men and 224 guns. Bulow's corps, which was 25,000 strong, had not joined him. But the field-marshal hoped to be reinforced by it or by the English army before the end of the action. But Bulow, through some error in the transmission of orders, was far in the rear; and the Duke of Wellington was engaged, as we have seen, with Marshal Ney. Blücher received early warning from Baron Müffling that the duke could not come to his assistance; but, as Müffling observes, Wellington rendered the Prussians the great service of occupying more than 40,000 of the enemy, who otherwise would have crushed Blücher's right flank. For not only did the conflict at Quatre Bras detain the French troops which actually took part in it, but d'Erlon received orders from Ney to join him, which hindered d'Erlon from giving effectual aid to Napoleon. Indeed, the whole of d'Erlon's corps, in consequence of conflicting directions from Ney and the emperor, marched and countermarched, during the 16th, between Quatre Bras and Ligny without firing a shot in either battle.

Blücher had, in fact, a superiority of more than 12,000 in number over the French army that attacked him at Ligny. The numerical difference was even greater at the beginning of the battle, as

Lobau's corps did not come up from Charleroi till eight o'clock. After five hours and a half of desperate and long-doubtful struggle, Napoleon succeeded in breaking the centre of the Prussian line at Ligny, and in forcing his obstinate antagonists off the field of battle. The issue was attributable to his skill, and not to any want of spirit or resolution on the part of the Prussian troops; nor did they, though defeated, abate one jot in discipline, heart, or hope. As Blücher observed, it was a battle in which his army lost the day but not its honor. The Prussians retreated during the night of the 16th and the early part of the 17th, with perfect regularity and steadiness. The retreat was directed not towards Maestricht, where their principal depots were established, but towards Wavre, so as to be able to maintain their communication with Wellington's army, and still follow out the original plan of the campaign. The heroism with which the Prussians endured and repaired their defeat at Ligny is more glorious than many victories.

The messenger who was sent to inform Wellington of the retreat of the Prussian army was shot on the way, and it was not until the morning of the 17th that the Allies, at Quatre Bras, knew the result of the battle of Ligny. The duke was ready at daybreak to take the offensive against the enemy with vigor, his whole army being by that time fully assembled. But on learning that Blücher had been defeated, a different course of action was clearly necessary. It was obvious that Napoleon's main army would now be directed against Wellington, and a retreat was inevitable. On ascertaining that the Prussian army had retired upon Wavre, that there was no hot pursuit of them by the French, and that Bulow's corps had taken no part in the action at Ligny, the duke resolved to march his army back towards Brussels, still intending to cover that city and to halt at a point in a line with Wavre, and there restore his communication with Blücher. An officer from Blücher's army reached the duke about nine o'clock, from whom he learned the effective strength that Blücher still possessed, and how little discouraged his ally was by yesterday's battle. Wellington sent word to the Prussian commander that he would halt in the position of

Mont St. Jean, and accept a general battle with the French, if Blücher would pledge himself to come to his assistance with a single corps of 25,000 men. This was readily promised; and after allowing his men ample time for rest and refreshment, Wellington retired over about half the space between Quatre Bras and Brussels. He was pursued, but little molested, by the main French army, which about noon of the 17th moved laterally from Ligny and joined Ney's forces, which had advanced through Quatre Bras when the British abandoned that position. The Earl of Uxbridge, with the British cavalry, covered the retreat of the duke's army with great skill and gallantry; and a heavy thunder-storm, with torrents of rain, impeded the operations of the French pursuing squadrons. The duke still expected that the French would endeavor to turn his right and march upon Brussels by the highroad that leads through Mons and Hal. In order to counteract this anticipated manoeuvre, he stationed a force of 18,000 men, under Prince Frederick of the Netherlands, at Hal, with orders to maintain himself there, if attacked, as long as possible. The duke halted with the rest of his army at the position near Mont St. Jean, which, from a village in its neighborhood, has received the ever-memorable name of the field of Waterloo.

Wellington was now about twelve miles distant, on a line running from west to east, from Wavre, where the Prussian army had now been completely reorganized and collected, and where it had been strengthened by the junction of Bulow's troops, which had taken no part in the battle of Ligny. Blücher sent word from Wavre to the duke that he was coming to help the English at Mont St. Jean, in the morning, not with one corps, but with his whole army. The fiery old man only stipulated that the combined armies, if not attacked by Napoleon on the 18th, should themselves attack him on the 19th. So far were Blücher and his army from being in the state of annihilation described in the boastful bulletin by which Napoleon informed the Parisians of his victory at Ligny. Indeed, the French emperor seems himself to have been misinformed as to the extent of loss which he had inflicted on the Prussians. Had he known in what good order and with what undiminished spirit they were retiring, he would scarcely have delayed sending a large force to press them in their retreat until noon on the 17th. Such, however, was the case. It was about that time that he confided to Marshal Grouchy the duty of pursuing the defeated Prussians and preventing them from joining Wellington. He placed for this purpose 32,000 men and 96 guns under his orders. Violent complaints and recriminations passed afterwards between the emperor and the marshal respecting the manner in which Grouchy attempted to perform this duty, and the reasons why he failed on the 18th to arrest the lateral movement of the Prussians from Wavre to Waterloo. It is sufficient to remark here, that the force which Napoleon gave to Grouchy (though the utmost that the emperor's limited means would allow) was insufficient to make head against the entire Prussian army, especially after Bulow's junction with Blücher. We shall presently have occasion to consider what opportunities were given to Grouchy during the 18th, and what he might have effected if he had been a man of original military genius.

But the failure of Grouchy was in truth mainly owing to the indomitable heroism of Blücher himself, who, though he had received severe personal injuries in the battle of Ligny, was as energetic and ready as ever in bringing his men into action again, and who had the resolution to expose a part of his army, under Thielman, to be overwhelmed by Grouchy at Wavre on the 18th, while he urged the march of the mass of his troops upon Waterloo. "It is not at Wavre, but at Waterloo," said the old field-marshal, "that the campaign is to be decided;" and he risked a detachment, and won the campaign accordingly. Wellington and Blücher trusted each other as cordially, and co-operated as zealously, as formerly had been the case with Marlborough and Eugene. It was in full reliance on Blücher's promise to join him that the duke stood his ground and fought at Waterloo; and those who have ventured to impugn the duke's capacity as a general ought to have had common-sense enough to perceive that to charge the duke with having won the battle of Waterloo by the help of the Prussians is really to say that he won it by the very means on which he relied, and without the expectation of which the battle would not have been fought.

Napoleon himself has found fault with Wellington[6] for not having retreated farther, so as to complete a junction of his army with Blücher's before he risked a general engagement. But, as we have seen, the duke justly considered it important to protect Brussels. He had reason to expect that his army could singly resist the French at Waterloo until the Prussians came up, and that, on the Prussians joining, there would be a sufficient force united under himself and Blücher for completely overwhelming the enemy. And while Napoleon thus censures his great adversary, he involuntarily bears the highest possible testimony to the military character of the English, and proves decisively of what paramount importance was the battle to which he challenged his fearless opponent. Napoleon asks, *"If the English army had been beaten at Waterloo, what would have been the use of those numerous bodies of troops, of Prussians, Austrians, Germans, and Spaniards, which were advancing by forced marches to the Rhine, the Alps, and the Pyrenees?"*[7]

The strength of the army under the Duke of Wellington at Waterloo was 49,608 infantry, 12,402 cavalry, and 5,645 artillerymen, with 156 guns.[8] But of this total of 67,655 men, scarcely 24,000 were British, a circumstance of very serious importance if Napoleon's own estimate of the relative value of troops of different nations is to be taken. In the emperor's own words, speaking of this campaign, "A French soldier would not be equal to more than one English soldier, but he would not be afraid to meet two Dutchmen, Prussians, or soldiers of the Confederation."[9] There were about 6,000 men of the old German Legion with the duke; these were veteran troops, and of excellent quality. Of the rest of the army the Hanoverians and Brunswickers proved themselves deserving of confidence and praise. But the Nassauers, Dutch, and Belgians were almost worthless; and not a few of them were justly suspected of a strong wish to fight, if they fought at all, under the French eagles rather than against them.

Napoleon's army at Waterloo consisted of 48,950 infantry, 15,765 cavalry, 7,232 artillery-men, being a total of 71,947 men and 246 guns.[10] They were the flower of the national forces of France; and of all the numerous gallant armies which that martial land has poured forth, never was there one braver, or better disciplined, or better led, than the host that took up its position at Waterloo on the morning of the 18th of June, 1815.

Perhaps those who have not seen the field of battle at Waterloo, or the admirable model of the ground and of the conflicting armies which was executed by Captain Siborne, may gain a generally accurate idea of the localities by picturing to themselves a valley between two and three miles long, of various breadths at different points, but generally not exceeding half a mile. On each side of the valley there is a winding chain of low hills, running somewhat parallel with each other. The declivity from each of these ranges of hills to the intervening valley is gentle but not uniform, the undulations of the ground being frequent and considerable. The English army was posted on the northern, and the French army occupied the southern ridge. The artillery of each side thundered at the other from their respective heights throughout the day, and the charges of horse and foot were made across the valley that has been described. The village of Mont St. Jean is situate a little behind the centre of the northern chain of hills, and the village of La Belle Alliance is close behind the centre of the southern ridge. The high road from Charleroi to Brussels (a broad paved causeway) runs through both these villages, and bisects, therefore, both the English and the French positions. The line of this road was the line of Napoleon's intended advance on Brussels.

There are some other local particulars connected with the situation of each army which it is necessary to bear in mind. The strength of the British position did not consist merely in the occupation of a ridge of high ground. A village and ravine, called Merk Braine, on the Duke of Wellington's extreme right, secured him from his flank being turned on that side; and on his extreme left, two little hamlets, called La Haye and Papellote, gave a similar though a slighter protection. Behind the whole British position is the extensive forest of Soignies. As no attempt was made by the French to turn either of the English flanks, and the battle was a day of straightforward fighting, it is chiefly important to see what posts there were in front of the British line of hills of which advantage could be taken either to repel or facilitate an attack; and it will be seen that there were two, and that each was of very great importance in the action. In front of the British right—that is to say, on the northern slope of the valley towards its western end—there stood an old-fashioned Flemish farmhouse called Goumont or Hougoumont, with out-buildings and a garden, and with a copse of beech-trees of about two acres in extent around it. This was strongly garrisoned by the allied troops; and while it was in their possession, it was difficult for the enemy to press on and force the British right wing. On the other hand, if the enemy could take it, it would be difficult for that wing to keep its ground on the heights, with a strong post held adversely in its immediate front, being one that would give much shelter to the enemy's marksmen, and great facilities for the sudden concentration of attacking columns. Almost immediately in front of the British centre, and not so far down the slope as Hougoumont, there was another farmhouse, of a smaller size, called La Haye Sainte,[11] which was also held by the British troops, and the occupation of which was found to be of very serious consequence.

With respect to the French position, the principal feature to be noticed is the village of Planchenoit, which lay a little in the rear of their right (*i.e.*, on the eastern side), and which proved to be of great importance in aiding them to check the advance of the Prussians.

Napoleon, in his memoirs, and other French writers, have vehemently blamed the duke for having given battle in such a position as that of Waterloo. They particularly object that the duke fought without having the means of a retreat, if the attacks of his enemy had proved successful; and that the English army, if once broken, must have lost all its guns and *matériel* in its flight through the forest of Soignies, that lay in its rear. In answer to these censures, instead of merely referring to the event of the battle as proof of the correctness of the duke's judgment, it is to be observed that many military critics of high authority have considered the position of Waterloo to have been admirably adapted for the duke's purpose of protecting Brussels by a battle; and that certainly the duke's opinion in favor of it was not lightly or hastily formed. It is a remarkable fact (mentioned in the speech of Lord Bathurst when moving the vote of thanks to the duke in the House of Lords) that, when the Duke of Wellington was passing through Belgium in the preceding summer of 1814, he particularly noticed the strength of the position of Waterloo, and made a minute of it at the time, stating to those who were with him that if it ever should be his fate to fight a battle in that quarter for the protection of Brussels, he should endeavor to do so in that position. And with respect to the forest of Soignies, which the French (and some few English) critics have thought calculated to prove so fatal to a retreating force, the duke, on the contrary, believed it to be a post that might have proved of infinite value to his army in the event of his having been obliged to give way. The forest of Soignies has no thicket or masses of close-growing trees. It consists of tall beeches, and is everywhere passable for men and horses. The artillery could have been withdrawn by the broad road which traverses it towards Brussels; and in the mean while a few regiments of resolute infantry could have held the forest and kept the pursuers in check. One of the best writers on the Waterloo campaign, Captain Pringle, well observes that "every person the least experienced in war knows the extreme difficulty of forcing infantry from a wood which cannot be turned." The defense of the Bois de Bossu near Quatre Bras on the 16th of June had given a good proof of this; and the Duke of Wellington, when speaking in after years of the possible events that might have followed if he had been beaten back from the open field of Waterloo, pointed to the wood of Soignies as his secure rallying place, saying, "They never could have beaten us so that we could not have held the wood against them." He was always confident that he could have made good that post until joined by the Prussians, upon whose co-operation he throughout depended.

As has been already mentioned, the Prussians, on the morning of the 18th, were at Wavre, about twelve miles to the east of the field of battle at Waterloo. The junction of Bulow's division had more than made up for the loss sustained at Ligny; and leaving Thielman, with about 17,000 men, to hold his ground as he best could against the attack which Grouchy was about to make on Wavre, Bulow and Blücher moved with the rest of the Prussians through St. Lambert upon Waterloo. It was calculated that they would be there by three o'clock; but the extremely difficult nature of the ground which they had to traverse, rendered worse by the torrents of rain that had just fallen, delayed them long on their twelve miles march.

An army, indeed, less animated by bitter hate against the enemy than were the Prussians and under a less energetic chief than Blücher, would have failed altogether in effecting a passage through the swamps into which the incessant rain had transformed the greater part of the ground through which it was necessary to move, not only with columns of foot, but with cavalry and artillery. At one point of the march, on entering the defile of St. Lambert, the spirits of the Prussians almost gave way. Exhausted in the attempts to extricate and drag forward the heavy guns, the men began to murmur. Blücher came to the spot and heard cries from the ranks of "We cannot get on." "But you must get on," was the old field-marshal's answer. "I have pledged my word to Wellington, and you surely will not make me break it. Only exert yourselves for a few hours longer, and we are sure of victory." This appeal from old "Marshal Forwards," as the Prussian soldiers loved to call Blücher, had its wonted effect. The Prussians again moved forward, slowly, indeed, and with pain and toil; but still they moved forward.

The French and British armies lay on the open field during the wet and stormy night of the 17th; and when the dawn of the memorable 18th of June broke, the rain was still descending heavily upon Waterloo. The rival nations rose from their dreary bivouacs and began to form, each on the high ground which it occupied. Towards nine the weather grew clearer, and each army was able to watch the position and arrangements of the other on the opposite side of the valley.

The Duke of Wellington drew up his army in two lines, the principal one being stationed near the crest of the ridge of hills already described, and the other being arranged along the slope in the rear of his position. Commencing from the eastward, on the extreme left of the first or main line, were Vivian's and Vandeleur's brigades of light cavalry, and the fifth Hanoverian brigade of infantry under Von Vincke. Then came Best's fourth Hanoverian brigade. Detachments from these bodies of troops occupied the little villages of Papelotte and La Haye, down the hollow in advance of the left of the duke's position. To the right of Best's Hanoverians, Bylandt's brigade of Dutch and Belgian infantry was drawn up on the outer slope of the heights. Behind them were the ninth brigade of British infantry under Pack; and to the right of these last, but more in advance, stood the eighth brigade of English infantry under Kempt. These were close to the Charleroi road and to the centre of the entire position. These two English brigades, with the fifth Hanoverian, made up the fifth division, commanded by Sir Thomas Picton. Immediately to their right, and westward of the Charleroi road, stood the third division, commanded by General Alten, and consisting of Ompteda's brigade of the king's German Legion and Kielmansegge's Hanoverian brigade. The important post of La Haye Sainte, which, it will be remembered, lay in front of the duke's centre, close to the Charleroi road, was garrisoned with troops from this division. Westward, and on the right of Kielmansegge's Hanoverians, stood the fifth brigade under Halkett; and behind, Kruse's Nassau brigade was posted. On the right of Halkett's men stood the English Guards. They were in two brigades, one commanded by Maitland and the other by Byng. The entire division was under General Cooke. The buildings and gardens of Hougoumont, which lay immediately under the height on which stood the British Guards, were principally manned by detachments from Byng's brigade, aided by some brave Hanoverian riflemen and accompanied by a battalion of a Nassau regiment. On a plateau in the rear of Cooke's division of Guards, and inclining westward towards the village of Merk Braine, were Clinton's second infantry division, composed of Adams's third brigade of light infantry, Du Plat's first brigade of the king's German Legion, and third Hanoverian brigade under Colonel Halkett.

The duke formed his second line of cavalry. This only extended behind the right and centre of his first line. The largest mass was drawn up behind the brigades of infantry in the centre, on either side of the Charleroi road. The brigade of household cavalry under Lord Somerset was on the immediate right of the road, and on the left of it was Ponsonby's brigade. Behind these were Trip's and Ghingy's brigades of Dutch and Belgian horse. The third Hussars of the king's German Legion were to the right of Somerset's brigade. To the right of these, and behind Maitland's infantry, stood the third brigade under Dornberg, consisting of the twenty-third English light dragoons and the regiments of light dragoons of the king's German Legion. The last cavalry on the right was Grant's brigade, stationed in the rear of the Foot Guards. The corps of Brunswickers, both horse and foot, and the tenth British brigade of foot were in reserve behind the centre and right of the entire position. The artillery was distributed at convenient intervals along the front of the whole line. Besides the generals who have been mentioned, Lord Hill, Lord Uxbridge (who had the general command of the cavalry), the Prince of Orange, and General Chassé were present and acting under the Duke.[12]

On the opposite heights the French army was drawn up in two general lines, with the entire force of the Imperial Guards, cavalry as well as infantry, in rear of the centre, as a reserve.

The first line of the French army was formed of the two corps commanded by Count d'Erlon and Count Reille. D'Erlon's corps was on the right, that is, eastward of the Charleroi road, and consisted of four divisions of infantry under Generals Durette, Marcognet, Alix, and Donzelot, and of one division of light cavalry under General Jaquinot. Count Reille's corps formed the left or western wing, and was formed of Bachelu's, Foy's, and Jerome Bonaparte's divisions of infantry and of Pire's division of cavalry. The right wing of the second general French line was formed of Milhaud's corps, consisting of two divisions of heavy cavalry. The left wing of this line was formed by Kellermann's cavalry corps, also in two divisions. Thus each of the corps of infantry that composed the first line had a corps of cavalry behind it; but the second line consisted also of Lobau's corps of infantry and Domont and Subervie's divisions of light cavalry; these three bodies of troops being drawn up on either side of La Belle Alliance and forming the centre of the second line. The third, or reserve, line had its centre composed of the infantry of the Imperial Guard. Two regiments of grenadiers and two of chasseurs formed the foot of the Old Guard under General Friant. The Middle Guard, under Count Morand, was similarly composed; while two regiments of voltigeurs and two of tirailleurs, under Duhesme, constituted the Young Guard. The chasseurs and lancers of the Guard were on the right of the infantry, under Lefebvre Desnouettes; and the grenadiers and dragoons of the Guards, under Guyot, were on the left. All the French corps comprised, besides their cavalry and infantry regiments, strong batteries of horse-artillery; and Napoleon's numerical superiority in guns was of deep importance throughout the action.

Besides the leading generals who have been mentioned as commanding particular corps, Ney and Soult were present, and acted as the emperor's lieutenants in the battle.

English military critics have highly eulogized the admirable arrangement which Napoleon made of his forces of each arm, so as to give him the most ample means of sustaining, by an immediate and sufficient support, any attack, from whatever point he might direct it, and of drawing promptly together a strong force, to resist any attack that might be made on himself in any part of the field.[13] When his troops were all arrayed, he rode along the lines, receiving everywhere the most enthusiastic cheers from his men, of whose entire devotion to him his assurance was now doubly sure. On the southern side of the valley the duke's army was also arrayed, and ready to meet the menaced attack.

Wellington had caused, on the preceding night, every brigade and corps to take up its station on or near the part of the ground which it was intended to hold in the coming battle. He had slept a few hours at his headquarters in the village of Waterloo; and rising on the 18th, while it was yet deep night, he wrote several letters, to the Governor of Antwerp, to the English Minister at Brussels, and other official personages, in which he expressed his confidence that all would go well; but, "as it was necessary to provide against serious losses should any accident occur," he gave a series of judicious orders for what should be done in the rear of the army in the event of the battle going against the Allies. He also, before he left the village of Waterloo, saw to the distribution of the reserves of ammunition which had been parked there, so that supplies should be readily forwarded to every part of the line of battle where they might be required. The duke, also, personally inspected the arrangements that had been made for receiving the wounded and providing temporary hospitals in the houses in the rear of the army. Then, mounting a favorite charger, a small thoroughbred chestnut horse, named "Copenhagen," Wellington rode forward to the range of hills where his men were posted. Accompanied by his staff and by the Prussian General Müffling, he rode along his lines, carefully inspecting all the details of his position. Hougoumont was the object of his special attention. He rode down to the southeastern extremity of its enclosures, and, after having examined the nearest French troops, he made some changes in the disposition of his own men who were to defend that important post.

Having given his final orders about Hougoumont, the duke galloped back to the high ground in the right centre of his position, and, halting there, sat watching the enemy on the opposite heights and conversing with his staff with that cheerful serenity which was ever his characteristic in the hour of battle.

Not all brave men are thus gifted; and many a glance of anxious excitement must have been cast across the valley that separated the two hosts during the protracted pause which ensued between the completion of Napoleon's preparations for attack and the actual commencement of the contest. It was, indeed, an awful calm before the coming storm, when armed myriads stood gazing on their armed foes, scanning their number, their array, their probable powers of resistance and destruction, and listening with throbbing hearts for the momentarily expected note of death; while visions of victory and glory came thronging on each soldier's highstrung brain, not unmingled with recollections of the home which his fall might soon leave desolate, nor without shrinking nature sometimes prompting the cold thought that in a few moments he might be writhing in agony, or lie a trampled and mangled mass of clay on the grass now waving so freshly and purely before him.

Such thoughts will arise in human breasts, though the brave man soon silences "the child within us that trembles before death," and nerves himself for the coming struggle by the mental preparation which Xenophon has finely called "the soldier's arraying his own soul for battle." Well, too, may we hope and believe that many a spirit sought aid from a higher and holier source, and that many a fervent, though silent, prayer arose on that Sabbath morn (the battle of Waterloo was fought on a Sunday) to the Lord of Sabaoth, the God of Battles, from the ranks whence so many thousands were about to appear that day before his judgment-seat.

Not only to those who were thus present as spectators and actors in the dread drama, but to all Europe, the decisive contest then impending between the rival French and English nations, each under its chosen chief, was the object of exciting interest and deepest solicitude. "Never, indeed, had two such generals as the Duke of Wellington and the Emperor Napoleon encountered since the day when Scipio and Hannibal met at Zama."

The two great champions who now confronted each other were equals in years, and each had entered the military profession at the same early age. The more conspicuous stage on which the French general's youthful genius was displayed, his heritage of the whole military power of the French republic, the position on which for years he was elevated as sovereign head of an empire surpassing that of Charlemagne, and the dazzling results of his victories, which made and unmade kings, had given him a formidable pre-eminence in the eyes of mankind. Military men spoke with justly rapturous admiration of the brilliancy of his first Italian campaigns, when he broke through the pedantry of traditional tactics and with a small but promptly wielded force shattered army after army of the Austrians, conquered provinces and capitals, dictated treaties, and annihilated or created states. The iniquity of his Egyptian expedition was too often forgotten in contemplating the skill and boldness with which he destroyed the Mameluke cavalry at the Pyramids and the Turkish infantry at Aboukir. None could forget the marvellous passage of the Alps in 1800, or the victory of Marengo, which wrested Italy back from Austria and destroyed the fruit of twenty victories which the enemies of France had gained over her in the absence of her favorite chief. Even higher seemed the glories of his German campaigns, the triumphs of Ulm, of Austerlitz, of Jena, of Wagram. Napoleon's disasters in Russia, in 1812, were imputed by his admirers to the elements; his reverses in Germany, in 1813, were attributed by them to treachery; and even those two calamitous years had been signalized by his victories at Borodino; at Lutzen, at Bautzen, at Dresden, and at Hanau. His last campaign, in the early months of 1814, was rightly cited as the most splendid exhibition of his military genius, when, with a far inferior army, he long checked and frequently defeated the vast hosts that were poured upon France. His followers fondly hoped that the campaign of 1815 would open with another "week of miracles," like that which had seen his victories at Montmirail and Montereau. The laurel of Ligny was even now fresh upon his brows. Blücher had not stood before him; and who was the adversary that now should bar the emperor's way?

That adversary had already overthrown the emperor's best generals and the emperor's best armies, and, like Napoleon himself, had achieved a reputation in more than European wars.

Wellington was illustrious as the destroyer of the Mahratta power, as the liberator of Portugal and Spain, and the successful invader of Southern France. In early youth he had held high command in India, and had displayed eminent skill in planning and combining movements, and unrivalled celerity and boldness in execution. On his return to Europe, several years passed away before any fitting opportunity was accorded for the exercise of his genius. In this important respect, Wellington, as a subject, and Napoleon, as a sovereign, were far differently situated. At length his appointment to the command in the Spanish Peninsula gave him the means of showing Europe that England had a general who could revive the glories of Crecy, of Poitiers, of Agincourt, of Blenheim, and of Ramillies. At the head of forces always numerically far inferior to the armies with which Napoleon deluged the Peninsula; thwarted by jealous and incompetent allies; ill supported by friends and assailed by factious enemies at home, Wellington maintained the war for seven years, unstained by any serious reverse, and marked by victory in thirteen pitched battles, at Vimiera, the Douro, Talavera, Busaco, Fuentes de Onoro, Salamanca, Vittoria, the Pyrenees, the Bidassoa, the Nive, the Nivelle, Orthes, and Toulouse. Junot, Victor, Massena, Ney, Marmont, and Jourdan — marshals whose names were the terror of Continental Europe — had been baffled by his skill and smitten down by his energy, while he liberated the kingdoms of the Peninsula from them and their imperial master. In vain did Napoleon at last despatch Soult, the ablest of his lieutenants, to turn the tide of Wellington's success and defend France against the English invader. Welington met Soult's manoeuvres with superior skill, and his boldness with superior vigor. When Napoleon's first abdication, in 1814, suspended hostilities, Wellington was master of the fairest districts of Southern France, and had under him a veteran army with which (to use his own expressive phrase) "he felt he could have gone anywhere and done anything." The fortune of war had hitherto kept separate the orbits in which Napoleon and he had moved. Now, on the ever-memorable 18th of June, 1815, they met at last.

It is, indeed, remarkable that Napoleon, during his numerous campaigns in Spain as well as other countries, not only never encountered the Duke of Wellington before the day of Waterloo, but that he was never until then personally engaged with British troops, except at the siege of Toulon, in 1793, which was the very first incident of his military career. Many, however, of the French generals who were with him in 1815 knew well, by sharp experience, what English soldiers were and what the leader was who now headed them. Ney, Foy, and other officers who had served in the Peninsula warned Napoleon that he would find the English infantry "very devils in fight." The emperor, however, persisted in employing the old system of attack, with which the French generals often succeeded against Continental troops but which had always failed against the English in the Peninsula. He adhered to his usual tactics of employing the order of the column, a mode of attack probably favored by him (as Sir Walter Scott remarks) on account of his faith in the extreme valor of the French officers by whom the column was headed. It is a threatening formation, well calculated to shake the firmness of ordinary foes, but which, when steadily met, as the English have met it, by heavy volleys of musketry from an extended line, followed up by a resolute bayonet charge, has always resulted in disaster to the assailants.[14]

It was approaching noon before the action commenced. Napoleon, in his memoirs, gives as the reason for this delay, the miry state of the ground through the heavy rain of the preceding night and day, which rendered it impossible for cavalry or artillery to manœuvre on it till a few hours of dry weather had given it its natural consistency. It has been supposed, also, that he trusted to the effect which the sight of the imposing array of his own forces was likely to produce on the part of the allied army. The Belgian regiments had been tampered with; and Napoleon had well-founded hopes of seeing them quit the Duke of Wellington in a body, and range themselves under his own eagles. The duke, however, who knew and did not trust them, had guarded against the risk of this by breaking up the corps of Belgians, and distributing them in separate regiments among troops on whom he could rely.

At last, at about half-past eleven o'clock, Napoleon began the battle by directing a powerful force from his left wing under his brother, Prince Jerome, to attack Hougoumont. Column after column of the French now descended from the west of the southern heights, and assailed that post with fiery valor, which was encountered with the most determined bravery. The French won the copse round the house, but a party of the British Guards held the house itself throughout the day. The whole of Byng's brigade was required to man this hotly contested post. Amid shell and shot, and the blazing fragments of part of the buildings, this obstinate contest was continued. But still the English were firm at Hougoumont, though the French occasionally moved forward in such numbers as enabled them to surround and mask this post with part of their troops from their left wing, while others pressed onward up the slope, and assailed the British right.

The cannonade, which commenced at first between the British right and the French left, in consequence of the attack on Hougoumont, soon became general along both lines; and about one o'clock Napoleon directed a grand attack to be made under Marshal Ney upon the centre and left wing of the allied army. For this purpose four columns of infantry, amounting to about 18,000 men, were collected, supported by a strong division of cavalry under the celebrated Kellermann, and seventy-four guns were brought forward ready to be posted on the ridge of a little undulation of the ground in the interval between the two principal chains of heights, so as to bring their fire to bear on the duke's line at a range of about seven hundred yards. By the combined assault of these formidable forces, led on by Ney, "the bravest of the brave," Napoleon hoped to force the left centre of the British position, to take La Haye Sainte, and then, pressing forward, to occupy also the farm of Mont St. Jean. He then could cut the mass of Wellington's troops off from their line of retreat upon Brussels, and from their own left, and also completely sever them from any Prussian troops that might be approaching.

The columns destined for this great and decisive operation descended majestically from the French range of hills, and gained the ridge of the intervening eminence, on which the batteries that supported them were now ranged. As the columns descended again from this eminence, the seventy-four guns opened over their heads with terrible effect upon the troops of the allies that were stationed on the heights to the left of the Charleroi road. One of the French columns kept to the east, and attacked the extreme left of the allies; the other three continued to move rapidly forward upon the left centre of the allied position. The front line of the allies here was composed of Bylandt's brigade of Dutch and Belgians. As the French columns moved up the southward slope of the height on which the Dutch and Belgians stood, and the skirmishers in advance began to open their fire, Bylandt's entire brigade turned and fled in disgraceful and disorderly panic; but there were men more worthy of the name behind.

In this part of the second line of the allies were posted Pack and Kempt's brigades of English infantry, which had suffered severely at Quatre Bras. But Picton was here as general of division, and not even Ney himself surpassed in resolute bravery that stern and fiery spirit. Picton brought his two brigades forward, side by side, in a thin, two-deep line. Thus joined together, they were not three thousand strong. With these Picton had to make head against the three victorious French columns, upwards of four times that strength, and who, encouraged by the easy rout of the Dutch and Belgians, now came confidently over the ridge of the hill. The British infantry stood firm; and as the French halted and began to deploy into line, Picton seized the critical moment. He shouted in his stentorian voice to Kempt's brigade: "A volley, and then charge!" At a distance of less than thirty yards that volley was poured upon the devoted first sections of the nearest column; and then, with a fierce hurrah, the British dashed in with the bayonet.

Picton was shot dead as he rushed forward, but his men pushed on with the cold steel. The French reeled back in confusion. Pack's infantry had checked the other two columns, and down came a whirlwind of British horse on the whole mass, sending them staggering from the crest of the hill and cutting them down by whole battalions. Ponsonby's brigade of heavy cavalry (the Union Brigade, as it was called, from its being made up of the British Royals, the Scotch Greys, and the Irish Inniskillings) did this good service. On went the horsemen amid the wrecks of the French columns, capturing two eagles and two thousand prisoners; onward still they galloped, and sabred the artillerymen of Ney's seventy-four advanced guns; then severing the traces and cutting the throats of the artillery horses, they rendered these guns totally useless to the French throughout the remainder of the day. While thus far advanced beyond the British position and disordered by success, they were charged by a large body of French lancers and driven back with severe loss, till Vandeleur's light-horse came to their aid and beat off the French lancers in their turn.

Equally unsuccessful with the advance of the French infantry in this grand attack had been the efforts of the French cavalry who moved forward in support of it, along the east of the Charleroi road. Somerset's cavalry of the English Household Brigade had been launched, on the right of Picton's division, against the French horse, at the same time that the English Union Brigade of heavy-horse charged the French infantry columns on the left.

Somerset's brigade was formed of the Life Guards, the Blues, and the Dragoon Guards. The hostile cavalry, which Kellermann led forward, consisted chiefly of cuirassiers. This steelclad mass of French horsemen rode down some companies of German infantry near La Haye Sainte and, flushed with success, they bounded onward to the ridge of the British position. The English Household Brigade, led on by the Earl of Uxbridge in person, spurred forward to the encounter, and in an instant the two adverse lines of strong swordsmen on their strong steeds dashed furiously together. A desperate and sanguinary hand-to-hand fight ensued, in which the physical superiority of the Anglo-Saxons, guided by equal skill and animated with equal valor, was made decisively manifest. Back went the chosen cavalry of France; and after them, in hot pursuit, spurred the English Guards. They went forward as far and as fiercely as their comrades of the Union Brigade; and, like them, the Household cavalry suffered severely before they regained the British position, after their magnificent charge and adventurous pursuit.

Napoleon's grand effort to break the English left centre had thus completely failed; and his right wing was seriously weakened by the heavy loss which it had sustained. Hougoumont was still being assailed, and was still successfully resisting. Troops were now beginning to appear at the edge of the horizon on Napoleon's right, which he too well knew to be Prussian, though he endeavored to persuade his followers that they were Grouchy's men coming to their aid.

Grouchy was, in fact, now engaged at Wavre with his whole force against Thielman's single Prussian corps, while the other three corps of the Prussian army were moving without opposition, save from the difficulties of the ground, upon Waterloo. Grouchy believed, on the 17th, and caused Napoleon to believe, that the Prussian army was retreating by lines of march remote from Waterloo upon Namur and Maestricht. Napoleon learned only on the 18th that there were Prussians in Wavre, and felt jealous about the security of his own right. He accordingly, before he attacked the English, sent Grouchy orders to engage the Prussians at Wavre without delay, and to approach the main French army, so as to unite his communication with the emperor's. Grouchy entirely neglected this last part of his instructions; and in attacking the Prussians whom he found at Wavre, he spread his force more and more towards his right, that is to say, in the direction most remote from Napoleon. He thus knew nothing of Blücher's and Bulow's flank march upon Waterloo till six in the evening of the 18th, when he received a note which Soult, by Napoleon's orders, had sent off from the field of battle at Waterloo at one o'clock, to inform Grouchy that Bulow was coming over the heights of St. Lambert, on the emperor's right flank, and directing Grouchy to approach and join the main army instantly, and crush Bulow *en flagrant délit*. It was then too late for Grouchy to obey; but it is remarkable that as early as noon on the 18th, and while Grouchy had not proceeded as far as Wavre, he and his suite heard the sound of heavy cannonading in the direction of Planchenoit and Mont St. Jean. General Gérard, who was with Grouchy, implored him to march towards the cannonade and join his operations with those of Napoleon, who was evidently engaged with the English. Grouchy refused to do so or even to detach part of his force in that direction. He said that his instructions were to fight the Prussians at Wavre. He marched upon Wavre, and fought for the rest of the day with Thielman accordingly, while Blücher and Bulow were attacking the emperor.[15]

Napoleon had witnessed with bitter disappointment the rout of his troops — foot, horse, and artillery — which attacked the left centre of the English, and the obstinate resistance which the garrison of Hongoumont opposed to all the exertions of his left wing. He now caused the batteries along the line of high ground held by him to be strengthened, and for some time an unremitting and most destructive cannonade raged across the valley, to the partial cessation of other conflict. But the superior fire of the French artillery, though it weakened, could not break the British line, and more close and summary measures were requisite.

It was now about half-past three o'clock; and though Wellington's army had suffered severely by the unremitting cannonade and in the late desperate encounter, no part of the British position had been forced. Napoleon determined to try what effect he could produce on the British centre and right by charges of his splendid cavalry, brought on in such force that the duke's cavalry could not check them. Fresh troops were at the same time sent to assail La Haye Sainte and Hougoumont, the possession of these posts being the emperor's unceasing object. Squadron after squadron of the French cuirassiers accordingly ascended the slopes on the duke's right, and rode forward with dauntless courage against the batteries of the British artillery in that part of the field. The artillery-men were driven from their guns, and the cuirassiers cheered loudly at their supposed triumph. But the duke had formed his infantry in squares, and the cuirassiers charged in vain against the impenetrable hedges of bayonets, while the fire from the inner ranks of the squares told with terrible effect on their squadrons. Time after time they rode forward with invariably the same result; and as they receded from each attack, the British artillery-men rushed forward from the centres of the squares, where they had taken refuge, and plied their guns on the retiring horsemen. Nearly the whole of Napoleon's magnificent body of heavy cavalry was destroyed in these fruitless attempts upon the British right. But in another part of the field fortune favored him for a time. Two French columns of infantry from Donzelot's division took La Haye Sainte between six and seven o'clock, and the means were now given for organizing another formidable attack on the centre of the allies.

There was no time to be lost: Blücher and Bulow were beginning to press upon the French right; as early as five o'clock, Napoleon had been obliged to detach Lobau's infantry and Domont's horse to check these new enemies. They succeeded in doing so for a time; but, as large numbers of the Prussians came on the field, they turned Lobau's right flank, and sent a strong force to seize the village of Planchenoit, which, it will be remembered, lay in the rear of the French right.

The design of the Allies was not merely to prevent Napoleon from advancing upon Brussels, but to cut off his line of retreat and utterly destroy his army. The defence of Planchenoit therefore became absolutely essential for the safety of the French, and Napoleon was obliged to send his Young Guard to occupy that village, which was accordingly held by them with great gallantry against the reiterated assaults of the Prussian left, under Bulow. Three times did the Prussians fight their way into Planchenoit, and as often did the French drive them out; the contest was maintained with the fiercest desperation on both sides, such being the animosity between the two nations that quarter was seldom given or even asked. Other Prussian forces were now appearing on the field nearer to the English left, whom also Napoleon kept in check by troops detached for that purpose. Thus a large part of the French army was now thrown back on a line at right angles with the line of that portion which still confronted and assailed the English position. But this portion was now numerically inferior to the force under the Duke of Wellington, which Napoleon had been assailing throughout the day, without gaining any other advantage than the capture of La Haye Sainte. It is true that, owing to the gross misconduct of the greater part of the Dutch and Belgian troops, the duke was obliged to rely exclusively on his English and German soldiers, and the ranks of these had been fearfully thinned; but the survivors stood their ground heroically, and opposed a resolute front to every forward movement of their enemies.

On no point of the British line was the pressure more severe than on Halkett's brigade in the right centre, which was composed of battalions of the 30th, the 33d, the 69th, and the 73d British regiments. We fortunately can quote from the journal of a brave officer of the 30th a narrative of what took place in this part of the field. The late Major Macready served at Waterloo in the light company of the 30th. The extent of the peril and the carnage which Halkett's brigade had to encounter may be judged of by the fact that this light company marched into the field three officers and fifty-one men, and that at the end of the battle they stood one officer and ten men. Major Macready's blunt, soldierly account of what he actually saw and felt gives a far better idea of the terrific scene than can be gained from the polished generalizations which the conventional style of history requires, or even from the glowing stanzas of the poet. During the earlier part of the day Macready and his light company were thrown forward as skirmishers in front of the brigade; but when the French cavalry commenced their attacks on the British right centre, he and his comrades were ordered back. The brave soldier thus himself describes what passed:

"Before the commencement of this attack our company and the grenadiers of the 73d were skirmishing briskly in the low ground, covering our guns and annoying those of the enemy. The line of tirailleurs opposed to us was not stronger than our own, but on a sudden they were reinforced by numerous bodies and several guns began playing on us with canister. Our poor fellows dropped very fast, and Colonel Vigoureux, Rumley, and Pratt were carried off badly wounded in about two minutes. I was now commander of our company. We stood under this hurricane of small shot till Halkett sent to order us in, and I brought away about a third of the light bobs; the rest were killed or wounded, and I really wonder how one of them escaped. As our bugler was killed, I shouted and made signals to move by the left, in order to avoid the fire of our guns and to put as good a face upon the business as possible.

"When I reached Lloyd's abandoned guns, I stood near them for about a minute to contemplate the scene: it was grand beyond description. Hougoumont and its wood sent up a broad flame through the dark masses of smoke that overhung the field; beneath this cloud the French were indistinctly visible. Here a waving mass of long red feathers could be seen; there, gleams as from a sheet of steel showed that the cuirassiers were moving; 400 cannon were belching forth fire and death on every side; the roaring and shouting were indistinguishably commixed—together they gave an idea of a laboring volcano. Bodies of infantry and cavalry were pouring down on us, and it was time to leave contemplation; so I moved towards our columns, which were standing up in square. Our regiment and 73d formed one, and 33d and 69th another; to our right beyond them were the Guards, and on our left the Hanoverians and German Legion of our division. As I entered the rear face of our square I had to step over a body, and, looking down, recognized Harry Beere, an officer of our grenadiers, who about an hour before shook hands with me, laughing, as I left the columns. I was on the usual terms of military intimacy with poor Harry—that is to say, if either of us had died a natural death, the other would have pitied him as a good fellow, and smiled at his neighbor as he congratulated him on the step; but seeing his herculean frame and animated countenance thus suddenly stiff and motionless before me (I know not whence the feeling could originate, for I had just seen my dearest friend drop, almost with indifference), the tears started in my eyes as I sighed out, 'Poor Harry!' The tear was not dry on my cheek when poor Harry was no longer thought of. In a few minutes after, the enemy's cavalry galloped up and crowned the crest of our position. Our guns were abandoned, and they formed between the two brigades, about a hundred paces in our front. Their first charge was magnificent. As soon as they quickened their trot into a gallop, the cuirassiers bent their heads so that the peaks of their helmets looked like vizors, and they seemed cased in armor from the plume to the saddle. Not a shot was fired till they were within thirty yards, when the word was given and our men fired away at them. The effect was magical. Through the smoke we could see helmets falling, cavaliers starting from their seats with convulsive springs as they received our balls, horses plunging and rearing in the agonies of fright and pain, and crowds of the soldiery dismounted, part of the squadron in retreat, but the more daring remainder backing their horses to force them on our bayonets. Our fire soon disposed of these gentlemen. The main body reformed in our front, and rapidly and gallantly repeated their attacks. In fact, from this time (about four o'clock) till near six, we had a constant repetition of these brave but unavailing charges. There was no difficulty in repulsing them, but our ammunition decreased alarmingly. At length an artillery wagon galloped up, emptied two or three casks of cartridges into the square, and we were all comfortable.

"The best cavalry is contemptible to a steady and well-supplied infantry regiment; even our men saw this, and began to pity the useless perseverance of their assailants, and, as they advanced, would growl out, 'Here come these fools again!' One of their superior officers tried a *ruse de guerre,* by advancing and dropping his sword, as though he surrendered; some of us were deceived by him, but Halkett ordered the men to fire, and he coolly retired, saluting us. Their devotion was invincible. One officer whom we had taken prisoner was asked what force Napoleon might have in the field, and replied with a smile of mingled derision and threatening, '*Vous verrez bientôt sa force, messieurs!*' A private cuirassier was wounded and dragged into the square; his only cry was, '*Tuez donc, tuez, tuez moi, soldats!*' and as one of our men dropped dead close to him, he seized his bayonet and forced it into his own neck; but this not despatching him, he raised up his cuirass and, plunging the bayonet into his stomach, kept working it about till he ceased to breathe.

"Though we constantly thrashed our steel-clad opponents, we found more troublesome customers in the round shot and grape, which all this time played on us with terrible effect and fully avenged the cuirassiers. Often as the volleys created openings in our square would the cavalry dash on, but they were uniformly unsuccessful. A regiment on our right seemed sadly disconcerted, and at one moment was in considerable confusion. Halkett rode out to them, and, seizing their color, waved it over his head and restored them to something like order, though not before his horse was shot under him. At the height of their unsteadiness we got the order to 'right face' to move to their assistance; some of the men mistook it for 'right about face,' and faced accordingly, when old Major M'Laine, 73d, called out, 'No, my boys, it's "right face"; you'll never hear the right about as long as a French bayonet is in front of you!' In a few moments he was mortally wounded. A regiment of light dragoons, by their facings either the 16th or 23d, came up to our left and charged the cuirassiers. We cheered each other as they passed us; they did all they could, but were obliged to retire after a few minutes at the sabre. A body of Belgian cavalry advanced for the same purpose, but on passing our square they stopped short. Our noble Halkett rode out to them and offered to charge at their head; it was of no use; the Prince of Orange came up and exhorted them to do their duty, but in vain. They hesitated till a few shots whizzed through them, when they turned about and galloped like fury, or, rather, like fear. As they passed the right face of our square the men, irritated by their rascally conduct, unanimously took up their pieces and fired a volley into them, and 'many a good fellow was destroyed so cowardly.'

"The enemy's cavalry were by this time nearly disposed of, and as they had discovered the inutility of their charges, they commenced annoying us by a spirited and well-directed carbine fire. While we were employed in this manner it was impossible to see farther than the columns on our right and left, but I imagine most of the army were similarly situated: all the British and Germans were doing their duty. About six o'clock I perceived some artillery trotting up our hill, which I knew by their caps to belong to the Imperial Guard. I had hardly mentioned this to a brother officer when two guns unlimbered within seventy paces of us, and, by their first discharge of grape, blew seven men into the centre of the square. They immediately reloaded, and kept up a constant and destructive fire. It was noble to see our fellows fill up the gaps after every discharge. I was much distressed at this moment; having ordered up three of my light bobs, they had hardly taken their station when two of them fell, horribly lacerated. One of them looked up in my face and uttered a sort of reproachful groan, and I involuntarily exclaimed, 'I couldn't help it.' We would willingly have charged these guns, but, had we deployed, the cavalry that flanked them would have made an example of us.

"The *vivida vis animi*—the glow which fires one upon entering into action—had ceased; it was now to be seen which side had most bottom, and would stand killing longest. The duke visited us frequently at this momentous period; he was coolness personified. As he crossed the rear face of our square a shell fell amongst our grenadiers, and he checked his horse to see its effect. Some men were blown to pieces by the explosion, and he merely stirred the rein of his charger, apparently as little concerned at their fate as at his own danger. No leader ever possessed so fully the confidence of his soldiery: wherever he appeared, a murmur of 'Silence! Stand to your front! Here's the duke!' was heard through the column, and then all was steady as on a parade. His aides-de-camp, Colonels Canning and Gordon, fell near our square, and the former died within it. As he came near us late in the evening, Halkett rode out to him and represented our weak state, begging his Grace to afford us a little support. 'It's impossible, Halkett,' said he. And our general replied, 'If so, sir, you may depend on the brigade to a man.' "

All accounts of the battle showed that the duke was ever present at each spot where danger seemed the most pressing, inspiriting his men by a few homely and good-humored words and restraining their impatience to be led forward to attack in their turn. "Hard pounding this, gentlemen: we will try who can pound the longest," was his remark to a battalion on which the storm from the French guns was pouring with peculiar fury. Riding up to one of the squares, which had been dreadfully weakened and against which a fresh attack of French cavalry was coming, he called to them: "Stand firm, my lads; what will they say of this in England?" As he rode along another part of the line, where the men had for some time been falling fast beneath the enemy's cannonade without having any close fighting, a murmur reached his ear of natural eagerness to advance and do something more than stand still to be shot at. The duke called to them: "Wait a little longer, my lads, and you shall have your wish." The men were instantly satisfied and steady. It was, indeed, indispensable for the duke to bide his time. The premature movement of a single corps down from the British line of heights would have endangered the whole position, and have probably made Waterloo a second Hastings.

But the duke inspired all under him with his own spirit of patient firmness. When other generals besides Halkett sent to him begging for reinforcements, or for leave to withdraw corps which were reduced to skeletons, the answer was the same: "It is impossible; you must hold your ground to the last man, and all will be well." He gave a similar reply to some of his staff who asked instructions from him, so that, in the event of his falling, his successor might follow out his plan. He answered, "My plan is simply to stand my ground here to the last man." His personal danger was indeed imminent throughout the day; and though he escaped without injury to himself or horse, one only of his numerous staff was equally fortunate.[16]

Napoleon had stationed himself during the battle on a little hillock near La Belle Alliance, in the centre of the French position. Here he was seated, with a large table from the neighboring farmhouse before him, on which maps and plans were spread; and thence with his telescope he surveyed the various points of the field. Soult watched his orders close at his left hand, and his staff was grouped on horseback a few paces in the rear.[17] Here he remained till near the close of the day, preserving the appearance at least of calmness, except some expressions of irritation which escaped him when Ney's attack on the British left centre was defeated. But now that the crisis of the battle was evidently approaching, he mounted a white Persian charger, which he rode in action because the troops easily recognized him by the horse's color. He had still the means of effecting a retreat. His Old Guard had yet taken no part in the action. Under cover of it he might have withdrawn his shattered forces and retired upon the French frontier. But this would only have given the English and Prussians the opportunity of completing their junction; and he knew that other armies were fast coming up to aid them in a march upon Paris, if he should succeed in avoiding an encounter with them and retreating upon the capital. A victory at Waterloo was his only alternative from utter ruin, and he determined to employ his Guard in one bold stroke more to make that victory his own.

Between seven and eight o'clock the infantry of the Old Guard was formed into two columns, on the declivity near La Belle Alliance. Ney was placed at their head. Napoleon himself rode forward to a spot by which his veterans were to pass; and as they approached he raised his arm, and pointed to the position of the allies, as if to tell them that their path lay there. They answered with loud cries of "*Vive l'empéreur!*" and descended the hill from their own side into that "valley of the shadow of death," while their batteries thundered with redoubled vigor over their heads upon the British line. The line of march of the columns of the Guard was directed between Hougoumont and La Haye Sainte, against the British right centre; and at the same time, Donzelot and the French, who had possession of La Haye Sainte, commenced a fierce attack upon the British centre, a little more to its left. This part of the battle has drawn less attention than the celebrated attack of the Old Guard; but it formed the most perilous crisis for the allied army; and if the Young Guard had been there to support Donzelot, instead of being engaged with the Prussians at Planchenoit, the consequences to the allies in that part of the field must have been most serious. The French tirailleurs, who were posted in clouds in La Have Sainte, and the sheltered spots near it, picked off the artillery-men of the English batteries near them; and, taking advantage of the crippled state of the English guns, the French brought some field-pieces up to La Haye Sainte, and commenced firing grape from them on the infantry of the allies, at a distance of not more than a hundred paces. The allied infantry here consisted of some German brigades, who were formed in squares, as it was believed that Donzelot had cavalry ready behind La Haye Sainte to charge them with, if they left that order of formation. In this state the Germans remained for some time with heroic fortitude, though the grape-shot was tearing gaps in their ranks, and the side of one square was literally blown away by one tremendous volley which the French gunners poured into it. The Prince of Orange in vain endeavored to lead some Nassau troops to the aid of the brave Germans. The Nassauers would not or could not face the French; and some battalions of Brunswickers, whom the Duke of Wellington had ordered up as a re-enforcement, at first fell back until the duke in person rallied them and led them on. Having thus barred the farther advance of Donzelot, the duke then galloped off to the right to head his men who were exposed to the attack of the Imperial Guard. He had saved one part of his centre from being routed, but the French had gained ground and kept it, and the pressure on the allied line in front of La Haye Sainte was fearfully severe, until it was relieved by the decisive success which the British in the right centre achieved over the columns of the Guard.

The British troops on the crest of that part of the position, which the first column of Napoleon's Guards assailed, were Maitland's brigade of British Guards, having Adams's brigade on their right. Maitland's men were lying down, in order to avoid, as far as possible, the destructive effect of the French artillery, which kept up an unremitting fire from the opposite heights, until the first column of the Imperial Guard had advanced so far up the slope towards the British position that any further firing of the French artillery-men would have endangered their own comrades. Meanwhile, the British guns were not idle; but shot and shell ploughed fast through the ranks of the stately array of veterans that still moved imposingly on. Several of the French superior officers were at its head. Ney's horse was shot under him, but he still led the way on foot, sword in hand. The front of the massy column now was on the ridge of the hill. To their surprise, they saw no troops before them. All they could discern through the smoke was a small band of mounted officers. One of them was the duke himself. The French advanced to about fifty yards from where the British Guards were lying down, when the voice of one of the group of British officers was heard calling, as if to the ground before him, "Up, Guards, and at them! "It was the duke who gave the order; and at the words, as if by magic, up started before them a line of the British Guards four deep, and in the most compact and perfect order. They poured an instantaneous volley upon the head of the French column, by which no less than three hundred of those chosen veterans are said to have fallen. The French officers rushed forward, and, conspicuous in front of their men, attempted to deploy them into a more extended line, so as to enable them to reply with effect to the British fire. But Maitland's brigade kept showering in volley after volley with deadly rapidity. The decimated column grew disordered in its vain efforts to expand itself into a more efficient formation. The right word was given at the right moment to the British for the bayonet-charge, and the brigade sprung forward with a loud cheer against their dismayed antagonists. In an instant the compact mass of the French spread out into a rabble, and they fled back down the hill pursued by Maitland's men, who, however, returned to their position in time to take part in the repulse of the second column of the Imperial Guard.

This column also advanced with great spirit and firmness under the cannonade which was opened on it, and, passing by the eastern wall of Hougoumont, diverged slightly to the right as it moved up the slope towards the British position, so as to approach the same spot where the first column had surmounted the height and been defeated. This enabled the British regiments of Adams's brigade to form a line parallel to the left flank of the French column, so that while the front of this column of French Guards had to encounter the cannonade of the British batteries, and the musketry of Maitland's Guards, its left flank was assailed with a destructive fire by a four-deep body of British infantry, extending all along it. In such a position, all the bravery and skill of the French veterans were vain. The second column, like its predecessor, broke and fled, taking at first a lateral direction along the front of the British line towards the rear of La Haye Sainte, and so becoming blended with the divisions of French infantry, which, under Donzelot, had been pressing the allies so severely in that quarter. The sight of the Old Guard broken and in flight checked the ardor which Donzelot's troops had hitherto displayed. They, too, began to waver. Adams's victorious brigade was pressing after the flying Guard, and now cleared away the assailants of the allied centre. But the battle was not yet won. Napoleon had still some battalions in reserve near La Belle Alliance. He was rapidly rallying the remains of the first column of his Guards, and he had collected into one body the remnants of the various corps of cavalry, which had suffered so severely in the earlier part of the day. The duke instantly formed the bold resolution of now himself becoming the assailant, and leading his successful though enfeebled army forward, while the disheartening effect of the repulse of the Imperial Guard on the rest of the French army was still strong, and before Napoleon and Ney could rally the beaten veterans themselves for another and a fiercer charge. As the close approach of the Prussians now completely protected the duke's left, he had drawn some reserves of horse from that quarter, and he had a brigade of Hussars under Vivian fresh and ready at hand. Without a moment's hesitation he launched these against the cavalry near La Belle Alliance. The charge was as successful as it was daring; and as there was now no hostile cavalry to check the British infantry in a forward movement, the duke gave the long-wished-for command for a general advance of the army along the whole line upon the foe. It was now past eight o'clock, and for nearly nine deadly hours had the British and German regiments stood unflinching under the fire of artillery, the charge of cavalry, and every variety of assault that the compact columns or the scattered tirailleurs of the enemy's infantry could inflict. As they joyously sprung forward against the discomfited masses of the French, the setting sun broke through the clouds which had obscured the sky during the greater part of the day, and glittered on the bayonets of the allies while they poured down into the valley and towards the heights that were held by the foe. The duke himself was among the foremost in the advance, and personally directed the movements against each body of the French that essayed resistance. He rode in front of Adams's brigade, cheering it forward, and even galloped among the most advanced of the British skirmishers, speaking joyously to the men and receiving their hearty shouts of congratulation. The bullets of both friends and foes were whistling fast around him; and one of the few survivors of his staff remonstrated with him for thus exposing a life of such value. "Never mind," was the duke's answer —"never mind, let them fire away; the battle's won, and my life is of no consequence now." And, indeed, almost the whole of the French host were now in irreparable confusion. The Prussian army was coming more and more rapidly forward on their right; and the Young Guard, which had held Planchenoit so bravely, was at last compelled to give way. Some regiments of the Old Guard in vain endeavored to form in squares and stem the current. They were swept away and wrecked among the waves of the flyers. Napoleon had placed himself in one of these squares: Marshal Soult, Generals Bertrand, Drouot, Corbineau, De Flahaut, and Gourgaud were with him. The emperor spoke of dying on the field, but Soult seized his bridle and turned his charger round, exclaiming, "Sire, are not the enemy already lucky enough?" With the greatest difficulty, and only by the utmost exertion of the devoted officers round him. Napoleon cleared the throng of fugitives and escaped from the scene of the battle and the war, which he and France had lost past all recovery. Meanwhile the Duke of Wellington still rode forward with the van of his victorious troops, until he reined up on the elevated ground near Rossomme. The daylight was now entirely gone; but the young moon had risen, and the light which it cast, aided by the glare from the burning houses and other buildings in the line of the flying French and pursuing Prussians, enabled the duke to assure himself that his victory was complete. He then rode back along the Charleroi road towards Waterloo; and near La Belle Alliance he met Marshal Blücher. Warm were the congratulations that were exchanged between the allied chiefs. It was arranged that the Prussians should follow up the pursuit and give the French no chance of rallying. Accordingly the British army, exhausted by its toils and sufferings during that dreadful day, did not advance beyond the heights which the enemy had occupied. But the Prussians drove the fugitives before them in merciless chase throughout the night. Cannon, baggage, and all the *matériel* of the army were abandoned by the French; and many thousands of the infantry threw away their arms to facilitate their escape. The ground was strewn for miles with the wrecks of their host. There was no rear-guard; nor was even the semblance of order attempted. An attempt at resistance was made at the bridge and village of Genappe, the first narrow pass through which the bulk

of the French retired. The situation was favorable; and a few resolute battalions, if ably commanded, might have held their pursuers at bay there for some considerable time. But despair and
panic were now universal in the beaten army. At the first sound of
the Prussian drums and bugles, Genappe was abandoned and
nothing thought of but headlong flight. The Prussians, under
General Gneisenau, still followed and still slew; nor even when the
Prussian infantry stopped in sheer exhaustion, was the pursuit
given up. Gneisenau still pushed on with the cavalry; and by an
ingenious stratagem made the French believe that his infantry
were still close on them, and scared them from every spot where
they attempted to pause and rest. He mounted one of his drum-
mers on a horse which had been taken from the captured carriage
of Napoleon, and made him ride along with the pursuing cavalry
and beat the drum whenever they came on any large number of
the French. The French thus fled, and the Prussians pursued,
through Quatre Bras and even over the heights of Frasne; and
when at length Gneisenau drew bridle, and halted a little beyond
Frasne with the scanty remnant of keen hunters who had kept up
the chase with him to the last, the French were scattered through
Gosselies, Marchiennes, and Charleroi, and were striving to regain
the left bank of the river Sambre, which they had crossed in such
pomp and pride not a hundred hours before.

Part of the French left wing endeavored to escape from the
field without blending with the main body of the fugitives who
thronged the Genappe causeway. A French officer who was
among those who thus retreated across the country westward of
the highroad has vividly described what he witnessed and what he
suffered. Colonel Lemonnier-Delafosse served in the campaign
of 1815 in General Foy's staff, and was consequently in that part
of the French army at Waterloo which acted against Hougoumont
and the British right wing. When the column of the Imperial
Guard made their great charge at the end of the day, the troops
of Foy's division advanced in support of them, and Colonel
Lemonnier-Delafosse describes the confident hopes of victory

and promotion with which he marched to that attack, and the
fearful carnage and confusion of the assailants, amid which he
was helplessly hurried back by his flying comrades. He then
narrates the closing scene: —

"Near one of the hedges of Hougoumont farm, without even
a drummer to beat the *rappel,* we succeeded in rallying under the
enemy's fire 300 men: they were nearly all that remained of our
splendid division. Thither came together a band of generals.
There was Reille, whose horse had been shot under him; there
were d'Erlon, Bachelu, Foy, Jamin, and others. All were gloomy
and sorrowful, like vanquished men. Their words were, —'Here
is all that is left of my corps, of my division, of my brigade: I,
myself.' We had seen the fall of Duhesme, of Pelet-de-Morvan, of
Michel—generals who had found a glorious death. My general,
Foy, had his shoulder pierced through by a musket-ball; and out
of his whole staff two officers only were left to him, Cahour
Duhay and I. Fate had spared me in the midst of so many dangers, though the first charger I rode had been shot and had
fallen on me.

"The enemy's horse were coming down on us, and our little
group was obliged to retreat. What had happened to our division
of the left wing had taken place all along the line. The movement
of the hostile cavalry, which inundated the whole plain, had
demoralized our soldiers, who, seeing all regular retreat of the
army cut off, strove each man to effect one for himself. At each
instant the road became more encumbered. Infantry, cavalry, and
artillery were pressing along pell-mell: jammed together like a
solid mass. Figure to yourself 40,000 men struggling and thrusting
themselves along a single causeway. We could not take that way
without destruction; so the generals who had collected together
near the Hougoumont hedge dispersed across the fields. General
Foy alone remained with the 300 men whom he had gleaned from
the field of battle, and marched at their head. Our anxiety was to
withdraw from the scene of action without being confounded with
the fugitives. Our general wished to retreat like a true soldier.

Seeing three lights in the southern horizon, like beacons. General Foy asked me what I thought of the position of each. I answered, 'The first to the left is Genappe; the second is at Bois de Bossu, near the farm of Quatre Bras; the third is at Gosselies.' 'Let us march on the second one, then,' replied Foy,' and let no obstacle stop us — take the head of the column, and do not lose sight of the guiding light.' Such was his order, and I strove to obey.

"After all the agitation and the incessant din of a long day of battle, how imposing was the stillness of that night! We proceeded on our sad and lonely march. We were a prey to the most cruel reflections; we were humiliated, we were hopeless; but not a word of complaint was heard. We walked silently as a troop of mourners and it might have been said that we were attending the funeral of our country's glory. Suddenly the stillness was broken by a challenge — '*Qui vive?*' 'France!' 'Kellermann!' 'Foy!' 'Is it you, general? come nearer to us.' At that moment we were passing over a little hillock, at the foot of which was a hut, in which Kellermann and some of his officers had halted. They came out to join us. Foy said to me, 'Kellermann knows the country: he has been along here before with his cavalry; we had better follow him.' But we found that the direction which Kellermann chose was towards the first light, towards Genappe. That led to the causeway which our general rightly wished to avoid. I went to the left to reconnoitre, and was soon convinced that such was the case. It was then that I was able to form a full idea of the disorder of a routed army. What a hideous spectacle! The mountain torrent, that uproots and whirls along with it every momentary obstacle, is a feeble image of that heap of men, of horses, of equipages, rushing one upon another; gathering before the least obstacle which dams up their way for a few seconds, only to form a mass which overthrows everything in the path which it forces for itself. Woe to him whose footing failed him in that deluge! He was crushed, trampled to death! I returned and told my general what I had seen, and he instantly abandoned Kellermann and resumed his original line of march.

"Keeping straight across the country, over fields and the rough thickets, we at last arrived at the Bois de Bossu, where we halted. My general said to me: 'Go to the farm of Quatre Bras and announce that we are here. The emperor or Soult must be there. Ask for orders, and recollect that I am waiting here for you. The lives of these men depend on your exactness.' To reach the farm I was obliged to cross the highroad: I was on horseback, but nevertheless was borne away by the crowd that fled along the road, and it was long ere I could extricate myself and reach the farmhouse. General Lobau was there with his staff, resting in fancied security. They thought that their troops had halted there; but, though a halt had been attempted, the men had soon fled forward, like their comrades of the rest of the army. The shots of the approaching Prussians were now heard; and I believe that General Lobau was taken prisoner in that farmhouse. I left him to rejoin my general, which I did with difficulty. I found him alone. His men, as they came near the current of flight, were infected with the general panic and fled also.

"What was to be done? Follow that crowd of runaways? General Foy would not hear of it. There were five of us still with him, all officers. He had been wounded at about five in the afternoon, and the wound had not been dressed. He suffered severely; but his moral courage was unbroken. 'Let us keep,' he said,' a line parallel to the highroad, and work our way hence as we best can.' A foot track was before us, and we followed it.

"The moon shone out brightly, and revealed the full wretchedness of the tableau which met our eyes. A brigadier and four cavalry soldiers, whom we met with, formed our escort. We marched on; and, as the noise grew more distant, I thought that we were losing the parallel of the highway. Finding that we had the moon more and more on the left, I felt sure of this, and mentioned it to the general. Absorbed in thought, he made me no reply. We came in front of a windmill, and endeavored to procure some information; but we could not gain an entrance or make any one answer, and we continued our nocturnal march. At last we entered a village, but found every door closed against us, and were obliged to use threats in order to gain admission into a single house. The poor woman to whom it belonged, more dead than alive, received us as if we had been enemies. Before asking where we were, 'Food, give us some food!' was our cry. Bread and butter and beer were brought, and soon disappeared before men who had fasted for twenty-four hours. A little revived, we asked, 'Where are we? what is the name of this village?' — 'Vieville.'

"On looking at the map, I saw that in coming to that village we had leaned too much to the right, and that we were in the direction of Mons. In order to reach the Sambre at the bridge of Marchiennes, we had four leagues to traverse; and there was scarcely time to march the distance before daybreak. I made a villager act as our guide, and bound him by his arm to my stirrup. He led us through Roux to Marchiennes. The poor fellow ran alongside of my horse the whole way. It was cruel but necessary to compel him, for we had not an instant to spare. At six in the morning we entered Marchiennes.

"Marshal Ney was there. Our general went to see him, and to ask what orders he had to give. Ney was asleep; and, rather than rob him of the first repose he had had for four days, our general returned to us without seeing him. And, indeed, what orders could Marshal Ney have given? The whole army was crossing the Sambre, each man where and how he chose; some at Charleroi, some at Marchiennes. We were about to do the same thing. When once beyond the Sambre, we might safely halt; and both men and horses were in extreme need of rest. We passed through Thuin; and finding a little copse near the road, we gladly sought its shelter. While our horses grazed, we lay down and slept. How sweet was that sleep after the fatigues of the long day of battle, and after the night of retreat more painful still! We rested in the little copse till noon, and sat there watching the wrecks of our army defile along the road before us. It was a soul-harrowing sight! Yet the different arms of the service had resumed a certain degree of order amid their disorder; and our general, feeling" his strength revive, resolved to follow a strong column of cavalry which was taking the direction of

Beaumont, about four leagues off. We drew near Beaumont, when suddenly a regiment of horse was seen debouching from a wood on our left. The column that we followed shouted out, The Prussians! the Prussians!' and galloped off in utter disorder. The troops that thus alarmed them were not a tenth part of their number, and were in reality our own 8th Hussars, who wore green uniforms. But the panic had been brought even thus far from the battle-field, and the disorganized column galloped into Beaumont which was already crowded with our infantry. We were obliged to follow that *débâcle*. On entering Beaumont we chose a house of superior appearance, and demanded of the mistress of it refreshments for the general. 'Alas!' said the lady, 'this is the tenth general who has been to this house since this morning. I have nothing left. Search, if you please, and see.' Though unable to find food for the general, I persuaded him to take his coat off and let me examine his wound. The bullet had gone through the twists of the left epaulette, and, penetrating the skin, had run round the shoulder without injuring the bone. The lady of the house made some lint for me; and without any great degree of surgical skill I succeeded in dressing the wound.

"Being still anxious to procure some food for the general and ourselves, if it were but a loaf of ammunition bread, I left the house and rode out into the town. I saw pillage going on in every direction: open caissons, stripped and half broken, blocked up the streets. The pavement was covered with plundered and torn baggage. Pillagers and runaways, such were all the comrades I met with. Disgusted at them, I strove, sword in hand, to stop one of the plunderers; but, more active than I, he gave me a bayonet stab in my left arm, in which I fortunately caught his thrust, which had been aimed full at my body. He disappeared among the crowd, through which I could not force my horse. My spirit of discipline had made me forget that in such circumstances the soldier is a mere wild beast. But to be wounded by a fellow countryman after having passed unharmed through all the perils of Quatre Bras and Waterloo! — this did seem hard, indeed. I was trying to return to General Foy, when another horde of flyers burst into Beaumont, swept me into the current of their flight, and hurried me out of the town with them. Until I received my wound I had preserved my moral courage in full force; but now, worn out with fatigue, covered with blood, and suffering severe pain from the wound, I own that I gave way to the general demoralization and let myself be inertly borne along with the rushing mass. At last I reached Landrecies, though I know not how or when. But I found there our Colonel Hurday, who had been left behind there in consequence of an accidental injury from a carriage. He took me with him to Paris, where I retired amid my family and got cured of my wound, knowing nothing of the rest of political and military events that were taking place."

No returns ever were made of the amount of the French loss in the battle of Waterloo; but it must have been immense, and may be partially judged of by the amount of killed and wounded in the armies of the conquerors. On this subject both the Prussian and British official evidence is unquestionably full and authentic. The figures are terribly emphatic.

Of the army that fought under the Duke of Wellington nearly 15,000 men were killed and wounded on this single day of battle. Seven thousand Prussians also fell at Waterloo. At such a fearful price was the deliverance of Europe purchased.

By none was the severity of that loss more keenly felt than by our great deliverer himself. As may be seen in Major Macready's narrative, the duke, while the battle was raging, betrayed no sign of emotion at the most ghastly casualties; but, when all was over, the sight of the carnage with which the field was covered, and, still more, the sickening spectacle of the agonies of the wounded men who lay moaning in their misery by thousands and tens of thousands, weighed heavily on the spirit of the victor, as he rode back across the scene of strife. On reaching his headquarters in the village of Waterloo, the duke inquired anxiously after the numerous friends who had been round him in the morning, and to whom he was warmly attached. Many, he was told, were dead; others were lying alive, but mangled and suffering, in the houses round him. It is in our hero's own words alone that his feelings can be adequately told. In a letter written by him almost immediately after his return from the field, he thus expressed himself: "My heart is broken by the terrible loss I have sustained in my old friends and companions and my poor soldiers. Believe me, nothing except a battle lost can be half so melancholy as a battle won. The bravery of my troops has hitherto saved me from the greater evil; but to win such a battle as this of Waterloo, at the expense of so many gallant friends, could only be termed a heavy misfortune but for the result to the republic."

It is not often that a successful general in modern warfare is called on, like the victorious commander of the ancient Greek armies, to award a prize of superior valor to one of his soldiers. Such was to some extent the case with respect to the battle of Waterloo. In the August of 1818, an English clergyman offered to confer a small annuity on some Waterloo soldier, to be named by the duke. The duke requested Sir John Byng to choose a man from the second brigade of Guards, which had so highly distinguished itself in the defense of Hougoumont. There were many gallant candidates, but the election fell on Sergeant James Graham, of the light company of the Coldstreams. This brave man had signalized himself throughout the day in the defense of that important post, and especially in the critical struggle that took place at the period when the French, who had gained the wood, the orchard, and detached garden, succeeded in bursting open a gate of the courtyard of the chateau itself, and rushed in in large masses, confident of carrying all before them. A hand-to-hand fight, of the most desperate character, was kept up between them and the Guards for a few minutes; but at last the British bayonets prevailed. Nearly all the Frenchmen who had forced their way in were killed on the spot; and, as the few survivors ran back, five of the Guards, Colonel Macdonnell, Captain Wyndham, Ensign Gooch, Ensign Hervey, and Sergeant Graham, by sheer strength, closed the gate again, in spite of the efforts of the French from without, and effectually barricaded it against further assaults. Over and through the loopholed wall of the courtyard the English garrison now kept up a deadly fire of musketry, which was fiercely answered by the French, who swarmed round the curtilage like ravening wolves. Shells, too, from their batteries were falling fast into the besieged place, one of which set part of the mansion and some of the outbuildings on fire. Graham, who was at this time standing near Colonel Macdonnell at the wall, and who had shown the most perfect steadiness and courage, now asked permission of his commanding officer to retire for a moment. Macdonnell replied, "By all means, Graham; but I wonder you should ask leave now." Graham answered, "I would not, sir, only my brother is wounded, and he is in that outbuilding there, which has just caught fire." Laying down his musket, Graham ran to the blazing spot, lifted up his brother, and laid him in a ditch. Then he was back at his post, and was plying his musket against the French again before his absence was noticed, except by his colonel.

Many anecdotes of individual prowess have been preserved; but of all the brave men who were in the British army on that eventful day, none deserves more honor for courage and indomitable resolution than Sir Thomas Picton, who, as has been mentioned, fell in repulsing the great attack of the French upon the British left centre. It was not until the dead body was examined after the battle that the full heroism of Picton was discerned. He had been wounded on the 16th, at Quatre Bras, by a musket-ball, which had broken two of his ribs and caused also severe internal injuries; but he had concealed the circumstance, evidently in expectation that another and greater battle would be fought in a short time, and desirous to avoid being solicited to absent himself from the field. His body was blackened and swollen by the wound, which must have caused severe and incessant pain; and it was marvellous how his spirit had borne him up, and enabled him to take part in the fatigues and duties of the field. The bullet which, on the 18th, killed the renowned leader of "the fighting division" of the Peninsula entered the head near the left temple, and passed through the brain; so that Picton's death must have been instantaneous.

One of the most interesting narratives of personal adventure at Waterloo is that of Colonel Frederick Ponsonby, of the 12th Light Dragoons, who was severely wounded when Vandeleur's brigade, to which he belonged, attacked the French lancers, in order to bring off the Union Brigade, which was retiring from its memorable charge. The 12th, like those whom they rescued, advanced much farther against the French position than prudence warranted. Ponsonby, with many others, was speared by a reserve of Polish lancers, and left for dead on the field. It is well to refer to the description of what he suffered (as he afterwards gave it, when almost miraculously recovered from his numerous wounds), because his fate, or worse, was the fate of thousands more; and because the narrative of the pangs of an individual, with whom we -an identify ourselves, always comes more home to us than a general description of the miseries of whole masses. His tale may make us remember what are the horrors of war as well as its glories. It is to be remembered that the operations which he refers to took place about three o'clock in the day, and that the fighting went on for at least five hours more. After describing how he and his men charged through the French whom they first encountered, and went against other enemies, he states:

"We had no sooner passed them than we were ourselves attacked, before we could form, by about 300 Polish lancers, who had hastened to their relief, the French artillery pouring in among us a heavy fire of grape, though for one of our men they killed three of their own.

"In the mêlée I was almost instantly disabled in both arms, losing first my sword, and then my reins; and followed by a few men, who were presently cut down, no quarter being allowed, asked, or given, I was carried along by my horse, till, receiving a blow from a sabre, I fell senseless on my face to the ground.

"Recovering, I raised myself a little to look around, being at that time, I believe, in a condition to get up and run away; when a lancer, passing by, cried out, *'Tu n'es pas mort, coquin!'* and struck his lance through my back. My head dropped, the blood gushed into my mouth, a difficulty of breathing came on, and I thought all was over.

"Not long afterwards (it was impossible to measure time, but I must have fallen in less than ten minutes after the onset) a tirailleur stopped to plunder me, threatening my life. I directed him to a small side pocket, in which he found three dollars, all I had; but he continued to threaten, and I said he might search me: this he did immediately, unloosing my stock and tearing open my waist coat, and leaving me in a very uneasy posture.

"But he was no sooner gone than an officer bringing up some troops, to which probably the tirailleur belonged, and happening to halt where I lay, stooped down and addressed me, saying he feared I was badly wounded; I said that I was, and expressed a wish to be removed to the rear. He said it was against their orders to remove even their own men; but that if they gained the day (and he understood that the Duke of Wellington was killed, and that some of our battalions had surrendered), every attention in his power would be shown me. I complained of thirst, and he held his brandy-bottle to my lips, directing one of the soldiers to lay me straight on my side and place a knapsack under my head. He then passed on into action — soon, perhaps, to want, though not receive, the same assistance; and I shall never know to whose generosity I was indebted, as I believe, for my life. Of what rank he was, I cannot say: he wore a great-coat. By and by another tirailleur came up, a fine young man, full of ardor. He knelt down and fired over me, loading and firing many times, and conversing with me all the while." The Frenchman, with strange coolness, informed Ponsonby of how he was shooting, and what he thought of the progress of the battle. "At last he ran off, exclaiming, 'You will probably not be sorry to hear that we are going to retreat. Good day, my friend.' It was dusk," Ponsonby adds, "when two squadrons of Prussian cavalry, each of them two deep, came across the valley and passed over me in full trot, lifting me from the ground and tumbling me about cruelly. The clatter of their approach, and the apprehensions they excited, may be imagined; a gun taking that direction must have destroyed me.

"The battle was now at an end, or removed to a distance. The shouts, the imprecations, the outcries of '*Vive l'empereur!*' the discharge of musketry and cannon, were over; and the groans of the wounded all around me became every moment more and more audible. I thought the night would never end.

"Much about this time I found a soldier of the Royals lying across my legs—he had probably crawled thither in his agony; and his weight, his convulsive motions, and the air issuing through a wound in his side, distressed me greatly; the last circumstance most of all, as I had a wound of the same nature myself.

"It was not a dark night, and the Prussians were wandering about to plunder; the scene in 'Ferdinand Count Fathom' came into my mind, though no women appeared. Several stragglers looked at me, as they passed by, one after another, and at last one of them stopped to examine me. I told him as well as I could, for I spoke German very imperfectly, that I was a British officer, and had been plundered already; he did not desist, however, and pulled me about roughly.

"An hour before midnight I saw a man in an English uniform walking towards me. He was, I suspect, on the same errand, and he came and looked in my face. I spoke instantly, telling him who I was, and assuring him of a reward if he would remain by me. He said he belonged to the 40th, and had missed his regiment; he released me from the dying soldier, and, being unarmed, took up a sword from the ground and stood over me, pacing backward and forward.

"Day broke; and at six o'clock in the morning some English were seen at a distance, and he ran to them. A messenger being sent off to Hervey, a cart came for me, and I was placed in it, and carried to the village of Waterloo, a mile and a half off, and laid in the bed from which, as I understood afterwards, Gordon had been just carried out. I had received seven wounds; a surgeon slept in my room, and I was saved by excessive bleeding."

Major Macready, in the journal already cited, justly praises the deep devotion to their emperor which marked the French at Waterloo. Never, indeed, had the national bravery of the French people been more nobly shown. One soldier in the French ranks was seen, when his arm was shattered by a cannon-ball, to wrench it off with the other; and, throwing it up in the air, he exclaimed to his comrades, "*Vive l'empereur jusqu' à la mort!*" Colonel Lemonnier-Delafosse mentions in his "Memoires" that, at the beginning of the action, a French soldier who had had both legs carried off by a cannon-ball was borne past the front of Foy's division, and called out to them, "*Ce n'est rien, camarades! Vive l'empereur! Gloire à la France!*" The same officer, at the end of the battle, when all hope was lost, tells us that he saw a French grenadier, blackened with powder and with his clothes torn and stained, leaning on his musket and immovable as a statue. The colonel called to him to join his comrades and retreat; but the grenadier showed him his musket and his hands and said, "These hands have with this musket used to-day more than twenty packets of cartridges: it was more than my share. I supplied myself with ammunition from the dead. Leave me to die here on the field of battle. It is not courage that fails me, but strength." Then, as Colonel Delafosse left him, the soldier stretched himself on the ground to meet his fate, exclaiming, "*Tout est perdu! pauvre France!*" The gallantry of the French officers at least equalled that of their men. Ney, in particular, set the example of the most daring courage. Here, as in every French army in which he ever served or commanded, he was "*le brave des braves.*" Throughout the day he was in the front of the battle, and was one of the very last Frenchmen who quitted the field. His horse was killed under him in the last attack made on the English position; but he was seen on foot, his clothes torn with bullets, his face smirched with powder, striving, sword in hand, first to urge his men forward, and at last to check their flight.

There was another brave general of the French army, whose valor and good conduct on that day of disaster to his nation should never be unnoticed when the story of Waterloo is recounted. This was General Pelet, who, about seven in the evening, led the first battalion of the 2d regiment of the Chasseurs of the Guard to the defense of Planchenoit, and on whom Napoleon personally urged the deep importance of maintaining possession of that village. Pelet and his men took their post in the central part of the village, and occupied the church and church-yard in great strength. There they repelled every assault of the Prussians, who in rapidly increasing numbers rushed forward with infuriated pertinacity. They held their post till the utter rout of the main army of their comrades was apparent and the victorious Allies were thronging around Planchenoit. Then Pelet and his brave Chasseurs quitted the churchyard and retired with steady march, though they suffered fearfully from the moment they left their shelter, and Prussian cavalry as well as infantry dashed fiercely after them. Pelet kept together a little knot of 250 veter-ans, and had the eagle covered over and borne along in the midst of them. At one time the inequality of the ground caused his ranks to open a little, and in an instant the Prussian horsemen were on them and striving to capture the eagle. Captain Siborne relates the conduct of Pelet with the admiration worthy of one brave soldier for another: —

"Pelet, taking advantage of a spot of ground which afforded them some degree of cover against the fire of grape by which they were constantly assailed, halted the standard-bearer, and called out, '*À moi, Chasseurs! Sauvons l'aigle, ou mourons autour d'elle!*' The Chasseurs immediately pressed around him, form-ing what is usually termed the rallying square, and, lowering their bayonets, succeeded in repulsing the charge of cavalry. Some guns were then brought to bear upon them, and subse-quently a brisk fire of musketry; but notwithstanding the awful sacrifice which was thus offered up in defense of their precious charge, they succeeded in reaching the main line of retreat, favored by the universal confusion, as also by the general obscurity which now prevailed, and thus saved alike the eagle and the honor of the regiment."

French writers do injustice to their own army and general when they revive malignant calumnies against Wellington and speak of his having blundered into victory. No blunderer could have successfully encountered such troops as those of Napoleon and under such a leader. It is superfluous to cite against these cavils the testimony which other Continental critics have borne to the high military genius of our illustrious chief. I refer to one only, which is of peculiar value on account of the quarter whence it comes. It is that of the great German writer Niebuhr, whose accurate acquaintance with every important scene of modern as well as ancient history was unparalleled, and who was no mere pedant, but a man practically versed in active life, and had been personally acquainted with most of the leading men in the great events of the early part of this century. Niebuhr, in the passage which I allude to, after referring to the military "blunders" of Mithridates, Frederick the Great, Napoleon, Pyrrhus, and Hannibal, uses these remarkable words: "The Duke of Wellington is, I believe, the only general in whose conduct of war we cannot discover any important mistake." Not that it is to be supposed that the duke's merits were simply of a negative order, or that he was merely a cautious, phlegmatic general, fit only for defensive warfare, as some recent French historians have described him. On the contrary, he was bold even to audacity when boldness was required. "The intrepid advance and fight at Assaye, the crossing of the Douro, and the movement on Talavera in 1809, the advance to Madrid and Burgos in 1812, the action before Bayonne in 1813, and the desperate stand made at Waterloo itself, when more tamely prudent generals would have retreated beyond Brussels, place this beyond a doubt."

The overthrow of the French military power at Waterloo was so complete that the subsequent events of the brief campaign have little interest, Lamartine truly says: "This defeat left nothing undecided in future events, for victory had given judgment. The war began and ended in a single battle." Napoleon himself recognized instantly and fully the deadly nature of the blow which had been dealt to his empire. In his flight from the battle-field he first halted at Charleroi, but the approach of the pursuing Prussians drove him thence before he had rested there an hour. With difficulty getting clear of the wrecks of his own army, he reached Philippeville, where he remained a few hours, and sent orders to the French generals in the various extremities of France to converge with their troops upon Paris. He ordered Soult to collect the fugitives of his own force and lead them to Laon. He then hurried forward to Paris, and reached his capital before the news of his own defeat. But the stern truth soon transpired. At the demand of the Chambers of Peers and Representatives, he abandoned the throne by a second and final abdication on the 22d of June. On the 29th of June he left the neighborhood of Paris, and proceeded to Rochefort in the hope of escaping to America; but the coast was strictly watched, and on the 15th of July the ex-emperor surrendered himself on board of the English man-of-war *Bellerophon*.

Meanwhile the allied armies had advanced steadily upon Paris, driving before them Grouchy's corps and the scanty force which Soult had succeeded in rallying at Laon. Cambray, Peronne, and other fortresses were speedily captured; and by the 29th of June the invaders were taking their positions in front of Paris. The Provisional Government, which acted in the French capital after the emperor's abdication, opened negotiations with the allied chiefs. Blücher, in his quenchless hatred of the French, was eager to reject all proposals for a suspension of hostilities, and to assault and storm the city. But the sager and calmer spirit of Wellington prevailed over his colleague; the entreated armistice was granted; and on the 3d of July the capitulation of Paris terminated the war of the battle of Waterloo.

On closing our observations on this, the last of the Decisive Battles of the World, it is pleasing to contrast the year which it signalized with the one that is now passing over our heads. We have not (and long may we be without) the stern excitement of the struggles of war, and we see no captive standards of our European neighbors brought in triumph to our shrines. But we behold an infinitely prouder spectacle. We see the banners of every civilized nation waving over the arena of our competition with each other in the arts that minister to our race's support and happiness, and not to its suffering and destruction.

> "Peace hath her victories
> No less renowned than War;"

and no battle-field ever witnessed a victory more noble than that which England, under her sovereign lady and her royal prince, is now teaching the peoples of the earth to achieve over selfish prejudices and international feuds, in the great cause of the general promotion of the industry and welfare of mankind.

ENDNOTES

PREFACE

[1] See Bolingbroke "On the Study and Use of History," vol. ii., p. 497 of his collected notes.

[2] Polyb., lib. ix., sect. 9.

[3] See Montesquieu, "Grandeur et Décadence des Romains," p. 35.

CHAPTER I

[1] The historians, who lived long after the time of the battle, such as Justin, Plutarch, and others, give ten thousand as the number of the Athenian army. Not much reliance could be placed on their authority, if unsupported by other evidence; but a calculation made for the number of the Athenian free population remarkably confirms it. For the data of this see Boeckh's "Public Economy of Athens," vol. i., p. 45. Some Μέτοικοι probably served as Hoplites at Marathon, but the number of resident aliens at Athens cannot have been large at this period.

[2] Mr. Grote observes (vol. iv., p. 464) that "this volunteer march of the whole Platæan force to Marathon is one of the most affecting incidents of all Grecian history." In truth, the whole career of Plataea, and the friendship, strong, even unto death, between her and Athens, form one of the most affecting episodes in the history of antiquity. In the Peloponnesian war the Platæans again were true to the Athenians against all risks, and all calculation of selt-interest; and the destruction of Platæa was the consequence. There are few nobler passages in the classics than the speech in which the Platæan prisoners of war, after the memorable siege of their city, justify before their Spartan executioners their loyal adherence to Athens. See Thucydides, lib. iii., sees. 53–60.

[3] At the battle of Platæa, eleven years after Marathon, each of the eight thousand Athenian regular infantry who served them was attended by a light-armed slave. — Herod., lib. viii., 27, 28, 29.

⁴ Ἀθηναῖοι πρῶτοι ἀνέσχοντο ἐσθῆτά τε Μηδικὴν ὁρέοντες, καὶ τοὺς ἄνδρας ταύτην ἐσθημένομς. τέως δὲ ἦν τοῖσι Ἕλλησι καὶ οὔνομα τῶν Μήδων φόβος ἀκοῦσαι.— HERODOTUS, lib. iv., c. 112 Ἀί δέ γνῶμαι δεδουλωμέναι ἁπάντων ἀνθρώπων ἦσαν οὕτω πολλὰ καὶ μεγάλα καὶ μάχιμα γένη καταδεδουλωμένη ἦν ἡ Περσῶν ἀρχή.— PLATO, Menexenus.

⁵ Herodotus, lib. vi., c. 103.

⁶ Ib.

⁷ See the character of Themistocles in the 138th section of the first book of Thucydides, especially the last sentence. Καί τὸ ξύμπαν εἰπεῖν φύσεως μὲν δυνάμει μελέτην δὲ βραχύτητι κράτιστος δὴ οῆτος αὐτοσχεδιάζειν τὰ δέοντα ἐγένετο.

⁸ Herodotus, lib. vi., sec. 109. The 116th section is to my mind clear proof that Herodotus had personally conversed with Epizelus, one of the veterans of Marathon. The substance of the speech of Miltiades would naturally become known by the report of some of his colleagues. The speeches which ancient historians place in the mouths of kings and generals are generally inventions of their own; but part of this speech of Miltiades bears internal evidence of authenticity. Such is the case with the remarkable expression, Ἥν δὲ ξυμβάλωμεν πρίν τι καὶ σαθρὸν Ἀθηναίων μετεξετέροιοι ἐγγενέσθαι, θεῶν τὰ ἴσα νεμό ντων, οἷοι τε ἐσμεν περιγενέσθαι τῆ συμβαλῆ. This daring and almost irreverent assertion would never have been coined by Herodotus, but it is precisely consonant with what we know of the character of Miltiades; and it is an expression which, if used by him, would be sure to be remembered and repeated by his hearers.

⁹ Ἐπὶ ῥητοῖς γέρασι πατρικαὶ Βασιλείαι.— THUCYD. lib. i., sec. 12.

¹⁰ See the tenth volume of the "Journal of the Royal Asiatic Society."

¹¹ Herod., lib. v., c. 96.

¹² Æschines in Ctes., p. 522, ed. Reiske. Mitford, vol. i., p. 485. Æchines is speaking of Xerxes, but Mitford is probably right in considering it as the style of the Persian kings in their proclamations. In one of the inscriptions at Persepolis, Darius terms himself" Darius, the great king, king of kings, the king of the many-peopled countries, the supporter also of this great world." In another, he styles himself "the king of all inhabited countries." (See "Asiatic Journal," vol. x., pp. 287 and 292, and Major Rawlinson's Comments.)

¹³ Ἀθηναῖοι μὲν νῦν ηὔξηντο δηλοῖ δὲ οὐ κατ᾽ ἕν μόνον ἀλλὰ πανταχῆ ἡ Ἰσηγορίη ὡς ἔστι χρῆμα σπουδαῖον εἰ καὶ Ἀθηναῖοι τμραννευόμενοι μὲν οὐδαμοῦ τῶν σφέας περιοικεό ντων ἔσαν τὰ πολέμια ἀμείνομς ἀπαλλάχθεντες δὲ τμράννων μακρῷ πρῶτοι ἐγέννντο δηλοῖ ὦν ταῦτα ὅτι κατεχόμενοι μὲν ἐθενοκάκεον, ὡς δεσπότη ἐργαζόμενοι ἐλευθερωθέντων δὲ αὐτὸς ἕκαστος ἑωυτῷ προθυμέετο κατεργάζεσθαι,— HEROD., lib. v., c. 87.

Mr. Grote's comment on this is one of the most eloquent and philosophical passages in his admirable fourth volume.

The expression Ἰσηγορίη χρῆμα σπουδαῖον is like some lines in old Barbour's poem of "The Bruce":

"Ah, Fredome is a noble thing;
Fredome makes man to haiff lyking,
Fredome all solace to men gives.
He lives at ease that freely lives."

[14] It is remarkable that there is no other instance of a Greek general deviating from the ordinary mode of bringing a phalanx of spearmen into action until the battles of Leuctra and Mantinea, more than a century after Marathon, when Epaminondas introduced the tactics which Alexander the Great in ancient times, and Frederic the Great in modern times, made so famous, of concentrating an overpowering force to bear on some decisive point of the enemy's line, while he kept back, or, in military phrase, refused, the weaker part of his own.

"Persæ," 402.

[15] Persæ, 402.

[16] Ἀλλ' ὅμως ἀπωσόμεσθα ξὺν θεοις πρὸς ἑσπέρα.

— ARISTOPH., *Vespæ*, 1085.

[17] Ἐμαχόμεσθ' αὐτοῖσι, θυμον ὀξίνην πεπωκοτές,
Στὰς ἀνὴρ παρ' ἀνδρ' ὑπ' ὀργῆς τὴν χελύνην ἐσθίων
Ὑπὸ δὲ τῶν τοξευμάτων οὐκ ἦν ἰδεῖν τὸν οὐρανὸν.

—ARISTOPH., *Vespæ*, 1082.

[18] See the description in the 62d section of the ninth book of Herodotus of the gallantry shown by the Persian infantry against the Lacedæmonians at Platæa. We have no similar detail of the fight at Marathon, but we know that it was long and obstinately contested (see the 113th section of the sixth book of Herodotus, and the lines from the Vespæ already quoted), and the spirit of the Persians must have been even higher at Marathon than at Platæa. In both battles it was only the true Persians and the Sacæ who showed this valor; the other Asiatics fled like sheep.

[19] The flying Mede, his shaftless broken bow; The fiery Greek, his red pursuing spear; Mountains above, Earth's, Ocean's plain below, Death in the front, Destruction in the rear! Such was the scene.— BYRON'S CHILDE HAROLD.

[20] Mitford well refers to Cr?cy, Poitiers, and Agincourt as instances of similar disparity of loss between the conquerors and the conquered.

[21] Pausanias states, with implicit belief, that the battle-field was haunted at night by supernatural beings, and that the noise of combatants and the snorting of horses were heard to resound on it. The superstition has survived the change of creeds, and the shepherds of the neighborhood still believe that spectral warriors contend on the plain at midnight, and they say they have heard the shouts of the combatants and the neighing of the steeds. See Grote and Thirlwall.

[22] It is probable that the Greek light-armed irregulars were active in the attack on the Persian ships, and it was in this attack that the Greeks suffered their principal loss.

[23] The commonplace calumnies against the Athenians respecting Miltiades have been well answered by Sir Edward Lytton Bulwer in his "Rise and Fall of Athens," and Bishop Thirlwall in the second volume of his "History of Greece;"

but they have received their most complete refutation from Mr. Grote in the fourth volume of his History, p. 490, et seq., and notes. I quite concur with him that, "looking to the practice of the Athenian dicastery in criminal cases, that fifty talents was the minor penalty actually proposed by the defenders of Miltiades themselves as a substitute for the punishment of death. In those penal cases at Athens where the punishment was not fixed beforehand by the terms of the law, if the person accused was found guilty, it was customary to submit to the jurors subsequently and separately the question as to amount of punishment. First, the accuser named the penalty which he thought suitable; next, the accused person was called upon to name an amount of penalty for himself, and the jurors were constrained to take their choice between these two, no third gradation of penalty being admissible for consideration. Of course, under such circumstances, it was the interest of the accused party to name, even in his own case, some real and serious penalty — something which the jurors might be likely to deem not wholly inadequate to his crime just proved; for, if he proposed some penalty only trifling, he drove them to prefer the heavier sentence recommended by his opponent" The stories of Miltiades having been cast into prison and dying there, and of his having been saved from death only by the interposition of the prytanis of the day, are, I think, rightly rejected by Mr. Grote as the fictions of after ages. The silence of Herodotus respecting them is decisive. It is true that Plato, in the Gorgias, says that the Athenians passed a vote to throw Miltiades into the Barathrum, and speaks of the interposition of the prytanis in his favor; but it is to be remembered that Plato, with all his transcendent genius, was (as Niebuhr has termed him) a very indifferent patriot, who loved to blacken the character of his country's democratical institutions; and if the fact was that the prytanis, at the trial of Miltiades, opposed the vote of capital punishment, and spoke in favor of the milder sentence, Plato (in a passage written to show the misfortunes that befell Athenian statesmen) would readily exaggerate this tact into the story that appears in his text.

²⁴ Wordsworth's "Greece," p. 115.

²⁵ Thirlwall.

²⁶ Pæans of the Athenian Navy.

CHAPTER II

¹ Ἀεὶ καθεστῶτος τὸν ἥσσοο ὑπὸ δυνατωτέρου κατείργεσθαι. — THUC., i., 77.

² Thuc., lib. i., sec. 144.

³ Arnold's "History of Rome."

⁴ Lib. vi., sec. 36, et seq., Arnold's edition. I have almost literally transcribed some of the marginal epitomes of the original speech.

⁵ 1851.

⁶ Arnold, in his notes on the passage, well reminds the reader that Agathocles, with a Greek force far inferior to that of the Athenians at this period, did, some years afterward, very nearly conquer Carthage.

⁷ It will be remembered that Spanish infantry were the staple of the Carthaginian armies. Doubtless Alcibiades and other leading Athenians had made themselves acquainted with the Carthaginian system of carrying on war, and meant to adopt it. With the marvellous powers which Alcibiades possessed of ingratiating himself with men of every class and every nation, and his high military genius, he would have been as formidable a chief of an army of *condottieri* as Hannibal afterward was.

⁸ Alcibiades here alluded to Sparta itself, which was unfortified. His Spartan hearers must have glanced round them at these words with mixed alarm and indignation.

⁹ Thuc., lib. vi., sec. 90, 91.

¹⁰ The effect of the presence of a Spartan officer on the troops of the other Greeks seems to have been like the effect of the presence of an English officer upon native Indian troops.

¹¹ Ἦν μὲν γὰρ σελήνη λαμπρὰ ἑώρων δέ οὕτως ἀλλήλους ὡς ἐν σελήνη εἰκὸς τὴν μέν ὄψιν τοῦ σώματος προορᾶν τὴν δὲ γνῶσιν τοῦ οἰκείου ἀπίστεῖσθαι. — Thuc., lib. vii., 44. Compare Tacitus' description of the night engagement in the civil war between Vespasian and Vitellius. "Neutro inclinaverat fortuna, donec adultâ nocte, *luna ostenderet acies, falleretque*." — *Hist.*, lib. iii., sec. 23.

CHAPTER III

¹ De Staël.

² Arrian, lib. vii., ad finem.

³ "The Historie of the World," by Sir Walter Raleigh, Knight, p. 648.

⁴ See Count Montholon's "Memoirs of Napoleon."

⁵ See Arnold, Hist. Rome, ii., p. 406.

⁶ See Humboldt's "Cosmos."

⁷ See Mitford.

⁸ Mitford's remarks on the strategy of Darius in his last campaign are very just. After having been unduly admired as an historian, Mitford is now unduly neglected. His partiality and his deficiency in scholarship have been exposed sufficiently to make him no longer a dangerous guide as to Greek politics, while the clearness and brilliancy of his narrative, and the strong common sense of his remarks (where his party prejudices do not interfere), must always make his volumes valuable as well as entertaining.

⁹ See Niebuhr's "Hist. of Rome," vol. iii., p. 466.

¹⁰ See Niebuhr.

¹¹ See Layard's "Nineveh," and see Vaux's "Nineveh and Persepolis," p. 16.

¹² See Clinton's "Fasti Hellenici." The battle was fought eleven days after an eclipse of the moon, which gives the means of fixing the precise date.

[13] Kleber's arrangement of his troops at the battle of Heliopolis, where, with ten thousand Europeans, he had to encounter eighty thousand Asiatics in an open plain, is worth comparing with Alexander's tactics at Arbela. See Thiers' "Histoire du Consulat," &c., vol. ii., livre v.

[14] Ἀλλὰ καιῶς τὰς προσβολὰς αὐτῶν ἐδέχοντο οἱ Μακεδόνες, καὶ βίᾳ κατ᾽ ἴλα προσπίπτοντες ἐξώθουν ἐκ τῆς τάξεως. — ARRIAN, lib. iii., c. 13.

The best explanation of this may be found in Napoleon's account of the cavalry fights between the French and the Mamelukes. "Two Mamelukes were able to make head against three Frenchmen, because they were better armed, better mounted, and better trained; they had two pair of pistols, a blunder-buss, a carabine, a helmet with a visor, and a coat of mail; they had several horses, and several attendants on foot. One hundred cuirassiers, however, were not afraid of one hundred Mamelukes; three hundred could beat an equal number, and one thousand could easily put to the rout fifteen hundred, so great is the influence of tactics, order, and evolutions! Leclerc and Lasalle presented their men to the Mamelukes in several lines. When the Arabs were on the point of overwhelming the first, the second came to its assistance on the right and left; the Mamelukes then halted and wheeled, in order to turn the wings of this new line; this moment was always seized upon to charge them, and they were uniformly broken." — MONTHOLON's "History of Captivity of Napoleon," vol. iv., p. 70.

[15] I purposely omit any statement of the loss in the battle. There is a palpable error of the transcribers in the numbers which we find in our present manuscripts of Arrian, and Curtius is of no authority.

[16] There is at this present moment in the Great Exhibition at Hyde Park a model of a piratical galley of Labuan, part of the mast of which can be let down on the enemy, and form a bridge for boarders. It is worth while to compare this with the account of Polybius of the boarding bridges which the Roman admiral, Duillius, affixed to the masts of his galleys, and by means of which he won his great victory over the Carthaginian fleet.

CHAPTER IV

[1] Livy, lib. xxi., sec. I.

[2] Vol. iii., p. 62. See also Alison, *passim.*

[3] See Arnold, vol. iii., 387.

[4] Vol. ii., p. 447, Wesseling's ed.

[5] Lib. xxv., 22.

[6] See the "Periplus" of Hanno.

[7] Lib. xxv., 40.

[8] "Histoire Romaine." vol. ii., p. 40.

[9] "We advanced to Waterloo as the Greeks did to Thermopylæ: all of us without fear, and most of us without hope." — *Speech of General Foy.*

[10] Arnold, vol. iii., p. 61. The above is one of the numerous bursts of eloquence that adorn Arnold's last volume, and cause such deep regret that that volume should have been the last, and its great and good author have been cut off with his work thus incomplete.

[11] See the excellent criticisms of Sir Walter Raleigh on this, in his "History of the World," book v., chap. iii., sec. II.

[12] Hamilcar was surnamed Barcar, which means the Thunderbolt. Sultan Bajazet had the similar surname of Yilderim.

[13] Sir Walter Raleigh.

[14] The annalists whom Livy copied spoke of Nero's gaining repeated victories over Hannibal, and killing and taking his men by tens of thousands. The falsehood of all this is self-evident. It Nero could thus always beat Hannibal, the Romans would not have been in such an agony of dread about Hasdrubal as all writers describe. Indeed, we have the express testimony of Polybius that the statements which we read in Livy of Marcellus, Nero, and others gaining victories over Hannibal in Italy, must be all fabrications of Roman vanity. Polybius states, lib. xv., sec. 16, that Hannibal was never defeated before the battle of Zama; and in another passage, book ix., chap. 3, he mentions that after the defeats which Hannibal inflicted on the Romans in the early years of the war, they no longer dared face his army in a pitched battle on a fair field, and yet they resolutely maintained the war. He rightly explains this by referring to the superiority of Hannibal's cavalry, the arm which gained him all his victories. By keeping within fortified lines, or close to the sides of the mountains when Hannibal approached them, the Romans rendered his cavalry ineffective; and a glance at the geography of Italy will show how an army can traverse the greater part of that country without venturing far from the high grounds.

[15] Livy, lib. xxvii., c. 45.

[16] "Adparebat (quo nihil iniquius est) ex eventu famam habiturum." — LIVY, lib. xxvii., c. 44.

[17] Livy, lib. xxvii., c. 46.

[18] Most probably during the period of his prolonged consulship, from BC 104 to BC 101, while he was training his army against the Cimbri and the Teutons.

[19] "Historic of the World," by Sir Walter Raleigh, p. 946.

CHAPTER V

[1] Arnold's "Lectures on Modern History."

[2] See *post*, remarks on the relationship between the Cherusci and the English.

[3] Ranke.

[4] Tacitus, "Annals," ii., 88.

[5] I cannot forbear quoting Macaulay's beautiful lines, where he describes how similar outrages in the early times of Rome goaded the plebeians to rise against the patricians:

"Heap heavier still the fetters; bar closer still the grate;
Patient as sheep we yield us up unto your cruel hate.
But by the shades beneath us, and by the gods above,
Add not unto your cruel hate your still more cruel love.

*   *   *

Then leave the poor plebeian his single tie to life —
The sweet, sweet love of daughter, of sister, and of wife,
The gentle speech, the balm for all that his vex'd soul endures,
The kiss in which he half forgets even such a yoke as yours.
Still let the maiden's beauty swell the father's breast with pride;
Still let the bridegroom's arm enfold an unpolluted bride.
Spare us the inexpiable wrong, the unutterable shame,
That turns the coward's heart to steel, the sluggard's blood to flame;
Lest when our latest hope is fled ye taste of our despair,
And learn by proof, in some wild hour, how much the wretched dare."

[6] I am indebted for much valuable information on this subject to my friend, Mr. Henry Pearson.

[7] See Gibbon's description (vol. i., chap. i.) of the Roman legions in the time of Augustus; and see the description in Tacitus, "Ann.," lib. ii., of the subsequent battles between Cæcina and Arminius.

[8] The circumstances of the early part of the battle which Arminius fought with Cæcina six years afterwards evidently resembled those of his battle with Varus, and the result was very near being the same: I have therefore adopted part of the description which Tacitus gives ("Annal." lib. i., c. 65) of the last-mentioned engagement: "Neque tamen Arminius quamquam libero incursu, statim prorupit: sed ut hæsere cœno fossisque impedimenta, turbati circum milites; incertus signorum ordo; utque tali in tempore sibi quisque properus, et lentæ adversum imperia aures, irrumpere Germanos jubet, clamitans, 'En Varus, et eodem iterum fato victæ legiones!' Simul hæc, et cum delectis scindit agmen, equisque maxime vulnera ingerit; illi sanguine suo et lubrico paludum lapsantes, excussis rectoribus, disjicere obvios, proterere jacentes."

[9] "Lucis propinquis barbaræ aræ, apud quas tribunos ac primorum ordinum centuriones mactaverant." — TACITUS, ANN., lib. i., c. 61.

[10] It is clear that the Romans followed the policy of fomenting dissensions and wars of the Germans among themselves. See the thirty-third section of the "Germania" of Tacitus, where he mentions the destruction of the

Bructeri by the neighboring tribes: "Favore quodam erga nos deorum: nam ne spectaculo quidem prœlii invidere: super lx. millia non armis telisque Romanis, sed, quod magnificentius est, oblectationi oculisque ceciderunt. Maneat quæso, duretque gentibus, si non amor nostri, at certe odium sui: quando urgentibus imperii fatis, nihil jam præstare fortuna majus potest quam hostium discordiam."

[11] Florus expresses its effect most pithily: "Hâc clade factum est ut imperium quod in litore oceani non steterat, in ripâ Rheni fluminis staret," iv., 12.

[12] "Ann.," i., 57.

[13] In the Museum of Rhenish Antiquities at Bonn there is a Roman sepulchral monument, the inscription on which records that it was erected to the memory of M. Cœlius, who fell "*Bello Varwno.*"

[14] Dr. Plate, in "Biographical Dictionary," commenced by the Society for the Diffusion of Useful Knowledge.

[15] See Tacitus, "Ann.," lib. ii., sec. 88; Velleius Paterculus, lib. ii., sec. 118.

[16] Palgrave on the "English Commonwealth," vol. ii., p. 140.

[17] See Lappenburg's "Anglo-Saxons," p. 376. For nearly all the philological and ethnographical facts respecting Arminius, I am indebted to my friend, Dr. R. G. Latham.

[18] See Grim, "Deutsche Mythologie," 329.

[19] Written in 1851 when Germany was divided into numerous independent principalities.

[20] On the subject of this statue, I must repeat an acknowledgment of my obligations to my friend, Mr. Henry Pearson.

[21] The battle of Cannæ, BC 216 — Hannibal's victory over the Romans.

[22] Winfield — the probable site of the "*Herrmanschladt*"; see *supra.*

[23] Augustus was worshipped as a deity in his lifetime.

[24] See *supra*, p. 139.

[25] I have taken this translation from an anonymous writer in French two years ago.

CHAPTER VI

[1] Herbert's "Attila," book i.. line 13.

[2] See the Introduction to Ranke's "History of the Popes."

[3] See Prichard's "Researches into the Physical History of Man," vol. ii., p. 423.

[4] Arnold's "Lectures on Modern History," p. 35.

[5] See Prichard's "Researches into the Physical History of Mankind."

[6] Priscus apud Jornandem.

[7] See the narrative of Priscus.

[8] In the "Niebelungen Lied," the old poet who describes the reception of the heroine Chrimhild by Attila [Etsel], says that Attila's dominions were so vast that among his subject-warriors there were Russian, Greek, Wallachian, Polish, *and even Danish knights.*

[9] See a curious justification of Attila tor murdering his brother, by a zealous Hungarian advocate, in the note to Pray's "Annales Hunnorum," p. 117. The example of Romulus is the main authority quoted.

[10] Biographical Dictionary commenced by the Useful Knowledge Society in 1844.

[11] If I seem to have given fewer of the details of the battle itself than its importance would warrant, my excuse must be, that Gibbon has enriched our language with a description of it, too long for quotation and too splendid for rivalry. I have not, however, taken altogether the same view of it that he has. The notes to Mr. Herbert's poem of "Attila" bring together nearly all the authorities on the subject.

CHAPTER VII

[1] Vol. vii., p. 17 et seq. Gibbon's sneering remark, that it the Saracen conquests had not then been checked, "perhaps the interpretation of the Koran would now be taught in the schools of Oxford, and her pulpits might demonstrate to a circumcised people the sanctity and truth of the revelation of Mohammed," has almost an air of regret.

[2] "Philosophy of History," p. 331.

[3] "History of the Reformation in Germany," vol. i., p. 5.

[4] "History of the later Roman Commonwealth," vol. ii., p. 317.

[5] Λέονθ' ὡς δηρινθήτην,

'Ωτ' ὄρεος κορυφῇσι περὶ κταμένης ἐλάφοιο,

'Ἀμφω πεινάοντε, μέγα φρονέοντε μάχεσθον.

—Il., π'.756.,

'Ως δ' ὅτε σὺν ἀκάμαντα λέων ἐβιήσατο χάρμ,

Τώ τ' ὀρεός κορυφῇσι μέγα φρονέοντε μάχεσθον.

Πίδακος ἀμφ' ὀλίγης · ἐθέλουσί δε πιέμεν ἄμοφω ·

Πολλὰ δέ τ' ἀσθμαίνοντα λέωι ἐδάμασσε βιηφιν.

—Il., π'.823.

[6] Martel — The Hammer. See the Scandinavian Sagas for an account of the favorite weapon of Thor.

[7] "Lors issirent d'Espaigne li Sarrazins, et un leur Roi qui avoit nom Abdirames, et ont leur fames et enfans et toute leur substance en si grand plente que nus ne le prevoit nombrer ne estimer: tout leur harnois et quanques il avoient amenement avec entz, aussi comme si ils deussent toujours mes habiter en France."

[8] Tune Abdirrahman, multitudine sui exercitûs repletam prospiciens terram, &c. — Script. Gest. Franc., p. 785.

[9] The Arabian chronicles were compiled and translated into Spanish by Don Jose Antonio Condé, in his "Historia de la Dominacion de los Arabos en España," published at Madrid in 1820. Condé's plan, which I have endeavored to follow, was to preserve both the style and spirit of his Oriental authorities, so that we find in his pages a genuine Saracenic narrative of the wars in Western Europe between the Mohammedans and the Christians.

¹⁰ Of the Hegira.
¹¹ Probably the Loire.
¹² Hallam's "Middle Ages."
¹³ Hallam, *ut supra.*

CHAPTER VIII

¹ "History of Normandy and England," vol. i., p. 526.
² "Essais sur l'Histoire de France," p. 273 *et seq.*
³ Sec Guizot, *ut supra.*
⁴ Sismondi, "Histoire des Français," vol. iii., p. 174.
⁵ Rapin. "Hist. England," p. 164. See, also, on this point Sharon Turner, vol. iv., p. 72.
⁶ See in Snorre the Saga of Haraldi Hardrad.
⁷ Wace, "Roman de Rou." I have *nearly* followed his words.
⁸ Sir James Mackintosh's "History of England," vol. i., p. 97.
⁹ See Roger de Hoveden and William of Malmesbury, cited in Thierry, book iii.
¹⁰ William's customary oath.
¹¹ Thierry.
¹² In the preceding pages I have woven together the "purpureos pannos" of the old chronicler. In so doing I have largely availed myself of Mr. Edgar Taylor's version of that part of the "Roman de Rou" which describes the conquest. By giving engravings from the Bayeux Tapestry and by his excellent notes Mr. Taylor has added much to the value and interest of his volume.
¹³ The Conqueror's Chaplain calls the Saxon battle-axes "Sævissimæ secures."
¹⁴ As cited in the "Pictorial History."
¹⁵ See them collected in Lingard, i., 452 *et seq.;* Thierry, i., 299: Sharon on Turner, i., 82; and Histoire de Normandie, par Lieguet, p. 242.
¹⁶ Creasy's "Text-book of the Constitution," p. 4.
¹⁷ "Pictorial Hist. of England," vol. i., p. 28.

CHAPTER IX

¹ Plutarch. Vit. Them., 17.
² De Serres, quoted in the Notes to Southey's "Joan of Arc."
³ The occasional employment of artillery against slight defences, as at Jargeau in 1429, is no real exception.
⁴ "Respondit quod in partibus suis vocabatur Johanneta, et postquam venit in Franciam vocata est Johanna." — *Procès de Jeanne d'Arc,* i., p. 46.
⁵ Southey, in one of the speeches which he puts in the mouth of Joan of Arc, has made her beautifully describe the effect on her mind of the scenery in which she dwelt:

> "Here in solitude and peace
> My soul was nursed, amid the loveliest scenes
> Of unpolluted nature. Sweet it was,
> As the white mists of morning roll'd away,
> To see the mountain's wooded heights appear
> Dark in the early dawn, and mark its slope
> With gorse-flowers glowing, as the rising sun
> On the golden ripeness pour'd a deepening light.
> Pleasant at noon beside the vocal brook
> To lay me down, and watch the floating clouds,
> And shape to Fancy's wild similitudes
> Their ever-varying forms; and oh! how sweet,
> To drive my flock at evening to the fold,
> And hasten to our little hut, and hear
> The voice of kindness bid me welcome home."

The only foundation for the story told by the Burgundian partisan Monstrelet, and adopted by Hume, of Joan having been brought up as a servant, is the circumstance of her having been once, with the rest of her family, obliged to take refuge in an *auberge* in Neufchâteau for fifteen days, when a party of Burgundian cavalry made an incursion into Domremy. (See the "Quarterly Review" No. 138.)

[6] "Procès de Jeanne d'Arc," vol. i., p. 52.

[7] "Procès de Jeanne d'Arc," vol. i., p. 56.

[8] See Sismondi, vol. xiii., p. 114; Michelet, vol. v., livre x.

[9] See the description of her by Gui de Laval, quoted in the note to Michelet, p. 69; and see the account of the banner at Orleans, which is believed to bear an authentic portrait of the Maid, in Murray's "Handbook for France," p. 175.

[10] "Procès de Jeanne d'Arc," vol. i., p. 238.

[11] Id. ib.

[12] Hall, f. 127.

[13] "Journal du Siège d'Orléans," p. 87.

[14] Vol. x., p. 408.

[15] "Je voudrais bien qu'il voulût me faire ramener auprès mes père et mère, à garder leurs brebis et bétail, et faire ce que je voudrois faire."

[16] "Dès le commencement elle avait dit, 'Il me faut employer; je ne durerai qu'un an, ou guère plus.' "—MICHELET, x., p. 101.

[17] The whole of the "Procès de Condemnation et de Réhabilitation de Jeanne d'Arc" has been published in five volumes, by the Société de l'Histoire de France. All the passages from contemporary chroniclers and poets are added; and the most ample materials are thus given for acquiring full information on a subject which is, to an Englishman, one of painful interest. There is an admirable essay on Joan of Arc in the 138th number of the "Quarterly."

[18] See Cicero, de Divinatione, lib. i., sec. 41; and see the words of Socrates himself, in Plato, Apol. Soc.: Ὅτι μοι θεῖόν τι καὶ δαιμόνιον γίγνεται. Ἐμοτ δὲ τοῦτ ἔοτιν ἐκ παιδὸς ἀοξάμενον, φωνή τις γιγνομένη, κ. τ. λ.

CHAPTER X

[1] In Macaulay's Ballad on the Spanish Armada, the transmission of the tidings of the Armada's approach, and the arming of the English nation, are magnificently described The progress of the fire-signals is depicted in lines which are worthy of comparison with the renowned passage in the Agamemnon, which describes the transmission of the beacon-light announcing the fall of Troy from Mount Ida to Argos.

[2] See Ranke's "Hist. Popes," vol. ii., p. 135.

[3] Ranke, vol. ii., p. 172.

[4] Strype, cited in Southey's "Naval History."

[5] Copy of contemporary letter in the Harleian Collection, quoted by Southey.

[6] "Historic of the World," pp. 799–801.

[7] "Historic of the World," p. 791.

[8] Hakluyt's "Voyages," vol. i., p. 601.

[9] Vol. i., p. 602.

[10] See Strype, and the notes to the Life of Drake in the "Biographia Britannica."

CHAPTER XI

[1] "Quand Louis XIV. dit, 'l'Etat, c'est moi:' il n'y eut dans cette parole ni enflure, ni vantère, mais la simple énonciation d'un fait." — MICHELET, Hisfoire Moderne, vol. ii., p. 106.

[2] "History of European Civilization," Lecture 13.

[3] Bolingbroke, vol. ii., p. 378. Lord Bolingbroke's "Letters on the Use of History" and his "Sketch of the History and State of Europe" abound with remarks on Louis XIV. and his contemporaries, of which the substance is as sound as the style is beautiful. Unfortunately, like all his other works, they contain also a large proportion of sophistry and misrepresentation. The best test to use before we adopt any opinion or assertion of Bolingbroke's, is to consider whether in writing it he was thinking either of Sir Robert Walpole or of Revealed Religion. When either of these objects of his hatred was before his mind, he scrupled at no artifice or exaggeration that might serve the purpose of his malignity. On most other occasions he may be followed with advantage, as he always may be read with pleasure.

[4] Ibid., p. 378.

[5] Bolingbroke, vol. ii., p. 397.

[6] "Histoire Moderne," vol. ii., p. 106.

[7] Bolingbroke, vol. ii., p. 418.

[8] Ibid., p. 404.

[9] Ibid., p. 399.

[10] "Military History of the Duke of Marlborough," p. 32.

[11] Bolingbroke, vol. ii., p. 445.

[12] Marlborough might plead the example of Sylla 5n this. Compare the anecdote in Plutarch about Sylla when young and Nicopolis, κοινῆς μὲνεὐπόρου δὲ γμναικὸς and the anecdote about Marlborough and the Duchess of Cleveland, told by Lord Chesterfield, and cited in Macaulay's "History," vol. i., p. 461.

[13] "Siècle de Louis Quatorze."

[14] Bolingbroke, vol. ii., p. 445.

[15] Coxe's "Life of Marlborough."

[16] Coxe.

[17] "Marshal Villeroy," says Voltaire, "who had wished to follow Marlborough on his first marches, suddenly lost sight of him altogether, and only learned where he really was on hearing of his victory at Donauwert." — *Siècle de Louis XIV.*

[18] Coxe.

[19] Alison's "Life of Marlborough," p. 248.

CHAPTER XII

[1] "Progress of Russia in the East," p. 142.

[2] Bolingbroke's Works, vol. ii., p. 374. In the same page he observes how Sweden had often turned her arms southward with prodigious effect.

[3] The Hussite wars may, perhaps, entitle Bohemia to be distinguished.

[4] See Arnold's "Lectures on Modern History," pp. 36–39.

[5] "The idea of Panslavism had a purely literary origin. It was started by Kollar, a Protestant clergyman of the Sclavonic congregation at Pesth, in Hungary, who wished to establish a national literature by circulating all works, written in the various Sclavonic dialects, through every country where and of them are spoken. He suggested that all the Sclavonic *literati* should become acquainted with the sister dialects, so that a Bohemian, or other work, might be read on the shores of the Adriatic as well as on the banks of the Volga or any other place where a Sclavonic language was spoken; by which means an extensive literature might be created, tending to advance knowledge in all Sclavonic countries; and he supported his arguments by observing that the dialects of ancient Greece differed from each other like those of his own language, and yet that they formed only one Hellenic literature. The idea of an intellectual union of all those nations naturally led to that of a political one; and the Sclavonians, seeing that their numbers amounted to about one-third part of the whole population of Europe, and occupied more than half its territory, began to be sensible that they might claim for themselves a position to which they had not hitherto aspired.

"The opinion gained ground; and the question now is, whether the Slcavonians can form a nation independent of Russia, or whether they ought to rest satisfied in being part of one great race, with the most powerful member of it as their chief. The latter, indeed, is gaining ground among them; and some Poles are disposed to attribute their sufferings to the arbitrary will of the Czar, without extending the blame to the Russians themselves. These begin to think that, if they cannot exist as Poles, the best thing to be done is to rest satisfied with a position in the Sclavonic empire, and they hope that when once they give up the idea of restoring their country, Russia may grant some concessions to their separate nationality.

"The same idea has been put forward by writers in the Russian interest; great efforts are making among other Sclavonic people to induce them to look upon Russia as their future head, and she has already gained considerable influence over the Sclavonic populations of Turkey."—WILKINSON'S DALMATIA.

[6] Alison.

[7] Scott's "Life of Napoleon."

[8] Voltaire attests, from personal inspection of the letters of several public ministers to their respective courts, that such was the general expectation.

[9] Crighton's "Scandinavia."

[10] Malkin's "History of Greece."

[11] Koch's "Revolutions of Europe."

CHAPTER XIII

[1] Eutropius, lib. i., exordium.

[2] The original French of these passages will be found in the chapter on "Quelles sont les chances de durée de l'Union Américaine—Quels dangers la menacent." in the third volume of the first part of De Tocqueville, and in the conclusion of the first part. They are (with others) collected and translated by Mr. Alison, in his "Essays," vol. iii., p. 374.

[3] Macgregor's "Commercial Statistics," vol. iii., p. 13.

[4] Fresh stars have dawned since this was written.

[5] Arnold.

[6] Ἐὸνὅμαιμόν τε καὶ ὁμόγλωσσον, καὶ Θεῶν ἱδρύματά τε κοινὰ και θυσίαι, ἤθεά τε ὁμότροπα.—HERODOTUS, viii., 144.

[7] Lord Chatham.

[8] Lord Chatham's speech on the employment of Indians in the war.

[9] See, in the "Annual Register" for 1777, p. 117, the "Narrative of the Murder of Miss M'Crea, the daughter of an American Loyalist."

[10] Burke.

[11] Botta's "American War," book viii.

[12] Botta, book ix.

CHAPTER XIV

[1] Alison.

[2] See Niebuhr's Preface to the second volume of the History of Rome, written in October, 1830.

[3] Scott, "Life of Napoleon," vol. i., c. viii.

[4] Lamartine.

[5] Carlyle.

[6] See Scott, "Life of Napoleon," vol. i., c. xi.

[7] Some late writers represent that Brunswick did not wish to crush Dumouriez. There is no sufficient authority for this insinuation, which seems to have been first prompted by a desire to soothe the wounded military pride of the Prussians.

[8] See Lamartine, Hist. Girond., livre xvii. I have drawn much of the ensuing description from him.

[9] Alison, vol. iii., p. 323.

[10] Goethe's "Campaign in France in 1792," Farie's translation, p. 77.

CHAPTER XV

[1] See the excellent Introduction to Mr. Charles Knight's History of the "Thirty Years' Peace."

[2] See, for these numbers, Siborne's "History of the Campaign of Waterloo," vol. i., p. 41.

[3] Siborne, vol. i., chap. iii.

[4] See Montholon's "Memoirs," p. 45.

[5] The fifth corps was under Count Rapp at Strasburg.

[6] See Montholon's "Memoirs," vol. iv., p. 44.

[7] See Montholon's "Memoirs," vol. iv., p. 44.

[8] Siborne, vol. i., p. 376.

[9] Montholon's "Memoirs," vol. iv., p. 41.

[10] See Siborne, *ut supra*.

[11] Not to be confounded with the Hamlet of La Haye, at the extreme left of the British line.

[12] Prince Frederick's force remained at Hal, and took no part in the battle of the 18th. The reason for this arrangement (which has been much cavilled at) may best be given in the words of Baron Müffling: "The Duke had retired from Quatre Bras in three columns, by three chaussées; and on the evening of the 17th, Prince Frederick of Orange was at Hal, Lord Hill at Braine l'Alleud, and the Prince of Orange with the reserve at Mont St. Jean. This distribution was necessary, as Napoleon could dispose of these three roads for his advance on Brussels. Napoleon on the 17th had pressed on by Genappe as far as Rossomme.

On the two other roads no enemy had yet shown himself. On the 18th the offensive was taken by Napoleon on its greatest scale, but still the Nivelles road was not overstepped by his left wing. These circumstances made it possible to draw Prince Frederick to the army, which would certainly have been done if entirely new circumstances had not arisen. The duke had, twenty-four hours before, pledged himself to accept a battle at Mont St. Jean if Blücher would assist him there with one corps of 25,000 men. This being promised, the duke was taking his measures for defence, when he learned that, in addition to the one corps promised, Blücher was actually already on the march with his whole force, to break in by Planchenoit on Napoleon's flank and rear. If three corps of the Prussian army should penetrate by the unguarded plateau of Rossomme, which was not improbable, Napoleon would be thrust from his line of retreat by Genappe, and might possibly lose even that by Nivelles. In this case Prince Frederick, with his 18,000 men (who might be counted superfluous at Mont St. Jean), might have rendered the most essential service." See Müffling, p. 246, and the *Quarterly Review*, No. 178. It is also worthy of observation that Napoleon actually detached a force of 2,000 cavalry to threaten Hal, though they returned to the main French army during the night of the 17th.

¹³ Siborne, vol. i., p. 376.

¹⁴ See especially Sir W. Napier's glorious pictures of the battles of Busaco and Albuera. The *theoretical* advantages of the attack in column, and its peculiar fitness for a French army, are set forth in the Chevalier Folard's "Traité de la Colonne," prefixed to the first volume of his "Polybius." See also the preface to the sixth volume.

¹⁵ I have heard the remark made that Grouchy twice had in his hands the power of changing the destinies of Europe, and twice wanted nerve to act: first, when he flinched from landing the French army at Bantry Bay in 1796 (he was second in command to Hoche, whose ship was blown back by a storm), and, secondly, when he failed to lead his whole force from Wavre to the scene of decisive conflict at Waterloo. But such were the arrangements of the Prussian general that even if Grouchy had marched upon Waterloo, he would have been held in check by the nearest Prussian corps, or certainly by the two nearest ones, while the rest proceeded to join Wellington. This, however, would have diminished the number of Prussians who appeared at Waterloo, and (what is still more important) would have kept them back to a later hour.

There are some very valuable remarks on this subject in an article on the "Life of Blücher," usually attributed to Sir Francis Head. The Prussian writer, General Clausewitz, is there cited as "expressing a positive opinion, in which every military critic but a Frenchman must concur, that, even had the whole of Grouchy's force been at Napoleon's disposal, the duke had nothing to fear pending Blücher's arrival.

"The duke is often talked of as having exhausted his reserves in the action. This is another gross error, which Clausewitz has thoroughly disposed of (p. 125). He enumerates the tenth British brigade, the division of Chassé, and the cavalry of Collaert as having been little or not at all engaged; and he might have also added two brigades of light cavalry." The fact, also, that Wellington did not at any part of the day order up Prince Frederick's corps from Hal is a conclusive proof that the duke was not so distressed as some writers have represented. Hal is not ten miles from the field of Waterloo."

[16] "As far as the French accounts would lead us to infer, it appears that the losses among Napoleon's staff were comparatively trifling. On this subject, perhaps, the marked contrast afforded by the following anecdotes, which have been related to me on excellent authority, may tend to throw some light. At one period of the battle, when the duke was surrounded by several of his staff, it was very evident that the group had become the object of the fire of a French battery. The shot fell fast about them, generally striking and turning up the ground on which they stood. The horses became restive, and 'Copenhagen' himself so fidgety that the duke, getting impatient, and having reasons for remaining on the spot, said to those about him, 'Gentlemen, we are rather too close together— better to divide a little.' Subsequently, at another point of the line, an officer of artillery came up to the duke, and stated that he had a distinct view of Napoleon, attended by his staff; that he had the guns of his battery well pointed in that direction, and was prepared to fire. His Grace instantly and emphatically exclaimed 'No! no! I'll not allow it. It is not the business of commanders to be firing upon each other.' "—SIBORNE. How different is this from Napoleon's conduct at the battle of Dresden, when he personally directed the fire of the battery, which, as he thought, killed the Emperor Alexander, and actually killed Moreau.

[17] "Ouvrard, who attended Napoleon as chief commissary of the French army on that occasion, told me that Napoleon was suffering from a complaint which made it very painful for him to ride."—LORD ELLESMERE.

SUGGESTED READING

ARRIAN, FLAVIUS. *The Campaigns of Alexander.* New York: Penguin, 1977.

BRADBURY, JIM. *The Battle of Hastings.* Stroud, Glous : Sutton, 2001.

BUTTERFIELD, HERBERT. *The Whig Interpretation of History.* London: Bell and Sons, 1931.

CAESAR, JULIUS. *Gallic War.* Trans. Carolyn Hammond. Oxford: Oxford University Press, 1998.

CARTLEDGE, PAUL. *The Spartans.* New York: Overlook, 2003.

CHANDLER, DAVID. *Art of Warfare in the Age of Marlborough.* Cambridge, MA: Da Capo, 1994.

CONNOLLY, PETER. *Greece and Rome at War.* London: Greenhill, 1998.

DANDO-COLLINS, STEPHEN. *Caesar's Legion.* New York: John Wiley & Sons, 2002.

DEFOE, DANIEL. *A Short Narrative of the Life and Actions of His Grace John, Duke of Marlborough.* New Haven: Yale University Press, 1991.

DELBRUCK, HANS. *History of the Art of War Vol. 1: Warfare in Antiquity.* Trans. Walter Renfroe, Jr. Lincoln, NE: University of Nebraska Press, 1990.

---. *History of the Art of War Vol. 2: The Barbarian Invasions.* Trans. Walter Renfroe, Jr. Lincoln, NE: University of Nebraska Press, 1990.

---. *History of the Art of War Vol. 3: Medieval Warfare.* Trans. Walter Renfroe, Jr. Lincoln, NE: University of Nebraska Press, 1990.

---. *History of the Art of War Vol. 4: Dawn of Modern Warfare.* Trans. Walter Renfroe, Jr. Lincoln, NE: University of Nebraska Press, 1990.

DODGE, THEODORE A. *Alexander: A History of the Origin and Growth of the Art of War.* Cambridge, MA: Da Capo, 1996.

DUPUY, R. ERNEST, AND TREVOR N. DUPUY. *The Harper Encyclopedia of Military History. 4th edition.* New York: HarperCollins, 1993.

ENGLUND, PETER. *The Battle That Shook Europe: Poltava and the Birth of Russian Empire.* London: I.B. Taurus, 2003.

FALKNER, JAMES. *Great and Glorious days: The Duke of Marlborough's Battles.* London: Spellmount, 2002.

FORTESCUE, JOHN W. *The War of Independence: The British Army in North America 1775-1783.* London: Greenhill, 2001.

FOURACRE, PAUL. *The Age of Charles Martel.* Indianapolis, IN: Pearson Education, 2000.

FOX, ROBIN LANE. *Alexander the Great.* New York: Penguin, 1994.

FULLER, J.F.C. *A Military History of the Western World Vol. 1.* Cambridge, MA: Da Capo, 1987.

---. *A Military History of the Western World Vol. 2.* Cambridge, MA: Da Capo, 1987.

---. *A Military History of the Western World Vol. 3.* Cambridge, MA: Da Capo, 1987.

---. *The Generalship of Alexander the Great.* Cambridge, MA: Da Capo, 2004.

GABRIEL, RICHARD A. *The Great Armies of Antiquity.* Portsmouth, NH: Greenwood, 2002.

GOLDSWORTHY, ADRIAN. *Cannae.* London: Cassell, 2002.

GREEN, PETER. *Alexander of Macedon 356-323 BC.* Berkley, CA: University of California Press, 1992.

HERODOTUS. *Histories.* Trans. Aubrey De Selincourt. New York: Penguin, 2003.

HOWARTH, DAVID. *1066: The Year of Conquest.* New York: Penguin, 1981.

---. *The Voyage of the Armada.* Guilford, CT: Lyons Press, 2001.

HOWARTH, PATRICK. *Attila: King of the Huns.* New York: Barnes & Noble, 1995.

JIMENEZ, RAMON L. *Caesar Against the Celts.* Secaucus, NJ: Book Sales, 2001.

KAGAN, DONALD. *The Peloponnesian War.* New York: Viking, 2003.

KETCHUM, RICHARD M. *Saratoga: Turning Point of America's Revolutionary War.* New York: Henry Holt, 1999.

LIDDELL-HART, BASIL HENRY. *Scipio Africanus: Greater than Napoleon.* Cambridge, MA: Da Capo, 1994.

LIVY, TITUS. *The War with Hannibal.* Trans. Aubrey De Selincourt. New York: Penguin, 1972.

MATTINGLY, LEONARD H. *The Armada.* Boston, MA: Houghton Mifflin, 1972.

MORILLO, STEPHEN, ED. *Battle of Hastings: Sources and Interpretations.* Woodbridge, Suffolk: Boydell & Brewer, 1996.

OMAN, CHARLES W. A. *A History of the Art of War in the Middle Ages: 378-1278 AD, Vol. 1.* London: Greenhill, 1998.

---. *A History of the Art of War in the Middle Ages: 1278-1485 AD, Vol. 2.* London: Greenhill, 1998.

---. *A History of the Art of War in the Sixteenth Century.* London: Greenhill, 1999.

PATTERSON, BENTON RAIN. *Harold and William: The Battle for England, AD 1064-1066.* Lantham, MD: Rowman & Littlefield, 2001.

PEROWNE, STEWART. *Hadrian.* New York: Barnes & Noble Books, 1990.

PLUTARCH. *Plutarch on Sparta.* New York: Penguin, 1988.

---. *The Rise and Fall of Athens.* Trans. Ian S. Kilvert. New York: Penguin, 1972.

SCOTT, SAMUEL F. *From Yorktown to Valmy.* Boulder, CO: University Press of Colorado, 2003.

SEWARD, DESMOND. *The Hundred Years War: The English in France 1337-1453.* New York: Penguin, 1999.

SUMPTION, JONATHON. *The Hundred Years War: Trial by Battle, Vol. 1.* Philadelphia, PA: University of Pennsylvania Press, 1999.

---. *The Hundred Years War: Trial by Fire, Vol. 2.* Philadelphia, PA: University of Pennsylvania Press, 2001.

THUCYDIDES. *The History of the Peloponnesian War.* Trans. Rex Warner. New York: Penguin, 1972.

WARRY, JOHN GIBSON. *Warfare in the Classical World.* Norman, OK: University of Oklahoma Press, 1995.